D0153512

BEACONS OF LIBERTY

Before the Civil War, free African Americans and fugitive slaves crossed international borders to places like Canada, Mexico, and the Caribbean in search of freedom and equality. *Beacons of Liberty* tells the story of how these bold migrants catalyzed contentious debates over citizenship, racial justice, and national character in the United States. Blending fresh historical analysis with incredible stories of escape and rebellion, Elena K. Abbott shows how the shifting geography of slavery and freedom beyond U.S. borders helped to shape the hopes and expectations of black radicals, white politicians, and fiery reformers engaged in the American anti-slavery movement. Featuring perspectives from activists and risk-takers like Mary Ann Shadd, Martin Delany, and James C. Brown, *Beacons of Liberty* illuminates the critical role that international free soil played in the long and arduous fight for emancipation and racial justice in the United States.

Elena K. Abbott is a Seattle-based author, editor, and historian whose scholarship focuses on slavery and anti-slavery in the Atlantic world. She received her PhD from Georgetown University, where she was awarded the Harold N. Glassman Distinguished Dissertation Award in the Humanities.

BEACONS OF LIBERTY

International Free Soil and the Fight for Racial Justice in Antebellum America

Elena K. Abbott

CAMBRIDGE
UNIVERSITY PRESS

CAMBRIDGE
UNIVERSITY PRESS

University Printing House, Cambridge CB2 8BS, United Kingdom

One Liberty Plaza, 20th Floor, New York, NY 10006, USA

477 Williamstown Road, Port Melbourne, VIC 3207, Australia

314–321, 3rd Floor, Plot 3, Splendor Forum, Jasola District Centre,
New Delhi – 110025, India

79 Anson Road, #06–04/06, Singapore 079906

Cambridge University Press is part of the University of Cambridge.

It furthers the University's mission by disseminating knowledge in the pursuit of
education, learning, and research at the highest international levels of excellence.

www.cambridge.org
Information on this title: www.cambridge.org/9781108491549
DOI: 10.1017/9781108863681

© Elena K. Abbott 2021

This publication is in copyright. Subject to statutory exception
and to the provisions of relevant collective licensing agreements,
no reproduction of any part may take place without the written
permission of Cambridge University Press.

First published 2021

Printed in the United Kingdom by TJ Books Limited, Padstow Cornwall

A catalogue record for this publication is available from the British Library.

ISBN 978-1-108-49154-9 Hardback
ISBN 978-1-108-79845-7 Paperback

Cambridge University Press has no responsibility for the persistence or accuracy of
URLs for external or third-party internet websites referred to in this publication
and does not guarantee that any content on such websites is, or will remain,
accurate or appropriate.

Contents

CONTENTS

List of Figures, Maps, and Tables

FIGURES

MAPS

TABLE

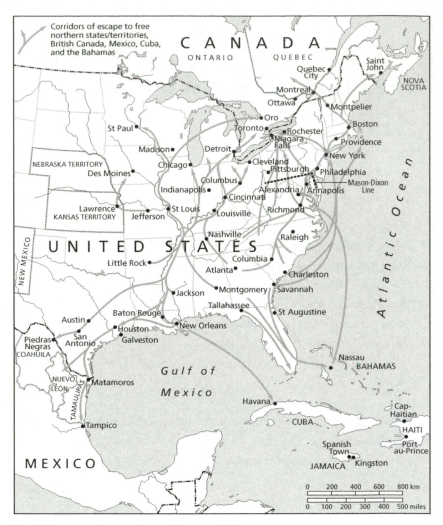

Map 1 Routes to Freedom in the Nineteenth Century

Introduction

N EARLY 1840, AN ENSLAVED MAN NAMED MADISON
Washington escaped from Virginia and made his way northward
all the way to Upper Canada (modern-day Ontario). A success story of the
so-called Underground Railroad, he lived for several months with Hiram
Wilson, a white missionary who had become famous among anti-slavery
advocates for his tireless work on behalf of fugitive slaves arriving in
Canada during the 1830s. Now a free man under British law, Madison
Washington nevertheless found that he could not live in freedom without
his wife, who remained enslaved in Virginia. So, Washington decided to
reverse the perilous route he had traveled to secure his freedom and
returned to the United States in 1841.

Sadly, his rescue attempt failed. Washington was re-captured and sold
to a slave-trader who put him on board a fast-moving brig, the *Creole*,
alongside 134 other enslaved men, women, and children. The ship was
engaged in the flourishing U.S. domestic slave trade, a lucrative business
that transported thousands of enslaved people from states like Virginia in
the Upper South to regions of intensive cotton and sugar production in
the expanding Deep South and Southwest. The *Creole* was scheduled to
carry Madison Washington and the rest of its enslaved human "cargo"
from Richmond, Virginia, along the Atlantic coast to New Orleans,
Louisiana.[1]

But the slave ship did not reach its destination. On November 7, 1841,
Washington led nineteen of the slaves aboard the *Creole* in a violent
rebellion. They overpowered the ship's crew and commandeered the
vessel. Once in command, Washington and his compatriots demanded
that the *Creole* be sailed into the port of Nassau on the British island of

New Providence (the Bahamas). Washington knew from his time in Canada that Great Britain, which had abolished slavery over the four-year period from 1834 to 1838, maintained a policy of freeing and protecting enslaved men and women who were able to cross into British territory. And this is exactly what happened. British officials in the city of Nassau immediately freed all but the nineteen leaders of the shipboard rebellion, and they eventually freed the leaders as well.[2]

While little is known about their lives after they engineered their emancipation, Madison Washington and the freed men, women, and children aboard the *Creole* were not soon forgotten. The *Creole* rebellion unfolded at the same time that abolitionism was picking up steam in the United States, with anti-slavery activists pitting themselves against powerful slaveholding interests in an ongoing battle to sway American public opinion toward their cause. The drama of a seafaring rebellion led by a self-liberated slave captured the imaginations of anti-slavery advocates, and the fact that British officials opted to free everyone on board in accordance with British law caused an uproar among southern slave-holders.[3] For American observers both for and against slavery, the event proved in no uncertain terms that the international borders separating slavery and freedom were both permeable and politically significant.

A decade later, in 1851, a free-born African American woman in her late twenties named Mary Ann Shadd left her family home in Pennsylvania and resettled in Canada West (formerly Upper Canada) after the enactment of the infamous 1850 Fugitive Slave Act. She was horrified by what the new law meant for the safety of free African Americans and for the future of slavery in the United States. The Fugitive Slave Act deputized all U.S. citizens to assist slave-catchers on the hunt for self-emancipated men and women, and it denied African Americans accused of being slaves the ability to contest their legal status in court. An expansion of the federal government's commitment to protecting southern enslavers' human "property," the Fugitive Slave Act put self-emancipated people in more danger than ever, and it escalated the threat that free black northerners might be kidnapped and sold illegally into southern bondage. Like thousands of other black northerners, Shadd decided to leave for Canada, where she knew that she would be safe from the predations of American enslavers and that British laws would not discriminate based on the color of her skin.[4]

Once across the U.S.–Canada border, Shadd proudly claimed an identity as a British subject and encouraged others to do the same. Yet from her new home, she still continued her tireless work as an activist against slavery in the United States. Like many free middle-class northerners, she espoused the idea of "racial uplift," the belief that African Americans' material and moral progress would diminish white racism and raise the social and political standing of African Americans in the United States. She believed, therefore, that African Americans needed opportunities to demonstrate their capacity to be free and equal members of society – and that they could do so only as British subjects.[5]

In Upper Canada, Shadd became a prominent newspaper editor (the first African American woman to do so) and used her fiery editorials to advocate for the abolition of American slavery and for the political advantages of black emigration away from the United States. She frequently compared her new home in Canada with other places where slavery had been outlawed in order to assess where African Americans could live most comfortably and fight American slavery most effectively. Weighing Canada against the British West Indies, Liberia, Haiti, Mexico, and South America, Shadd encouraged African Americans to join her in Upper Canada because it guaranteed them "impartial freedom" – meaning that they would be equal in the eyes of the law and accorded all the rights of British subjects. She believed that this distinction made the British province "the only ground on which [African Americans] can make despots feel the force of their words and actions," and a place from which activists could exert a "reflex influence" upon slavery in the United States.[6]

In other words, Shadd saw Upper Canada as far more than just an escape hatch from the United States in the wake of the Fugitive Slave Act. She saw it as a model for what it looked like when a powerful government was willing to guarantee the legal equality of all residents, and she saw it as a secure base camp from which black men and women could pursue socio-political change in the United States.

Mary Ann Shadd's anti-slavery emigrationism and Madison Washington's dramatic, transnational odyssey from slavery to freedom illustrate the significance of international "free soil" within the American anti-slavery movement of the nineteenth century. Beginning in the late eighteenth century, diverse anti-slavery efforts transformed Haiti, Sierra Leone, Liberia, Upper Canada, Mexico, some newly independent South American nations, Great Britain, and the British West Indies into places where anti-slave trade legislation and emancipation laws either immediately or gradually freed enslaved populations. These locations became "international free-soil havens" – places with the potential to free and protect self-emancipated men and women and offer equal standing for free African American emigrants.

Weaving together themes of black mobility, information circulation, jurisdictional dispute, and transnational abolitionism, this book investigates the individual and collective influence that these international free-soil havens had on the American anti-slavery movement over the fifty-year period between 1813 and 1863. Their influence was profound, variable, and complex. Over time, international free-soil havens developed into practical models of black freedom, offered concrete destinations where free and self-emancipated people could anticipate legal protection and equal standing, and became potent symbols of liberty in the fight against American slavery. Not only did they provide enslaved men and women, free people of color, and black and white anti-slavery advocates alternative possibilities to slavery and racism in the United States, they helped Americans develop and articulate ideas about national character, who belonged, and under what conditions. Free-soil havens abroad formed the international stage upon which the fight to end American slavery took place.

* * *

First identified by historians Sue Peabody and Keila Grinberg in 2011, the "principle of free soil" created significant but often overlooked boundaries between slavery and freedom on both sides of the Atlantic Ocean.[7] Unrelated to the American "Free-Soil Party" of the mid-nineteenth century, the concept of free soil in this context encompasses a far greater expanse of time and a much wider geographic field.[8] At surface level, it refers to places where slavery had already been curtailed or abolished, and where slaves could expect to be freed upon crossing the border. But this gets us only so far. Neither the characteristics nor the significance of international free-soil havens were static at any point in the nineteenth century. They were characterized by different forms of government, various approaches to anti-slavery legislation, differing degrees of anti-slavery sentiment, and varying levels of geopolitical power with which to police and enforce anti-slavery borders against neighboring pro-slavery interests. They also had complex internal social, political, and economic currents that shaped and changed them over time, just as the evolution of domestic politics in the United States regularly re-shaped the geography of slavery and black Americans' access to legal rights and protection.

Moreover, and perhaps more importantly, international free-soil havens were defined in different ways by different people in response to changing social conditions and evolving geopolitical relationships within and beyond the United States. Over time, international free-soil havens developed specific and distinct reputations among slaves, free black activists, and white anti-slavery advocates for their potential to harbor African Americans, influence the fight against U.S. slavery, and provide socio-economic opportunities for free people. Yet these reputations were always contingent. How different people viewed international free-soil havens and their relevance to the American anti-slavery project shifted in relationship to individuals' legal standing, the changing context of U.S. race relations, conditions on the ground in different free-soil locales, and the evolving landscape of slavery and freedom around the Atlantic.

For self-emancipated slaves, international free-soil havens offered destinations where, as fugitives from bondage, they expected to be freed and protected by local laws and international treaties. Enslaved people like Madison Washington frequently had some awareness of the evolving geography of freedom beyond the United States. In some cases, they learned of free-soil havens directly from enslavers who expressed frustration over their inability to retrieve or extradite lost "property" from across specific borders. In other cases, they learned from people who had personal experience or who had access to information. Escapees themselves were often able to pass along critical details about where to go, as well as who to trust and what perils to watch out for. A newspaper left where a literate slave might read it could become a conduit to the wider world. Individuals enslaved or employed in the overland and maritime transportation industries linking slave-based economies in the South and Southwest to northern and Caribbean markets could also connect enslaved workers to news and information. These nodes of communication and information exchange often took the form of rumor in enslaved communities, helping to create what historian Phillip Troutman has identified as "geopolitical literacy" among enslaved people.[9]

Still, the enormous risk of running away ensured that far-flung havens of freedom remained little more than a dream for the vast majority of enslaved African Americans. Furthermore, the majority of those who did escape bondage remained in the United States, either in free states north of the Ohio River or in urban spaces where they hoped to avoid recapture.[10] Nonetheless, enslaved people crossed international free-soil borders regularly throughout the nineteenth century. For some, international free-soil borders were simply closer than domestic free states, as was the case for enslaved people in the southwest who absconded across the border between the United States and Mexico. For others, especially in the wake of the 1850 Fugitive Slave Act, the increased security that specific international free-soil havens provided made the longer journey worth it. Whether they remained in bondage, escaped to free spaces within the United States, or crossed international borders, enslaved and self-emancipated people viewed international free-soil havens as places of hope and freedom that interrupted the geography of slaveholders' power.

For free African Americans, international free-soil havens meant something a bit different. First and foremost, they offered possible alternatives to the oppression and discrimination that people of color faced in the United States. Beginning in the early nineteenth century, it seemed increasingly clear to many free black northerners that the United States and its white citizenry remained staunchly opposed to extending the promises and protections of the U.S. Constitution to people of color – despite African Americans' ongoing efforts and activism to define themselves into the fabric of citizenship.[11] International free-soil havens, by contrast, seemed unburdened by the social and civic weight of slavery in the United States. As a result, they became sites for the development and trial of a range of political, social, and economic ideas related to black liberty and empowerment.

Throughout the nineteenth century, free-soil havens abroad inspired international black trade networks, alternative crop economies designed to undercut produce grown by slave labor, and the evolution of black nationalist thought and enterprise.[12] Particularly in moments of social and political rupture, like when states passed laws restricting black people's rights or when Congress passed the 1850 Fugitive Slave Act, free African Americans engaged in deep and sustained discussion about where they might go in order to experience meaningful freedom with equal standing before the law. Whether they left or, like the vast majority of free African Americans, stayed to fight for equality in the United States, free black people throughout the nineteenth century recognized international free-soil havens as a powerful force in the fight for racial justice.

Because international free-soil havens provided examples of black liberation – both as spaces where slavery had been immediately or gradually abolished and as places where free and self-emancipated people might experience liberty unfettered by the threat of capture or enslavement – anti-slavery advocates and reformers also saw them as key sites of study and social engineering. When neighboring empires and republics passed anti-slavery legislation and abolition laws, American anti-slavery advocates took note and took action. Black and white activists alike assiduously observed and assessed international free-soil havens in order to demonstrate the practicability of emancipation, and they evaluated the outcomes of other governments' emancipation processes in order to formulate specific arguments regarding how to dismantle slavery in the United States. These places, they argued, showed that the abolition of slavery was realistic, safe, and unlikely to cause the long-term economic damage forecasted by enslavers and their supporters.

Anti-slavery advocates and reformers also saw international free-soil havens as places to identify and even cultivate the legal practices and social interventions they believed would best support black freedom. They sent investigatory missions to places where slavery had been dismantled, offered philanthropic assistance to black communities, and advocated for black emigrants with local, regional, and imperial governments. Significantly, while evaluating and comparing the living conditions and socio-economic prospects facing people of African descent in disparate free-soil environments, black and white observers often reached contradictory conclusions about what practices and interventions were paramount for safeguarding black freedom – and what black freedom should even entail. African Americans tended to focus on all aspects of civic life, from access to education and economic opportunity to voting rights and the ability to hold public office. White observers tended to focus on administrative and legal mechanisms that guaranteed equality under the law, but not much else.

Although they did not always agree on what made international free-soil havens truly meaningful spaces of freedom, black and white anti-slavery advocates did agree that positive reports about the outcome of black freedom would contribute to the anti-slavery cause. Reflecting what historian Ibram X. Kendi has described as "uplift suasion," they believed that evidence of good behavior, industriousness, and success in freedom had the capacity to diminish racism and white opposition to abolition.[13] Laboring to prove what black people were capable of if the fetters of slavery and racism were removed, anti-slavery activists circulated their copious observations and conclusions with one another through the anti-slavery press. In the process, they defined the specific attributes that they believed made free soil "free" and that they believed would best contribute to emancipation if implemented in the United States.

The phenomenon of finding freedom across international borders was not new, however. Long before the term "free soil" entered the anti-slavery lexicon, knowledge that political borders and boundaries could be crossed in a gambit to secure one's freedom was already a familiar element of slavery's geopolitical landscape. In eighteenth-century North America, imperial powers held out the promise of freedom to one another's slaves in the hopes of undermining each other's economic and social security. During the ill-fated 1739 Stono Rebellion, for example, enslaved men and women marched from Britain's South Carolina colony toward neighboring Spanish Florida, responding to a well-known Spanish promise that freedom and protection would be granted to British slaves who converted to Catholicism.[14] Thirty-six years later, Dunmore's Proclamation of 1775 inspired thousands of "American" slaves to cross British military lines in an effort to secure their freedom during the American Revolution.[15]

It was in the aftermath of the political revolutions severing imperial powers from their overseas colonies, however, that international free-soil borders emerged as truly salient reference points within the geopolitical landscape of Atlantic slavery. As American, Haitian, and Spanish American revolutions began to redraw political borders in the late eighteenth and early nineteenth centuries, they created a growing and evolving map of freedom based on the new nations' varying commitments to the idea of universal liberty.[16] Simultaneously, the loss of thirteen mainland colonies encouraged British abolitionists to pursue anti-slave trade projects that focused on ending the transatlantic slave trade, including establishing a black colony in Sierra Leone.[17] These changing circumstances all contributed to the emergence of international free-soil havens that seemed increasingly relevant to enslavers, enslaved people, free African Americans, and white reformers in the United States.

Of course, spaces of freedom were not unique to international locales. After the American Revolution, black and white reformers in the United States – and enslaved people themselves – leveraged ambiguity around the issue of slavery in the new republic to create free spaces at the state level in places like Pennsylvania, Massachusetts, Vermont, and Rhode Island. Over time, state-level anti-slavery legislation in places like Connecticut and New York and the prohibition of slavery in states carved out of the Northwest Territory (Ohio, Indiana, Illinois, Michigan, Wisconsin) further expanded spaces of freedom within the nineteenth-century United States.[18] These zones of freedom were enormously important for both free and self-emancipated African Americans, offering potential safety from recapture and opportunities for collective organizing and activism around emancipation, racial justice, and citizenship rights. In some cases, they even functioned as domestic free-soil havens when enslaved people crossed specific state borders and lodged freedom suits in court, hoping to secure their liberty based on local laws.[19]

Yet there was a fundamental difference between domestic spaces of freedom and the international free-soil havens that began to dot the horizon beginning in the late eighteenth century. In the United States, freedom at the state level was always circumscribed by the fact that, at the federal level, the institution of slavery remained sanctioned and protected. Enslavers' reach into ostensibly free spaces was a point of major contention and concern throughout the antebellum era.[20] While the vast majority of free black people and self-emancipated men and women nevertheless remained within the United States, the particular significance and appeal of international free-soil havens stemmed from the fact that slavery had been abolished throughout the land and at the highest levels of government, providing a higher level of protection against re-enslavement and, in many places, equal standing for black people. In other words, international free-soil havens were important destinations and meaningful sites of American anti-slavery thought and activism in part because the promise of freedom in domestic spaces was curtailed by the fact that slavery was condoned and upheld at the national level.

Often, the significance of international free-soil havens had as much to do with the debates they inspired and the possibilities they represented as it did with the lived experiences of those who crossed their borders. When opportunities arose to emigrate to international free-soil locales, black communities across the northeast and mid-Atlantic gathered to discuss the practical and ideological implications of relocating to places where black liberty and equality were enshrined in law. While the overwhelming majority of free African Americans stayed to fight for "birthright citizenship" in the United States, the possibility of free-soil migration sparked intense debate within individual communities, at national conventions, and through the pages of the black newspaper press over the course of several decades.[21] Should African Americans leave the country or continue to fight for equality from their homes in the United States?[22] Would leading successful lives in free-soil havens prove the merits of black freedom and thereby contribute to achieving abolition in the United States, or would it ultimately strengthen the institution of slavery by removing its most vocal antagonists? What allegiance did African Americans owe the United States and the fight for equality within it when there were other places where they could experience equality immediately? As free-soil alternatives expanded beyond the United States, they facilitated important discussions among black communities about national identity and citizenship at a time when slavery remained a defining institution in American life.[23]

The prospect of international free-soil migration similarly tapped into diverse conversations held among white anti-slavery advocates.

Nineteenth-century anti-slavery advocacy encompassed a wide and evolving array of ideological outlooks on slavery, abolition, and the strategies by which freedom should be achieved. From abolitionists who wanted immediate, uncompensated emancipation to conservative anti-slavery thinkers who believed in more gradual approaches to dismantling the slave system, there was enormous ideological and political breadth among slavery's nineteenth-century opponents.[24] Many of these differences formed and hardened in relation to the possibilities presented by free-soil havens abroad. While abolitionists tended to focus on how the example and practical implementation of abolition abroad could be replicated (or improved upon) in the United States, the idea of relocating black people altogether proved to be particularly captivating for conservative white reformers, gradual anti-slavery advocates, and individuals who abhorred slavery but believed that there was no place in the United States for non-white people.[25]

For those who thought that the United States should adopt a gradual approach to emancipation, free-soil relocation projects functioned as a kind of safety valve, taking the pressure off the slave system. Relocating free black people outside the United States, in their perspective, offered the U.S. a chance to save itself from a violent "race war" like the Haitian Revolution. In the meantime, they believed, more conservative anti-slavery measures could be enacted. Many also believed that removing people of color from the United States would make anti-slavery legislation more palatable to white Americans while simultaneously protecting free black communities from the debilitating effects of white prejudice.

However, while many conservative white anti-slavery advocates honestly hoped that free-soil relocation would promote an eventual end to slavery, their ideas regarding the removal of black men, women, and children from the United States reflected the pervasive racism of most white Americans. They might have seen slavery as a moral evil that needed to be overcome, but that did not mean that they wanted to live side by side with African Americans in the United States. Moreover, conservative reformers' interest in black relocation resonated with many slaveholders, who saw free-soil relocation as a promising strategy to delay progress toward freedom by removing a dangerous anti-slavery demographic: freed slaves.

As self-emancipated people, free black men and women, and black and white anti-slavery advocates looked (and sometimes went) abroad to international free-soil havens, they defined and redefined what these places meant and why. Individually and collectively, free-soil spaces inspired and refined a wide range of ideas, opinions, experiences, and hopes over a half century. From a practical standpoint, free-soil havens often fell short of their promise – they rarely received as many migrants as anti-slavery enthusiasm made it seem, and they were largely unable to provide indisputable evidence of the positive socio-economic effects of emancipation. Many people who crossed international free-soil borders filled with hope eventually returned to the United States disappointed and disillusioned. Time and time again, discussion and debate regarding the relevance of international free soil to the fight against American slavery focused on the disparity between migrants' hopes and expectations and the reality of social prejudice, economic strain, and political upheaval that they often experienced abroad.

Nevertheless, these places figured into the anti-slavery imagination of freedom in powerful ways. Over time, as anti-slavery advocates discussed the implications of international free-soil havens for the future of American slavery, they developed a shared geopolitical language linking different places with a wide variety of phenomena such as escape, equality, free (non-slave) labor, economic opportunity, and anti-slavery violence. These places accrued substantial symbolic value within the American anti-slavery movement because, simply, people thought about them a lot. And thinking about them helped to structure the set of ideas they had about freedom.

By bringing disparate locations and many viewpoints into one field of analysis, this book offers the first evaluation of how international free-soil havens collectively affected a national anti-slavery movement. It stands on mighty shoulders, bringing together a vibrant body of scholarship on African American migration streams and transnational anti-slavery activism in the nineteenth century. Various forms of relocation, to use an umbrella term, brought African American migrants across diverse free-soil borders throughout the nineteenth century – although these migration streams were characterized by vastly different philosophies regarding black freedom.[26] This book draws from rich histories of the black-led *emigration* projects that brought black people to Haiti and Canada, as well as the burgeoning literature tracing the experiences of black emigrants crossing the southwest border into Mexico.[27] It also incorporates scholarship on the longstanding debates over *colonization* – the relocation projects to West Africa typically associated with the white-led American Colonization Society.[28] And it builds on a robust foundation of scholarship tracing the routes to freedom forged by self-emancipated men and women who crossed international borders by land and by sea to Canada, Mexico, the Caribbean, and even England, stirring enthusiasm from abolitionists and panic from slaveholders in equal measure.[29]

Anti-slavery activists also criss-crossed the Atlantic. Black and white abolitionists performed important advocacy work on British soil, and the British provided the American anti-slavery cause with powerful political, moral, and financial aid. In showing how international anti-slavery networks and the influence of British abolitionism shaped the contours of the long fight for freedom in the United States, this book follows in the footsteps of scholars like R. J. M. Blackett, Caleb McDaniel, Van Gosse, and Edward Rugemer.[30] People, aid, and ideas moved fluidly across international borders throughout the antebellum period, and, as scholars of these movements have shown, the history of the American anti-slavery movement simply cannot be told without these transnational connections.

Stitching together into one frame of analysis all the places that people went – and the networks, ideas, and migration streams they inspired – offers a new perspective on the anti-slavery movement in the United States. This approach not only offers a more complete reflection of how American activists, observers, emigrants, runaways, allies, and ideologues understood the geography of slavery and freedom in the world around them, it depicts how their various hopes, dreams, and expectations about freedom – as well as their strategies for how to achieve it – were often developed and honed by engaging with all these locales at once.

Charting the transnational geography informing how people conceptualized freedom beyond the borders of the United States, this book also reshapes an important and familiar narrative: the Underground Railroad to Canada. Both the Underground Railroad and Canada are powerful symbols of escape and freedom in U.S. cultural memory.[31] However, their close relationship in narratives of freedom has overshadowed the longer and more geographically diverse history of runaway slaves in North America and occluded the complex and uncertain process by which Canada *became* a powerful geographical reference point for abolitionist sentiment.

Placing the escape of self-emancipated slaves across the U.S.–Canada border into the context of the broader geopolitical currents dictating the practical and political relevance of different international free-soil borders allows for a more precise analysis of three interrelated phenomena: it shows how and why Canada became the premier international destination for self-liberated individuals; it illuminates how the *idea* of the Underground Railroad to Canada influenced anti-slavery activism in the United States; and it further contributes to our understanding of the enormous impact that border-crossing slaves had on national politics. Following in the footsteps of historical individuals like Madison Washington and Mary Ann Shadd, this book shows that Canada's significance within the American anti-slavery movement was fundamentally linked to an evolving geography of international free-soil havens and to the different visions of racial justice these spaces represented.

Bringing diverse migration streams into one field of analysis also expands our understanding of how nineteenth-century relocation projects affected ideas about national and political identities. While historians generally agree that African Americans' rejection of white-led colonization projects helped to forge a shared vision of identity and national belonging in the United States, my research reframes this analysis by suggesting that black political identity was formed as much through an *engagement* with the myriad opportunities presented by international free-soil spaces as it was by a rejection of colonization.[32] Examining the experiences of free-soil migrants abroad helped black Americans develop and articulate specific ideas regarding the value of American citizenship and what they wanted from the U.S. government.

At the same time, however, many white people in the United States, whether they considered themselves pro-slavery, anti-slavery, or entirely agnostic on the matter, felt that there was no room in the nation for free people of African descent. International free soil provided a strategy of rejection and exclusion. White Americans often saw black Americans as competition for labor and land, as harbingers of racial "amalgamation" or violence, or simply as unwelcome embodiments of difference and "otherness." They typically believed in black Americans' inherent inferiority and did not want them to be a part of the body politic. As a result, white people across the nation protested against abolitionism and any activism in support of racial equality, and many whites supported the forced relocation of freed slaves as a way to rid the country of non-white people. In short, white Americans throughout the nineteenth century exerted what anthropologist Arjun Appadurai has labeled a "predatory identity." They mobilized around the principle that the United States was a fundamentally "white" nation and saw the presence (and, worse, the potential equality) of free black people as a threat to the American national identity.[33] By advocating for the relocation of free African Americans to free-soil spaces abroad, conservative anti-slavery advocates represented the interests of white people committed to racial homogeneity and white supremacy.

* * *

The ability to translate information about international free-soil locales into distinct, concrete ideas about slavery, emancipation, and national identity was made possible by the fact that American anti-slavery observers regularly produced information about them. Modeling a form of fact-finding social inquiry that became the backbone of transatlantic reform movements in the nineteenth century, politicians, activists, migrants, missionaries, and newspaper editors studied migrant experiences abroad and reported on them in the form of pamphlets, books, and editorials.[34] Generating enormous quantities of material, they created what communications scholar Carolyn Calloway-Thomas describes as "a rigorous and comprehensive database for propaganda purposes."[35] In the process, this book demonstrates, anti-slavery advocates developed an information culture that emphasized the particular value of eyewitness testimonials and firsthand investigations. Trusted agents conducted investigatory missions and published their travel accounts, anti-slavery societies solicited information from on-site officials or other designated "experts," and individuals with personal experience delivered moving speeches on the lessons of international free soil at conventions, on lecture circuits, and in the halls of Congress. These free-soil reports and reflections were circulated far and wide through the anti-slavery press and its pro-slavery counterparts.

The widespread circulation of such material was facilitated by the fact that U.S. print culture was expanding rapidly during these years thanks to rising literacy rates, increased infrastructure, new technology, and a vigorous practice of reprinting that developed in the absence of copyright laws. Americans in far-flung locales connected with each other each time they picked up a newspaper. And with diverse experiences and viewpoints reaching into the homes of growing audiences, readers developed shared ideas about the world around them. They created dynamic communities of shared interest across great geographical divides.[36]

Rather than unifying the nation, however, these developments were accompanied by a deepening sense of division.[37] For their part, anti-slavery advocates created a veritable print industry around the practice of cataloging the sins of slavery and disseminating their opposition to it far and wide. The expansion of American print culture created for them what literary scholar Jeannine Marie DeLombard has called an "alternative tribunal" for putting slavery on trial before a reading public – and which has left behind a rich record of the conversations and practices that gave their movement life.[38]

Yet even as material printed and circulated for a public audience reveals the myriad ways that anti-slavery advocates gathered, developed, and shared ideas about international free-soil havens, there are inevitably some stories that an archive of published material does not capture. As historian Mary Niall Mitchell has shown, for example, personal letters produced by school children in New Orleans illuminate the particular resonance of Haiti and Mexico in the way that young Louisianans imagined freedom.[39] In addition, the fact that presses publishing anti-slavery material were located in the Northeast, Mid-Atlantic, and Midwest means that they generally slanted toward views and opinions circulating in those regions. While a broad focus on anti-slavery print culture does not fully account for such regional nuance or for unpublished reflections regarding international free soil, it does illuminate the scope and variety of free-soil conversations developing among an anti-slavery public increasingly interconnected through the national circulation of different forms of print media.

Anti-slavery advocates were also prolific writers. As historian Manisha Sinha aptly points out, "whatever [abolitionists] lacked in power, they made up for by outproducing their mighty opponents in newspapers, books, pamphlets, letters, diaries, memoirs, material, and artwork, creating a huge, complicated historical archive."[40] Thanks to massive and ongoing digitization projects at libraries, museums, and other repositories across the country, there are now more of these anti-slavery print artifacts available at the click of a button than one could hope to sift through in a lifetime. Online libraries, collections, and databases extend this project's reach far beyond the traditional research I conducted at brick-and-mortar institutions such as the National Archives of the United States and Canada, and at repositories such as the public libraries of Toronto and Boston. Digitized collections have, for example, allowed this project to bring together voices from sixty different newspapers encompassing a broad variety of viewpoints from across the United States. The wealth of archival sources now readily available enables this study to effectively recreate both the broad strokes and sharp detail of how nineteenth-century anti-slavery advocates understood the evolving geopolitics of Atlantic slavery and freedom.

The sheer volume of anti-slavery material available in this digital age presents unique methodological challenges, however, stemming from the de-textualized way they are typically navigated. Using keyword searches and their results can, in principle, lead historians to over-determine textual linkages and predispose them to see connections that may, in fact, have been more tenuous. Historians also risk missing data when using keyword searches because relevant material does not contain the precise words, phrases, or spelling used to conduct the search, or because optical character recognition software (OCR) may misread or simply miss relevant sources originally produced on nineteenth-century printing presses. And finally, digital archives – often presented in a document-by-document format – can obscure the original context in which the reading public actually met archival material.

Yet the potential limitations of such a large and potentially de-textualized archive are not insurmountable. In fact, as literary historian

Ryan Cordell has shown, digital archives are uniquely suited to help scholars identify patterns that transcend individual texts and authors to illuminate how reading publics saw the world around them.[41] In this case, keyword searches within digital archives immediately reveal the frequency with which anti-slavery advocates discussed free-soil havens in material printed for public consumption. Furthermore, once keyword search results have been carefully scrutinized to determine that each document is a substantively relevant source, the likelihood of missing data suggests that the "incidence frequency" of international free-soil havens being discussed in print was likely *higher* than keyword search returns indicate. Restricting search parameters can also reveal more detailed information. Tabulating how frequently different free-soil havens were discussed within specific newspapers, for example, demonstrates the regularity with which readers of the anti-slavery newspaper press encountered information about multiple locales in the pages of a single edition. Conducting targeted keyword searches across many newspapers simultaneously shows that specific information regarding international free-soil havens was commonly reprinted in newspapers from Maine to Maryland to Ohio.

Most importantly, however, this study uses keyword database searches to supplement, rather than supplant, a traditional historical methodology based on the close reading of many historical sources. In researching this book, I used keyword database searches to reveal important patterns regarding how ideas circulated and were shared through an expanding print network, *and* I conducted cover-to-cover examinations of anti-slavery newspapers, pamphlets, and books to illuminate what anti-slavery advocates from across North America thought about free-soil havens abroad and their relevance to the American anti-slavery movement.

* * *

When examined in light of international free-soil havens and the international geopolitics that gave rise to them, the timeline of American anti-slavery looks different than a more traditional, national periodization of U.S. history before the Civil War. This study begins and ends at moments when the U.S. government was presented with specific recommendations regarding the future of free African Americans that were formulated in relation to international free-soil opportunities. In 1813, a well-known African American northerner, Paul Cuffe, presented a petition to the U.S. Congress for financial support to help black emigrants relocate to Great Britain's Sierra Leone colony in West Africa. After England abolished the transatlantic slave trade in 1807, its Sierra Leone colony was on the front lines of British efforts to curb other nations' human trafficking, and Cuffe saw it as a promising free-soil locale for African Americans looking for better opportunities than they had in the United States.

Exactly fifty years later, in 1863, a wartime commission appointed by President Abraham Lincoln reported back with its recommendations regarding the future of former slaves freed by the Emancipation Proclamation. The commission's report was significantly influenced by interviews conducted with formerly enslaved men and women in Canada, all collected by a commissioner who believed that Canada could provide the most instructive guidance on the topic of black freedom. Framed by these episodes, this book introduces a timeline of the American anti-slavery movement that emphasizes the importance of international patterns and events reshaping the geography of Atlantic slavery and freedom in the nineteenth century.

In the last several decades, widespread interest in narratives of slavery and resistance has increased in the United States as Americans seek to understand and grapple with the many, often tragic, ways our nation's history of slavery and institutional racism still reverberates in our daily lives. Scholars, filmmakers, artists, activists, politicians, and the public continue to explore and examine the United States' long and continuing history of black oppression and resilience in order to see a path forward. In a sense, this study captures a fifty-year period in which nineteenth-century Americans were engaged in a similar process on an international scale. American men and women, black and white, looked out from the borders of the United States to draw hope and inspiration from the surrounding geopolitical landscape. As pockets of international free soil began to dot the horizon, they provided evidence that slavery could be eliminated and that racial justice could prevail.

Although anti-slavery advocates and reformers often disagreed about what lessons should be drawn from free-soil havens abroad, they did agree that studying the way these locales experienced the transition from slavery to freedom would prove instructive for dismantling slavery and achieving racial equality in the United States. As models, symbols, and destinations, international free-soil havens brought a transnational geography of slavery and freedom right into the heart of the American anti-slavery movement.

CHAPTER 1

Reform and Relocation: West Africa and Haiti in the Early Republic

... Let American people of color awake,
For Providence calls them to go and partake –
Ye despised and poor are invited to come,
And accept a delightful and permanent home;
Where room may be found for ten millions to dwell;
And all become thriving who aim to do well.

~ From "A Poem To the Free and Independent Haytiens"
J. Kenrick (1826)[1]

In December 1810, American sea captain, black activist, and prominent entrepreneur Paul Cuffe left for the shores of Freetown, Sierra Leone. He had become intrigued by the possibility of commercial and economic opportunities in the British anti-slave-trade colony and was determined to investigate how African Americans might benefit from them as migrants and trading partners.

Born in Massachusetts, Cuffe was the son of a formerly enslaved Akan man from West Africa and a Wampanoag woman. As a mariner and merchant, he had steadily worked his way up to become one of the wealthiest black men in the United States in the first two decades of the nineteenth century. He was also a Quaker. He maintained transatlantic trade and humanitarian networks with fellow members of the Society of Friends, and he was determined to fight racial injustice through benevolent work. Thanks to his connections in England, he had begun to envision Sierra Leone as the foundation for strong, black-led commercial ventures that would contribute to the economic uplift of black people on both sides of the Atlantic.[2]

Initially conceptualized in 1786 as a means of alleviating the conditions of poor black migrants in England following the American Revolution, Sierra Leone and the idea of a black colony in West Africa had briefly captured the imagination of black Americans in the late eighteenth century.[3] Richard Allen, a prominent minister, and over fifty of his fellow Philadelphians had even signed a petition addressed to the Second Federal Congress asking for government support for a similar endeavor. Yet the petition was never actually sent, and the issue lay dormant for the next twenty-five years.[4] Then, when England abolished the transatlantic slave trade in 1807, its Sierra Leone colony was suddenly on the front lines of British efforts to curb human trafficking by other nations. The epicenter of Britain's anti-slave-trade activities along the African coast, it was also the focal point of "legitimate commerce," an anti-slave-trade concept based on the belief that trade in African staple crops could undercut the trade in human beings.[5]

It was at this point in time that the colony piqued Paul Cuffe's interest. Looking toward Sierra Leone, he saw commercial opportunity in supporting legitimate commerce and promoting trade between the United States, Britain, and Sierra Leone. He also saw the benefits of encouraging the migration of African Americans to a place ostensibly free of racial prejudice – and where they could anchor an agricultural economy and trade network that would connect people of African descent across three continents.[6] And so, with the support of the African Institution – the administrative body overseeing the colony – Cuffe arrived in Sierra Leone in March 1811 to establish trade ties and explore the merits of supporting voluntary African American emigration to the region.

Cuffe spent several months discussing the colony's economic and labor needs with members of the African Institution in Sierra Leone and during an extended interval in England. He was deeply impressed by the colony's potential for trade, for emigration, and for racial uplift. When he returned to the United States, he delivered lectures in Baltimore, Philadelphia, and New York, and he printed a pamphlet to publicize the benefits of African American settlement in fledgling Freetown.[7] He even helped to establish

U.S. auxiliaries of the African Institution to encourage active recruitment and support for his emigration and trade ventures.

The War of 1812 curtailed the immediate impact of Cuffe's activities, but he was undeterred. Taking up the mantle where Richard Allen's Philadelphia meeting had left off in 1786, he sent a petition to Congress in 1813 requesting financial support to send emigrant families to the British colony. Citing his recent voyage, the support of leading British abolitionists, and his optimism that free black people were well disposed toward the project, he assured members of Congress that aid from the United States would directly promote civilization in Africa.[8] Although Cuffe's petition fell on deaf ears at the time, it marked an important first step in turning his dream of African American emigration to Sierra Leone into a real possibility.

As soon as the war ended in 1815, Cuffe launched a correspondence campaign to reestablish his project among a sizeable network of friends throughout the United States and Britain. His first order of business was to find colonists who were prepared to accompany him on a second voyage to Sierra Leone. Planning to sail later that year, he hoped for as many colonists as his ship could carry. Casting wide nets, he wrote to prominent black Philadelphians Richard Allen and James Forten, to his friend Peter Williams, Jr., the first African American minister of New York City's Protestant Episcopal Church, and to Daniel Coker, a black minister and schoolteacher in Baltimore, Maryland. He asked each of them for help in securing willing migrants to join him.

His efforts seemed to bear fruit. On March 21, 1815, a good friend and well-known teacher at Boston's African School, Prince Saunders, expressed his own interest in sailing to Sierra Leone and noted that he also knew of "several families who are very desirous to go to Africa to live." Six days later, Cuffe boasted to James Forten that he had found between ten and fourteen families ready to depart from Boston and "had application from New Haven, Rhode Island, and Providence."[9] Within just a few short months, Cuffe had ignited interest in his colonization plan up and down the New England seaboard.

Despite these pockets of enthusiasm, however, Cuffe's expansive vision for transporting African American emigrants to Sierra Leone never came to pass. Uncertain financing and reports of poor living conditions plagued his efforts to generate widespread involvement. In addition, the African

Institution itself came under fire due to accusations of mismanagement. In 1815, just as Cuffe was revamping his communication networks after the war, he and his British allies had to spend considerable time and energy fending off substantial negative publicity.[10]

Prior to his death in 1817, Cuffe had only managed to transport thirty-eight emigrants to the British colony.[11] And yet, while Cuffe never realized his vision of mass migration, his efforts to galvanize domestic and international interest in the economic and socio-political opportunities of colonization struck a chord among free African Americans and white reformers.[12] He set the wheels in motion for one of the most wide-ranging, controversial, and divisive issues in the anti-slavery movement of the nineteenth century: whether, how, and to what end black Americans might leave the United States.

In part, Cuffe's plan received sustained interest because meaningful freedom for black communities in the North, as well as the project of racial uplift that many black leaders hoped would pave the way for it, seemed more elusive than ever in the 1810s. Between 1810 and 1820, the free black population of the northeastern United States grew from approximately 75,000 to nearly 93,000, largely due to the gradual emancipation laws passed in the wake of the American Revolution.[13] The black population in Massachusetts alone grew to be seven times what it had been before American independence.[14] Yet public policy and private interest alike assumed that whites were still entitled to free black men and women's time, labor, and personal lives; that free black people were, to use the words of historian Joanne Pope Melish, "public resources."[15]

Patterns of social prejudice and labor discrimination intensified in tandem with the growth of free black communities. Black leaders like James Forten and Richard Allen were deeply concerned that violence against free African Americans in northern cities, the loss of suffrage rights, and diminishing economic opportunities were all foreboding signs that free black people's rights were being increasingly curtailed by legal and extra-legal means.[16] It is not surprising, then, that many free African Americans were receptive to Paul Cuffe's overtures – at least, in principle. Through the intercession of prominent black elites and directly through their own letters, potential emigrants regularly requested information about Paul Cuffe's upcoming plans.[17] Freedom in Sierra Leone, a colony established by the British as a wedge of freedom aimed right at the heart of the transatlantic slave trade, seemed a reasonable alternative for many to legal exclusion and social prejudice in the United States.

Before Cuffe died in 1817, his emigration plans also captured the interest of a white reformer, Robert Finley, a young evangelical Christian passionately committed to benevolent work and to the eradication of social evils. Concerned with what he saw as "wretchedness" among free black people in early 1816, Finley lamented that "every thing connected with their condition, including their colour, is against them; nor is there much prospect that their state can ever be greatly ameliorated while they shall continue among us."[18] After studying Britain's Sierra Leone experiment with great interest, he became increasingly convinced that black colonization seemed a promising strategy to simultaneously counteract what he saw as the deterioration of African Americans' social conditions in the United States and lift the burden of their support from white society. "Could not the rich and benevolent devise means to form a colony on some part of Africa, similar to the one at Sierra Leone," he wondered, "which might gradually induce many free blacks to go there and settle . . .?"[19]

To this end, Finley took the lead in establishing the "Society for the Colonization of Free People of Color of America" – or, simply, the American Colonization Society (ACS) – in late 1816. He argued that such an organization would not only siphon free black people out of the United States and allow African American emigrants to enjoy a "better situation," it would uplift African civilization through the settlement of "partially civilized and Christianized" migrants.[20] Reflecting the hopes of his contemporaries in London's African Institution, Finley imagined that an American counterpart to Britain's free colony in Africa would substantively improve social conditions for the migrants themselves and for those they left behind in the United States. Like many white advocates of black relocation, he also claimed that colonization would, eventually, lead to the end of slavery.[21]

The ACS was officially formed on December 21, 1816, in Washington, DC. It was an elite white affair comprising white reformers and white politicians. And yet, because of Finley's abiding interest in modeling his African colonization project on Sierra Leone, he was inspired to incorporate Paul Cuffe's expertise regarding the British colony into the ACS's mission right from the start. He recognized that Cuffe's experience sailing to and from Sierra Leone and drumming up enthusiasm for black migration was invaluable to a centralized effort to relocate African Americans en masse to western Africa. So, just prior to the society's founding, he solicited Cuffe's information and advice in the hopes of gathering geopolitical and geographic statistics on Sierra Leone and evaluating its "prospects of happiness" for African American colonists.[22]

Responding in early 1817, Cuffe encouraged Finley's "great, great and laborous [sic] task" and offered his perspective on the project. Commenting on Sierra Leone's geography, soil, population, and general health, he indicated that the population seemed to have grown between his voyages in 1811 and 1815, that there was a good harbor, and that arable land was advantageously situated near Freetown. He did note, however, that the soil itself was poor.[23] No doubt enthusiastic about the prospect of institutional support, Cuffe also sent his insights regarding Sierra Leone to Samuel John Mills, another leading figure in the newly formed ACS. To Mills, Cuffe specifically recommended that his friend, Peter Williams, Jr., be selected to oversee a voyage to Africa's western coast to seek an adequate location for the settlement of a new colony under American control.[24] In this, and in many other particulars, the ACS took Cuffe's advice.

Yet Finley and the ACS did not take to heart the entirety of Cuffe's impressions regarding colonization's potential, especially those regarding African Americans' political standing. Before expanding on any of the specific information Finley had requested on the colony's geography, Cuffe reminded his readers in clear terms that black migrants did not just relocate across the Atlantic Ocean for the arable land. Rather, he wrote, in Sierra Leone "they are instilled to every Proviledg [sic] of free born Citizens, and fill stations in their Courts."[25] His reminder went unheard. Cuffe was memorialized during the third annual meeting of the ACS for his efforts to encourage African American support of colonization,[26] but his observations on the significance of black emigrants' political rights and citizenship status were never incorporated into the ACS's thinking on the removal of African Americans from the United States. While reformers like Robert Finley and Samuel J. Mills hoped to improve what they saw as the degraded socio-economic conditions of free African Americans in the northern United States, they saw their work as a moral and material issue – not a political one.

When both Finley and Mills died in 1817 and 1818, respectively, the ACS's leadership shifted away from northern reformers altogether. By 1821, when the society purchased land in West Africa for its new colony, Liberia, its leadership had settled firmly in the hands of southern politicians. While reform-minded members professed that colonization would alleviate African Americans' social woes and therefore support the cause of gradual emancipation, it became increasingly clear that many of the ACS's members supported African colonization only because making relocation mandatory for all freed slaves would diminish the population of free African Americans in U.S. territory. White Americans' fears of slave majorities and free black populations had escalated precipitously after the Haitian Revolution (1791–1804), and the idea of colonizing freed slaves in Africa offered a way to diffuse what many whites viewed as the nascent threat of slave unrest and the unchecked growth of free black communities.[27] As powerful southerners like Kentucky Congressman Henry Clay took the society's reins, they therefore ensured that any burgeoning anti-slavery reformism within the society was nipped in the bud, warning that their participation specifically hinged on the group avoiding the "delicate question" of slavery.[28]

The shift toward southern leadership prompted vocal criticism of the ACS and of African colonization itself, most especially from within urban black communities.[29] Black leaders urged anti-slavery allies not to be fooled by the ACS's benevolent language: its mission, they argued, would directly hinder the cause of emancipation and cause irreparable harm to the cause of racial justice. Throughout the antebellum period, black communities across the northern and midwestern United States formed anti-colonization societies to protest against what they saw as a clear threat to black Americans' ongoing struggle to be seen and treated as U.S. citizens.[30]

The earliest and most resounding articulation of African American opposition to African colonization was an 1817 protest pamphlet titled, "Address to the humane and benevolent Inhabitants of the city and

county of Philadelphia."[31] Widely circulated throughout the northeastern United States, this well-known document was produced in the wake
of a meeting held by members of Philadelphia's black community on
August 10, 1817. Convened to discuss the issue of colonization, the
meeting drew a crowd of several thousand, large enough to fill the
capacious Mother Bethel AME Church, the religious epicenter of black
Philadelphia founded by Richard Allen in 1787. Although several of the
meeting's elite leaders, including James Forten and Richard Allen,
arrived sympathetic to the concept of colonization, it was clear that the
community at large felt unequivocally opposed to the ACS.[32] By the end
of the meeting, the attendees unanimously voted against supporting the
African colonization plan. They also voted that a pamphlet reflecting
their collective views on colonization and the ACS should be produced
and widely circulated.

The "Address," whose authorship is generally attributed to the meeting's chairman, James Forten, carefully states that it was signed by Forten
and the meeting's secretary, Russell Perrott, "on behalf of the meeting"
and in reflection of decisions "*Resolved Unanimously*" (emphasis in original). A true community document, the pamphlet was keenly concerned
with the relationship between black relocation and the eventual achievement of full emancipation. It argued that the ACS's relocation scheme
would strengthen slavery in the United States rather than weaken it, and
that support for colonization would ultimately undermine the cause of
emancipation. By diminishing the overall black population, the pamphlet warned, colonization would allow enslavers to secure remaining
bondspeople more effectively because they could use the threat of forced
colonization as the "heaviest of punishments." It would enable slaveholders to "enforce increased submission to their wishes and subjection
to their commands." In fact, the pamphlet argued, colonization would
alleviate enslavers' fears of a restive work force, as they would keep only
those deemed "tame and submissive" enslaved in the southern states.
According to Philadelphia's black community, the African colonization
plan would ensure nothing but "perpetual slavery and augmented sufferings" for those left behind in bondage.[33]

But the concern articulated in this pamphlet was not just for those
who remained enslaved. The attendees at the Philadelphia meeting

agreed that colonization would also fail to adequately prepare newly freed colonists for freedom, and thus guarantee their failure in Africa. In the early nineteenth century, most anti-slavery advocates – black and white alike – believed that education and religious ministry were necessary components of preparing slaves for freedom. The 1817 "Address" reflected a significant worry, therefore, that if colonizationists transported freed slaves overseas without first addressing their educational and spiritual needs, the newly freed men and women would be left vulnerable to "every suffering which can afflict the members of the human family."[34] By addressing the detrimental effects of African colonization on both enslaved individuals and freed colonists, the pamphlet argued in no uncertain terms that the plan was thoroughly antithetical to the goal of gradual emancipation and to the well-being of former slaves.

In the process of repudiating the ACS and rejecting colonization, this community document also articulated a specific vision of what meaningful freedom could look like in the United States. It asserted that African Americans in Philadelphia had no desire to leave their homes; they were only interested in improving their situation through the opportunities allowed *all* Americans by the Constitution and by established laws. Colonization, according to the pamphlet's framers, "is not asked for by us; nor will it be required by any circumstances, in our present or future condition; as long as we shall be permitted to share the protection of the excellent laws, and just government that we now enjoy, in common with every individual of the community."[35] Emphasizing the importance of positive law, constitutional rights, just government, and legal equality, the pamphlet identified what mattered most at a time when the meaning of citizenship itself was still fragmented and contested in the United States. In fact, the pamphlet's framers boldly used their rejection of African colonization to claim a specific legal relationship between African Americans and the American government that anticipated a version of citizenship which did not exist until after the Civil War.[36]

However, a close examination of the Philadelphia pamphlet also highlights a generally underappreciated facet of the meeting: there were limits to the participants' willingness to reject relocation in favor of their native soil. Repeatedly emphasizing the importance of laws and rights to the black community's well-being, the language of the pamphlet implied that relocation might yet be something that African Americans would consider *if* the essentials of meaningful freedom (rights, just government, equality) were no longer accessible in the United States. In other words, if migration abroad seemed to offer more freedom than being free in the United States. This qualification to the meeting's anti-colonization stance helps to explain why many African Americans who vociferously rejected colonization nevertheless continued to express interest in and support for competing relocation ideas over the next decade.

The first of these alternatives emerged nearly simultaneously with the formation of the ACS in the early nineteenth century: Haiti. A free black republic since the end of the long and bloody Haitian Revolution in 1804, Haiti became the most influential alternative for African American emigration in the late 1810s and 1820s. The idea first took shape in 1814 when the famous British abolitionist Thomas Clarkson proposed to King Henri Christophe of northern Haiti that he tap into the colonization movement in the United States and encourage African Americans to emigrate to the island nation. Not only would emigration help to develop a middle class in Haiti, Clarkson suggested, it might also encourage the United States government to extend diplomatic recognition to the new republic.[37]

In the following years, the emigration idea gained momentum thanks in part to the networks of interest that Paul Cuffe had developed around Sierra Leone. In Boston, Cuffe had found a particularly receptive audience for his Sierra Leone project in two men: Thomas Paul, the prominent founder of the African Baptist Church, and Prince Saunders, a young teacher at Boston's African School. With Cuffe's encouragement, Saunders and Paul became vocal advocates of West African emigration, and, in 1815, they sailed to Britain in an effort to secure financial backing from British abolitionists.[38] While in London, however, Prince Saunders refocused his attention from Sierra Leone to Haiti when Thomas Clarkson and fellow abolitionist William Wilberforce – both associated with the African Institution with whom Paul Cuffe had worked so closely – commissioned Saunders to act as advisor to Henri Christophe in northern Haiti.[39] Although Paul also became a strong supporter of Haitian emigration, the two parted ways in London. Paul continued to

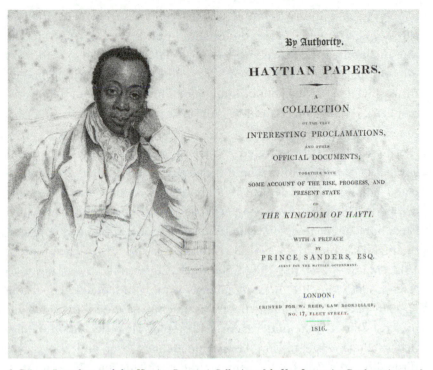

1 Prince Saunders and the *Haytian Papers: A Collection of the Very Interesting Proclamations and Other Official Documents, Together with Some Account of the Rise, Progress, and Present State of the Kingdom of Hayti* (London: W. Reed, 1816). Courtesy of the John Carter Brown Library.

pursue financing for the Sierra Leone project while Saunders accepted the new appointment in Haiti.[40]

By casting his lot with Clarkson, Wilberforce, and Henri Christophe, Saunders helped to promote and popularize the first emigration project sponsored by the Haitian government. He embraced the idea with gusto. In 1816, his very first year as advisor to Henri Christophe, he enthusiastically produced a 228-page book titled *Haytian Papers*, which he commissioned a London bookseller to publish (Figure 1).[41] Identifying himself as the "agent for the Haytian government" and adopting the courtesy title "esquire," Saunders touted Henri Christophe's Haiti and established himself as a leading authority on the island and its government. Convinced that Haiti offered an exciting opportunity for African American emigration, Saunders expounded upon the manners,

happiness, and industry found at all levels of society. He credited
Christophe with "the sincere desire, and firmly settled purpose" to elevate and improve the hearts and lives of all Haitians.[42] Read by reformers
in both England and the United States, the book's first edition proved
successful enough with a public hungry for information about the world's
first black republic that Saunders published a subsequent edition for his
American audience in 1818.[43]

The *Haytian Papers* offered readers a sample of state documents
curated by Saunders to promote the image of a confident and enlightened administration dedicated to stable governance and economic
prosperity. Included were extracts from the "Code Henri," in which
Christophe delineated new plantation labor laws designed to strengthen
the island's economy and social relations, and the text of Christophe's
1814 "Manifesto of the King," in which Christophe vowed never to
"compromise the honour, the liberty, or the independence of the
Haytian people."[44] Framing these documents, Saunders provided his
own assessment of life under Henri Christophe. He reflected on themes
that would emerge in anti-slavery commentary over and over again
throughout the nineteenth century: the character and disposition of
free black people; whether they made good subjects; whether the experiment of black self-government was a triumph; and how the government
could best facilitate the overall success of transitioning an enslaved
population into freedom. In the process of offering his perspective on
these matters, he emphasized the justice and equity of Christophe's
administration and argued that Haiti provided powerful proof that
black men were capable of strong and intelligent political leadership.

But Saunders did not stop there. While providing insight into
Christophe's administration, he also developed a strong argument in
favor of entrusting black liberty to a royalist government. It is not surprising that Saunders – particularly working as a liaison for the British – would
feel sympathetic toward Christophe's monarchy. The British government
had recently established pathways of freedom for African American slaves
during the War of 1812, just as it had famously done during and after the
American Revolution.[45] By contrast, the young United States seemed bent
on further restricting the freedom of its black inhabitants and limiting
republican liberty to white people. The protection afforded African

Americans by the British monarchy, even though such protection rarely extended to Britain's own black population, stood in stark contrast to the unfulfilled promises of American republicanism.

Published just as the two models of government, royalist and republican, seemed to offer African Americans increasingly disparate levels of civic inclusion, the *Haytian Papers* reflected Saunders's belief that a strong monarch had the power to protect black freedom more effectively than a "free" republic of enslavers. "The greatest happiness of a nation," he averred, was to have a king who could make the rights of his country and people respected abroad, and who governed with justice and equity at home. Saunders believed Henri Christophe to be just such a leader. "It is around this wise and valiant King, therefore, my brethren," he declared, "that we ought to rally and to fight until our latest breath to establish our rights, our liberty, and our independence!"[46]

While Prince Saunders's advocacy did encourage some black Americans to reach out to Haitian officials about the possible benefits of resettlement, it was a bit of a rocky start.[47] Notably, Christophe himself did not approve of Saunders publishing the *Haytian Papers*, and when Saunders described himself as an agent of the Haitian government, he did so without Christophe's permission. Moreover, Christophe took umbrage at Saunders's spendthrift lifestyle while he was having the book published in London. Before long, Saunders had fallen out of favor with the king entirely and was sent back to the United States.[48]

Nonetheless, interest in Saunders's perspective on Haiti had already taken hold. He had successfully established himself as an expert on the subject, and he could not have published for a more receptive audience than American anti-slavery advocates. His anti-slavery conservatism fit easily within the mold of gradual emancipationism to which most white anti-slavery advocates of the time adhered, and, significantly, his efforts to develop a viable emigration scheme to Haiti dovetailed with the formation of the ACS and its African relocation project.

Saunders's advocacy of Haitian emigration quickly caught the attention of the American Convention for Promoting the Abolition of Slavery and Improving the Condition of the African Race, the first and only national meeting of anti-slavery advocates in the United States at the time. Since it was first called to order in 1794, this biennial convention brought white delegates from independent state anti-slavery societies to Philadelphia to discuss key issues pertaining to the mission for gradual and total emancipation. Relying on moral influence, its delegates envisioned the convention as a central organization to advise anti-slavery societies and to mediate between anti-slavery interests and the federal government. After achieving initial success in petitioning the federal government to ban the transatlantic slave trade, the American Convention declined over time as a potent social and political force for anti-slavery reform. Yet, by providing a centralized venue for white anti-slavery advocates to try to direct organized anti-slavery activism, it continued to serve an important intellectual function for many anti-slavery advocates. Through its final meeting in 1839, delegates gathered from every state across the country to discuss what they agreed were the most pressing anti-slavery issues of the moment. Their decisions were communicated directly to state anti-slavery societies and circulated regularly in anti-slavery newspapers.[49]

In 1817, African colonization was one of the most pressing issues facing the organization. "The present is a very extraordinary and eventful moment," delegates wrote, as "some project for colonization appears to occupy the minds of a great multitude of our fellow citizens." Recognizing that opinions on the merits of colonization remained "various and unsettled," they wanted clarity on whether or not they should support the idea. In expectation that the issue would have "the most important consequences to the future welfare of our colored population," a seven-member subcommittee was convened to report on what further steps the Convention should take.[50] Feeling the "magnitude of the task," they initially decided to ignore the Haitian alternative, instead focusing their report exclusively on the African colonization plan promoted by the ACS. On this topic, they offered a recommendation of non-support, suggesting that the Convention ought to withhold its approval until *after* the gradual process of emancipation had been fully completed. Meeting just days before Philadelphia's black community convened at Mother Bethel AME Church, this centralized body of white anti-slavery advocates reached the same conclusion: African colonization would not advance the cause of abolition.

Yet convention delegates were not fully satisfied on the matter. At the request of two anti-slavery societies, a special meeting of the fifteenth Convention was held in December of the following year (1818) to focus more intensively on three key issues: colonization (listed first); the illegal slave trade; and the expansion of emancipationism in the United States.[51] In advance of the meeting, several member societies sent requests specifically asking for a broader focus than African colonization and the ACS. Noting that there had been several expensive failures of anti-slave-trade colonization schemes – yet another reason not to support the ACS in Africa – delegates wanted to hear more about the prospects of free African American emigration to *established* destinations.[52] Delegates from several anti-slavery societies requested information about Haiti, and the Abolition Society of Delaware confidently declared that there was "no congregated body who can obtain that information with as much facility as the Convention of the Abolition Societies."[53]

Responding to these requests, the American Convention invited the man who had established himself as the foremost authority on the present state of Haiti: Prince Saunders. Not only had Saunders recently published his American edition of the *Haytian Papers*, he had also been gaining the support of prominent black northerners like James Forten and Russell Perrott, both well known for having authored the anti-colonization pamphlet on behalf of Philadelphia's black community the previous year.[54] Arriving at the Convention's special meeting in 1818, Saunders struck while the iron was hot, providing detailed notes on Haiti's size, demographics, and export economy. "Among the various projects or plans which have been devised or suggested, in relation to emigration," he concluded, "there are none which appear to many persons to wear so much the appearance of feasibility, and ultimate successful and practical operation, as the luxuriant, beautiful and extensive island of Hayti."[55]

Yet there was one outstanding issue related to the prospect of black emigration that Saunders felt compelled to address: he asked the American Convention to adopt measures that would support the unification of Haiti under Henri Christophe (who controlled northern Haiti) and that would encourage the United States to extend political recognition to his kingdom, which it had yet to do. As Prince Saunders saw it, the division of Haiti into two governments destabilized the island's political security. Since 1807, southern Haiti and northern Haiti had been ruled by very different men with very different agendas. In the Kingdom of Northern Haiti, Henri Christophe's leadership was characterized by state-directed, forced plantation labor, his diplomatic agenda lay with the British, and he expressed no intention of intervening in the slavery of other nations. In the south, by contrast, President Alexandre Pétion and his successor, Jean-Pierre Boyer, led a republic that was characterized by personal and economic freedom, proved to be more receptive to French diplomatic overtures than British, and courted international disfavor by adopting an aggressive stance against slavery in surrounding regions.[56]

In fact, Pétion's policies in southern Haiti tapped directly into pro-slavery advocates' worst fears regarding the influence of Haiti and the Haitian Revolution in the Americas: he had established southern Haiti as a free-soil zone, offering legal protection to people enslaved elsewhere.[57] In 1817, just one year prior to Prince Saunders's presentation to the American Convention, seven runaway slaves had absconded from British Jamaica to southern Haiti, likely because they had heard stories about freedom and state protection in Pétion's jurisdiction. They were not disappointed. Deferring to the 1816 Haitian Constitution, which conferred the status of "Haitian" on all people of African or Indian descent residing on the island, Pétion rebuffed British authorities' efforts to have the seven men returned to the Jamaican slaveholder.[58]

In Saunders's view, Pétion's republic was responsible not only for jeopardizing international political support for Haiti, but also for undermining the cause of gradual emancipation by increasing enslavers' hostility toward it. In the *Haytian Papers*, he had put great effort into refuting the general perception of post-revolution Haiti as violent, unstable, and debt-ridden. He had also specifically reassured readers that Henri Christophe would not intervene in the internal affairs of neighboring powers on the topic of slavery.[59] Now, in front of the American Convention, Saunders once again reminded delegates of the pressing need for unification. He wanted his audience to understand that unification under Christophe, rather than Pétion, would be more likely to promote international alliances in support of gradual emancipation. Moreover, he believed that such a reunification would allow the island to fulfill its potential as a politically stable asylum for black Americans. "If the two rival governments of Hayti were consolidated into one well balanced pacific power," he argued, "there are many hundreds of the free people in the New England and middle states, who would be glad to repair there immediately to settle."[60]

Unfortunately for Saunders, his intentions misfired. His call for the American Convention to support Haitian political unification overshadowed his speech's promotion of the emigration scheme. The Convention resolved only that its president would begin corresponding with Britain's African Institution and other influential philanthropists to discuss how best to bring both sides of the island under one government. Although they agreed that the goal of this effort would be to "render that island a safe asylum for such free people of color in the United States and elsewhere, as may choose to emigrate to it," they did not weigh in with an explicit endorsement of Haitian emigration – either for individual migrants or as a step toward the greater project of gradual emancipation.[61]

Notably, attendees of the Convention's special meeting were far less ambivalent on the topic of African colonization. To speak on the subject, they invited Saunders's dear friend James Forten, the wealthy businessman who had long been a prominent figure in Philadelphia's black community. As co-author of the 1817 "Address," he was also a highly visible opponent of colonization. On December 12, 1818, Forten arrived with Saunders in front of the American Convention to provide a general account of the conditions of free African Americans in Philadelphia. Since a cornerstone of both the African and Haitian relocation plans was the argument that conditions for African Americans in the United States were poor and increasingly insurmountable, Forten testified as to whether circumstances were, in fact, so dire – and whether African Americans themselves saw relocation as a reasonable solution.

What Forten provided was a powerful indictment against African colonization that echoed the views collectively articulated by Philadelphia's black community the year before. Moved by his words, the special committee of the American Convention reiterated, in more detail, the collective opposition earlier expressed during their organization's regular meeting. Declaring itself "forcibly impressed with the conviction" that African colonization would have "fatal consequences," the special committee agreed that colonization's effects on the condition of both free people and slaves would be "greatly injurious."[62] To supplement their conclusions, they reproduced the entirety of Forten's 1817 co-authored anti-colonization pamphlet for inclusion at the end of the "circular address" they subsequently sent to every abolition and manumission society in the United States. The opposition of free black people themselves thus became Exhibit A in the American Convention's recommendation against supporting the African colonization scheme.

General disapproval among African Americans and the opposition of a centralized body of white anti-slavery advocates did not prevent the ACS from moving forward, however. In late 1821, it purchased land in West Africa for its Liberia colony and slowly began making headway in the field of white public opinion. Nevertheless, it remained the object of substantial debate for decades to come, and its Liberian enterprise never shook the taint of early accusations that colonization served pro-slavery interests. By contrast, Haitian emigration continued to be promoted by many free African Americans as a black-led alternative to African colonization that could contribute to the cause of racial uplift. Haitian emigration also tantalized those white reformers who harbored deep reservations about the ACS, but who believed that black relocation was the best option for improving the conditions of free African Americans and paving the way for gradual emancipation. Despite the frustration that Prince Saunders must have felt when the American Convention's special meeting concluded without producing a united resolution to encourage Haitian emigration, his speech before the delegates nonetheless increased the visibility of the idea among a national network of anti-slavery advocates.

One man Saunders had certainly inspired was Evan Lewis. A member of the Abolition Society of Delaware who had attended the American Convention's special meeting in 1818, Lewis was so intrigued by the prospect of black emigration to Haiti that he decided to travel to the island himself to learn more about its politics, economy, and society. On October 19, 1819, Lewis wrote directly to Henri Christophe, enumerating the reasons for his proposed visit. First, he wanted to go on behalf of potential emigrants. Patronizingly self-assured that African Americans would have "naturally looked to [American Convention delegates] for advice," Lewis felt himself obliged to see if "a plan could be devised" that would ensure the future happiness and prosperity of black emigrants on the island. Second, he wrote of his commercial interest in visiting Haiti. Much as Paul Cuffe had in Sierra Leone, Lewis saw both material benefit and ideological importance in supporting a "free-produce" economy. He asserted that many people, particularly among the Society of Friends to which he belonged, were interested in procuring coffee and sugar produced by free men and wanted to establish a commercial relationship with free Haitian farmers.[63] And, finally, while visiting the islands on these two points of business, he hoped to behold a novel sight: "the operations of a regularly organized government, and political and civil institutions [that have] for their object the happiness and improvement of a people whom the powers of Christendom have so long and unjustly oppressed." He believed that such a government had the capacity to demonstrate to all nations that black people were as "capable of equal attainments" as whites.[64]

Despite his enthusiasm, Evan Lewis's trip never got off the ground. In 1820, not long after his letter would have arrived, Haiti's political terrain fundamentally altered with the death of Henri Christophe. Two years later, the island unified under the republican leadership of Jean-Pierre Boyer, Pétion's successor in the south. The monarchical government extolled by Prince Saunders had come to a permanent end.

At first, it was unclear whether Boyer would welcome the prospect of African American emigration to the island. But, like Christophe, he came to recognize that emigration could help to secure international political standing and bolster the island's economy by expanding its labor force. In 1824, Boyer therefore decided to extend his own invitation, investing approximately $300,000 to pay for the transportation and initial support of African American emigrants willing to work as agriculturalists and skilled laborers in the island republic.[65] With the Haitian emigration idea now back on firm footing, black and white reformers immediately renewed their efforts to learn what the island had to offer. Without missing a beat, Evan Lewis announced that he was resuscitating his plan to sail for Haiti on a fact-finding mission – though it remains unclear whether this second proposed trip was any more successful in launching than his first.[66]

Where Henri Christophe's overtures to potential emigrants had piqued interest, Jean-Pierre Boyer's invitation sparked significant enthusiasm. As historian Sara Fanning has shown, Boyer's offer enticed African American migrants from all walks of life, from prominent individuals like the Reverend Richard Allen's son, John, to an urban laundress from New York named Hannah Quincy. In all, approximately six thousand free African Americans took advantage of the emigration offer, leaving their homes in a gambit to improve their material conditions in Haiti.[67]

Although these migrants accounted for only a small fraction of the approximately 144,000 free African Americans living in the North and Mid-Atlantic at the time, the opportunity they embraced received substantial coverage in the anti-slavery press.[68] Some of the most enthusiastic reports of Haitian emigration made their way to readers through the pages of the *Genius of Universal Emancipation,* one of the premier anti-slavery newspapers of the 1820s. The paper's editor, Benjamin Lundy, shared the American Convention's censure of African colonization, but regularly examined other black emigration ideas and assessed their potential for weakening the American slave system. Publishing for several years out of Greenville, Tennessee, before moving his operation to Baltimore, Maryland, Lundy was a Quaker who brought his religiously based advocacy of gradual emancipation to readers on a regular basis.[69] With his abiding interest in black relocation, his anti-slavery advocacy and editorial interests reflected a distinctly transnational geography that only became more pronounced as the decade progressed.

By 1825, Lundy had become a passionate believer in the idea that international free-soil emigration would contribute to the achievement of gradual emancipation in the United States. He was therefore determined to "make it his business to collect information, and to notice every material incident, relative to the removal of the colored people, from the United States, to Hayti, Africa, and elsewhere." He was similarly committed to recording the proceedings of the various abolition, emigration, and colonization societies that were proliferating around the United States.[70] He was always on the lookout for information to share. Remarking on Evan Lewis's proposed voyage in 1824, Lundy was delighted to note that Lewis would sail "for the purpose of ascertaining the moral state and condition of the people; their susceptibility of improvement, and the propriety of sending a portion of our colored population there." He expected to "derive much interesting informa- tion" to share with his readers.[71] By mid-decade, his reports on the anti- slavery potential of free-soil emigration had become a central component of his newspaper, and, in part due to energetic support from the American Convention, the *Genius* became the dominant forum for anti- slavery news and views in the United States.[72]

No relocation plan seemed to be more practicable and timely to Lundy than that of Haitian emigration. He believed that it would have a direct influence on abolitionism in the United States and felt obliged to furnish his readers with a thorough assessment of its feasibility. "Justice demands," he wrote, "that it shall be thoroughly investigated ... for the political salvation of thousands and perhaps millions of human beings depends on it."[73] In its 1824–1825 run, every single issue of the *Genius* reprinted emigrants' letters from the island or included an extended discussion of Haiti's conditions and prospects.

One of Lundy's dominant arguments was that emigrating to Haiti would improve migrants' social conditions and economic prospects by saving them from their "degraded condition" in the United States. In Haiti, he wrote, "all would be placed strictly upon an equality; where [free people of color] would no longer be tantalized with the idea of mental inferiority; and where, of course, they would feel themselves released from the fancied chains of moral abasement."[74] More than anything else, however, the driv- ing force of his pro-emigrationism always remained his belief that relocation would "open a door for the release and final enfranchisement" of those still in bondage in the United States. "Indeed," Lundy assured his readers, "were I not fully persuaded that the measure will be calculated to have this effect, I should have considered the matter comparatively unimportant, and hardly worthy of our serious attention."[75]

To encourage support for Haitian emigration among his readers, Lundy looked to the eyewitness accounts of emigrants themselves. He was convinced that their letters furnished evidence of "vital importance" and was determined to devote a "considerable portion" of each issue to them.[76] In 1825, he published "Letters from Hayti," a column containing glowing firsthand accounts of the island received at his offices either directly from Haiti or from emigrants' friends and families. They uniformly remarked on the fine climate, the abundance of food, the soil's fertility, farmers' high prospects, and the safety of the voyage. When Charles W. Fisher – a young graduate of New York's African Free School and a recent emigrant to Haiti – ended a letter to his father with a practical and political exhortation for others to follow in his footsteps, Lundy made sure to publish it. "I now invite my African brothers and sisters to come over to this fruitful soil and enjoy its productions among their Haytian brethren," wrote Fisher, "and to aid in supporting an African government, in an African nation. – Come on, my fellow Africans – and eat *free bread*, and drink *free water*."[77]

Although Lundy readily admitted that not every letter was so positive, he assured his readers that for each negative account he received there were nearly 100 from emigrants "highly gratified" with their new situation. The sheer volume of evidence corroborating his optimistic views of Haitian emigration was his best argument in support of the idea.

While free black northerners were, indeed, quite enthusiastic about the idea of Haitian emigration through 1824 and into 1825, the tide of public opinion began to shift as the months progressed. Many emigrants found that the reality of their new lives as Haitian laborers did not match their hopes and expectations, and opponents of the emigration plan enthusiastically circulated news of their disappointment.[78] According to negative accounts, Haitian emigrants were not, in fact, welcomed to the island with open arms, and the Haitian government did not fulfill its liberal promises of republican citizenship. Some reports even alleged that Haitian emigrants had essentially become hostages, not allowed to leave once settled on the island and not permitted to write letters to the United States.[79]

Pro-slavery advocates jumped at the opportunity to publicize unhappy reports from the island, sensing that emigration to this nearby locale posed a threat to the stability of the U.S. slave system. Supporters of the ACS were also thrilled to broadcast bad news from emigrants, recognizing that broad-based enthusiasm for Haitian emigration posed the biggest roadblock to securing widespread support for the ACS's Liberian colonization project.[80]

By early 1825, reports that emigrants were being treated unfairly in Haiti achieved enough traction in the U.S. press that much of

Benjamin Lundy's energy in the *Genius* was recalibrated to contradict the damaging reports. And, just as Paul Cuffe had when responding to allegations of emigrants' poor conditions in Sierra Leone, Lundy countered detractors' impressions with vigor. He drew upon his abundant collection of emigrant letters to provide proof-positive confirmation of emigration's salutary benefits. The abundance of happy correspondents, he claimed, proved "to a certainty" that negative reports were no more than rumors circulated for the "basest of purposes" by those who professed to value republican freedom while supporting slavery.[81] Over the next year, Lundy pursued a prolific defense of Haiti as he attempted to counteract what he saw as pernicious pro-slavery efforts to undermine the Haitian emigration project at every turn.

Assisting Lundy in this endeavor was the Reverend Loring D. Dewey. A member of the ACS, Dewey had become a leader of the Haitian emigration movement in 1824 after establishing a correspondence with President Boyer. He became convinced that African Americans would be better off in Haiti than in Liberia and had encouraged the Haitian president to provide the political and financial backing necessary to support African American resettlement. Dewey faced substantial censure from the ACS, both for his defection to a scheme that was seen as the biggest obstacle hindering the organization's success and for having presented himself to Boyer as an official agent of the ACS – which he was not.[82] Undaunted, Dewey organized the Society for Promoting the Emigration of Free Persons of Colour to Hayti and published the sum of his correspondence with Boyer in a small book that anti-slavery advocates read with interest. It even inspired one reader to pen a poem in honor of the "*Isle of the Free*" for publication in Benjamin Lundy's newspaper.[83] Dewey's efforts were crucial to the quick, successful emigration of the several thousand enthusiastic African Americans who left the United States in the mid-1820s.[84]

Like Lundy, Loring Dewey recognized that the initial success of Haitian emigration in 1824 was endangered by 1825. No matter how much Lundy dismissed negative press as malicious rumor, the dissatisfaction of returnees and the obvious failure of the idea of Haitian relocation to encourage slaveholders to manumit their slaves all took a significant toll.[85] Unwilling to abandon the project, however, Dewey determined to make a fact-finding expedition to Haiti in early 1825 in an effort to discover for himself and report firsthand on the conditions and prospects of Haitian emigrants. Touring the island for four months, he took stock of emigrants' circumstances in their new home and sent his observations back to his correspondents in the United States.

His news was good. Spending February near the city of Cape Haytian, he found that upward of 700 arrivals had been "received according to the promise of [the Haytian] government," had mostly become land-holders in or near the city, and were generally satisfied and in good health. Staple crops grew plentifully and with such little effort that he was convinced the 3 acres furnished each emigrant by the Haitian government was equal to 10 acres of American soil. Markets abounded, the climate was temperate, and cattle and swine ran wild in abundance. He concluded that Haiti was a particularly favorable destination for industrious young emigrants who were prepared to work diligently on the land in return for enjoying their "natural rights and privileges."[86]

Due to his prominence in the emigration effort, Dewey's positive reflections on Haitian emigration were eagerly reprinted in newspapers from Baltimore to Maine.[87] Yet the campaign to promote Haitian emigration continued to prove an uphill battle, especially in the face of waning support from potential emigrants themselves. Making it harder still, at least 200 dissatisfied emigrants returned from Haiti at the end of the summer, and as many as a third of all emigrants may have returned over the next several years. Frustrated, Dewey complained bitterly that potential emigrants were discouraged by the return of what he characterized as a fraction of the 6,000 who had left for the island over the previous year.[88]

More than ever, conflicting information proliferated, and most of it stemmed from the eyewitness accounts of individuals who had either visited or emigrated to the island. With no clear consensus about what or who to believe, emigration societies began circumventing the partisan testimony of Loring Dewey and the returnees by commissioning their own independent, exploratory investigations to furnish the information they needed about life in Haiti. The "Cincinnati Haytian Union," for example, which had been formed in Ohio by free African Americans,

sent an "intelligent agent" to Haiti at their own expense. The organization's central mission was to ascertain "correct intelligence of the nature
of the soil and the climate" before deciding whether they wished to
advocate the Haitian relocation plan. To that end, they expected their
agent to gather information and report back by the following spring, at
which point they would "do all in their power" to facilitate emigration if –
and only if – their agent's information proved favorable.[89] Similarly,
when determining whether to use Haiti as a relocation site for former
slaves on the occasion of their manumission, the 1826 Committee of the
Yearly Meeting of Friends in North Carolina sent three agents of their
own to investigate. North Carolina's Quakers committed to sending
newly freed slaves to the island nation only if their agents reported
favorably.[90]

By 1826, Benjamin Lundy himself saw the utility of launching an
investigatory expedition to navigate the morass of conflicting testimony.
Not only had it become clear that reports from satisfied emigrants could
not fully counter negative accounts in the court of public opinion,
President Boyer himself had pulled away from the emigration arrangement. He had discovered that money earmarked for the emigrants was
being embezzled and mismanaged on several fronts, he was tired of
emigrants' complaints, and he began to worry that African American
emigrants might become too significant a force within the island's
unstable political landscape.[91]

So, Lundy jumped at the chance to kill two birds with one stone. Leaving
behind his pregnant wife, he boarded a ship bound for Haiti to discern
firsthand the condition of Haitian emigrants and to entreat the Haitian
government to continue financing African American relocation. The result
was a glowing six-part account of his journey titled, simply, "Hayti," in which
he offered his readers data "from whence the most rational conclusion can
be drawn."[92] Modeling the developing information culture in which eyewitness accounts furnished by informed individuals were respected for their
"truth," Lundy's investigatory expedition and firsthand reflections were
crucial to his continued promotion of Haitian emigration.

In addition to providing anti-slavery emigrationists with confidence in
their support of Haitian emigration, fact-finding expeditions of the sort
launched by Lundy, the North Carolina Friends, and the Cincinnati

Haytian Union also helped people develop specific hypotheses about the abundance of contradictory experiences reported by emigrants. Lundy had long claimed in the pages of the *Genius* that Haitian emigrants dissatisfied with their experiences on the island had left the United States with inflated and unreasonable expectations of what they would find. Not only did his island visit confirm his faith in this analysis, other investigatory agents reached the same conclusion. Emigrant dissatisfaction, in the view of the North Carolinian contingent, stemmed from emigrants' unreasonable expectations of gaining office or of "living an easy life."[93] Only emigrants prepared to work industriously *as agriculturalists*, they agreed, would find success in their new homes. Those unprepared to be farmers, by contrast, would find themselves dissatisfied with life in the black republic.

Ironically, as historian Chris Dixon points out, black northerners opposed to emigration regularly worried that the emigration movement was depriving African American communities of their most educated and talented members – those least likely, according to the North Carolina contingent, to find satisfaction as farmers.[94] Initially, Lundy declared that this disparity was actually for the best, as a successful emigration movement could not rest on the shoulders of lesser men. Yet when disgruntled emigrants returned en masse, Lundy joined other white emigrationists in concluding that their dissatisfaction stemmed from their inability or unwillingness to make do as farmers.

Indeed, the reaction of many white reformers to the returning emigrants illuminates the limits of their imagination regarding what black freedom could look like, even in a free-soil haven abroad. While they certainly believed that emigration to free soil might offer free African Americans and former slaves better living conditions than were available to them in the United States, they often fell far short of imagining the kinds of opportunities that African Americans envisioned for themselves. What the returnees saw as a lack of opportunity for skilled, educated emigrants, white reformers often saw as a lack of patience, a want of industry, and a clear indication that emigrants had "over-wrought" expectations for their new lives.[95] "Hope and fancy are always on the wing," Lundy wrote, "tempting men to aspire to that which would be most congenial to their wishes, without first endeavoring to be worthy of promotion, and without waiting for what they conceive to be the too tardy operations of industry, to acquire wealth."[96] Yet the precipitous decline of support for Haitian emigration among free black northerners suggests that, on the whole, they had little interest in living in a place that limited their professional opportunities to that of farmer – even in exchange for the guarantee of equal rights and privileges. When free African Americans left for free soil, they expected to experience a society that valued the breadth of what they had to offer.

Still, Haiti and the *idea* of Haitian emigration as a black-led alternative to African colonization remained important in African American thought long after the stream of enthusiastic volunteers dried up in the mid-1820s. As the first example of international free soil where slavery was completely abolished on a national scale, Haiti provided a reference point for articulating a politics of freedom that included citizenship, equal rights, and civil liberties. By extolling the Haitian government's provision of citizenship rights to all residents, African Americans were able to argue that equal citizenship under the law could and should be a cornerstone of republican government. Moreover, by upholding Haiti's government and society as an example of black people's potential to flourish in freedom, African Americans were able to demonstrate the salutary effects of universal emancipation. Simply put, for African Americans at the tail end of the 1820s, Haiti became both a symbol and a model of freedom to be emulated in the United States – rather than a free-soil haven to move to.[97]

In no place is Haiti's ongoing symbolic importance among African Americans in the late 1820s more readily seen than in the pages of *Freedom's Journal*, the first black-owned, black-operated newspaper in the United States. Established in New York City as a forum for northern African Americans to share their views and advocate for racial justice, it ran for two years from 1827 to 1829, with an estimated 800 subscribers among both African Americans and white sympathizers. Yet the actual readership was likely much wider, as people shared the journal, read it in subscribing libraries, or listened as it was read aloud. Like the *Genius of Universal Emancipation*, it was also read by members of the American Convention for Promoting the Abolition of Slavery, which subscribed to two copies.[98] In addition to contributing to the moral, religious, and intellectual uplift of northern free black people, the *Journal* aimed to bring together African American voices from across the United States so "that plans which apparently are beneficial may be candidly discussed and properly weighed."[99] The newspaper's two founding editors, Samuel Cornish and John Brown Russwurm, were sensitive to the "benevolent feelings" of many white sympathizers, but felt that the time had come for African Americans to speak for themselves and "plead [their] own cause."[100]

Freedom's Journal first entered publication three years after the peak wave of African American emigration to Haiti in 1824. Tellingly, while both Samuel Cornish and John Brown Russwurm had been early boosters of Haitian emigration in the mid-1820s, neither still advocated the idea when they founded the *Journal* in 1827. Cornish had been a member of New York's Haytian Emigration Society and a prominent proponent of emigration, but he had become disillusioned by the unsavory reports of returning migrants in 1825. Russwurm, who was born in Jamaica and then educated in Canada, had intended to become a doctor and actually emigrate to Haiti himself. The first black graduate from Maine's Bowdoin College in 1826, he had delivered a lengthy oratory praising the island at his college commencement ceremony. By the end of the year, however, he had changed his mind and decided against the move.[101]

Despite the two editors' general disenchantment with the Haitian emigration plan, Haiti made regular appearances in the *Journal*'s news column and editorials from the start of its two-year run. Either through reference to its revolution, its national heroes, its system of government, or its ongoing significance to pro-emigrationists, *Freedom's Journal* used Haiti as a foil to discuss ideas about freedom, abolition, and governance in the United States.[102] In its first year alone, the *Journal* included substantive discussion of Haiti in eighteen of its forty-two issues. Not only did it celebrate Haiti as the model of true republican liberty, it lauded evidence from the island that demonstrated black people's capacity for self-governance and intellectual achievement.[103] In the words of an early contributor: "We have seen the establishment of an independent nation by men of our own color; the world has seen it; and its success and durability are now placed beyond doubt."[104] Even when reprinting less decisive reflections on Haiti's success as a durable, independent nation, Cornish and Russwurm selected material that highlighted Haiti's salutary example of black potential.[105]

Ideas about Haiti printed in *Freedom's Journal* perfectly capture the complexity of a decade in which American reformers struggled to untangle how international free soil might affect the fight for black freedom and racial justice in the United States. The formation and evolution of free soil in both Haiti and West Africa reflected growing concern about the place of free African Americans in the United States, and it set the stage for black and white reformers alike to debate whether migration might speed or stall the decline of American slavery, what role the government should play in safeguarding the interests of free African Americans, and if free African Americans even had a place in the nation's future. The debates were contentious and the stakes were high, and, as the pages of leading anti-slavery newspapers demonstrate, the ideological significance of discussing free-soil relocation ideas far outpaced the marginal rate of actual departures among free African Americans.

And yet, as the 1820s drew to a close, racism in the United States seemed to be growing ever deeper. So, even as West Africa and Haiti played a defining role in how American reformers had come to conceptualize black freedom and the struggle to achieve it, it was with a new set of hopes and expectations – and facing a new set of challenges – that they looked abroad to a growing array of international free-soil havens in the decade to come.

CHAPTER 2

Exit and Expansion: The Search for Legal Equality in a Time of Crisis

A secret influence is imperceptibly conveyed from the land of Bolivar to the miserable slaves. It invites them to freedom. You cannot intercept that influence. You may build a wall to heaven . . . and still you cannot resist it.

~ Rev. Hoyt, Potsdam, New York, July 4, 1826[1]

* * *

Yet Christian's curses round him roll,
His Brother loves him not,
Where goes he? Lo, the polar star
A beacon shines before;
He leaves his native land afar,
To tread a Monarch's shore,
He goes to take at Britain's hand
The boon his home denies.

~ From "The Fugitive," Anonymous (1836)[2]

James C. Brown was born in Virginia around the year 1796. The son of a white man and an enslaved mixed-race woman, Brown inherited his mother's legal status. At a young age, he was taken to Kentucky – along with his brother and sister – where he was "hired out" at the age of fifteen to a Captain George Smith. Promised his freedom in exchange for serving as a fifer, the teenaged Brown found himself with Captain Smith's soldiers at the famous Battle of Tippecanoe in 1811. He survived the confrontation with Tecumseh's warriors, but, as it turned out, his own battle for freedom had only just begun. Rather than being freed as promised, Brown had to work as a hired-out slave until he was able to purchase his freedom. He worked as a mason for six years until, at the age of twenty-one, he purchased his freedom for $1,800.

But living as a free man in a "slave country" was not easy, and Brown was distressed by the violence and prejudice that surrounded him. Years later, he still remembered the story of a local freeman named Freeribbon who had been framed for a murder he did not commit. Freeribbon had initially been sentenced to hang, but he was given a reprieve on the condition that he be "sent away to some Spanish mine," there to labor for the rest of his days. After twenty years, Freeribbon was finally exonerated when a local white man confessed on his deathbed that he had been paid to plant the evidence by three local men – one a congressman, one a colonel, and one a "gentleman." Freeribbon returned from the mines alive but "heart-broken," his story a testament to the vulnerability of free African Americans living in a slave state.[3]

So, it was not long after purchasing his freedom that Brown began to consider leaving Louisville. But where to go? In 1819, following advice received from Benjamin Lundy, the anti-slavery newspaper editor, Brown traveled southwest into the province of Texas in New Spain, where he hoped to discover "suitable situations for free people of color."[4] But he was dissuaded from removing permanently to the area upon learning that a local councilman expected the region to develop into a "great cotton and sugar-growing country." The official also informed him that "the majority of the council were opposed to having a free coloured settlement in Texas, and it would be useless for [him] to look further."[5]

In the wake of his uninspiring trip to Texas, Brown simply decided to move north across the Ohio River. In the mid-1820s, he moved himself and his family from Louisville, Kentucky, to Cincinnati, Ohio. They joined a small-but-growing community of free African Americans in town, and he quickly became a "leading spirit" within it.[6]

In spite of his high hopes, however, his stay in Cincinnati did not last long.

In 1829, the first year of Andrew Jackson's presidency, Ohio's state legislators made an announcement that reverberated through African American communities across the nation. Responding to white discomfort over the state's growing free black population, they announced that Ohio's longstanding Black Laws would be enforced, effective the following year. Although largely ignored and unused since they first went on the books in 1804 and 1807, the Black Laws offered a sure-fire way to undermine the civil rights of black Ohioans and to underscore race as a barrier to American citizenship and equality.[7] Beginning in 1830, enforcement of the state's laws would force African Americans in Ohio to withdraw from military and jury service, deny them the right to bear arms, and require them to register themselves with the state and post a costly bond to ensure their good behavior.[8]

James C. Brown, like thousands of other free African Americans throughout the state, faced a grim choice. He could stay in his home and experience the sting of discriminatory legislation, or he could leave his adopted state in the hope of finding a more welcoming environment elsewhere. It was a difficult decision, but the answer soon became clear. Over the course of several nights in mid-August 1829, violent anti-black rioting ripped through the city's African American neighborhoods. Mobs numbering 200–300 attacked black Cincinnatians and destroyed many of their homes and businesses. Despite the community's appeals for protection, elected officials were slow to respond and no police protection was provided.[9] By late 1829, as many as half of Cincinnati's 3,000 free black residents – James C. Brown among them – had decided to leave the city.

Once again, Brown was forced to consider where he should go to start anew. But this time, he was not alone. As black Cincinnatians considered their options in the aftermath of the riots, Brown emerged as a leading voice in the large group debate about what locations might offer a safer and more welcoming environment.

Brown recalled several decades later that some attendees suggested relocating to Texas. The option, possibly on his counsel, was not pursued. But when Brown suggested they consider Canada, the idea elicited enough interest that the group organized a "Colonization Society," of which Brown was made president. With Brown at the helm, the

Colonization Society's Board of Directors made contact with the Lieutenant-Governor of Upper Canada (now Ontario), purchased a large tract of land, and established a settlement. Eventually, they named their settlement Wilberforce, in honor of the British champion against the slave trade, William Wilberforce. Although only a fraction of the expected participants made it all the way to Wilberforce, roughly 600 of the men and women who left Cincinnati in the summer of 1829 followed Brown north to resettle across the U.S.–Canada border.[10]

Many historians have told the story of this emigration stream from Cincinnati to Upper Canada, as it laid the foundation for subsequent black emigration northward to the British "land of freedom" along the Underground Railroad. Yet the story of *why* Cincinnati's free black population chose Upper Canada as the site of their relocation in 1829 is less widely understood.[11] Why was the Texas option considered and subsequently rejected? Why were Liberia and Haiti, the two most frequently discussed free-soil locales during the 1820s, seemingly not brought up at all during the Cincinnati meeting? What made Upper Canada, at the time a marginal province of a powerful slave-owning empire, seem like a place for free African Americans to experience a more satisfactory form of freedom than was available to them in the U.S. North?

Answering these questions not only opens a window into understanding the complex decisions of place, race, and citizenship facing free African Americans in the late 1820s, it offers an essential and overlooked explanation for Canada's subsequent importance within American anti-slavery thought and activism. It shows that the Upper Canadian government only articulated a commitment to free-soil protectionism as a direct response to the black Cincinnatians' self-advocacy. Free African Americans spurred Upper Canada's emergence as an international free-soil locale in the late 1820s and, by doing so, helped anti-slavery advocates with diverse ideological beliefs develop evermore specific ideas about how to abolish slavery in the United States and what freedom should look like in its wake.

Framing this Canadian emigration story as both a product and a process of international free-soil comparison, it becomes clear that free-soil locales abroad – as symbols and as actual destinations – had important, concrete effects on American anti-slavery thought and action.

During the late 1820s and early 1830s, discussions about Mexico and Canada joined the ongoing debates over Liberia and Haiti that had absorbed anti-slavery advocates' attention for over a decade. As African Americans "voted with their feet," they inserted their own ideas about what freedom meant into the narrative of American anti-slavery. In the process, their efforts to carve out a meaningful vision of freedom within a growing international free-soil landscape galvanized and strengthened the two most significant shifts within anti-slavery culture in the early 1830s: the expansion of immediatism as a mainstream anti-slavery ideology and the widening influence of black protest voices within white anti-slavery efforts.

* * *

Although the Black Laws and anti-black riots of 1829 prompted that year's large-scale migration of African Americans away from Cincinnati, it was not the first time the city's black residents had expressed interest in the possibilities of relocation. In the early 1800s, the growing city's myriad labor opportunities had made it a magnet for free black migration.[12] But racism grew apace with Cincinnati's black community. Like their counterpart communities in the northeastern United States, African Americans and local anti-slavery advocates in Cincinnati began investigating and weighing whether participating in free-soil relocation projects might offer free people a better life.

In 1824, when interest in Haitian emigration peaked in the United States, a group of African Americans formed the "Cincinnati Haytien Union" to consider whether the island might provide a promising alternative to Ohio's growing anti-black sentiment.[13] Despite some interest, the Haitian option failed to achieve widespread appeal in Cincinnati, and only a small number of free African Americans seem to have relocated from there to the black republic.[14] Then, in 1826, white Cincinnatians formed a state auxiliary to the ACS – though the organization made little headway over the next three years. Its members were unable to raise enough money to support potential migrants' long sea voyage, and free black Ohioans themselves considered the white-led option to be "entirely out of the question."[15] Cincinnati was clearly immersed in the nationwide debates over black relocation, and, by the summer of 1829, the young border town's black inhabitants already had years of careful consideration regarding which projects – if any – they thought would benefit Ohio's free people.

Steeped in what historian Nikki Taylor has identified as a dual tradition of emigrationism and self-determinism, many members of Cincinnati's African American populace remained interested in forming a "separate society" even after the Haitian and Liberian projects failed to secure their support.[16] To some, self-segregation seemed the only way to adequately protect themselves from the daily effects of racism and inequality. Such was the case for Lewis Woodson, a black Ohioan, who penned his perspective on the matter in an 1829 letter to the editor of the *Ohio Monitor*. The goal of separating from white America, he wrote, was to "entirely alter our condition" and establish "perfect equality." Once resettled away from white society, he contended, African Americans could be "free from the looks of scorn and contempt – free from fraud – and in fine, free from all the evils attendant on partial and unequal laws."[17]

While Lewis Woodson hoped that such a settlement could be established somewhere within Ohio, the editor of the *Ohio Monitor*, David Smith, had different ideas. Modeling the conservative white reformism that had inspired the formation of the ACS in 1816, Smith expressed his belief that removal outside the United States would ultimately prove to be more beneficial. He suggested that Africa, Haiti, South America, or Mexico were places where African Americans would be more likely to find the political freedom that men like Lewis Woodson longed for. However, he conceded, if free African Americans were initially unwilling to "leave their native land," he thought that Woodson's proposed settlement in Ohio could act as a "nursery" for people who would ultimately see the socio-political benefits of leaving altogether.[18]

While Smith's response vastly underestimated most African Americans' desire that their "native land" should remain their permanent home, his letter nonetheless reflects the fact that there were certainly more international options for African American migrants seeking socio-political standing in 1829 than there had been just a few years earlier. The international frontier of freedom now expanded across independent Mexico and South America, and it piqued the interest of reformers whose enthusiasm for the Haitian and Liberian relocation projects had begun to waver.

The expansion of freedom in Mexico and South America stemmed from the imperial conflicts that severed ties between Spain and most of its colonies in the early decades of the nineteenth century. Movements that began with the goal of establishing greater colonial autonomy gave way to full-scale wars for independence during the 1810s and 1820s. By 1833, the political map of Mexico and South America had been redrawn, with Spain having lost all its American colonies except Cuba and Puerto Rico.

The success of anti-Spanish independence movements in South America and Mexico resulted in the formation of new republican nations dedicated to the revolutionary ideas of liberty and equality. Some regions passed local anti-slavery legislation in the 1810s, and many of the national governments formed in the 1820s made freedom for slaves and racial harmony a component of their core republican identities.[19] As early as 1816, the famous revolutionary leader Simón Bolívar pledged to Alexandre Pétion of Haiti that he would abolish slavery in all territory he liberated in Venezuela. Made in exchange for a substantial amount of material support from Pétion, Bolívar's wartime promise set the tone for how the former colonies of Spain addressed slavery in the wake of their independence movements.[20] Lawmakers passed legislation to free enslaved men and women – often through gradual and compensated processes – in Gran Colombia (Colombia, Venezuela, northern Peru, and Ecuador, 1821), Chile (1824), the Federal Republic of Central America (1824), and Mexico (1829). Although none of these laws actually abolished slavery outright, they established legal pathways to freedom and were generally regarded as methods to facilitate the eventual demise of the slave system.[21]

In the United States, observers watched with interest as these new republics enacted a range of anti-slavery measures.[22] For American reformers with more conservative aims, the shifting political terrain encouraged longstanding hopes that Spanish American independence could stem the tide of the transatlantic slave trade. In 1818, for example, the American Convention for Promoting the Abolition of Slavery and Improving the Condition of the African Race – the same meeting visited by Prince Saunders regarding the promise of Haiti – sent a memorial to Congress requesting that the United States make the abolition of the transatlantic slave trade a requirement for the new, independent nations to receive diplomatic recognition.[23]

But while some reformers saw Spanish American independence as an opportunity for the United States to support anti-slavery initiatives through diplomacy, others felt that the willingness of newly independent South American nations to pass anti-slavery legislation was, rather, an indictment against the United States. Famous Prussian scientist and travel writer Alexander von Humboldt, for example, looked at what the new Spanish American republics had done for the "extinction of slavery" and saw a reflection of the United States through a glass, darkly. In his view, the new nations' "prudent" decision to enact anti-slavery legislation in the wake of their independence movements underscored the fact that the young United States, at the national level, had not.[24] According to Humboldt, anti-slavery legislation in the former Spanish colonies provided a positive example of freedom for other nations to follow.

It certainly did not go unnoticed that slaves themselves might see it that way. In an 1826 Fourth of July speech, the Reverend Hoyt of Potsdam, New York, declared that "a secret influence" was being "conveyed from the land of Bolivar to the miserable slaves" of the United States, counteracting the efforts of slave owners to make "the poor black believe it right to thus oppress him." The influence of freedom in the former Spanish colonies, Hoyt warned, was imperceptible and unstoppable. Like Haiti, the new republics were a beacon of hope inviting slaves to slough off their bonds.[25] Hoyt's speech made clear that the frontier of freedom was marching toward the United States and would arrive either in the form of insurrection or legislative action. "You cannot intercept that influence," he proclaimed. "You may build a wall to heaven ... and still you cannot resist it."[26]

Although there is little evidence to suggest that the South American anti-slavery initiatives incited the insurrectionary zeal that Hoyt anticipated in the United States, it is clear that American slaves were quite aware of the shifting political landscape to the south and southwest. In particular, they paid close attention to the various anti-slavery policies implemented in nearby Mexican territory both before and after Mexico won its independence from Spain in 1821. Between 1803 and 1812, slaves often crossed the border into Spanish territory, though the exact number of such departures remains unknown (see Appendix). In a savvy and not uncommon strategy to try and destabilize its neighbor, Spain enticed enslaved laborers away from adjacent U.S. territory by promising freedom to runaway slaves who crossed the border.[27] While this practice was a persistent thorn in the side of American slaveholders, it was just a prelude to the more momentous shift that accompanied the anti-Spanish independence movement across the border: the rise of anti-slavery sentiment and legal action.

The history of anti-slavery legislation during Mexico's independence movement is far from straightforward, but it had powerful ramifications for how enslaved people and slave owners in the United States viewed Mexico and its government. The first push for emancipation in conjunction with independence came in 1810, when Miguel Hidalgo y Costilla launched a famous but ill-fated revolt against Spanish rule. As part of his vision for republican independence and universal liberty, he promulgated a general emancipation decree freeing all slaves in Mexico. Unfortunately, his vision and his decree died with him the following year. Then, when Mexico finally achieved its independence in 1821, revolutionary leader Augustín de Iturbide made another nod toward the anti-slavery cause by freeing all slaves who had fought with the republican army. Iturbide did not, however, implement a general – or even gradual – emancipation effort, and progress thereafter came only in fits and starts. Over the next several years, anti-slavery initiatives struggled against pro-slavery interests and the powerful diplomatic efforts of American slaveholders living in Texas.[28]

Throughout the 1820s, as the Mexican government sorted out whether slavery had a future in the new nation, it passed inconsistent and limited legislation at the national and state levels. A prohibition against importing slaves was passed at the national level in 1823, for example, but that same year the Mexican government offered sizable land grants to American settlers bringing in large numbers of enslaved people. In the state of Saltillo, the government allowed for a six-month period of slave importation in 1824, but the passage of a six-month "sunset" period for the practice in 1827 suggests that the first law's time limitation was inadequately enforced.

Yet strides were made throughout the decade. In September 1827, at the same time that Mexico's national government enacted a second non-importation law, it simultaneously passed a gradual abolition law ensuring that "no one shall be born a slave in the state." Then, in 1829, the Mexican government finally committed itself to a general emancipation decree outlawing slavery. But still the law's effect was hampered by a significant caveat: it did not, in fact, outlaw slavery in all Mexico's territories. Rather, thanks to the persistent pro-slavery diplomacy of slave-holding Americans who had been resettling in the fertile land across the southwestern U.S.–Mexico border, the emancipation decree applied to all of Mexico except Texas.[29]

In spite of these inconsistencies, however, Mexico's anti-slavery initiatives were making U.S. slaveholders feel vulnerable. Although there is no clear indication of how many U.S. slaves sought freedom across the U.S.–Mexico border in the 1820s, it is clear that enslaved people in the southwest viewed Mexico as a land of freedom and that American enslavers felt deep consternation at the border's permeability.[30] In 1829, a correspondent identified simply as "Americanus" wrote a letter to the *St. Louis Beacon* pointing out just how little there was to stop runaway slaves from crossing into Mexican Texas. He worried that Louisiana, Arkansas, Mississippi, Tennessee, Kentucky, and Missouri were all at significant risk. Comparing the flight of fugitives across the southwestern international border to the northern border shared with Canada, Americanus determined that geography played a significant role in the loss of slaves across the Mexican border. Referring to the Fugitive Slave Clause of the U.S. Constitution, he explained that slaves fleeing toward Canada had to cross several states that were "bound to deliver up fugitives." This necessity greatly increased the "difficulties and distance" of reaching free soil under the British flag. By contrast, he argued, escape across the U.S.–Mexico border was "easy and certain" due to the "contiguity of territory" and the "free navigation of our rivers."[31]

In truth, it was nowhere near as easy to escape to Mexico as concerned slaveholders felt it to be. Focusing on the many perils of running away through the southwest borderlands, historian Makela Audain notes that runaway slaves faced a harsh landscape with little hope of help from sympathetic whites. Harsh weather, rough terrain, rugged ecology, and human and animal predators imperiled every journey.[32] Moreover, as historian James David Nichols reminds us, the permeability of the border often worked both ways: pursuers could cross the border just as readily as runaway slaves themselves. While laws passed in the wake of the Texas Revolution (1836) and the U.S.–Mexican War (1846–1848) meant that Mexico would at least try to protect runaways once they crossed the border, there were certainly no guarantees in the first decades of the nineteenth century.[33]

Nonetheless, hoping to stem what seemed like a rising tide of escape to the "notorious" haven for runaway slaves, slaveholders demanded that the federal government intervene on their behalf. In late 1826, an alarmed Henry Clay, the well-known statesman from Kentucky, wrote to President John Quincy Adams on behalf of the House of Representatives and its members' slaveholding constituents. He wanted to ascertain "whether any measures [had] been taken, by instructions to our Minister in Mexico, or otherwise, to obtain the runaway negro slaves from Louisiana and elsewhere." What he discovered was both reassuring and concerning. The U.S. government had, in fact, been negotiating a treaty with Mexico since September 1825 for the return of fugitive slaves. But the negotiations had not been going well. While Clay applauded the U.S. government's efforts to negotiate a treaty and remained optimistic regarding their outcome at least through February 1827, the treaty was eventually withdrawn because Mexico failed to ratify it by the end of that year.

Under pressure from pro-slavery interests such as those represented by Clay, negotiations began anew. By February 1828, a treaty between the U.S. government and the United Mexican States was once again under consideration. But this time, slaveholders' efforts to shore up the south-western border by diplomatic means had the exact opposite effect of what they were hoping for. Rather than simply failing to ratify the treaty in a timely fashion as they had the year prior, the Mexican government positively resolved that it would not ratify a treaty that included a stipulation for the return of fugitive slaves.[34] The diplomatic failure only confirmed that the U.S.–Mexico border was a boundary between slavery and freedom and a beacon for enslaved African Americans.

Meanwhile, as enslavers fought to contain the threat of having free soil nearby, anti-slavery advocates sought to make the most of it. As free soil expanded in Mexico and South America during the 1820s, anti-slavery advocates in the United States leveraged the examples of their Spanish-American neighbors to support specific arguments in favor of emancipation and racial justice. Some observations highlighted the socio-political outcomes of black freedom. Readers of *Freedom's Journal*, for example, were informed in 1827 that the South American experience of emancipation proved that it was not African Americans' natural inheritance to live in "ignorance, poverty, and degradation."[35] Rather, evidence from the former Spanish colonies showed that people of African descent, once emancipated and granted all the rights and privileges of citizenship, were "not a whit inferior· to [their] fairer brethren."[36] Other observations highlighted the economic benefits of emancipation, such as eyewitness accounts from Mexico that seemed to support the theory that "free" labor (meaning "non-slave" labor) could successfully sustain an agricultural economy previously based on slavery. Benjamin Lundy of the *Genius of Universal Emancipation* drew on the observations of a British envoy in Mexico to make this latter point, concluding that "the labor of slaves will never bear a competition with that of free men, when fairly treated."[37]

If comparison and observation indicated what the United States could expect were it to follow a similar anti-slavery path, some observers went so far as to suggest that the standard of free (non-slave) labor established in the nearby republics would, itself, lead to the dissolution of slavery in the United States. One correspondent to the *New York Observer* expected that the "introduction of the highest agricultural improvements" by the "enlightened governments" of independent, emancipated places like the Republic of Colombia, Mexico, and Haiti would lower the market rate of produce and render slave labor comparatively unprofitable.[38] While historians have shown that such expectations regarding the incompatibility of slavery, capitalism, and the global market economy were fundamentally wrong, anti-slavery advocates in the 1820s optimistically leapt at the opportunity to link their anti-slavery ideas to evidence of eco-nomic innovation and growth.[39]

Whether it was the growing reputation of former Spanish colonies as havens of freedom or the positive impressions contained in nationally circulated and widely reprinted newspapers like the *Genius* and the *New York Observer*, there were a number of factors that likely encouraged members of Cincinnati's black community to consider Mexican Texas as a potential site for resettlement in the summer of 1829. Although Mexico was still technically several months away from officially abolishing slavery, it had certainly made significant strides toward ending slavery within its borders. Moreover, the diplomatic broils that arose when fugitive slaves crossed the southwest border seemed to confirm the impression that Mexico was a land of freedom. One optimistic observer went so far as to declare that Mexico, for all intents and purposes, was "a non-slave-holding empire, and will remain so."[40]

In the end, however, enthusiasm for what Mexico and its South American counterparts might mean for U.S. slaves and slavery was not enough to sway the black Cincinnatians toward endorsing Mexican emigration. In fact, there was as much to fear as there was to applaud in the newspaper press of the 1820s, and it is reasonable to conjecture that the men and women who gathered in 1829 worried that the on-the-ground reality of living in Mexico would not live up to the expectations of hopeful anti-slavery advocates in the United States. First of all, not all press coverage of the diplomatic negotiations between the United States and Mexico in the 1820s emphasized the latter's unwillingness to sign a treaty containing an extradition clause for the return of American slaves. Rather than reporting the good news that Mexico had twice rejected such a clause, many newspapers between 1827 and 1829 instead reprinted congressional accounts of the process, which emphasized that treaty efforts were ongoing and that U.S. statesmen remained optimistic that an agreement could be reached.[41] Cincinnati's potential emigrants were largely composed of legally free Ohioans who were therefore less likely to be affected by an extradition clause for the return of fugitive slaves, yet the possibility that such a treaty might be ratified may have discouraged their faith in Mexico's commitment to its black inhabitants.

In addition, newspapers in the United States reported that Mexico's post-independence political landscape remained volatile. *Freedom's Journal*, which was certainly read by free black readers in Cincinnati, reported on January 1, 1829, that intelligence from Mexico was "not of a nature to give pleasure to those who have conceived high ideas of the future prospects of the Hispano-American governments." The article described streets swarming with violent beggars and state violence becoming the main means of subduing the populace. The author asserted that force and violence, rather than elections, were placing control of the government in the hands of a "new despot every few years."[42]

Combined with the fact that Mexico's anti-slavery legislation shifted with each of the republic's successive regimes between 1821 and 1829, Mexico likely seemed too uncertain a choice for the black Ohioans seeking a new home. To James C. Brown, in particular, it may have seemed that little had changed in Mexico since his travels through Texas ten years earlier.

* * *

But what inspired Brown to offer up Canada as an alternative once Mexico had been rejected? Why did it capture the attention of the Cincinnati meeting's attendees more effectively than did Mexico, Liberia, or Haiti? And, most importantly, why did they ultimately choose Upper Canada – modern-day Ontario – despite the fact that it had garnered virtually no national attention as a free-soil emigration option in the years preceding 1829?

By exploring the black Ohioans' decision to resettle across the U.S.–Canada border as an extension of a story that includes their consideration and subsequent rejection of other free-soil options, two important and underappreciated facets of Canadian emigration come to light. First, it becomes clear that self-liberated men and women played a foundational role in building and securing the reputation of Upper Canada, specifically, as a secure free-soil haven long before the Underground Railroad became a significant phenomenon. Second, we see that the British government promised African Americans equality under the law in Upper Canada because of the black Cincinnatians' efforts to carve out an asylum consonant with their own definition of freedom. Security, stability, autonomy, opportunity, and, most importantly, legal equality were key components of how the black Ohioans defined freedom for themselves and their community, and they were determined that this was the kind of freedom they would experience under the British flag.

When James C. Brown encouraged his friends and neighbors to consider Canada, he no doubt recalled a terrifying experience that made him painfully aware of Canada's growing reputation as a free-soil destination for fugitive slaves. Not long after he had moved to Ohio in the mid-1820s, Brown returned to his former home in Louisville, Kentucky, to settle some unfinished business. In his absence, it turned out that a local Quaker had been forging free passes for runaway slaves so they could make their way to Canada. Unbeknownst to Brown, the Quaker had invoked his name as a liaison in Cincinnati, urging fugitives to find him after crossing the Ohio River so he could assist them on their northward journey. Just prior to Brown's return, local whites had entrapped the Quaker by coercing an enslaved young man to feign a need for help getting to Canada. Brown's name came up in the proceedings.

Unaware either of the Quaker's activities or of the man's recent arrest, Brown was unexpectedly swept up in the affair upon his arrival in Kentucky. He was seized by several local white men who demanded he bear witness against the Quaker. If Brown refused, they threatened, they would drag him into the woods and give him 900 lashes – a punishment that would surely kill him. As they had with the young man forced into entrapping the Quaker, the white men insisted that Brown's testimony should explicitly identify Canada as the fugitive slaves' destination. Fearing for his life in the face of such coercion and violence, Brown fled Louisville that night by stowing away on a steamboat.[43]

Although information about self-liberated slaves fleeing to Canada received little mention in the newspaper press prior to 1829, it was abundantly clear to Brown in the moment of his harrowing misadventure that both slaves and enslavers in the Upper South saw British North America as a free-soil haven. And slaveholders had good reason to feel threatened by Canada. For several decades, slavery and freedom had been a growing geopolitical issue at the U.S.–Canada border, where competing moral and economic imperatives rode the crest of Anglo-American diplomatic relations.

It began in 1772, when Lord Mansfield's famous *Somerset* decision determined that chattel slavery was not supported by English law. Although the decision technically only applied to England itself, public opinion held that it outlawed slavery in Britain's mainland North American colonies as well.[44] In perception, if not in law, this was the first indication that the U.S.–Canada border could interrupt slaveholders' power over the individuals they enslaved. Then, in the wake of both the American Revolution and the War of 1812, the British transported thousands of African Americans – many of them runaway slaves – to Nova Scotia. Twice over, the British offered freedom and protection to African Americans who crossed British lines during wartime, and twice over they stood by their promises despite substantial protest from the new United States.[45] Many of the "Black Loyalists" – those who were transported to Nova Scotia in the wake of the American Revolution – subsequently relocated to Sierra Leone due to the inhospitable climate and difficult social relations they faced in Nova Scotia. Yet the British decision to settle African Americans under their protection in Canada promoted the general perception that the *Somerset* decision did, indeed, apply to mainland British North America. More a product of Anglo-American politics than a reflection of widespread anti-slavery sentiment, these wartime decisions helped to formulate the U.S.–Canada border as a boundary line between slavery and freedom and fashioned the British as powerful protectors of black liberty despite their ongoing commitment to slavery in the West Indies.[46]

Unlike Nova Scotia, Upper Canada was not a destination for the American Revolution's Black Loyalists or for refugees from the War of 1812. And, unlike Nova Scotia, it was not a place that symbolized the unique legacy of black loyalism and Britain's power to honor its wartime promises to African Americans. Nevertheless, the border between the United States and Upper Canada had a rich history of imperial border crossing that was equally significant, if more generally overlooked.

This story began with the enactment of two key pieces of legislation on either side of the Detroit River, which was the imperial boundary bifurcating Michigan Territory (U.S.) and Upper Canada. In 1787, the United States passed the Northwest Ordinance, preventing slaves from being imported into new territories northwest of the Ohio River. Six years later, in 1793, the provincial government of Upper Canada passed its Act Against Slavery. This latter piece of legislation did not actually abolish slavery – or even emancipate a single slave – but it did establish a policy against the introduction of more slaves into the province.[47] As soon as these territorial policies against slave importation had been enacted, enslaved people from either side of the U.S.–Canada border began crossing the Detroit River in the hope of freeing themselves by reaching the other side.[48]

In the first decade of the nineteenth century, Canadian slaveholders had as much to lose through such border-crossing activity as did American slaveholders. Deteriorating Anglo-American relations during this period meant that neither side's government was keen to assist in the recapture of the other's runaway slaves. Although it remains unclear just how many runaway slaves crossed the border during this time and they were likely few in number overall (see Appendix), the number of runaways grew precipitously on both sides of the river as it became clear that flailing diplomacy made them difficult to retrieve. As a result of fugitive slaves' efforts to define the U.S.–Canada border as a gateway to freedom, slavery dwindled in the Detroit River Valley on both sides of the border until it disappeared altogether in the 1810s.[49]

Yet an end to slavery at the local level was only the tip of the iceberg. To the horror of American slaveholders, fugitive slaves from the United States continued making their way north from regions much farther south than the Detroit River Valley in order to cross the international border. Information that Upper Canada offered asylum to American slaves passed by word-of-mouth into the Upper South during the early years of the nineteenth century. Following the War of 1812, the rumor was substantiated by the return of American soldiers from Upper Canada to places like Virginia and Kentucky. In light of Britain's decision to protect black refugees who were transported to Nova Scotia after the war, information about border-crossing slaves probably seemed particularly threatening.[50]

The hope of freedom encouraged runaway slaves from Upper South states such as Kentucky, Virginia, and Tennessee to try their luck. Before long, the Upper Canadian border developed a free-soil reputation among both slaves and slave owners that was comparable to the Mexican border in the southwest. As early as 1815, anti-slavery advocates in the Western Reserve of Ohio (the northeast corner) provided "aid and directions" to fugitive slaves crossing the region toward Upper Canada. Prominent abolitionist Elizur Wright, Jr., who spent his early childhood in the area, remembered that many white settlers looked on these self-emancipated travelers with compassion and opened their doors to them as they passed through.[51] While no doubt exaggerated, abolitionists in southern Ohio claimed to have helped over 1,000 slaves make their way from the Upper South toward Canada by 1817.[52]

Prior to 1830, self-emancipated slaves arrived in Upper Canada hoping for protection against marauding slave-catchers and for ready employment in the region's burgeoning tobacco industry. In fact, the connection between self-emancipated slaves and the region's tobacco agriculture was strong enough that some American supporters of Canadian resettlement believed that they were responsible for introducing the crop.[53]

These early runaway arrivals frequently relocated just across the border, establishing small settlements on the Detroit River, the Niagara River, and around Lake Erie. Those who were able to make an even longer trek could, after 1819, travel all the way up to the distant shores of Lake Simcoe, where the government established a small settlement for black veterans of the War of 1812.[54] But for most, the extra distance was too far. Most newcomers preferred to settle closer to the U.S.–Canada border.[55] The largest of the early communities of African American emigrants formed in Amherstburg and nearby Colchester. By 1827, these towns had amassed a combined black population of nearly 600 people. Other towns hosting noticeable, if small, black populations by the 1820s included Welland, St. Catharines, Windsor, London, Chatham, Dresden, Oro, and Toronto, each of which continued to be magnet destinations for fugitives seeking to settle near earlier arrivals (Map 2).[56]

As slaves from the Upper South made their way toward the international border with increasing frequency, the alarm of American

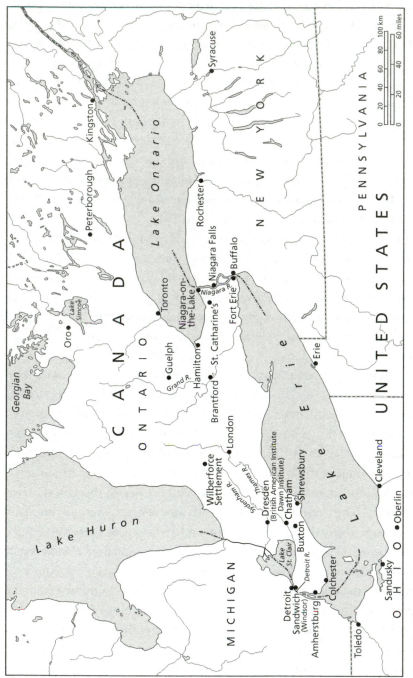

Map 2 Southwestern Upper Canada/Canada West

slaveholders – like those who threatened James C. Brown in Louisville – grew precipitously. They recognized, quite rightly, that successful border-crossings were turning Canada into a powerful symbol of freedom even for slaves in the Deep South, for whom Upper Canada was not a realistic destination. As a result, southern slaveholders lobbied the federal government to intervene on their behalf at the U.S.–Canada border – just as they had in regard to Mexico. International diplomacy, they hoped, would help them recapture lost "property" and nip in the bud Upper Canada's symbolic status as a land of freedom.

In 1819, however, slaveholders' first effort to leverage federal diplomacy backfired spectacularly. It was a difficult year. As the United States rapidly expanded westward, problems arose and tensions flared. The U.S. economy entered a period of crisis known as the Panic of 1819, which was precipitated in part by the frontier land boom and excessive lending by the Second Bank of the United States. Meanwhile, heated debates over whether slavery should or should not be restricted in the United States' newest territories came to a head. The result was the famous Missouri Compromise, which effectively established a sectional line determining where slavery could or could not expand.[57]

At the time, future president of the United States John Quincy Adams was still the Secretary of State in James Monroe's administration. And it was to him, in the midst of these national crises, that enslavers from Tennessee clamored for assistance on the matter of international slave diplomacy when several slaves escaped from Tennessee into Upper Canada in 1819. On the slaveholders' behalf, Adams reached out to the British Ambassador in Washington, DC, who, in turn, forwarded Adams's request for the return of the slaves to Upper Canada's provincial government. Contrary to the Tennessean slaveholders' hopes, however, the Canadian province's attorney-general forcefully rejected Adams's overture. Writing back that the self-emancipated slaves had "the right to personal freedom" in Upper Canada, the attorney-general asserted that their legal status in the United States had no bearing on their legal status in Upper Canada. Citing the "Law of England as the rule of decision," he then warned that any Americans attempting to "infringe upon this right" would face legal consequences.[58]

This decision was momentous. Rather than disrupting Upper Canada's growing reputation as a free-soil haven by returning runaway slaves to the United States, Upper Canada's attorney-general actually committed his province to a free-soil policy that – while previously practiced at the local level – had not yet been formally established as official government policy. The inadvertent outcome of U.S. pro-slavery diplomacy was to transform the international border into a geopolitical wall preventing U.S. slaveholders from reclaiming fugitive slaves.

Unsurprisingly, U.S. slaveholders refused to accept the matter as settled. In the 1820s, Kentucky slaveholders, in particular, regularly pressured the U.S. government to re-enter negotiations for the return of self-emancipated individuals. This time around, however, they hoped the United States would circumvent provincial lawmakers in Upper Canada and go directly through London. In 1821, Kentucky Congressman William Brown presented a memorial from the Kentucky General Assembly to the U.S. House of Representatives, requesting that the U.S. government "invite the attention of the British Government" to the ongoing issue of Canadian free soil. "Many negroes and persons of color," the memorial stated, had escaped from Kentucky across the international border, "tend[ing] greatly to the injury of the people." The blame for this state of affairs, the memorial suggested, was easily attributable to the Canadian policy of "concealing and countenancing slaves that thus escape." Kentucky's General Assembly felt sure that if the situation was not soon addressed, there were likely to be "unhappy consequences" between American citizens and British-Canadian subjects.[59]

Although a technicality in the memorial's composition forced Kentucky Congressman Brown to withdraw this particular document in 1821, Anglo-American diplomacy on the topic of fugitive slaves remained an ongoing concern at the state and federal levels. In both 1825 and 1827, the Kentucky General Assembly again reached out through its state Congressmen to "invok[e] the interposition of the general government" on slaveholders' behalf.[60] By this time, John Quincy Adams had become president and Henry Clay, the famous Kentucky statesman, had taken over as Secretary of State. In response to the concern repeatedly expressed by the General Assembly of his home state, Clay worked closely with the American Minister to Great Britain, Albert Gallatin, to find an acceptable arrangement.

Clay was determined to make a treaty for the mutual surrender of fugitive slaves across the U.S.–Canada border. However, the fact that slavery had dwindled to the point of near-absence in Upper Canada meant that the practical effects of such a treaty would be rather one-sided. So, Clay told Albert Gallatin to sweeten the deal by negotiating for the mutual surrender of military and naval deserters. Gallatin was to assure the British that they would "obtain the advantage" in such an agreement. A treaty agreement for the "restoration" of military and naval fugitives, he believed, would more than compensate for the "practical operation of an article for the mutual delivery of fugitives from labor." Echoing the Kentucky General Assembly's concern regarding the "unhappy consequences" that might arise from Upper Canada's refusal to return fugitive slaves to the United States, Clay told Gallatin to emphasize that a treaty, or at the very least a formal directive to Upper Canada to return American slaves, would "cultivate good neighborhood" between the two countries.[61]

The result of Clay's efforts was another letdown for U.S. slaveholders. In 1827, over a year after the initiation of Gallatin's efforts with the British government, Gallatin admitted that he was making very little headway. On the matter of fugitive slaves, he found that "the state of [British] public opinion" was so strong that "no administration would, or could, admit in a treaty, a stipulation such as was asked for."[62] The British government stood firmly behind Upper Canada's non-extradition policy.

This information enraged Clay, who subsequently adopted a more ominous tone with Gallatin's successor, James Barbour. In 1828, when Clay directed the new Minister to Great Britain to broach the issue once again, he urged Barbour to remember that "the evil is a growing one, and is well calculated to disturb the good neighborhood which we are desirous of cultivating with the adjacent British provinces." He continued, "It is almost impossible for the two governments, however well disposed, to restrain individual excesses and collisions which will arise out of the pursuit of property on the one side, and the defense on the other, of those who have found an asylum."[63] Clay's words reflected James C. Brown's experience in Louisville just a few years earlier: Kentucky slaveholders were willing to use whatever means necessary to staunch the flow of self-liberated slaves to Upper Canada.

By December 1828, the press had picked up the story of the U.S. diplomatic stalemate. Henry Clay's correspondence with Gallatin and Barbour first made its way into *Niles' Weekly Register*, then into the *Genius of Universal Emancipation*, and, by mid-January of the following year, it reached the front page of *Freedom's Journal.*[64] It was exciting news for anti-slavery advocates, and John Brown Russwurm, editor of *Freedom's Journal*, made sure its significance was not lost on his readers. "It has never been our happy lot to present so interesting a sheet to [readers'] perusal," he wrote. He rejoiced to find the British "so firm and positive" in their protection of self-liberated men and women. Noting that Albert Gallatin was generally regarded as a formidable diplomat, he emphasized that the man's failure in this case only proved how truly unmovable the British were on the topic of fugitive slave extradition.[65]

Of course, pro-slavery advocates saw things quite differently. As one pro-slavery editorial pointed out, "hundreds (if not thousands) of slaves have escaped from Virginia and Kentucky into Upper Canada," and the failure of U.S. diplomacy meant that there was "no regulation by which they can be surrendered to their masters."[66]

The British government's public commitment to protecting self-liberated men and women in the 1810s and 1820s built Upper Canada's reputation as a free-soil haven at the very same time as other locales' free-soil security seemed increasingly fragile. Rumor and hope encouraged runaway slaves to strike out for Upper Canada, and the media's coverage of the United States' failed diplomacy confirmed their success and inspired new efforts. Just as importantly, the security of Upper Canadian free soil in the late 1820s stood in stark contrast to the ominous forecast elsewhere. While Mexico ultimately decided not to sign a treaty stipulating that it must return fugitive slaves to the United States, neither did it formally refuse to extradite them.[67]

Not even Haiti was immune from international pressure when it came to returning runaway slaves. In 1826, just two years after inspiring the emigration of thousands of free African Americans, President Boyer signed a diplomatic treaty with Britain in which he agreed that Haiti would return any slaves from British territory who sought sanctuary in his country.[68] This was also an ill omen for the safety of runaways from the United States. There had been rumors that runaway slaves from the U.S. had been able to make their way to the island alongside legal emigrants, and American slaveholders were keen to make Congress "interpose the national arm for the preservation of this species of property."[69] While few, if any, specific complaints were made, Boyer's decision to return self-emancipated people to slavery in the British colonies was a promising sign for U.S. slaveholders hoping to hem in potential runaways. By signing the treaty with Great Britain in 1826, Boyer affirmed that Haiti would no longer be at the vanguard of free-soil activism. For free and fugitive African Americans alike, its reputation as a resettlement locale was at low ebb by the end of the decade.

While the story of the treaty between Haiti and Great Britain illuminates the limits of free soil for a young island nation struggling to achieve international recognition and a stabilized economy, it is also a stark reminder of the marked contrast dictating British policy in its mainland Canadian colonies and its sugar-producing colonies in the Caribbean. In Upper Canada, where slavery was almost entirely defunct and had little effect on the British economy, Great Britain was more than happy to thumb its nose at the United States by offering free-soil sanctuary to runaway slaves. In the West Indies, however, where sugar production on islands like Jamaica, Barbados, and Antigua was still a mainstay of the British colonial economy, there was no question of condoning self-emancipation. Yet choosing to ignore the imperial double standard by which the British government strong-armed an extradition treaty with Haiti for the return of its own fugitive slaves, African Americans and U.S. anti-slavery advocates celebrated the political calculus whereby Britain decided to protect American runaways in Upper Canada. By 1829, enslaved people's savvy efforts to claim freedom across an international border where they were protected as part and parcel of broader geopolitical contests made Upper Canada seem an unassailable asylum of freedom.

More than anything else, it was likely this reputation for protecting self-liberated men and women that encouraged Cincinnati's free African Americans to contemplate whether Upper Canada might make a good home for them as well. In fact, when James C. Brown first recommended Upper Canada to other black Cincinnatians in 1829, he did so expressly with the hope that the British province might provide "an asylum for ourselves, our wives, and children."[70] They needed a destination where they would not be unwelcome due to the color of their skin, where they could earn a living, and where policies regarding the return of fugitive slaves would not put them at risk of being accused by underhanded enslavers of being runaway "property." Even among the Canadian provinces, Upper Canada seemed the best bet. While Nova Scotia had been the center of black loyalism in the British Empire after the American Revolution and through the War of 1812, it had gradually become a less welcoming space for brown-skinned residents. Many of the early emigrants, the Black Loyalists, decided to relocate even further abroad to the British colony of Sierra Leone on the coast of West Africa. By contrast, Upper Canada had established a history of quietly welcoming black migrants as useful contributors to local agricultural production.[71]

And yet, despite providing a safe haven for men and women made suddenly and violently unwelcome in their former home, there was no reason to think that the *quality* of freedom for free people in Upper Canada would be any different than it was in Ohio. In Ohio, slavery had been illegal since 1803, but free people were still not considered equal citizens. Similarly, as 200 petitioners indicated to the provincial lieutenant governor in 1828, African Americans in Upper Canada remained to "a great measure excluded" from the "many privileges" delineated by the Province's constitution.[72] As in Ohio, African Americans were free in Upper Canada, but barred from political participation. When the Cincinnatians looked north, therefore, they would have seen a familiar landscape of legal – but not equal – freedom.

In this light, it makes sense that the *Ohio Monitor* omitted Upper Canada from its 1829 list of locales where African Americans "would enjoy political freedom." At the time of the exchange between Lewis

Woodson, who advocated for a separate black settlement within Ohio, and the paper's editor, who responded by encouraging international emigration, Upper Canada was fundamentally different from the other sites on the editor's list of recommendations. Whereas Haiti, Mexico, and the new South American republics had each undergone some sort of revolutionizing process as a part of their independence movements, Canada remained a loyal part of the slaveholding British Empire. Moreover, while Great Britain had conferred subject status on black war veterans of the American Revolution and the War of 1812, there had been no effort to fundamentally rethink the legal status of free people of color within the empire (as would eventually happen in 1833 with the enactment of gradual emancipation).[73]

In short, while Canada's reputation for protecting runaway slaves likely encouraged Brown and his compatriots to consider it, there was no indication that free black residents would experience any more civic inclusion than they did in the free states of the United States. And when Brown and his fellow Cincinnatians met to discuss potential emigration options, they were not looking for a new home where they would again be excluded from formal citizenship. They hoped to find "some place to live free from the trammels of unsocial and unequal laws."[74]

Rather than simply continuing their search and looking elsewhere, however, the group took an unprecedented action: they contacted the representative of the British crown in Upper Canada directly. James C. Brown, as president of the group's newly formed Colonization Society, wrote a letter directly to Sir John Colborne, Lieutenant Governor of Upper Canada, in order to determine exactly what kind of "asylum" free people might find in the province known for protecting runaway slaves.[75] The letter was delivered in person by several of the Colonization Society's board members so that they could simultaneously conduct their own firsthand assessment of the province's potential.

The group was well received. The delegates were pleased to report that the country was "beautiful and fertile," and that Colborne was very amenable to their interest in emigrating to the province. He not only assured them that the black Ohioans were welcome and that there was land aplenty to accommodate their resettlement, he was prepared to help them choose between three districts for their settlement location.[76] Most importantly, Colborne assured the Cincinnatians that Upper Canada would extend to them all the rights and privileges of British subjects, without regard to color, as long as they remained "true and loyal" to their new home.[77]

Extended in person and in written correspondence to Brown, Colborne's guarantee that free African Americans would enjoy equal legal and civil rights in Upper Canada was momentous. His guarantee fundamentally re-envisioned the relationship between Great Britain and black settlers. The past ten years of diplomatic negotiation had established that self-emancipated slaves would be protected under the British flag, but Colborne's guarantee expanded Upper Canada's obligation toward African American emigrants, free and fugitive, to include legal equality in addition to protection. Ultimately, it was Colborne's response to the Cincinnati Colonization Society that convinced the Cincinnatians that it was Upper Canada, rather than another state or a different free-soil haven, that offered them the most promising future.[78]

Brown never forgot "the benevolence of the Governor of Canada." He claimed to have kept Colborne's response letter as a prized possession for several decades.[79] And contemporary commentators were quick to note that potential emigrants "appear[ed] to be elevated at the prospect of possessing equal rights and privileges."[80] Within a decade of the Ohio exodus, in fact, the contents of Sir John Colborne's letter to the black Cincinnatians had become something of a legend: "Tell the Republicans on your side of the line that we do not know men by their color. If you come to us, you will be entitled to all the privileges of the rest of his Majesty's subjects."[81] With Colborne's guarantee in hand, members of the Cincinnati Colonization Society began to put all the necessary pieces in place for a speedy relocation, catapulting Canada onto the map of the American anti-slavery movement and setting the stage for what would soon come to be known as the Underground Railroad.

CHAPTER 3

Departure and Debate: Free Black Emigration to Canada and Mexico

About six thousand of us went to Hayti . . . but we found that a settlement there did not suit our extensive population. Thus you see that the Lord is opening a way for us to pack up and march off, without crossing the seas, to Canada, and I hope soon, to the Texas, or some neighboring province.

~ A Colored Citizen of Brooklyn, *The Liberator*, April 7, 1832[1]

In the April 1830 edition of the *Genius of Universal Emancipation*, Benjamin Lundy shared a report on the "colony in Canada." Just a few months earlier, the delegates of the Cincinnati Colonization Society had worked with the Canadian Land Company to purchase a large swath of land located 50 miles from Lake Erie. Nestled along the banks of the Grand River, it was, reportedly, close to two flourishing Dutch and Quaker settlements.[2] Noting that African Americans in the middle and northern states were showing enormous interest in the settlement, Lundy confidently declared that "a very extensive emigration" would soon take place. "There is now no doubt," he wrote, "that they will be admitted to the full enjoyment of their civil and religious privileges."[3] Not two years later, he remained confident that there had been no project so full of promise since the idea of colonization had first emerged in the United States. He had seen the area where the settlement was located himself and found it "very suitable for those accustomed to our climate."[4]

And yet the process of resettling on the newly purchased land never lived up to expectations. Although Lundy, like James C. Brown, had good reason for optimism, only a mere fraction of the numbers either man expected ever made their way to the new township site. Of the 2,700

Cincinnatians Brown had originally projected, no more than 460 made the long trek across the border.[5]

Financial difficulty was one likely cause. In a series of notices in the *Daily Cincinnati Gazette,* Brown encouraged the public to make charitable donations toward the emigration project. Some interested emigrants, he declared, were unable to afford the trip because of their difficulty finding employment in Cincinnati. Although "anxious to get away," they were "without the means even to commence their journey."[6] Many more were likely hesitant to court the hardship of emigrating to a new settlement. The precious few who joined James C. Brown – which he estimated at five or six families from Cincinnati and another fifteen families from Boston – faced enormous adversity. The difficulty of clearing dense Canadian forest and the lack of adequate farmland led to extreme suffering, with one observer noting that the migrants spent their first year in acute destitution and "a state of actual starvation." It is unsurprising that many Ohio refugees decided to resettle elsewhere within the United States or in established Canadian towns and cities rather than making their way to the fledgling settlement on the Grand River.[7]

Although the settlement did not live up to its founders' hopes (and eventually failed altogether), it did persevere through its early years. Thanks to sheer will and substantial philanthropy from allies in the United States, the settlers survived and eventually renamed their home in honor of William Wilberforce, the famed British abolitionist. Moreover, despite their small number and perilous welfare, the residents of the "Wilberforce colony" became a cause célèbre in American antislavery circles. The Cincinnatians' northward migration captured the attention of American observers and propelled Upper Canada into a place of national significance in the United States.

For many, the settlement of African Americans across the Canadian border was a matter of grave concern. White people from Ohio and elsewhere expressed alarm that there might be unintended, unwanted consequences as a result of African Americans' decision to find asylum in British territory. It reignited a fear voiced after the Anglo-American wars that Britain's practice of welcoming black veterans and refugees would someday lead to these emigrants fighting for Britain against the United

States.[8] Nearly twenty years after the momentous mass migration from Cincinnati, Frederick Douglass recalled this fear playing out in newspapers and journals across the free states. Almost as soon as news of the Canada plan became public, he recalled, people began "teeming with objections and censures against the Legislature and state of Ohio." Observers agreed that by implementing the Black Laws, Ohio's legislature had "over-shot the mark." It had failed to take into account the cost of "supplying the dominions of a powerful enemy with robust able-bodied men" – men who might "one day retaliate upon this country with terrible consequences."[9]

The Cincinnati city government itself harbored this concern. Fearing that every man, woman, and child who crossed the U.S.–Canada border was equivalent to "a sword drawn against the United States," the mayor summoned Brown to his office in an effort to avert disaster. Meeting with Brown just before his departure from Cincinnati, the mayor begged him to "stay any action" while the city advocated for the repeal of the Black Laws at the state level. Needless to say, Brown paid no attention.[10]

For many, the emigration of African Americans across the U.S.–Canada border inspired interest and hope rather than fear. American reformers and anti-slavery advocates immediately recognized the significance of Sir John Colborne's decision to offer equality under the law, and they anticipated that the experience of the Wilberforce settlers could potentially affect people's perceptions about black freedom in the United States. As British abolitionist Charles Stuart expressed in a widely read pamphlet, black settlers "shall be setting the whites of the United States an example, on their own borders, and under their own eyes, of righteous superiority to criminal prejudice." They would show that the races could "intermingle happily," and thus encourage Americans to abolish slavery within their own border.[11]

As anti-slavery advocates eagerly followed and promoted the settlers' progress, Upper Canada became more than a refuge; it became a critically important experiment in black freedom. After a decade of contentious debate surrounding the competing relocation plans and anti-slavery merits of Haiti and Liberia, Upper Canada presented a promising alternative whose reputation was premised on equal citizenship, voluntary emigration, economic opportunity, and cultural similitude. If successful, the Wilberforce settlement would undermine pro-slavery arguments that black men and women were collectively unprepared and unfit for freedom. Leading anti-slavery newspapers like Benjamin Lundy's *Genius of Universal Emancipation* and William Lloyd Garrison's *The Liberator* were keen to print all the news and views they could about it, and a hungry audience was keen to gobble up information. As Lundy astutely noted, "whatever relates to the new settlement in Canada, must excite the attention, not only of our free colored population, but of the country more generally."[12]

The newly established free-soil haven – as a symbol of legal equality and as an actual destination – perfectly captured the needs of an anti-slavery movement in transition. In the early 1830s, the zeitgeist of American anti-slavery swung from gradualism, a philosophy characterized by elite-driven efforts to eradicate slavery through legal reform and individual manumission, toward immediatism – a new phase of organization, activism, and ideas that emphasized broad-based mobilization, moral outrage, and public protest to achieve the immediate release of all enslaved people from bondage. Radical "abolitionism," as this form of activism was called, was a product of religious revivalism, expanding political participation, and African American activism. It was also a response to increasing evidence – such as Ohio's 1829 decision to enforce its Black Laws – that gradualism was not producing results.[13]

William Lloyd Garrison, a white anti-slavery advocate who had been mentored and inspired by Benjamin Lundy, is typically described as launching the movement in the United States through the publication of his newspaper, *The Liberator*, in 1831.[14] Like Lundy, he had previously been a proponent of gradualism, but his first issue of *The Liberator* rejected this mode of anti-slavery thinking as a "popular but pernicious doctrine."[15]

As many historians have noted, Garrison was inspired to this change of heart by engaging with black activists from Baltimore to Boston.[16] Among the voices guiding his transformation was that of writer and activist David Walker, author of the widely read 1829 pamphlet, *Appeal to the Colored People of the World*. Writing from his home in Boston, Walker – a former agent for *Freedom's Journal* – denounced the moral and political hypocrisy of slaveholders. He condemned slavery for having rendered African Americans "the most degraded, wretched, and abject set of beings that ever lived since the world began," and he encouraged African Americans – free and enslaved – to fight for freedom and racial justice.[17] His fiery appeal, along with the efforts of other African

American activists, helped move William Lloyd Garrison and like-minded white reformers toward a radical form of anti-slavery more closely aligned with the goals of African American activists.

The cause of immediate, uncompensated abolition swiftly grew into an organized movement with enormous visibility relative to the modest number of reformers actively contributing to its mission. With a vim and vigor bred of moral purpose and fostered by national organization, abolitionists in the early 1830s were transformed into what historian James Brewer Stewart has called "whirlwinds of agitation."[18] Attempting to sway hearts and minds throughout the nation, they gave public lectures, organized community meetings, and rallied the power of the press to spread their message and unite like-minded reformers. Most famously in these early years of organized immediatism, they flooded the South with abolitionist reading material in the "Great Pamphlet Campaign" of 1835.[19]

A key component of immediate abolitionism was the rejection of African colonization and any similar efforts to make black freedom contingent on the removal of African Americans from the United States. Although African American antipathy toward the white-led ACS was by no means new, Walker's *Appeal* – which included a denunciation of the organization – helped convince white reformers like Garrison that the rejection of both African colonization and the ACS was essential to the cause of immediate emancipation.[20] For more conservative white reformers, however, this was uncomfortable territory. Labeled by historian Richard Newman as a "key transitional topic" for reformers shifting from gradualism to immediatism,[21] the issue of colonization exposed the racist underbelly of anti-slavery advocates who could only fathom the idea of African American freedom if it was outside the United States.

Antagonists of the ACS were deeply concerned, therefore, that the organization was only gaining momentum as time wore on. A decade after the ACS had first been formed in Washington, DC, the organization had been steadily building support in the North during the second half of the 1820s and was growing nationally. Initially, it had struggled to maintain a thriving membership after Philadelphia's free black community and the American Convention for Promoting the Abolition of

Slavery and Improving the Condition of the African Race had agreed that Liberian colonization would likely perpetuate American slavery and social prejudice. It reached its nadir, or what historian P. J. Staudenraus labeled its "crisis years," in 1823–1824.[22] During that time, the ACS divided internally along sectional lines, with pro-slavery and anti-slavery members unable to agree on whether gradual emancipation should be among the organization's objectives. Furthermore, the upsurge in Haitian emigrationism – and the clear preference among African American communities for the Haitian option – compromised the ACS's ability to rally widespread popular support.

But everything changed for the ACS in 1825. At the very same time as returning migrants began to cast a pall over Haiti's emigration prospects, the ACS managed a successful campaign to revamp its public image. Ralph R. Gurley, a white Connecticut reformer, was named the ACS's new corresponding secretary. Almost single-handedly, he bolstered the organization's interregional membership and reinvigorated interest in colonization. Using a savvy combination of grassroots public relations strategies to gain momentum and support, Gurley gave Liberia a second wind and brought it surging back onto the mental map of anti-slavery advocates. By the end of the 1820s, even the majority of the American Convention's members supported the idea.[23]

One of Gurley's most significant innovations was the publication of a central ACS news organ, the *African Repository and Colonial Journal*. Published on a monthly basis from March 1, 1825, through 1919, the *African Repository* published the ACS's annual meeting minutes, articles on the governance and administration of Liberia, general interest pieces on the people and customs of West Africa, and promising information on the expansion of colonizationist sentiment. "We must conceal nothing from public view, tear away every veil, and expose the dark as well as bright spots of our object," Gurley declared at the ACS's 1825 annual meeting.[24] The *African Repository* did its job well. African colonization became the go-to plan for many white reformers who believed mass relocation was the only plausible way to galvanize anti-slavery sentiment in the United States. They saw little that concerned them about shipping former slaves away from the land of their birth to the distant shores of coastal West Africa.

While the ACS steadily increased white support for its efforts to relocate freed slaves to Liberia, it also pressed its efforts to woo potential migrants from among free people in the north and south. In what seemed like a coup for ACS promoters in 1829, they even convinced John Brown Russwurm, the prominent editor of *Freedom's Journal*, to join their ranks. During *Freedom's Journal's* two-year run (1827–1829), John Brown Russwurm and his co-editor, Samuel Cornish, had maintained an official stance of non-support for the colonization project. With African colonization a leading concern among African Americans, the paper had consistently offered an illuminating cross-section of pro- and anti-colonization perspectives. But the majority of *Freedom's Journal* readers were staunchly opposed to the idea of African colonization – and appreciated that the editors were, too. It came as an enormous and unwelcome surprise to many, therefore, when Russwurm published a lengthy editorial professing his change of heart in February 1829. Increasingly concerned about African Americans' prospects in the United States, Russwurm described the U.S. as a land where "we cannot enjoy the privileges of citizen, for reasons known and felt daily." It was, he believed, time to look elsewhere.[25]

Russwurm's seemingly sudden embrace of colonization was a lightning rod in the debate over African relocation in 1829. His reversal enraged and alienated many of the black northerners who had spent over a decade fighting against it. Some even depicted him as a race traitor.[26] But Russwurm held his ground. Assuring his readers that he had read every article he could find on the topic, he had become convinced that free African Americans would never be granted full and equal citizenship in the United States. He had also come to share the belief that emancipation would never take place unless freed slaves could "be removed as fast as they drop their galling chains, to some other land besides the free states."[27] So, in late September 1829, six months after shuttering *Freedom's Journal*, Russwurm sailed across the Atlantic Ocean under the auspices of the ACS.[28] He settled in Liberia, where he became the editor of the colony's newspaper, the *Liberia Herald*.

Russwurm was a prime example for the ACS to show that their relocation plan *could* and *did* inspire the voluntary participation of free African Americans. Not only did he choose to move to Liberia, he made it very clear that it was a conscious and well-considered choice among all available options. In 1829, three years after the rise and fall of his desire to resettle in Haiti, Russwurm described Liberia as a land "where we may enjoy all the rights of freemen; where everything will tend to call forth our best and most generous feelings – in a word, where we may not only feel as men, but where we may also act as such."[29] Writing from his new home in 1832, Russwurm continued to remark upon the expanding free-soil landscape and what it meant for African Americans: "Where then will the thousands of free persons of color, and the thousands of slaves, whose masters stand ready to free them, flee for shelter?" he asked. "Can they *all* go to Canada?" He found the possibility laughable. "Will they flee to Hayti?" he continued, with equal skepticism. "The experiment has been tried, and hundreds have returned back with these words in their mouths, 'if we are to be slaves, let us be slaves in America.'" Even in the midst of the positive attention that the Ohio exodus brought to Upper Canada, Russwurm applauded twenty-two former Ohioans who had recently sailed for Liberia instead.[30]

Against the strong current of growing white support for the ACS, many African Americans in the early 1830s fully rejected all relocation projects that removed people of African descent from the United States. A group who met together in Pittsburgh's African Methodist Episcopal Church, for example, was determined to stay and fight for equality and racial justice. Characterizing themselves as "citizens of these United States," they pledged their lives, fortunes, and honor not to support relocation of any sort to Africa, Upper Canada, or Hayti.[31] More frequently, however, black communities voiced generous support for Upper Canada once it emerged as a prospective destination in 1829. Not only was it a place where African Americans would be granted legal equality, it was – like Haiti had been in the mid-1820s – a promising and self-directed alternative to the ACS. At gatherings held to protest the ACS from New York and New Jersey to Pennsylvania and Ohio, free black people raised their voices to affirm that they would support – and in some cases even encourage – emigration to Upper Canada.[32] As a group of free African Americans from Columbia, Pennsylvania, declared, nothing could induce them to leave for Liberia, but they would support emigrants in Canada because the British province was "far more consonant with [their] views."[33]

In fact, support for Upper Canada quickly became part and parcel of the fight against colonization. Not only did it provide an alternative place of asylum without the coercive overlay of the ACS, it offered clear evidence that many of the ACS's racist talking points were simply wrong. Nearly as soon as the Wilberforce settlement was established in the early 1830s, Upper Canada became a ready reference point within anti-slavery circles for disputing specific pro-colonization claims regarding why African Americans were better suited for living elsewhere.

One such claim was that freed black people from southern slave states were better suited to warm, equatorial climates than they were to the more temperate zones of the northern United States. "Can it be doubted," exclaimed an ACS supporter advocating Liberian emigration in 1827, "whether or not the climate of Africa is congenial to her own descendants!"[34] Drawing from the same racist pseudoscience used by slaveholders to argue that people of African descent were better able than Europeans to labor in the warm climates where staple crops like sugar and cotton grow, colonization supporters purported that the Liberia colony provided the most physically healthy environment for people of African descent.[35] Although counter-evidence abounded in the form of healthy black communities in the urban North and in the high death rate of black Liberian colonists, the ACS clung tenaciously to its position.[36]

Reports of emigrants' well-being in the cold climate of Upper Canada not only offered additional proof that African Americans' physical health was suited just fine to northern temperatures, they offered a poignant contrast to Liberia, which opponents of colonization often characterized as a disease cesspool bringing migrants to an early grave.[37] Of course, the argument went both ways: the ACS did not hesitate to depict the cold Upper Canadian climate as so "uncongenial" to the health of African Americans that "nothing but dire necessity could induce them to live there."[38] But the evidence that African Americans could comfortably live in climates depicted as even colder than the northern United States was compelling, and it supported anti-colonization arguments. Nobody said it better than British abolitionist Charles Stuart. In an excoriation of his fellow British national, the pro-ACS physician Thomas Hodgkin, Stuart simply noted that "men are not palm trees."[39]

For some observers, the prospect of Canadian emigration also provided a moving counterpoint to the ACS claim that sending freed African Americans to Liberia would help civilize and Christianize the African continent. According to a meeting of African Americans in Brooklyn, New York, this ACS talking point was nothing but hot air. "Sending a parcel of uninstructed, uncivilized, and unchristianized people, to the western coast of Africa, with bibles in their hands, to teach the natives the truths of the gospel, social happiness, and moral virtue, is mockery and ridicule in the extreme." By contrast, they suggested, Upper Canada offered emigrants *themselves* the "opportunity to become civilized and Christianized" – an opportunity this group of well-educated men and women clearly assumed that former slaves would require. As a Christian country where "prejudice has not such an unlimited sway" as it did in the United States, Upper Canada struck them as a superior destination for black migrants if the concern was the spiritual and moral health of former slaves.[40]

In addition to countering the basic propositions bolstering the ACS's rise in popularity among gradual abolitionists, many anti-slavery advocates saw in Upper Canada a powerful way to talk about the importance of equal citizenship in the United States. Anti-slavery observers were quick to juxtapose the prejudice of Ohio's Black Laws (and of U.S. attitudes more generally) with Upper Canada's extension of legal equality to African American settlers. Benjamin Lundy, for one, did not mince words when he blamed the "despotism of a republican government" for driving the Cincinnatians to seek refuge "under the more liberal policy of an enlightened monarchy."[41] A mainstay of anti-slavery news articles about Canadian emigration throughout the antebellum period, this kind of comparison highlighted the hypocrisy of structural racism in the United States (where the government professed to be "the most *free* and most liberal in the world") and reignited old discussions about the relationship between free African Americans and the state.[42]

What was the obligation of the state to its black inhabitants, observers wondered, and what kind of government best protected the liberty of all?

In the 1820s, the unification of Haiti under Boyer's administration and the emergence of new republics in the aftermath of the former Spanish colonies' independence movements allowed anti-slavery advocates to castigate the United States for its selective reading of republican liberty. Unlike other republics, the United States had failed to at least *try* living up to the values of liberty and equality for all. Now, with Upper Canada's promise of color-blind equality, it appeared to many that Britain's liberal monarchy was actually the better guarantor of legal rights typically associated with American republicanism.

By facilitating important political critiques ultimately aimed at encouraging the United States to treat black people as equal citizens, the prospect of Canadian emigration provided a means for free African Americans to link the here-and-now experience of legal equality in Upper Canada with the hope of achieving the same outcome in the United States. This link was, for example, a driving impulse in the formation of the American Society of Free Persons of Color, a national association of black leaders and activists. Inspired to gather in the aftermath of the Ohio Black Laws, participants assembled for the first time in Philadelphia in 1830. Meeting annually for the next five years and then regularly through the end of the American Civil War, the Society became the backbone of the Colored Conventions movement, which brought black men and women together at the state and national level throughout the nineteenth century to discuss strategies for achieving racial justice across the United States.[43]

When the Society first met on September 20, 1830, it was with the intention of purchasing land and establishing a settlement in Upper Canada. Such a course, delegates agreed, would be "a great advantage to the people of color." Although the Society decided to proceed independently from James C. Brown and the Wilberforce settlement, its aims were the same. Its leaders believed that a settlement in Upper Canada would serve two interconnected purposes: providing an asylum for African Americans forced from their homes by white prejudice, and furthering the project of racial uplift in the United States. The economic opportunities and apparent lack of social prejudice in Upper Canada would, they expected, allow the "diligent student" to "take their stand as men," and doing so would cultivate the necessary conditions for promoting the future prosperity – and moral and political standing – of African Americans generally.[44]

A year after their inaugural meeting, delegates were happy to report that their efforts to recruit and support settlers were working. Their friends and funds were "daily increasing," and even their most sanguine expectations had been outperformed by leaps and bounds. "Already have our brethren purchased eight hundred acres of land," they reported, "and two thousand of them have left the soil of their birth, crossed the lines, and laid the foundation for a structure which promises to prove an asylum for the colored population of these United States." Even Austin Steward, the man who had acted as co-vice president at the Society's inaugural meeting, had left his home in Rochester, New York, to make a fresh start across the border.[45]

In truth, the group's estimate that 2,000 settlers had crossed the border by 1831 was likely an overstatement, but high estimates were common in the first several years of Canadian resettlement. Accounts differ on the overall black population in Upper Canada, but a preeminent historian on the topic argues that the population of Wilberforce alone likely never rose above 200, and the overall population of the region never rose above 1,000 in total.[46] However, the specific estimate of 2,000 produced in the course of the 1831 Colored Convention served an important purpose: it was used to show that as many black settlers had gone to Canada in the space of one year as had gone to Liberia in over a decade. Circulated in the anti-slavery press for over twelve months, it proved a highly marketable comparison despite the fact that 2,000 migrants still accounted for only 1.6 percent of the Northeast's free black population of 125,214.[47]

Throughout the northern United States, observers' immediate and widespread interest in Canadian resettlement only grew. Thriving emigration societies were organized in major cities, and – as similar associations had previously done for Haiti – each society dispatched its own agents to Upper Canada to assess its potential and report back. Hezekiah Grice, a prominent black Baltimorean and founding father of the Colored Conventions movement, even produced a 25-cent map to assist potential emigrants and society agents by detailing the settlement territory and the various routes to get there.[48] Newspapers like the

Genius of Universal Emancipation noted this enthusiasm and regularly reported that "extensive preparations" were underway for "vast numbers" of further emigrants to make their way across the border.[49] Even observers in Upper Canada who realized that emigration was not yet as great as had been represented in American newspapers nonetheless perpetuated the notion that "a very extensive emigration will very soon take place."[50]

As a temporary home while waiting for socio-legal change in the United States or as a permanent destination big enough to hold all who wanted to leave, Upper Canada had become a recognizable asylum. It was a place of refuge and equality – two characteristics that emigration proponents consistently emphasized throughout the antebellum period. Even African Americans who remained adamant that American-born black people should remain in their native land recognized that Upper Canada was an important escape hatch for the truly oppressed among their number.[51]

There were good reasons for observers to feel such enthusiasm. Settlers' health, the climate, the organization of religious establishments, the soil's productivity, and the availability of educational resources were all subjects on which Upper Canada won winning marks in the public arena. Also in its favor, observers pointed out, was that it did not take enormous expense to get to Canada, or expose settlers to the "danger of the sea."[52] As William Lloyd Garrison himself declared, Upper Canada was the optimal destination for those needing to flee the United States.[53]

However, despite general fervor for Upper Canada as an emigration destination for free African Americans, a counterpoint to African colonization, and a positive example of black freedom, not all news from Upper Canada was good. In particular, the settlement at Wilberforce was struggling. Although the settlement's supporters tried to downplay migrants' reliance on financial assistance, it was clear that Wilberforce was finding it difficult to achieve full economic independence. It continued to require the largesse of American allies to stay above water.[54] While strong justifications could easily be made for soliciting philanthropic aid based on the merits of the project and the mettle of the migrants – it was, after all, "one of the most noble enterprises that ever was started" – fundraising became more difficult after evidence of fraud and mismanagement hit the news in 1831.[55]

It started as a political rivalry between two of Wilberforce's leading members: Israel Lewis and Austin Steward, both early settlers in Wilberforce and members of the Board of Trustees. Beginning in 1831, reports began to circulate in American newspapers that Lewis had mismanaged funds he had solicited from American donors as an official agent of the settlement.[56] It seemed that philanthropic pledges were not reaching the town's coffers, and Steward was sure that the blame lay at Lewis's doorstop. Over the next two years, Lewis, Steward, and their various supporters reached out through various anti-slavery newspapers to defend themselves and attack each other.[57] While attempting to defend their personal reputations, however, they tarnished that of Wilberforce. Although Lewis resigned his post as agent in 1832, the scandal continued to be reported for another year and tainted the settlement's public image considerably.[58]

And Wilberforce was not alone. Nearly simultaneously, it emerged that a scurrilous character was posing as an official agent for another new Canadian settlement. Traveling the northeastern United States, he reportedly embezzled the funds he solicited on the town's behalf.[59]

Scandals threatened the stability of young black settlements in Canada and undermined the anti-slavery public's trust in their management. Yet, among all the fledgling settlements, anti-slavery advocates continued to support and promote Wilberforce with singular tenacity. It was, as Benjamin Lundy put it, "the most important."[60] As the first self-directed African American settlement in Upper Canada – and the most well-known by name – it was critical that Wilberforce succeed. One leading abolitionist even urged the Wilberforce Board of Trustees to keep their embattled leadership and financial woes under wraps.[61] Rather than trying to impose a code of silence, however, the most committed supporters of Canadian emigration took more practical approaches. A well-known African American leader from Albany, the Reverend Nathaniel Paul, moved his entire family across the border to support, assess, and report on emigrants' efforts in their new communities. His presence alone inspired confidence. Benjamin Lundy assured his readers that black settlements in Upper

Canada were likely to prosper, despite scandal, because individuals with Nathaniel Paul's "intelligence" had "gone thither."[62]

General optimism and good public relations continued to over-shadow damaging reports in the early 1830s. Positive, even celebratory information outpaced negative news coming out of Upper Canada as well-known African American emigrants like Nathaniel Paul, Austin Steward, and James C. Brown strove to cultivate Upper Canada's reputation as a land of freedom, equality, and opportunity. It did not hurt, either, that both Lundy and William Lloyd Garrison each put their stamp of approval on Canadian emigration. As he had several years earlier when committing his support to Haitian emigration, Lundy even visited Upper Canada in order to base his views on perso-nal experience. Touring Wilberforce and surrounding areas in early 1832, he printed his travel notes, general observations, and overall opinions in his newspaper. He found much to like, from the soil and weather to what he described as a distinct lack of social prejudice.[63] Describing Lundy as "our indefatigable and inquisitive friend," Garrison then reprinted Lundy's description of his trip in *The Liberator*.[64] For those in the slave states with no choice but to "fly elsewhere," Garrison agreed that Upper Canada was the best alterna-tive because it was close, shared a common language, and granted black emigrants equal rights.[65]

Both Lundy and Garrison garnered Upper Canada considerable pub-licity as a promising site of black freedom and secured the province's growing reputation as a preferable locale for free black emigrants relative to other international free-soil destinations.[66] For the first half of the 1830s, in fact, Upper Canada fully eclipsed other free-soil locales in the imaginations of most American anti-slavery advocates. "It would seem that they all forget both *Hayti* and *Africa*," mused Lundy, "and I do not wonder at it."[67] In the eyes of many reformers and potential migrants, the fact that Upper Canadian emigration was voluntary and directed by African Americans themselves distinguished it from the ACS's Liberian relocation efforts. And the fact that none had yet returned dissatisfied with their experience of the British province cast it in better light than Haiti, whose reputation continued to suffer in the wake of returning migrants.

Yet, almost lost in the hubbub over Upper Canada, another free-soil destination started to build momentum, as well: Mexico. Just months after James C. Brown and his fellow Cincinnatians had rejected Mexico as a resettlement option in 1829, President Vicente Guerrero of Mexico finally abolished slavery outright after a decade of confusing and inconsistent anti-slavery legislation. While intensive lobbying from slaveholding Americans in Texas resulted in that territory's exemption from the general abolition, a subsequent law passed in April 1830 prevented any new immigration of Americans – including the importation of more slaves. Although news of this deepening commitment to emancipation did not immediately inspire a mass wave of emigration among free African Americans, it was enough to ignite interest.

It certainly caught the attention of "A Free Colored Floridian." In a letter first published in the *New-York Daily Advocate*, the *Working Man's Advocate*, and the *African Sentinel*, the author – identifying himself only by color and location – laid out a thorough rationale for Mexican emigration. First and foremost, he wrote, its border with the southern United States made it especially convenient for free people of color in the southern states. He also noted that the familiar climate made it more amenable to southern emigrants who would find Canada's cold climate "uncongenial." He expected land to be available at a good rate, describing the country as a boundless horizon of uninhabited or thinly settled opportunity, and he anticipated that migrants could easily tap into a crop economy where "there is little or no winter to kill the vegetables."

Of most importance, however, was the author's assessment of Mexico's social and political character relative to people of color. He depicted the country as "*entirely free from all prejudice against complexion*" because the people were "mostly colored" themselves. Moreover, he pointed out that Mexico's constitution and laws "*recognized no difference of merit on account of color*" (all emphasis in original). Asserting that free people of color had only ever asked for constitutional protection for themselves and their property, Mexico seemed more than capable of delivering.[68]

To "A Free Colored Floridian," this last point was particularly noteworthy when taking stock of the free-soil landscape abroad. Although he acknowledged that the British Constitution governing Canada offered "ample guarantee" against prejudice and injustice, he did not trust it to last. "Canada is only a Provincial Government," he pointed out, "and may, at some future period not far distant, lose the advantages of that protection." With Upper Canada's provincial status in mind, he asked readers for their good wishes and financial support for emigrating to Mexico instead – and hoped that some enterprising soul would take the first step of contacting the Mexican government to obtain lands for settlement.[69]

It was Benjamin Lundy who heard the call. Republishing the letter in October 1831, Lundy described the views of "A Free Colored Floridian" as "enlarged and liberal." While he noted that the author's arguments were particularly applicable to those residing in the South, his imagination was thoroughly captured. In late summer and fall of that year, he printed a three-part series introducing Mexico's politics, economy, religion, and social outlook according to recent authors on the topic.[70] Then, in 1832, he took what became the first of his own investigatory trips to the country. As historian Trish Loughran puts it, "Where others wrote of and to and for distant populations, Lundy walked among them."[71] Making his way first to Louisiana and then across the Sabine River into Texas, he arrived in Mexico at the end of June. Contrasting this journey with his recent tour of Canada, he reflected that he had "traveled mostly on foot in Canada in the coldest of the winter, and in Louisiana and Texas in the hottest of the summer".[72]

Throughout his travels in Texas, he met with slave-owning white Americans. Acknowledging that their treatment of enslaved people varied little from what it was in the United States, Lundy was undeterred in his efforts to read the landscape in favor of potential emigration. Texas was just one part of Mexico, he argued. And, in any case, he felt sure that the Texan exemption to Mexico's general abolition would soon come to an end. He was thrilled by the possibilities of Mexican emigration: the general health of the country, the good climate, the comparatively small cost of moving there, and the trade potential of tapping into its agricultural and commercial economies. He was particularly inspired by the prospect of demonstrating, side by side against southern slaveholders, the value of free (non-slave) labor in producing sugar, cotton, rice, and

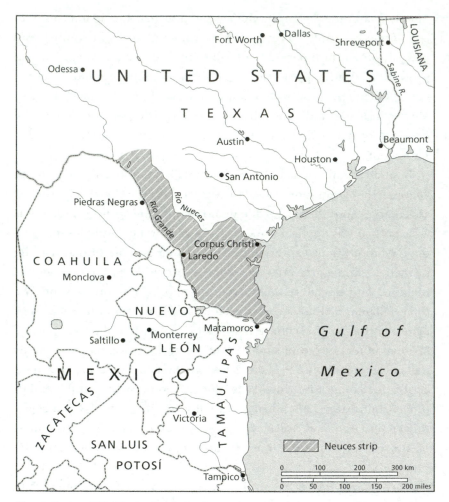

Map 3 Eastern U.S.–Mexico Borderlands

other cash crops. He had no doubt that growing these products would quickly make emigrants wealthy and further prove to observers in the United States that black people could easily "rise above the degradation that slavery and prejudice has imposed on [them]."[73]

From that point on, Lundy's interest only grew. As much as he recognized and contributed to reformers' enthusiasm for Upper Canada, his passion for Mexico soon surpassed his support for the British province. Between 1832 and 1836, Lundy developed a full-fledged plan for establishing a new settlement in Mexico for free and manumitted African

Americans.[74] Trying to drum up support among potential settlers and philanthropists, he devoted regular columns to the topic and took two more expeditions to explore the country in 1833 and 1834–1835. Throughout, he made careful journal entries to build his case for Mexican emigration, noting in detail his meetings with various black emigrants and his impressions of the land and people.

Eventually, Lundy settled on a location for his colony in the State of Tamaulipas, to the south of Texas.[75] He was particularly struck by the thriving community of African Americans he met there in the town of Matamoros, just across the Rio Grande (Map 3). Many hailed from Louisiana, but several came from as far away as Pennsylvania. All gainfully employed, Lundy was impressed by what he described as their intelligence, their respectability, and their general financial state. Not only did he find them well disposed toward his idea for a colony, many of them contributed to his own financial support as he made his way on foot to Victoria (the capital of Tamaulipas) to submit his request for a land grant. Moreover, he was as impressed by the region's rich agricultural potential as he had hoped to be. Staying in Matamoros through winter at the tail end of 1834, he was pleased to see that the vegetable gardens were still growing well, with no sign of first frost by late December. He marveled at the lettuce, cabbages, and onions, and noted that there was still "lots of beautiful looking corn, waist high."[76]

His enthusiasm was unstoppable. He happily noted that most everyone he met on his travels seemed to support his idea for a settlement. It did not give him any pause when he was informed by his new friends in Matamoros that they faced racist incidents around town. At a ball held in mid-November, 1834, for example, a fight broke out when a white clerk called a group of black men "d—d n—rs" and declared that they ought not to be present. The next month, Lundy discovered, two "genteel young black men" had been denied a drink at the bar of "one of the most dashing hotels of the city." The bar-keeper informed them that he did not keep a public house for the "negroes."[77]

Not even the Texas Revolution of 1835–1836 stemmed Lundy's passion. As white, slaveholding colonists took up arms to create an independent Texas where the legality of slavery would not be subject to the Mexican government's anti-slavery leanings, he clung tenaciously to his belief that slavery's days were numbered in the region. Even as the conflict erupted around him, he traveled hundreds of miles south to Victoria. Once he arrived in early March 1835, he waited for over a week beneath the city's snow-tipped mountains to meet with the governor, whose focus was drawn northward to the tense situation in Texas. Despite the delay, Lundy was eventually given permission to settle 250 families on 30 leagues of land. And so, with a light heart, he made his way on foot back to the United States.[78]

In the wake of his tour, Lundy was driven by the singular purpose of encouraging support for his Mexican emigration plan. He even reimagined his newspaper as a "vehicle of information" for it.[79] But reactions to his project had been mixed from the start. From some corners, he received positive feedback. A friend residing in Wilberforce received news of Lundy's project with pleasure. He believed that a colony to the south would only increase the number of enslaved African Americans who "may yet taste the sweets of liberty."[80] And there are certainly indications that Lundy's efforts to illuminate Mexico's potential increased public interest in the southwestern republic as an alternative to the United States. In December 1831, a "large and respectable meeting" of African Americans in Cincinnati noted that their "rights as freemen" would be equally secure in Canada *or* Mexico, and the following February a Trenton, New Jersey, meeting followed suit.[81]

In one of the most enthusiastic responses printed in the anti-slavery press, "A Colored Female of Philadelphia," affirmed that, given the opportunity, she would move to Mexico over all the other options available to her. She would not be taken to Africa, she wrote, "were the society to make me queen of the country." Nor would she agree to move to any quarter of Upper Canada outside the urban centers. Among her reasons for this decided preference was that she had learned that there were 8 million people of color in Mexico and only 1 million whites. Asserting the likelihood that "amalgamation" would further darken the country's complexion, she anticipated that Mexico would, ere long, become "one entire colored nation." In addition, she was inspired by the promise of economic opportunity. "The soil is rich and fertile," she wrote, "which will contribute to our wealth." With wealth would come respectability, she believed, and the ability to aspire to more than was possible in the United States.[82]

Perhaps Lundy's most well-known supporter, however, was John Quincy Adams. After losing out on a second term of his presidency to Andrew Jackson, Adams became one of only two former U.S. presidents to serve in Congress after leaving the White House. From his seat in the U.S. House of Representatives, he took note of Lundy's interest in Mexico and maintained a correspondence with him through the last months of the Texas Revolution. Convinced by Lundy that Mexico could promote the cause of anti-slavery in the United States, Adams requested that Lundy send him translations of all Mexico's laws, decrees, and ordinances relating to the abolition of slavery and the slave trade. He also entreated Lundy to continue publishing on the subject with the promise that he would refer to Lundy's work on the floor of the House of Representatives "in such manner as will call the attention of its members and of the public."[83]

Yet, on the whole, Lundy's plans were not well received. For a start, the looming conflict over the issue of slavery between the Mexican government and American slaveholders in Texas territory was hard to overlook. Although President Vicente Guerrero had caved to mounting pressure from Texas slaveholders to exempt the territory, Mexico's abolition of slavery in 1829 greatly exacerbated tensions. Significantly, the Texas exemption rendered Mexican abolition relatively symbolic. Debt peonage, an often coercive and abusive indentured servitude, was a far more common form of labor extraction in most of the country, and there were very few enslaved people left in Mexico *outside* Texas when the abolition law passed.[84]

Yet, as historian James David Nichols points out, it did not take long for slaveholders to see a correlation between Mexican abolitionism and the difficulties they had with runaway slaves. Taking advantage of both the Mexican government's and many Mexican people's willingness to help and protect them, people enslaved in Texas often ran away to the states of Tamaulipas or Coahuila – to the border towns and villages that dotted the Rio Grande or to areas within Texas that lay outside the control of the Texan colonists.[85] Despite a difficult journey to get there, hundreds of enslaved people from Louisiana and Texas found pathways to de facto freedom in Mexican territory, and it did not take long for the escalating conflict between slave-owning Anglo-Texan settlers and the Mexican government to boil over.[86] After a successful rebellion, the Republic of Texas emerged as an independent slaveholding entity in 1836.

In addition, while Mexico was celebrated as a place of racial equality, the ability to establish legal standing as a Mexican citizen was not straight-forward – a fact that Lundy generally ignored. To become citizens, emigrants were required to have an occupation and to have resided in Mexico for at least three years.[87] Until then, black emigrants were vulner-able. They could be jailed and stripped of civil rights, and they were often forced to accept roles assigned to them by the government or face extradition. For many, including emigrants who arrived in Tampico, Tamaulipas, from New Orleans in the late 1830s, this meant serving in the national militia. While many self-emancipated slaves readily took up arms during the conflict with Texas in exchange for their freedom, African Americans who were already free in the United States may have felt that the exchange rate on legal equality tipped more immediately in their favor elsewhere.[88]

But the most significant challenge that Lundy faced while promoting his Mexico settlement was more personal in nature. As a longtime proponent of gradual emancipation and relocation as strategies to increase broad-based support for abolition, his advocacy of Mexico struck many immediate abolitionists as nothing more than a new colo-nization scheme concocted by a white reformer. Criticism ran deep enough that Lundy felt called upon to defend his intentions.[89] Admitting at the third annual Colored Convention that his aims had been "misapprehended" by members, he clarified that he was not cut from the same cloth as supporters of the ACS. His goal, he declared, was and always had been the "total and unconditional abolition of slavery," as well as the elevation of African Americans to "perfect equality of privilege (moral, political, and religious) with the whites, in the land of [their] birth." He just wholeheartedly believed that *voluntary* emigra-tion to places where equality was already established by law would help to achieve this goal by setting an example – without requiring the removal of any sizeable number of African Americans to a distant land.[90]

While Lundy's explanation was generally well received, he was nonetheless unable to win widespread support from either the African American community or from white abolitionists. He was never able to establish a colony on the land granted him by the Mexican government, and the idea simply fizzled out outside Louisiana and the southwest. When it came to the emigration of free people, general interest in Mexico paled in comparison with the activism promoting Upper Canada; when it came to the idea of colonizing manumitted slaves elsewhere, only Liberia garnered significant support.

Yet by differentiating between and comparing these disparate free-soil alternatives as *potential* destinations for free black emigrants, reformers of all colors and ideological stripes were able to develop increasingly informed arguments about what made a given place (in the words of Benjamin Lundy) "more free and equal."[91] And as emigrants and travelers passed information back to the United States from abroad, black and white abolitionists and potential migrants used it to articulate the specific tenets of freedom they deemed critical to African American uplift and equality: security, political stability, economic opportunity, and – most importantly – equality under the law.

As the free-soil landscape continued to expand in ways that caught the attention of anti-slavery advocates and reformers in the first half of the 1830s, Upper Canada seemed to be the resounding winner. The promise of legal equality, the availability of land and opportunity, the power of the British Empire to protect and defend, and a familiar linguistic and religious culture made the notion of emigrating to Upper Canada more appealing for many than the idea of resettling in places with political upheaval or virulent disease. Although the government found itself unable to fully deliver on its guarantees, as we will see in Chapter 5, Upper Canada had become the indisputable beacon of freedom even before Great Britain had committed itself to general emancipation in its western empire.

CHAPTER 4

Assessing Abolition: Investigating the Results of British Emancipation

If in Jamaica, why not Carolina?

~ William Lloyd Garrison, *The Liberator*, June 1, 1838[1]

* * *

The West India experiment is an imperfect development of the abolition principle, good and evil are therefore mingled with its results.

~ Commentary on West Indian Emancipation, *The Philanthropist*, April 14, 1837[2]

In 1833, 1.3 million people throughout England signed petitions demanding the immediate emancipation of slavery in the British colonies. One such petition, a massive document carrying 187,000 names, was delivered to Parliament on May 14, the very same day that Lord Edward Stanley introduced an emancipation bill into the House of Commons. After three months of debate over the logistics of such a popular measure, the bill was passed into law on August 29.

In the end, the British Act of Abolition was a compromise. It legislated for the gradual (rather than immediate) release of 800,000 men, women, and children from slavery over a four- to six-year "apprenticeship" period, and it provided slaveholders with monetary compensation to the tune of £20 million for the loss of their human "property." Furthermore, slaves and their anti-slavery allies had to wait nearly an entire year for this gradual process to begin, which was plenty of time for hopeful anticipation and dire prediction to wage war on both sides of the Atlantic before even a single person had been freed. Would the commencement of

British emancipation inspire widespread, violent reprisals against former slaveholders? Would a gradual, four- to six-year de-institutionalization of slavery help to keep laborers from abandoning the plantations? Could former slaves be adequately prepared through the so-called "apprentice-ship system" to become productive wage laborers?

In the words of Lord Edward Stanley himself, British emancipation was a "mighty experiment." Under intense international scrutiny, the British West Indies became the barometer to determine whether an emancipated labor force could sustain the productive value of agricultural, cash-crop economies.[3]

As historian David Brion Davis has noted, news of British emancipation hit the United States "like a political and social tsunami."[4] While free spaces seemed to be making inroads into the geography of Atlantic slavery – in Haiti, in West Africa, in the formerly Spanish Americas, and in Upper Canada – the abolition of slavery throughout the British Americas was especially noteworthy to American observers. It signified the first peacetime effort of a powerful slave-owning empire to dismantle a lucrative labor system on the basis of morality and public opinion. Moreover, with the brief exception of the French in the West Indies prior to Napoleon's reinstallation of slavery in 1802, Britain was the first empire to commit itself to governing a majority black, formerly enslaved population in the Americas. Perhaps most significantly of all, Britain was also culturally and economically comparable to the United States. As a result, Americans closely monitored the socioeconomic effects of emancipation in Britain's western empire, worrying about the industry and honesty of wage laborers, gauging whether landowners were economically successful when they paid their laborers, and watching for any sign that emancipating slaves would result in violent reprisals against former slaveholders or their property.

As pro-slavery and anti-slavery advocates alike looked to the British West Indies to assess the outcome of an emancipation process engineered and implemented by an imperial government against the wishes of a powerful, wealthy, pro-slavery lobby, the region became a battleground of observation and evaluation. For American slaveholders, British emancipation not only seemed to confirm their worst fears about anti-slavery's effects on the economic and social stability of the islands, it extended the network of international free-soil borders across which they might permanently lose their slave "property." Slaveholders therefore hoped to prove that emancipation in the West Indies was a failure. If they could show that it had a devastating impact on the sugar economy, it would vindicate their conviction that slavery was in the United States' economic best interest.

Moreover, if the living conditions of newly freed men, women, and children turned out to deteriorate in a waged labor economy – which slaveholders anticipated they would – it would support slaveholders' growing efforts to portray slavery as a paternalistic and humanitarian institution. Their efforts to re-brand slavery as a "positive good" (to use John C. Calhoun's infamous words, spoken in 1837) emerged in the 1830s as a reaction to the rising tide of American abolitionism. Slaveholders sought to square their reliance on slavery with emerging ideas about humanitarianism by arguing that slaveholders' benevolent oversight of slaves' physical and spiritual lives ensured the well-being of the southern economy and of the slaves themselves.[5] If slaveholders could convincingly demonstrate that British emancipation was a harbinger of socio-economic catastrophe, it might nip the growing pressure of international abolitionism in the bud.

By contrast, anti-slavery advocates celebrated Britain's decision to abolish slavery and anticipated its broader effects on Atlantic slaveholding. They watched with excitement as hundreds of thousands of men, women, and children stepped into freedom and rejoiced at the geopolitical pressure that the West Indian islands exerted on American slaveholders. The abolition of slavery throughout the British Empire could, they hoped, serve as an inspiration and a paradigm for the destruction of slavery in the United States. With a will to make it so, they used North America's expanding print culture to bring free-soil information into the homes of armchair abolitionists. Employing overlapping strategies of social investigation and rhetorical argument to demonstrate that emancipation in the West Indies was a success, they worked tirelessly to undermine pro-slavery propaganda and fearmongering. They documented aspects of Britain's emancipation model that they thought worked well and identified elements that they hoped to improve upon, all in the hopes of convincing the American public that the British example could and should be emulated in the United States.

For anti-slavery advocates, one of the most significant aspects of British emancipation was how it unfolded. Although the British Act of Abolition provided for a structured gradual emancipation process in order to minimize changes to plantation agriculture and colonial society, the implementation of this momentous change varied from place to place. Islands like Jamaica and Barbados grudgingly implemented the multi-year apprenticeship period stipulated by London lawmakers. By contrast, islands like Antigua and Bermuda decided to disregard the apprenticeship concept, opting instead to implement full and immediate emancipation for all bondspeople beginning on August 1, 1834.[6] As a result of these variations, British emancipation offered observers a side-by-side comparison of two specific models for emancipating slaves: immediate and unconditional versus gradual and conditional.

The difference between these two approaches struck right at the heart of a key ideological rift within the anti-slavery movement. In the 1830s, the rise of immediate abolitionism divided the ranks of American reformers over which approach to support. While reformers worked cooperatively to show that emancipation was working, generally speaking, the two models unfolding simultaneously in the British West Indies provided the opportunity to compare and debate the relative merits of both anti-slavery strategies in real time.

In the end, however, the outcome of emancipation became a matter of debate rather than a matter of record for slaveholders and anti-slavery advocates alike. There was no shortage of information from the British Caribbean islands, but the ideological leanings of American observers influenced whose information they believed and how they interpreted what they heard. Reflecting a nineteenth-century version of "fake news" culture, readers of information from the West Indies were predisposed to believe any anecdotal evidence in support of what they hoped to see, and they rejected as untrue any information at odds with their expectations. Thus, the same political concerns that made the stakes so high for both sides of the debate also fundamentally shaped how each side interpreted the information available to them.

Those inclined to believe that British emancipation was an unmitigated socio-economic disaster did not lack for evidence. They could glean it from the pages of planter-friendly Caribbean newspapers, from correspondence reprinted in U.S. newspapers, and from West Indian planters visiting the United States. From a planter visiting Philadelphia from Jamaica, for example, a local newspaper editor learned that Kingston's white population "labored under the most dreadful apprehensions of a revolt," as well as the fact that planters felt their compensation by the British government was not enough to save them (and the economy more generally) from financial disaster.[7] The editor of the *New Hampshire Patriot and State Gazette*, meanwhile, had read recent information about the "most miserable state of things in the British islands" and informed his readers that nearly a tenth of St. Vincent's 9,000 "negro laborers" had been "brought up for correction." In addition, the report read, buildings and manufacturing facilities were "constantly being destroyed by incendiaries." It seemed that the result of emancipation was that white inhabitants suffered "great dissatisfaction and gloomy forebodings," preventing them from enjoying peace, contentment, or happiness.[8]

Grim accounts were so ubiquitous during the apprenticeship period that renowned travel writer and anti-slavery advocate Joseph Kimball could not help but ask if there were any who had *not* heard them:

> Who that has read the New York Courier, or its neighbor the Commercial, or the African Repository, or the Boston Recorder, or its echo prints in Maine, New Hampshire and Vermont, or the thousand and one other proslavery papers, from Duff Green's Telegraph and the Washington Globe, down to Paul Pry and the New Hampshire Patriot, have not been horrified with the pictures of the idleness, poverty, misery, insubordination, crime, and destruction which those sage-papers asserted would attend and have attended emancipation in the British West Indies?[9]

Of considerable concern to many American observers was the anecdotal evidence that former slaves, once freed, were leaving the plantations or simply refusing to work. Reports from nearly every island indicated that "apprentices" could not be convinced to work at the pace required for plantation agriculture. In Jamaica, planters reported that apprentices were beginning to "expect all things." In their estimation, the newly apprenticed laborers were demanding "every advantage of the slave, and the free man too; to abate two thirds of his work, and have his compensation trebled."[10] In Barbados, the refusal of laborers to work as hard as planters required resulted in such friction that the planters called in soldiers to quell what they saw as insubordination.[11] There was significant concern that former slaves would not work "for love or money . . . and no means were at hand to compel them to do so."[12]

It seemed clear to anti-abolitionists that this was an inevitable outcome of the British Act of Abolition, which both set the number of hours former slaves were required to work and empowered laborers (in principle) to set limits on their labor obligations. In one detailed analysis of the economic ramifications of emancipation, the *Richmond Enquirer* described the representative plantation of Shrewsbury in Savannah-la-Mer, Jamaica. Where the 400-person, formerly enslaved labor force had previously produced an average of three hogsheads of sugar per week, "apprenticed" laborers only produced one hogshead per week due to their collective refusal to work beyond six o'clock in the evening. This work stoppage also threatened production in the boiling houses, where overseers resorted to bribing apprentices to work overnight so that nothing would be spoiled.[13] According to such reports, apprentices' collective resistance to slave-like labor demands clearly had a considerable impact on planters' ability to profit and contradicted anti-slavery arguments regarding the economic viability of free (non-slave) labor.

While Americans regularly read unsavory reports about the breakdown of labor relations, authority, and economic production, the top concern for many was the safety of the former owners in the wake of British emancipation. They feared that loosening the bonds of slavery would inevitably result in anti-white violence, and they had powerful examples to draw from. The bloody history of the Haitian Revolution continued to cast an alarming shadow across American memory. As William Lloyd Garrison noted in August 1834, "Nothing is more common than to hear the condition of St. Domingo or Hayti appealed to, as proof of the inexpediency of emancipation. If we propose at once to substitute the mild sway of law for the tyrannous domination of individual avarice, we are warned of the HORRORS OF ST. DOMINGO, *as if liberty, and not slavery*, had shed all the blood that once drenched that now *happy* island."[14]

Fear that Haiti's bloody history might be repeated was so strong that pro-slavery pundits could easily draw on it for dramatic effect. When predicting that Jamaica's white planters might leave the island for economic reasons, for example, the pro-slavery *Richmond Enquirer* took the opportunity to remind its readers that Haiti had also become inhospitable to whites. Ignoring the fact that economically motivated relocation was hardly the same as the threat of racial genocide, the newspaper declared ominously, "Every body knows that the St. Domingo emancipation was the extermination of the whites and the white government."[15]

Since race war seemed a plausible outcome of emancipation, anti-abolitionists were hyper-attentive to every indication of violence in the West Indies. Just prior to August 1, 1834, an anecdote arrived from Jamaica in which an enslaved man promised retributive justice for being punished. Having just been "reproved by his master," the enslaved man reportedly exclaimed, "Ah masss [sic], me to be free 1st August, and you is de first man dat I shall lick."[16] In St. Kitts, meanwhile, an overseer was reported to have been publicly and severely beaten by former slaves after trying to quell a disturbance. The governor himself had fled the scene to avoid receiving similar treatment.[17]

With accounts of "insolence" and "unrest" trickling in from the West Indian islands, many wondered if American slaves would cultivate similar animosity toward their former owners if the United States followed in Britain's footsteps. "If such are the ruinous consequences of conditional, partial emancipation *there*," asked one news editor, "what would be the inevitable effect of the total and immediate emancipation of the ignorant hordes at the *South?*" The answer, in his estimation, required no "pretensions to prophetic skill": immediate emancipation in the United States would cause "*insurrection, pillage, massacre, desolation and death.*"[18]

Fear that freedom would lead inevitably to violence made it easy for pro-slavery advocates to depict abolitionists in the United States as harbingers of bloodshed. As historian Edward Rugemer has shown, the history of slave rebellions in the early 1800s deepened many white Americans' genuine belief that abolitionism would catalyze slave uprisings. A Barbadian rebellion in 1816, a South Carolinian conspiracy in 1822, an 1823 uprising in

Demerara, and near-simultaneous insurrections in Jamaica and Virginia in 1831 had all been preceded by public debate over slavery.[19]

To many American slaveholders, it seemed clear that the example of British emancipation had only emboldened those whose ever more radical anti-slavery activity threatened the safety and stability of the southern way of life. Eminent southern politician and colonizationist Henry Clay, in fact, lamented that the emancipation of slaves "in the islands adjacent to our country" was the *principal* cause of abolitionist zeal in the United States during the 1830s. The influence could hardly be helped, he supposed, as "the similarity of laws, in language, in institutions, and in common origin, between Great Britain and the United States" meant that "no great measure of national policy can be adopted in the one country without producing a considerable degree of influence in the other."[20]

As abolitionist activity became more visible and increasingly radical in the mid-1830s, it felt vital for slaveholders to counter the alarming influence of British emancipation in order to stymie the spread of anti-slavery sentiment. When abolitionist women sent petitions to Congress advocating the end of slavery and the slave trade in the District of Columbia, for example, Henry Clay blamed the precedent of British emancipation and was determined to undercut it. In a speech delivered on the Senate floor, he warned against drawing parallels between any successes of abolitionism in the West Indies and the potential to replicate them in the United States. First, he reminded his fellow senators, the British experiment was yet "undecided" among all but the most "superficial" observers. Second, the U.S. Constitution prevented Congress from exercising the "unlimited" powers of the British Parliament, which had abolished slavery only by withholding (he asserted) adequate political representation from West Indian planters. And third, he argued that support for abolition had only taken root in England because there was a wide ocean separating the parent country from the newly freed population. In sum, he concluded that abolitionists in the United States were misguided to draw hope from the British precedent. The ink abolitionist women spilled on petitions was unlikely to amount to anything more than a "prelude to the shedding of the blood of their brethren."[21]

According to South Carolina Governor George McDuffe, however, the prelude was already over. The threat of abolitionist-inspired bloodshed felt very immediate in the wake of radical abolitionists' massive 1835 campaign to blanket the South with anti-slavery pamphlets – and he believed British emancipation to be both the root cause and the cautionary tale. The lesson he drew from the British precedent was that abolitionist incursions into the South must be stopped by any means necessary. Britain's "suicidal legislation," he fumed, could easily be compared with a neglected spark among combustible materials. It would speedily become a "sweeping torrent of fiery desolation, which no human power can arrest or controul [sic]."[22] Insinuating that British agents might be traveling the South and inciting abolitionist "outrages," McDuffe called on South Carolina's lawmakers to lead the way in demanding local, state, federal, and even international legal measures to stop abolitionist activity. In a fiery appeal to the state's General Assembly, he declared it their "solemn and responsible duty" to punish those who would endanger the peace. Warning of West Indian planters' recent experience against abolitionist incursions, he pointed out their regret that they had "neglected to hang up the first of these political missionaries."[23]

Against this background of increasing hostility, American reformers were determined to present British emancipation as a positive event that would vindicate and encourage steadfast anti-slavery activism in the United States. Indeed, for many anti-slavery advocates, British emancipation was important specifically because it demonstrated that abolition could be enacted in the face of powerful opposition. For some, this meant moral suasion – the strategy of appealing to people's higher nature. Inspired by the success of British anti-slavery advocates, one letter writer asked, "Are we using all the moral means which God has placed in our power wholly and speedily to remove this national evil?"[24] For others, the example of British emancipation demonstrated the power of political pressure. The *New Hampshire Sentinel* noted that if "the action and policy of our free States" were "directed wholly to convince the South of the injustice of slavery," a similar outcome could be accomplished in the United States as had been achieved in the West Indies.[25] If the British could abolish slavery, many hoped, surely the United States could do the same with an enthusiastic application of anti-slavery activism.

Yet with both the pro-slavery press and powerful pro-slavery politicians warning against the myriad threats posed by British emancipation, anti-slavery leaders of all ideological persuasions fought an uphill battle to present a convincingly optimistic picture of West Indian freedom. So, from the beginning of the apprenticeship period, they employed several overlapping strategies to neutralize the pro-slavery perspective and elevate their own. One of the earliest tactics anti-slavery leaders deployed was to cast doubt on the intentions and believability of reports describing emancipation in negative terms. "For some months to come," William Lloyd Garrison informed his readers in August 1834, "we may expect to see in the newspapers, falsehoods of all sizes, and misrepresentations of every complexion, in relation to the state of things in the British Colonies." After all, he continued, "editors who do not hesitate to deal in calumny and fiction, respecting abolitionists and men of color in this land, to prop up American slavery, cannot be expected to speak the truth habitually, with reference to the conduct of the emancipated slaves abroad."[26] Sharing Garrison's perspective that unsatisfactory reports should be viewed with suspicion, many abolitionists simply refused to believe any allegation that emancipation was a social and economic failure.

Like their pro-slavery counterparts, abolitionists did not lack for evidence to demonstrate that their expectations were being met. It was simply a matter of weeding out conflicting information and deciding who or what to believe. And for many, information seemed more "trustworthy" and "accurate" if it demonstrated the positive outcome that they hoped for. The New York Young Men's Anti-Slavery Society offers an illustrative example of this selective belief in action. In 1834, the Society produced a pamphlet addressed to their fellow citizens insisting that "lying newsmakers" were responsible for the proliferation of pessimistic reports about emancipation. By contrast, the Society assured their readers, they had access to sources that were more "direct," "recent," and "respectable" than those cited by pro-slavery papers. Practically speaking, their pamphlet did not actually provide any identifying information for the sources cited. Their reliability seemed to stem only from the fact that they corroborated what the Society wanted to believe (in this instance, that freed laborers worked "better" than their enslaved counterparts).

For this reason alone, the New York Young Men's Anti-Slavery Society felt confident disregarding the gloomy portrayals of West Indian freedom circulating among American readers.[27]

Not all positive information had to be taken on faith, however. Amid the sea of conflicting accounts from the West Indies, there was certainly a steady supply of specific, attributable evidence corroborating the hopes and expectations of anti-slavery readers. Foremost among these were Caribbean newspapers that printed government, rather than planter, perspectives on emancipation and apprenticeship. Providing a veneer of legitimacy absent from the apocalyptic forebodings of disgruntled planters, government information gleaned from colonial newspapers provided anti-slavery editors with firsthand information that was generally deemed reliable enough to reprint or quote from – when the news was good.[28] Similarly, abolitionists tended to prefer positive reports gathered by British observers. Many reformers believed that British perspectives, like the colonial governments' observations, could not be written off as abolitionist propaganda. In the words of New York judge William Jay, they could be "extensively circulated & read without suspicion & prejudice."[29] Anti-slavery newspapers like the weekly *New York Evangelist* – a small publication edited by abolitionist and Presbyterian reformer Joshua Leavitt – could thus accurately label promising news from British and Caribbean sources as "secular intelligence."[30]

Still, relying on intelligence from Caribbean newspapers, in particular, could be a tricky business. First of all, the sense of their legitimacy swung both ways. As we have seen, anti-abolitionists found it just as easy and useful to find *negative* reports to reprint from West Indian newspapers. Moreover, anti-slavery papers – especially the smaller ones – were often unable to access the Caribbean reports they hoped would deliver good news. This limited access was a product of nineteenth-century newspaper production, which relied heavily on reprinting. On the one hand, reprinting was a cornerstone strategy for small or local newspapers to expand the geographic scope of their content. Thanks to the narrow definition of what was considered copyrightable material, newspaper reports (seen as facts, and therefore public property) were regularly clipped and reprinted throughout the United States.[31] Reprinting was, in fact, deemed to be so important to the dissemination of knowledge that the U.S. Postal Service allowed newspapers to exchange copies with each other free of charge.[32] However, this practice often meant that smaller newspapers relied on whatever items the bigger papers had already selected as noteworthy. This was particularly an issue when it came to foreign news packets, as the bigger papers had more extensive and immediate access to news from abroad. The subjective choices that larger newspapers made about what news to print could therefore unduly shape the information printed by smaller newspapers throughout the United States.

Joshua Leavitt's *New York Evangelist* provides a clear example of how this inconsistent access to Caribbean newspapers might affect publishers' ability to relay foreign news items regarding emancipation to their readers. In one week's selection of "Secular Intelligence," Leavitt expressed particular gratitude to the *Daily Advertiser* for the information it extracted from West Indian newspapers regarding former slaves' willingness to perform agricultural labor following emancipation. Before reprinting the relevant reports, however, he noted with frustration that another domestic paper he frequently relied on for foreign correspondence had received the exact same Caribbean newspaper (the *Bermuda Royal Gazette*), yet had published none of it because the editor had found "nothing interesting."[33] Editors of small anti-slavery publications like Leavitt's clearly recognized that reporting firsthand information from West Indian newspapers was a sound strategy for rebutting pro-slavery portrayals of emancipation's outcome, but they were often restricted to whatever intelligence larger newspapers deemed important enough to extract and publish.

It should come as no surprise, therefore, that reformers turned to a familiar tactic of information gathering. During the four-year period of Britain's gradual emancipation, American anti-slavery organizations capitalized on the burgeoning practice of sending agents to investigate free-soil spaces and entrusting select individuals to produce reliable eye-witness accounts documenting the results of abolition. Traveling on behalf of associations whose members expected that their observations had the capacity to challenge and sway the expectations of invested readers, investigatory agents tapped into a phenomenon that sociologist Judith Adler has identified as the "cultural prestige" of travel.[34]

Their reports were, in a sense, performances for an eager public. They authoritatively weighed in on the industry and honesty of wage laborers, attested to the myriad economic benefits that accrued to landowners who paid their laborers fairly, and confirmed that free people were committed to education, enterprise, and religion. Each report presented, through the inclusion of particular anecdotes and the exclusion of others, a coherent set of seemingly impartial observations that would collectively support the writer's conclusions about emancipation. Their texts garnered significant respect within abolitionist communities because they were imbued with the seeming immutability of "facts" established by firsthand observation, and any interpretive slant was acceptable because the agents selected for this work were deemed trustworthy and informed.

For the American Union for the Relief and Improvement of the Colored Race, a small and relatively impoverished organization founded in 1835, a firsthand look at the British experiment aligned with their central mission to "spare no pains, and no reasonable expense, in the work of investigating, and collating, and publishing to the world in the form of clear statements and undeniable deductions, all the facts that can be ascertained" related to the "condition of the Colored Race."[35] Committed to gradual – rather than immediate – emancipation as a means of improving the lives of African Americans, the American Union believed that examining the social and economic results of abolition where it had already taken place was the key to determining "by what process it may be most safely and happily accomplished."[36]

To that end, the American Union commissioned a man named Sylvester Hovey to scout the British Caribbean on their behalf. A former professor of mathematics and natural philosophy at Amherst College, Massachusetts, Hovey had recently returned from several months spent on the Danish island of St. Croix when he agreed to sail again on behalf of the American Union in 1836. Something of an ideological free agent, he openly disavowed any affiliation with either abolitionism or the colonization movement. He was not even a member of the American Union. He did, however, harbor deep sympathy for the cause of gradual emancipation. Convinced that a detailed study of both immediate emancipation and gradual apprenticeship in the British colonies would prove invaluable should the United States itself move toward abolition, he agreed to tour the British islands for several months in 1836 and 1837.[37]

Although ill-health prevented a speedy publication of his findings, Hovey's optimistic 200-page report was well received when it finally came to print in 1838. *Letters from the West Indies. Relating Especially to the Danish Island St. Croix, and to the British Islands Antigua, Barbados, and Jamaica* was lauded in the anti-slavery press for its "unusual degree of candor, industry, sound judgment and discriminating observation."[38] In fact, some believed that his unaligned position likely gave his work more credibility among readers who "consider abolitionism *conclusive* evidence of falsehood."[39] However, while Hovey's book was met with approbation in anti-slavery circles and was excised for reprint in the abolitionist press, its delayed publication meant that its significance within the movement was ultimately overshadowed by a contemporaneous publication of another text: *Emancipation in the West Indies* by Joseph Kimball and James Thome.[40]

Emancipation in the West Indies was produced on behalf of the American Anti-Slavery Society (AASS). The hub of American abolitionism, the society had been founded in Philadelphia in 1833 and had auxiliary societies throughout the northern and western regions of the United States. Like the American Union, the AASS recognized the importance of commissioning trusted agents to conduct fact-finding missions in the British West Indies. Its Executive Committee had no doubt that eyewitness information would provide compelling evidence that abolition was safe and that immediate emancipation produced the most successful results.

The AASS had first contemplated sending an agent to the West Indies in 1835, when co-founder Elizur Wright tapped fellow abolitionist William Jay for the job. But Jay had declined. A prominent New York judge and the son of a founding father, Jay had already published a book that year in support of immediate emancipation. He felt that his high-profile abolitionist sentiment would render his observations suspect to anyone not previously convinced on the subject. In addition, he did not think that sending *any* American agent could effectively challenge the pro-slavery narrative. He believed the best course of action would be to rely on British abolitionists and parliamentary reports for information of a "more official & authentic character."[41] Temporarily stymied, it was not until the following year that the AASS's Executive Committee successfully commissioned two agents for their cause: Joseph H. Kimball, Esq., and Rev. James A. Thome.[42]

On November 31, 1836, Thome and Kimball began a high-profile, six-month West Indian tour to collect vital "facts and testimony" on the outcome of emancipation in the British islands. Kimball was the well-known editor of Concord, New Hampshire's *Herald of Freedom*, and it was perhaps because of this experience that he became the voice of the team during the expedition itself. He penned letters for an abolitionist audience eager for information, and his observations were regularly printed and re-printed throughout the anti-slavery press.[43] Kimball's anecdotes and opinions were deemed so significant, in fact, that the newly established black abolitionist paper, *The Colored American*, ran a front-page series highlighting his Caribbean correspondence during its first three months of publication in 1837. It also printed periodic selections throughout the year. Thanks to Kimball's correspondence, readers read up-to-the-minute reports on how agricultural practices were shifting due to the immediate abolition of slavery in Antigua, on the political aptitude of former slaves and their ability to make informed voting decisions in island elections, and on what a traveler might see of local color and social practices were they to "seek the freedom and freshness" of the (perfectly safe) countryside.[44]

When Kimball's already ill-health gave out upon their return, however, it was James Thome who spearheaded the process of preparing their observations for widespread publication in book form. A native of Kentucky and the reformed son of a wealthy slave owner, the young Rev. Thome was an early southern convert to abolitionism, a prolific anti-slavery orator, and an experienced anti-slavery traveling agent in the U.S. West. He was also a resident of the newly established Oberlin College, a religious institute in Ohio committed to social justice and activism.[45] Yet, even armed with this experience and dedication, the process of single-handedly organizing the observations and testimony collected during the journey took Thome longer than the AASS's Executive Committee had hoped. The pair returned to New York in June 1837, but it was not until March 1838 that the society was able to publish Thome and Kimball's *Emancipation in the West Indies: A Six Months' Tour in Antigua, Barbadoes, and Jamaica in the Year 1837.*[46]

It was worth the wait. It came to readers replete with the agents' firsthand observations and encounters, interviews with "public men, planters, and other responsible individuals," and written correspondence sent by island officials. Printed just prior to Sylvester Hovey's well-reviewed account of the islands, Thome and Kimball's much-anticipated book quickly became the most important and widely read source of information about West Indian emancipation in the United States. The full publication amounted to 480 pages of accumulated evidence on the workings of emancipation and the apprenticeship system, and a condensed version of 126 pages was available in cheap pamphlet form. The latter was priced at approximately 18 cents to promote its wide circulation and included the request that purchasers send it along to a friend after their own perusal.[47]

Emancipation in the West Indies even caught the attention of prominent individuals not publicly affiliated with abolitionism. William Lloyd Garrison was quite pleased, for example, to publish book endorsements penned by high-profile figures such as the governors of Massachusetts and Connecticut. Although these men did not (for the time being) identify with the abolitionist cause, they admitted that Thome and Kimball's observations in the West Indies provided valuable information regarding the benefits and potential of slave emancipation.[48] As the *Herald of Freedom* declared, "it is getting to be somewhat fashionable to be convinced of the proprieties of anti-slavery, by reading the interesting and beautiful Journal of Thome and Kimball."[49] Even when one African American critic noted that neither Thome nor Kimball could possibly "consult the interests of colored men as well as could agents of our own selection," they nonetheless conceded the authors "the credit of affording ample information regarding those Islands on the topics connected with their mission."[50] The book's cultural and evidentiary significance peaked in the year of its publication, just prior to the early ending of the apprenticeship system on August 1, 1838, but *Emancipation in the West Indies* remained a recognizable authority on West Indian emancipation throughout the antebellum period.[51]

From the comfort of their living rooms, readers were provided a front-row seat to "the three grand phases" of emancipation in the British Caribbean colonies as seen through the firsthand witness of trusted travelers. Although Hovey, Kimball, and Thome stopped at numerous islands (including the Danish islands of St. Thomas and St. Croix), their various publications focused on the three islands that best reflected the disparate outcomes of British emancipation: Antigua, Barbados, and Jamaica. Antigua exemplified the working of immediate and complete abolition; Barbados represented where the apprenticeship system seemed to be working best; and Jamaica seemed to epitomize the failings of the apprenticeship model.

These distinctions arose from the content of the news emerging from Caribbean papers in the first two years of the apprenticeship period. News from the small island of Antigua universally seemed to agree that immediate emancipation had proceeded peacefully and with little detriment to the island's plantation economy.[52] By contrast, news from Jamaica generally depicted conflict, work stoppages, and general disaffection among the so-called apprentices.[53] And in Barbados, the transition from slavery to apprenticeship was reported to be "generally barren of incident," despite occasional grumblings that conditions were getting "worse and worse" and early reports that a "strong rural police had been established."[54] As Hovey succinctly put it, anyone acquainted with the subject would agree that the three islands fairly represented the two systems of emancipation and would recognize the universal applicability of evidence gathered from them.[55]

The specific topics under scrutiny were wide-ranging, reflecting nearly every point of debate between abolitionists and anti-abolitionists in the Anglo-Atlantic. Regarding the preparedness of slaves for freedom, the agents assessed whether former slaves in the West Indies were peaceful and obedient to the law; whether they demonstrated religious piety and moral fiber; if they exhibited temperance; whether they were "manageable" as laborers; if they were honest, industrious, and polite; and whether they demonstrated an aptitude for education. Regarding the economic outcome of emancipation, they examined whether waged ("free") labor was more or less expensive than slave labor, how the productivity of emancipated and apprenticed laborers compared with their productivity as slaves, how emancipation affected real estate prices on the islands, and whether there had been a boost to other forms of trade and industry. And, finally, they investigated whether emancipation had shifted more amorphous categories of social well-being such as racial prejudice, feelings of security among planters, and happiness among former slaves.

Significantly, the investigatory agents did not expend much effort interviewing formerly enslaved men and women for relevant information. Instead, they prioritized the accumulation of testimony from white planters and island officials. While Thome and Kimball did incorporate informal exchanges held with apprentices and free people into their narrative, it is clear in both works that those most affected by the two emancipation systems were not considered experts on their own experience.

The two most important conclusions that the collected observations and testimony seemed to support were that abolition was a safe and beneficial proposition, and that the West Indian experiment provided valuable information about the best way to dismantle slavery in the United States. On the safety and socio-economic benefits of emancipation, the two texts provided such similar anecdotes and testimony that one review called them "essentially the same."[56] The texts agreed that emancipation was more likely to prevent insurrection than cause it, and that the disturbances attending apprenticeship in some locales stemmed from former masters and misguided officials abusing the system. They also agreed that there was little difficulty in obtaining waged labor from former slaves, that free labor was cheaper than slave labor, and that planters who had given apprenticeship a fair chance now preferred free labor to slave. And, finally, they asserted optimistically that "the emancipated people are perceptibly rising in the scale of civilization, morals, and religion."[57] The individual anecdotes provided by the authors differed somewhat in detail, but their testimony agreed on the broad strokes.

Yet they did not readily agree on whether their observations supported immediate or gradual emancipation. Thome and Kimball excoriated apprenticeship even at its most successful, arguing that it "cheats the slave of his freedom, cheats the planter of his gains, cheats the British nation of its money, and robs the world of what else might have been a glorious example of immediate and entire emancipation."[58] Moreover, they believed that the Antiguan example, where planters abolished slavery outright for political rather than moral reasons, demonstrated that American slaveholders could similarly be persuaded to emancipate slaves without actually repenting the sin of slaveholding itself.[59] By contrast, Hovey defended Britain's gradual emancipation plan, arguing that the results of apprenticeship's "intermediate state" demonstrated its "sound sense and practical wisdom."[60] Like Thome and Kimball, Hovey documented myriad ways that Jamaican planters, in particular, regularly abused apprenticeship laws to extort extra labor from the formerly enslaved, but he did not believe that either enslavers or those they enslaved could be expected to make a successful transition from one system to another overnight.

In the hands of abolitionist readers, however, Hovey's conclusions hardly mattered. What was more important was how his information could be used. As Joshua Leavitt put it, Hovey's text embodied "a great amount of important information" and was "a valuable work to read in connection with Thome and Kimball." Yet his reasoning in favor of apprenticeship, Leavitt declared, was simply "not sufficient to establish its propriety against even the facts which he narrates."[61] Indeed, by distinguishing between the contents of Hovey's journal and the man's personal assessment of apprenticeship, abolitionists were able to apply a circular logic of reliability that ultimately lent credibility to their support for immediate emancipation. They argued that Hovey's professed ideological neutrality was a testament to his evidence's merit. Then they showed that his ideologically neutral evidence corroborated Thome and Kimball's testimony. Since Thome and Kimball's evidence supported immediate abolition, Hovey's same evidence could not possibly support his personal conclusions to the contrary. Therefore, it could be assumed that Hovey's support for apprenticeship and gradualism was ideologically motivated and should be dismissed, even while his evidence itself held continuing value. Illustrating the point, *The Liberator* printed extensive testimony from Hovey's book but entirely ignored Hovey's interpretation of his own evidence, asking, "Do not the following confessions look as if the slaves were *ready* for freedom, for *immediate* emancipation?"[62]

Inexhaustible founts of ideological conviction were bolstered by eye-witness observations, and together they contributed to anti-slavery efforts to dismantle, piece by piece, the dominant narrative that emancipation would end in failure and violence. But on August 1, 1838, it seemed that the ultimate vindication of abolitionism came to pass in the form of an early end to apprenticeship in the British West Indies. While American agents had been traveling the British islands to collect observations and evidence, prominent British abolitionists had been doing the same. In 1837, Joseph Sturge and Thomas Harvey conducted an extensive tour of the British islands to collect detailed accounts of apprenticeship on behalf of the British public. Like Thome and Kimball, Sturge and Harvey concluded that immediate emancipation produced better economic and social results in Antigua than did the abuse-riddled system of apprenticeship in Jamaica. And, like Thome and Kimball's *Emancipation in the West Indies*, the extensive volume Sturge and Harvey published on their return to England proved a great success. *The West Indies in 1837* was already in its second edition when Sturge presented its contents to a committee of the House of Commons, and it contributed significantly to galvanizing a popular anti-slavery campaign for the early end of apprenticeship.[63]

Although Sturge and Harvey's book made comparatively little impact on a U.S. audience, likely due to the contemporaneous popularity of Thome and Kimball's work, the early end of apprenticeship itself did.[64] It seemed to corroborate American abolitionists' view that immediate, rather than gradual, emancipation was a better model. And yet, even cut short, the four-year period of apprenticeship also fulfilled the hopes of those who believed in gradual emancipation. Overall, they could argue, the process prevented violence and economic collapse, and the cash compensation provided to West Indian planters actually stimulated new investment in land and plantation technology. Moreover, the combination of British sugar protections and rising sugar prices in London more than compensated planters for the simultaneous drop in production they experienced after 1834. (Notably, the sugar output of Antigua, where immediate emancipation had been enacted in 1834, also remained steady throughout the apprenticeship period.)[65]

Clearly, abolition had neither depressed the sugar industry nor bank-rupted the planters. And observers in both England and the United States agreed that apprenticeship had raised the standard of living for formerly enslaved people in both material and religious respects. The only significant problem observers saw was with the former slaveholders in Jamaica, who continued to exploit apprentices' bodies and time in spite of the government's efforts to curtail abuses.

The end of the apprenticeship period in 1838 did not signal an end to debate, however. Instead, observers turned their attention to focus more particularly on Jamaica, gauging whether things would iron out over time in the British Caribbean's most difficult colonial case. A substantially larger island (approximately twenty-five times the size of Antigua), Jamaica was neither demographically nor politically typical of the British West Indian islands. Yet it was the model for British post-emancipation policy because of its economic importance, and so became the test case for evolving ideas about what freedom should look like in a former slave colony.[66] So, in spite of the relative socio-economic stability of islands like Antigua, American observers followed the gaze of their British counterparts and looked to Jamaica to determine the long-term effects of emancipation.

What they saw was an entrenched planter class using every strategy they could to control black Jamaicans' labor, as well as a sugar economy struggling under the pressure of antagonistic labor relations. After August 1, 1838, planters maintained their power through their contin-ued control of local legislatures. No longer encumbered by the appren-ticeship laws designed to prevent labor abuses, planters were able to enact a series of oppressive laws aimed at regulating laborers' spatial mobility and controlling their labor. This was a critical step for them, because bound Jamaicans during apprenticeship had already started saving money in order to purchase freeholds away from the plantations where they had been enslaved and apprenticed.[67] In a concerted effort to keep former slaves on plantations and keep labor costs low, planters throughout the British West Indies passed laws restricting emigration and criminalizing vagrancy, established new taxes to pressure freed peo-ple into wage labor, used exploitative contracts to ensure laborers' dependency, and developed new police and prison systems to regulate and punish labor infractions.[68] Nearly ten years later, an American missionary to Jamaica noted that "slavery still exist[ed] in all but name" long after freedom was legally established.[69]

Planters erected this new edifice of legal oppression due to their (not-unwarranted) fear that formerly enslaved people would abandon the plantations when possible. Yet the slave-like labor, wage, and spatial coercion they perpetuated not only failed to halt the development of independent communities, it actually sped the departure of laborers from plantations in the colonies where the availability of land made alternatives possible. While the lack of available land in Antigua, St. Kitts, and Barbados prevented freed people from fleeing the plantations in those colonies, the relative availability of land in Jamaica, Trinidad, and British Guiana allowed them to leave plantations in greater numbers. This "flight" from the plantations led to a rapid development of an independent peasantry and a vibrant alternative economy beyond the control of the plantations. At least 21 percent of Jamaica's apprenticed population had become residents on peasant freeholds by 1842, and one contemporary estimate suggested that only a third of formerly enslaved plantation workers remained on the estates by 1846.[70] Some individuals were able to save enough money to purchase small landholdings despite the islands' rising land prices.[71] Others "clubbed together" to purchase collective freeholds.[72]

Resident missionaries also interjected themselves in plantation politics by helping formerly enslaved individuals move away from direct planter control. Armed with the dual purpose of evangelization and civilization, Baptist and Wesleyan missionaries positioned themselves as mediators between planters and emancipated laborers by purchasing large tracts of land that they allotted into individual plots to form independent villages. The Rev. James Phillippo, who established the first such community at a town site called Sligoville, confidently asserted that these communities played a crucial post-emancipation function by creating a content peasantry immune to the coercive intentions of the planter class.[73] Although residency in the villages demanded strict adherence to the missionaries' dual religious and imperialist objectives, these communities provided black Jamaicans with much-needed institutional support during the post-emancipation period.[74] The missionaries encouraged resident peasants to supplement agricultural work on their own land with wage labor on surrounding properties, but free villages were widely despised by planters for siphoning away their resident labor force.

Observers following the Jamaican case from the shores of the United States would have been familiar with the island's antagonistic labor relations, the interventions of Christian missionaries into plantation politics, and the fact that laborers' defection from sugar plantations into independent villages was contributing to an economic crisis. In a series of published letters sent from Jamaica to Henry Clay, British abolitionist and investigatory traveler Joseph John Gurney reflected at length on the rapid changes to the island's socio-economic landscape. An avowed abolitionist, Gurney generally depicted the island's transition to full freedom in the best light possible, recognizing the significance of Jamaica's success to the cause of anti-slavery. But even he could not fail to note that black Jamaicans "the length and breadth of the island" had been driven by planters' oppression "to seek for themselves a new home, either by moving to other properties, or by purchasing little freeholds on the neighboring mountains." Recognizing the impact of laborers' disaffection on the sugar economy, he noted that the only estates to maintain their prosperity were those on which planters chose *not* to implement the coercive labor policies that so consistently alienated newly freed workers.[75]

By presenting a significant socio-economic issue as an easily fixable problem caused by the planters themselves, Gurney joined anti-slavery advocates in providing positive evidence that emancipation – if done properly – benefitted planters and workers alike. But not even this optimistic representation of the island's post-emancipation labor conditions could paper over the fact that the Jamaican sugar economy was in trouble. Jamaica had produced 11 percent of the world's cane sugar in 1830, yet was producing only 3 percent in 1840 when Joseph John Gurney's letters to Henry Clay were published. By 1851, its production had further dropped, topping out at only 2 percent.[76] To compound the problem for planters, Britain's enactment of the 1846 Sugar Duties Act ended the metropole's protection of colonial sugar, placing it in competition with sugar produced in the slave-driven sugar economies of places like Brazil and Cuba.

Jamaican planters' sense that they were unable to secure adequate supplies of labor from the island's formerly enslaved residents prompted the colonial legislature to pursue innovative labor-recruiting schemes. The bulk of Jamaican efforts to secure labor involved indentured labor from the East Indies and the legalized semi-slavery of so-called "Liberated Africans" who were released in the West Indies from illegal transatlantic slave-trading vessels captured by the British Navy.[77] However, Jamaica's colonial legislature was highly aware that additional laborers could also be secured from their neighbors on the North American mainland.

Tapping into the emigration debates that African Americans had been knee deep in since the 1820s, Jamaican planters attempted to secure the labor of free black people willing to relocate from the United States to the British Caribbean. Responding to planters' panicked demands for workers, the Jamaican colonial legislature passed an immigration act on April 11, 1840, allocating £50,000 per year to support immigration between 1840 and 1843. The legislation provided free passage and provisions for all emigrants, supported them for a limited time after their arrival, and exempted them from military duty. Once in Jamaica, emigrants would meet with agents to ensure they were directed in the choice of their pursuits. The allocated funds also paid for Jamaican commissioners to travel to the United States to promote the emigration project and publicize its benefits.[78]

While the legislation specified that the promotion of Jamaican emigration should occur by "avoiding all misrepresentation, and explaining the real advantages which the emigrant may derive by accepting," agents on the ground were quite prepared to encourage emigration by downplaying the socio-economic problems that made planters so desperate to recruit foreign workers in the first place.[79] Edmund A. Grattan, for example, an emigration agent active in Boston in 1841, claimed that every visitor welcomed into Jamaica would agree that "the comforts enjoyed by the laboring class of that island are exceeded by none in the world." Grattan cited Joseph John Gurney's letters to Henry Clay in support of abolitionism as "trustworthy evidence" of the "gratifying" condition and "rapidly increasing prosperity" to be found throughout the island. Most telling, however, was Grattan's appeal to African Americans' desire for equality. Reflecting a keen understanding of what was ultimately at stake for African Americans in the emigration debates, Grattan noted that "the point of view in which Jamaica stands pre-eminently inviting to the colored class of the United States, is the free and full enjoyment of those rights and privileges to which their white brethren justly attach so much importance." He assured potential migrants (despite abundant evidence to the contrary) that the island was free from the influence of prejudice.[80]

In the end, the Jamaica planters were only successful in enticing a small number of African Americans to Jamaica in the early 1840s. On November 12, 1840, the *Isabella* arrived in Kingston from Baltimore carrying fourteen African Americans, and, only six days later, fifteen more African Americans arrived from Philadelphia on board the *Vesper*.[81] Many of the individuals on these two vessels were described as "servants," but included in their number were carpenters, barbers, black-smiths, farmers, and sailmakers.[82] Yet, overall, responses to Jamaican emigration appeals were quite tepid. Despite their dubious efforts to downplay endemic issues on the island, the agents' promotion of Jamaican emigration could not help but bring planters' concerns about a labor shortage more immediately to the attention of American observers. And anti-slavery advocates were quick to point out that such a labor deficit might not exist but for the planters' own poor treatment of the resident labor force.[83] In March 1841, nearly a year after Jamaica passed its immigration act, Jamaican resident George Davison asserted that there had been no further arrival of African American emigrants beyond those few from the mid-Atlantic.[84] At most, there were 480 American men and women living in Jamaica by 1844, but because the census of that year did not distinguish between Americans of European and African descent, the overall number of African Americans living in Jamaica by 1844 was probably much lower.[85]

While Jamaica's notoriously poor labor relations were likely a significant factor in the low rates of black emigration to the island, it is also possible that the scheme failed to pick up steam because it came late to the table. By the time the Jamaican legislature passed the Emigration Act in April 1840, a similar project launched by Trinidadian planters had already been introduced, assessed, and largely rejected in the United States. Trinidad had first begun wooing African Americans to emigrate in early 1839, and the question of whether to support the notion was quickly picked up by the New York-based newspaper *The*

Colored American. Between the summers of 1839 and 1841, the paper's editor, Charles B. Ray, led the charge of public debate. He regularly published information and opinions about the Trinidadian recruitment efforts, beginning with an appeal crafted specifically for the newspaper by the island's recruitment agent, a prominent former slaveholder named William Burnley.[86] Noting that the "subject of emigration has lately excited much inquiry among our friends," Ray moderated an extensive discussion between Burnley and the paper's readers. He also published correspondence written by informed observers and shared editorials expressing his own hopes and concerns on the topic.[87]

Initially, Ray was ready to provide a modicum of support to the prospect of Trinidadian emigration. Although he believed no country provided as many advantages to African Americans as the country of their birth, he acknowledged that certain classes of people could benefit from emigrating to Caribbean islands, where neither legal persecution nor prejudice would present insurmountable barriers to advancement. Perhaps remembering the dissatisfaction of the emigrants who returned from Haiti in the decade prior, Ray believed that only the "*right kind*" of emigrants should be encouraged to relocate to the West Indies. Assuring readers that West Indian emigration would provide "constant employment and good wages" for farmers and "rough mechanics," the newspaper emphasized the importance of emigrating only if one had the "capacity and willingness to work in the *field* with a *hoe.*"[88]

Quickly, however, his already limited support waned. By October 1839, he felt pessimistic about "the course of things" with respect to Trinidad and cautioned readers not to "headlong blunder" into the arms of recruiters. He encouraged them to wait "until well qualified *scientific agents* have been sent out to examine the whole matter and report."[89] And on April 11, 1840, when a friend returned from a trip to "investigate matters" in Trinidad, Ray decided to cut all ties with the project unequivocally. This trusted informant reported that emigrants were "sickly and extremely dissatisfied and disheartened." Considering themselves deceived, they desired to return to the United States.[90]

Yet Charles B. Ray did not speak for everyone when he rejected Trinidadian emigration. In Baltimore, large-scale political meetings were held among African Americans beginning in late 1839. Living in a slave state with a large free population, black Baltimoreans felt the tug of emigrationism. Maryland's lawmakers made it easy, allocating money to support the investigatory travels of two men, Nathaniel Peck and Thomas Price, to Trinidad and Guiana on behalf of the black community at large. Discovering that the islands might offer opportunities for economic independence in addition to equal rights, Peck and Price catalyzed the emigration of several hundred African Americans from Baltimore to Trinidad and Guiana from early 1840 through 1841. Pleased with their success, Peck and Price submitted a "counter statement" to *The Colored American*, challenging Charles B. Ray's negative assessment of the project by reminding readers that the islands offered the legal equality denied black people in the United States.[91]

The emigration of black Baltimoreans only fueled Charles B. Ray's opposition to the idea. By February 1841, his animus had grown so vociferous that he believed few things had more prominently occupied the pages of his paper in the year previous than his efforts to "expose the rottenness, the deceptiveness of this scheme." Even in relation to other "systems of emigration," he asserted, the Trinidadian project possessed a "ruinous tendency to the cause of our people."[92] He was persuasive. Agents for Trinidad and Guiana were unable to make further headway outside of Maryland, and the project was essentially dead in the water.

Emerging just at the tail end of the heated debates over Trinidadian emigration in the pages of *The Colored American*, it is no surprise that the Jamaican emigration scheme had difficulty taking off. Anti-slavery advocates in the United States largely distrusted Jamaican recruitment efforts from the first, and what little was printed about Jamaican emigration did not reflect well on the island.[93] *The Liberator* reported the story of James G. Barbadoes, for example, who had been a "most prominent abolitionist known among the people of color" in the United States. Engaged to work on a silk plantation, Barbadoes had perhaps been recruited by Samuel Whitmarsh, a prominent silk grower from Massachusetts. Whitmarsh had been commissioned by the Jamaican government a year earlier to recruit free black emigrants and "introduce the silk culture." Enticed by the opportunity, Barbadoes moved his family to Jamaica in 1841. Sadly, however, both Barbadoes and two of his children died not long after their arrival, and his family's misfortunes were counted among the "sufferings, the miseries, the death-destroying process" awaiting emigrants in Jamaica.[94]

Even in less dramatic circumstances, African Americans in Jamaica reportedly experienced the same low wages and oppression that characterized the lives of former slaves who remained on Jamaican plantations. According to observers, food and land were too expensive relative to plantation laborers' low wages, the religious establishments maintained a "Negro pew" for colored parishioners, and "education privileges" were no better than in the United States. Reports suggested that white prejudice was virtually absent – so long as colored residents remained firmly within the "lowest caste of laborers." According to a black missionary named Nancy Prince who traveled through Jamaica in 1841, many could be found daily soliciting the American Consul to send them home.[95] Reflecting on the state of the island and his pessimism regarding African American emigration, Jamaican resident George Davison reported his belief that "common laborers cannot live [in Jamaica]" simply because they "cannot get good wages."[96]

While most prominent African American leaders and newspaper editors regarded Jamaican emigration in the 1840s as "a gross and scandalous delusion from beginning to end," others recognized that there were alternative ways to capitalize on and support the newly free island's economic potential.[97] For some, the solution was to invest in transatlantic black enterprise, tapping into the legacy of men like Paul Cuffe, who had devoted his later years to the effort of establishing black trade networks that would benefit black people around the Atlantic. This was certainly how noted black activist and self-liberated slave J. W. C. Pennington saw it when he connected with a group of like-minded individuals in Kingston, Jamaica, in the mid-1840s. Together, they came up with the idea of forming a society called the Jamaica Hamic Association to support black enterprise. Writing to a member of the National Colored Convention in 1847 – perhaps to Pennington himself, who by then had become a member of the Colored Convention's Committee on Commerce – members of the Jamaica Hamic Association elaborated on the need for black-owned commercial ventures between the United States and Jamaica. Noting that there was great demand in Jamaica for American products, the members of the association believed that if a black network of producers and merchants were to enter into trade, it would have an enormous impact on elevating black people's quality of life and furthering the cause of racial uplift – both in Jamaica and in the United States. The 1847 National Colored Convention agreed, declaring that the idea would be "of mutual benefit and advantage."[98]

Still, when it came to the idea of economic opportunity for African Americans in Jamaica, emigration was the number-one topic – and it received failing marks. Nonetheless, the West Indian emigration projects collectively acted as an important foil for anti-slavery advocates to articulate what constituted meaningful freedom – as well as the opportunity to weigh the outcome of West Indian freedom against it. Weighing in on the Trinidadian emigration controversy playing out in the pages of *The Colored American*, Samuel Cornish (the well-known newspaper editor of *Freedom's Journal* and the *Friend of Man*) noted that of 500 people who expressed interest in emigrating, he found "*not a single one* willing to make his living by working *in the sun with his hoe*." While many were willing to work for the planters for a brief period of time, they hoped and expected to then "go on [their] own hook," establishing themselves as independent freeholders working for themselves.[99] Based on the broad condemnation of West Indian emigration due to emigrants' limited opportunities and reports of unhappy living conditions, it was not enough that slavery had been abolished and that legal equality was guaranteed. African Americans wanted respectable wages for their labor, they wanted educational opportunities, they wanted social equality, and they wanted to work for themselves.

By rejecting West Indian emigration projects, African Americans and their anti-slavery allies navigated a thin line between their ongoing desire to demonstrate the success of Britain's emancipation and their recognition that it had not worked well enough for emigrants to make a life in any of the new free-soil islands. Demoralizing evidence that free people faced ongoing abuse and difficulty – as well as the increasing evidence of Jamaica's economic woes – made anti-slavery advocates' defense of British emancipation's positive outcome seem tenuous.

And yet, the fact that Great Britain had abolished slavery against the will of powerful pro-slavery interests never ceased to be a cause worth celebrating. African American communities held "First of August" celebrations each year across North America throughout the antebellum period, commemorating the enactment of Great Britain's path-breaking legislation.[100] British West Indian emancipation had freed 800,000 people from bondage and provided a powerful example for how the same could be done in the United States. It had also deepened the sense among African Americans and anti-slavery activists that Great Britain was the most stalwart international ally in the fight against slavery – a beacon of hope for emancipation in the United States.

CHAPTER 5

Reputations and Expectations: Assessing Migrant Life in Upper Canada

Are they loyal subjects of the government? 2d. As a people are they as honest, as industrious, as temperate and well behaved as the white citizens? 3d. In proportion to their numbers are criminal cases more numerous among them than among the whites? Do any of them beg from door to door, or depend on public charity for sustenance; and if so, are such cases more numerous proportionately than among the whites?

~ Hiram Wilson, from a questionnaire to British Canadian officials regarding "the colored man in Canada," January 26, 1837[1]

In 1837, at the very same time that Joseph Kimball and James Thome were traveling through the British West Indies on behalf of the American Anti-Slavery Society, a well-known white reformer named Hiram Wilson was busily collecting information about the condition and conduct of African American emigrants in Upper Canada. Whereas Thome and Kimball were tasked with uncovering the outcome of emancipation in the black-majority British sugar islands, the AASS desired Wilson to illuminate how effectively African Americans blended into a white society akin to the U.S. North.

A Christian and an anti-slavery activist, Wilson garnered widespread attention when he was tapped by the AASS to be their investigatory agent in Upper Canada. He was the perfect candidate. In 1836, after graduating from Ohio's Oberlin Theological Seminary, he had accepted $25 from the school's president, Charles Finney, to perform a "tour" of Upper Canada's African American communities. He had been so deeply touched by the experience that he had moved there in order to devote the remainder of his life to helping the black emigrants.

His aims in Upper Canada were varied and ambitious. He intended to ascertain the migrants' spiritual and temporal condition, to assess their needs, to relieve their suffering, to educate the uneducated, to support their "mental and moral elevation," and to "collect such facts as will have an important bearing on the subject of slavery and of emancipation."[2] His wide-ranging objectives dovetailed perfectly with the aims of the AASS. Combined with the support he received for his missionary work from black and white reformers alike, Wilson quickly became a recognized authority on the subject of black life in Upper Canada.[3]

By sending investigatory agents simultaneously to the West Indies and to Upper Canada, the AASS sought to hone its ideas about black freedom at a tense moment in the anti-slavery struggle. British emancipation had raised slaveholders' fears to boiling point, and, at the same time, the increasing support for immediate emancipation among American abolitionists spurred an intense backlash in both North and South. The personal safety of white and black abolitionists was as threatened by widespread racism as it was by pro-slavery activism. African American communities across the country were targeted by violent mobs, anti-slavery printers were attacked and their printing presses destroyed, and the U.S. House of Representatives took the controversial step of passing a "Gag Rule" in 1836 that banned abolitionist petitions from being read in session.[4] While such reactionary anti-abolitionism illustrates how endangered many white people felt by growing abolitionist sentiment in the United States, it was black communities and their abolitionist allies who came increasingly under fire.

Against the backdrop of this dangerous political climate, the AASS realized that exploring emancipation in two very different socio-political environments could provide powerful ammunition in the battle for hearts and minds. While the ongoing appraisal of emancipation's socio-economic effects in the West Indies allowed anti-slavery advocates to counter powerful pro-slavery arguments in opposition to abolition in the United States, the migration of African Americans to Upper Canada (or Canada West, as it became known in 1841[5]) facilitated important conversations about black freedom in a white-majority society. Although the reality of black life in Canada was frequently more difficult than migrants hoped and their supporters anticipated, black migrants in

Canada offered anti-slavery advocates an opportunity to rejoice in the freedom of African Americans and assess what institutions and policies best facilitated their success.

Ever since the first Colored Convention of 1830 reported that 2,000 emigrants had followed in the footsteps of James C. Brown and left for Canada, it had appeared to Americans that the number of black emigrants seeking asylum across the United States' northern border was growing fast. In truth, it is difficult to determine with any certainty how many people actually entered the province during the 1830s and 1840s because contemporary observers overestimated the numbers of both free and fugitive emigrants for political purposes. It is also difficult to assess how many free migrants accounted for the rising population level versus self-emancipated fugitives on the run. Emigrants themselves may have further confused the issue, either because they were able (and chose to) pass as white or because they claimed free status for fear that they might still be in danger from slave catchers, even across the border.[6] Nevertheless, the AASS asserted in 1837 that Upper Canada had an African American population of "about ten thousand, almost entirely fugitives from American oppression."[7] Three years later, a census conducted for submission to the first British and Foreign Anti-Slavery Convention (held in 1840) indicated that no fewer than 13,511 "colored" residents lived in Upper Canada and that this population "chiefly" comprised "fugitives from the great prison-house of southern bondage."[8] (See Appendix.)

Reports of overall population numbers continued to grow precipitously through the 1840s. Even the most conservative estimates suggested that no fewer than 281 African Americans emigrated across the border each year between 1842 and 1847.[9] But much higher estimates abounded. Hiram Wilson himself reported to the AASS that 700–800 fugitives had crossed the border between 1839 and 1840 alone, and that he expected close to a thousand to arrive in the following year.[10] In 1841, several journals reported that the *Montreal Courier* had placed Canada's runaway population at 20,000 – although even Wilson, who often received criticism for inflating population numbers, did not think that Canada's black population had reached that high until 1848.[11] In mid-1843, he believed Canada's black population to be closer to 16,000, an estimate that still reflected incredible growth over a few short years.[12]

While it was quite clear to observers that African American migrants were resettling across the border in large numbers, it was less clear to them what black emigrants actually experienced as free people of color living in British Canada. Were their expectations of finding legal equality and freedom from oppression met? And, if so, how did equality and social opportunity affect black emigrants' community standing and prospects in a society that otherwise bore a striking resemblance to the U.S. North? For potential migrants and for reformers convinced that the Canadian example could positively influence the American anti-slavery struggle, information on these topics was crucial.

Emigrants themselves were quick to recognize that American reformers were hungry for on-the-ground information about the treatment and condition of black emigrants in Upper Canada, and they knew that they could make a positive impact with their perspectives. Black men like Western Graves and Jehu Jones wrote letters for publication in the American anti-slavery press lauding Canadian society. Writing to William Lloyd Garrison and readers of *The Liberator* from his new home in Toronto, Graves declared that Canada provided "liberty and equality to all subjects alike," and he informed his audience that black emigrants were quick to transform themselves into loyal British subjects because of it. Using the paper to communicate with "friends and acquaintances" still in Philadelphia, Graves affirmed that he himself was likewise transformed and had "relinquished all desire of returning."[13]

Meanwhile, in a letter to Charles B. Ray of *The Colored American,* Jehu Jones expressed surprise that so many black northerners remained in the United States. Having moved to Toronto in 1839 to escape financial hardship and social prejudice in New York, he found that men of color were truly free in Upper Canada. Due to the equal laws in his adopted home, he informed his readers, "every American disability falls at your feet."[14]

Indeed, black emigrants often raised their voices from their new homes to extoll their experience of racial justice in Upper Canada. In 1838, a group of prominent African Americans in Toronto even gathered together to generate and share their collective perspective on the "true state of the coloured population of Canada." Comprising self-emancipated slaves and free migrants – including the well-known James C. Brown of the original Ohio emigrants – the group produced a set of resolutions for publication in all newspapers "friendly to the cause of human rights, especially the Anti-Slavery Journals in the United States and in England." They resolved that Upper Canada was a true "asylum for the oppressed," and they agreed that migrants lived in a state of "perfect contentment" due to Britain's provision of equal laws to all.[15] According to them, Upper Canada fully measured up to its reputation.

Even as black emigrants penned and publicized their own perspectives on the reality of life in Upper Canada, however, it was Hiram Wilson's reflections on black life in the British province that received the widest distribution in the anti-slavery press. At first, like his counterparts working in the West Indies, Hiram Wilson prioritized the insights provided by local (white) officials when he reported back to the AASS in 1837. Soliciting the perspectives of several prominent Upper Canadians on how African Americans fared in the province, he sent a questionnaire asking whether African American emigrants were loyal subjects, whether they seemed honest, industrious, and temperate, and whether they were "as well behaved as the white citizens." In addition, he asked how the rate of black criminality compared with the rate of white criminality, and whether the numbers of African Americans who depended on public charity were comparable with those of whites in similar circumstances. Receiving exceptionally favorable replies from several high-profile individuals, Wilson sent the respondents' letters along to abolitionists awaiting information in the United States. Abolitionists could read these perspectives on emigrants' "good behavior and value as citizens" either in the report of the AASS's fourth annual meeting or by perusing the abstracts that were reprinted in anti-slavery newspapers from New York to Ohio.[16]

Over the next several years, however, Wilson became much more attentive to ensuring that he amplified the voices of black emigrants themselves. In a letter addressed to the *Michigan Observer*, he reminded readers that those who had escaped the clutches of American slavery "had the best opportunity for knowing what slavery is." Upper Canada was, he noted, full of "TEN THOUSAND COMPETENT WITNESSES" against the horrors of slavery. Their testimony could elevate the hitherto "superficial" understanding of northern abolitionists about the horrors they fought against.[17] Even when white northern readers patronizingly spoke of the "artless manner" in which self-emancipated slaves shared their testimony, Wilson's efforts brought African Americans' own perspectives on their self-liberation to the attention of anti-slavery advocates who might otherwise have discounted the voices of those they purported to help.[18]

Fueled by a deep sense of purpose, Wilson regularly responded to information requests from regional anti-slavery societies across the United States and wrote letters directly to editors of anti-slavery publications.[19] Just as James Thome and Joseph Kimball were highly aware that their notes from the West Indies would be used to weigh in on the future of anti-slavery activism in the United States, so too was Wilson highly attentive to how his representation of Canadian liberty could assist in the fight against American slavery. "I am persuaded that the multitude of *facts* I have gathered among the people of color of this province," he wrote, "will greatly subserve the anti-slavery cause, and ought immediately to come before the public."[20] He relished evidence of African Americans' "marvelous transformation from the condition of chattels to the dignity of British freemen." His letters frequently related anecdotal success stories of individual migrants, shared positive testimony from "white neighbors," and emphasized his belief that African Americans, if freed by the U.S. government, "would make as useful citizens [in the United States] as they now do on British territory."[21]

He also shared that black men and women supported anti-slavery activism in the United States from their adopted home, noting that many black emigrants offered financial support to the Upper Canada Anti-Slavery Society. Having just recently been formed in January 1837, the society's mission was to spread abolitionism throughout the province of Upper Canada and the northern United States – a cause to which many emigrants contributed between $5 and $10 per family.[22]

Yet as Wilson continued to fill his letters with observations and anecdotes, his depiction of what black migrants experienced in Upper Canada gradually deviated from the positive portrayals produced by men like Western Graves and Jehu Jones. There were two reasons for this. The first was that Wilson frequently wrote from towns and villages far afield from Toronto, where he witnessed migrants struggle with hardships less likely to be met either by free black northerners who relocated with financial resources or by fugitive slaves who made their way to the province's main urban center.[23] The second was that his correspondence was steeped in the overlapping imperatives he navigated as a missionary, as an avowed abolitionist, and as a white interloper in black communities. Reflecting an imperialistic impulse typical of missionaries working among freed slaves and native Africans in the Atlantic world, Wilson justified his mission among the emigrants by emphasizing that their generally uneducated and impoverished condition necessitated his spiritual guidance and philanthropic intervention.[24]

He walked a fine line. As an anti-slavery reformer and a true believer in African American potential, he made sure to clarify that he considered what he saw as black emigrants' unhappy state to be the product of enslavement in the United States and prejudice in Upper Canada. This mode of thinking fell firmly within a tradition common among many white abolitionists of identifying slavery as an "environmental" explanation for perceived racial difference.[25] At the same time – lest his words be interpreted to suggest that slavery had rendered African Americans fundamentally unfit for freedom – he underscored the fact that he found their "moral and mental condition" to be better than he expected based on their former lives as chattel. While balancing these overlapping assessments of black emigrants in Upper Canada, he also made regular appeals to readers for the financial contributions necessary to keep his work afloat.[26]

On the one hand, Wilson's letters consistently offered anti-slavery readers reassuring accounts of emigrants' conditions in Canada during the late 1830s. In July 1837, for example, Wilson was pleased to report that self-emancipated migrants were largely "a noble-minded, industrious, thriving people; unassuming, unoffending in their demeanor, and more temperate in their habits than their white neighbors." Anti-slavery newspaper editors readily accepted and repeated his report. Three months later, after reading Wilson's evaluation of emigrant life, the editor of Boston's *New England Spectator* summarized the information for his readers, indicating that black men and women in Canada rarely became public charges, readily took advantage of educational

opportunities, and were "rising in respectability, intelligence and property." Based on Wilson's observations, the editor assessed that "no
other class of inhabitants provide for themselves more uniformly
than they."[27]

Yet Wilson's correspondence also revealed substantial difficulty.
Reflecting on success and hardship in equal measure, Wilson com-
mended the 120 black residents of the northwest village of Oro for
having carved out a comfortable life for themselves and for living in
such a way that white neighbors could attest to their honesty, quiet-
ness, and self-sufficiency – especially since they had arrived entirely
destitute in a snow-packed region populated only by bears and
wolves. The government had granted them land on condition that
they "perform settlement duties," but had given them no provisions
with which to do so. By contrast, once these earliest black settlers had
established a modicum of infrastructure, the government encouraged
white families to move to the area by allotting them land, providing
a year's provision, and employing the black residents to build their
cabins.[28]

Hiram Wilson began worrying about such disparities from his
earliest days in the province, expressing concern that "public prejudice in [Upper Canada] is much the same as in the states." More
often than not, it seemed, he was right. In fact, prejudice had nipped
at black emigrants' heels from the start. Acting on petitions sent by
two separate towns, Upper Canada's House of Assembly (Lower
House) had passed a series of resolutions in 1830 in which they
expressed their opposition to unrestricted migration from across
the border and the legal equality of those who arrived. While they
affirmed that they felt no uneasiness over the "law of nature" obligat-
ing Upper Canada to protect individual fugitives from their pursuers,
they were unequivocal in their belief that the sudden and possibly
unlimited migration of free African Americans was "dangerous to the
peace and comfort of [the province's] inhabitants." They argued that
emigrants had become unwelcome where they "approach[ed] an
equality with whites" in the United States, so it was logical to expect
that "disasters" would "flow from the same cause in this Province."[29]
In the end, the Lower House's lawmakers were unsuccessful in

excluding black migrants and questioning their equal standing as citizens, but their efforts set a worrisome precedent.[30]

By the time Hiram Wilson arrived in the province six years later, it seemed that unwelcoming white Canadians had found other ways to discriminate against African Americans. While African Americans were "protected in their persons and property," Wilson noted, they were frequently "denied those advantages which are calculated to refine and elevate the human character."[31] His chief concern was that administrators in Upper Canada did not provide black emigrants with equitable access to education. Schools in the late 1830s and 1840s became a lightning rod for white Canadians' discomfort with the growing population of self-emancipated men and women in their midst, and Upper Canada's educational structure provided a mechanism for exclusion. Until 1844, education was decentralized and locally directed. It placed decisions in the hands of tax-paying property owners and trustees elected by school parents, which provided an easy way for white-majority communities – particularly those in more rural areas – to formally or informally discriminate against black children.[32] Black children were regularly prevented from attending white schools, either due to overtly segregationist policies or because non-integrated settlement patterns meant that schools were too far for children of color to attend.[33]

African Americans' limited access to education in Upper Canada exposed a deep gulf between the legal equality promised by the British-Canadian government and the social equality expected by black emigrants. In Toronto, educational inequity posed enough of a problem in 1837 that a group of African Americans reached out to Dr. Thomas Rolph, a prominent British anti-slavery advocate, to help pressure the British imperial government into providing adequate teachers and access to public schools for black migrants.[34]

In the township of Hamilton, black emigrants were desperate enough to petition the newly arrived Governor-General, Charles Metcalfe, for help. According to a petition sent in 1843, black students were being denied entry to public schools, a right that their equal status as British subjects should have guaranteed them. Just as upsettingly, black children in Hamilton were frequently addressed with derogatory terms, and local whites regularly threw dangerous items at them. Pointing to their collective allegiance to the British flag and their status as tax-paying British subjects, the Hamilton petitioners asserted that they had every right to send their children to the town's public schools. They expressed confidence that Metcalfe, as "her majesty's representative" in Canada, would rectify the situation and ensure that they would be able to "enjoy our rights in this province."[35]

Governor-General Metcalfe was, indeed, concerned to hear that Hamilton's black population was being excluded from adequate schooling. He forwarded the Hamiltonians' petition to Rev. Robert Murray, the Assistant Superintendent of Upper Canada, who, in turn, demanded answers from George Tiffany, the President of Hamilton's Board of Police. Foreshadowing the ways that modern police forces are tasked with upholding systems premised on structural inequity, the Board of Police was the agency in charge of collecting local school assessments (taxes). And Tiffany's response was troublingly ambivalent. Describing local whites' racism, Tiffany warned that both teachers and parents had expressed an expectation that any attempt to desegregate Hamilton's schools would cause white parents to pull their children out.[36] Although a far cry from the virulence of white parents in Amherstburg, who stated a preference for cutting off their own children's heads over allowing them to be educated alongside black students, Tiffany indicated that white Hamiltonians' likely removal of their children from public schools had unsustainable implications for local tax revenue. It was therefore unlikely that the community's schools would be desegregated.[37]

Whether through negligence or prejudice, the Hamilton case made it clear that the inequality of provincial education belied black emigrants' expectations of what it meant to be a British subject in Canada.

Responding to this longstanding and pernicious form of structural inequity, Hiram Wilson made the education of self-liberated individuals his main philanthropic and missionary concern when he arrived in Upper Canada. In 1837, using his own limited financial resources and requesting financial support from American reformers, he established a new organization, the Canada Mission, to build schools and distribute religious texts for black emigrants throughout the province. By summer 1839, he had helped to establish ten schools, each run by an "ardently pious" collection of predominantly female teachers.[38]

His efforts to rectify the educational disparity felt by African American emigrants received support and praise from American reformers, who generally agreed that education and religion would help pave the way for racial justice. They recognized that a lack of educational opportunities in Upper Canada/Canada West had the potential to severely undercut the social elevation of black emigrants once they had escaped from the U.S. "house of bondage."[39]

In fact, as the black population of Upper Canada continued to grow through the 1830s and 1840s, so too did American anti-slavery advocates' awareness that their philanthropy could help to bolster the British province's political capital in the fight against American slavery. As famed abolitionist editor William Lloyd Garrison noted in 1843, the financial and moral support of fugitive slaves in Canada could have "a very important bearing on the total and speedy abolition of slavery in [the United States]."[40] In addition to "elevating" formerly enslaved men and women, whom he characterized as "generally in a very destitute condition, without money, without clothing, and without any place where to shelter themselves or to obtain the means of subsistence," he believed that supporting missionary work among them would, in time, furnish "well-educated colored youth, to take the field as lecturers and agents in the cause of universal emancipation."[41]

To this end, abolitionists began fundraising efforts to support black emigrants in Canada. In addition to extensive fundraising in the United States, these efforts brought many abolitionists – especially African American abolitionists – across the Atlantic to England. One of the first well-known black abolitionists to sail for England was the Rev. Nathaniel Paul, who had moved from Albany, New York, to the Wilberforce settlement soon after its founding. In 1832, he departed from Wilberforce for a four-year sojourn in Great Britain, raising thousands of dollars in England and Scotland for the support of black emigrants in Canada.[42] Many more renowned African American abolitionists followed in his wake, becoming the principal representatives of the American anti-slavery movement abroad throughout the 1830s and 1840s.[43]

The connections forged by abolitionists in Great Britain provided enormous financial and moral support for black emigrants in Canada, as well as for the twin causes of American anti-slavery and racial justice more generally. Not only did fundraising result in British support for vigilance committees, schools, and churches, the experience of traveling in Great Britain furnished black travelers with the unforgettable experience of being treated as equals at the heart of the British empire.[44] While it was a common experience to be targeted by racism aboard transatlantic steamships while *getting* to British shores, African Americans frequently felt the omnipresent burden of anti-black prejudice removed entirely once there.[45] As historian Elizabeth Stordeur Pryor suggests, it was the sensory experience of moving through public spaces without being accosted by various forms of racism that truly allowed black activists "to embody the full scope of what equality and citizenship could mean for themselves and for other people of color back home."[46]

Interestingly, despite the fact that Great Britain seemed to offer the racial tolerance that felt increasingly elusive in British Canada, England did not become a notable free-soil destination for black emigrants prior to 1850 and the passage of the Fugitive Slave Act. Fewer than a hundred black activists went to the British Isles between 1833 and the 1860s, and those who visited generally did not stay. They toured and lectured to raise money for projects in the United States and Canada, then returned to continue the fight for racial justice in North America.[47] Nonetheless, as the moral center of abolitionism, a source of financial aid for abolitionists, and a place where black sojourners could experience freedom from racism, Britain had an almost unassailable reputation as a leader in the fight for black freedom and as a model for what it should look and feel like once achieved.

Back in Canada, Hiram Wilson was able to expand his mission among the black emigrants throughout the 1840s due to the energetic fundraising activities of abolitionist supporters at home and abroad. But it was thanks to the largesse of philanthropy from Great Britain, in particular, that he was able to spearhead the purchase of 200 acres of land in 1841 for a new school: the British American Institute of Science and Industry. Located along the Sydenham River approximately 60 miles northeast of

Detroit, it quickly became a hub of activity. Nearly as soon as ground was broken on Wilson's school, a new community named Dawn developed around it.[48]

Wilson provided the American anti-slavery press with regular, widely circulated reports about how many "star-led" runaways made their way to Dawn, their conditions upon arrival, and the efforts made to ensure their success. In addition to overseeing their practical and religious education, he assured American reformers that a major goal of the British American Institute was to cultivate "upon the Anti Slavery battle ground colored champions who will wage a successful warfare ... by narrating their awful experiences of slavery."[49] In the end, unfortunately, Dawn proved to be a mismanaged affair that Wilson himself left in 1849. Yet during his tenure in the community, he remained committed to demonstrating for American supporters that formerly enslaved people – with a bit of intervention and guidance – made upstanding citizens and neighbors in a white-dominant society.

Still, some anti-slavery advocates doubted the value of focusing so much energy on uplifting African American communities in Upper Canada. In an 1843 letter to well-known white activist Maria Weston Chapman, fellow abolitionist Frances Drake worried that women's efforts to solicit charity for the Canada Mission were getting in the way of fundraising efforts that she believed would more directly counter slavery. "They think they must do something for the cause," she wrote, "as they claim to be anti-slavery." But, in her eyes, women who devoted themselves to Canada were either insufficiently abolitionist or deficient in moral courage, squandering their efforts on those already free in Canada instead of daring to "scatter light" on the subject of slavery itself. "How long think you," she asked Chapman skeptically, "before they will abolish slavery if they go on with the work in their way?"[50]

At least one vocal critic also argued that philanthropy directed toward Upper Canada sent the wrong message. Referring to Wilson's fundraising efforts as "specious humbug," a black emigrant named Peter Gallego claimed that the Canada Mission "misrepresents [emigrants'] real condition, by holding them up to the world as a *population of beggars*." Gallego, who had graduated from the University of Toronto since moving to Canada, characterized Wilson's negative depictions of black emigrants as inaccurate and offensive. He worried that they had the potential to discredit the project of racial uplift and was convinced that "no inconsiderable portion of the colored refugees" felt the same. He guaranteed readers that people of color in Upper Canada did, in fact, have equal access to education, and that they generally lived in more comfortable circumstances than any other class of emigrants on the entire continent. He adamantly rejected the notion, therefore, that philanthropic aid was necessary to assist self-emancipated slaves, and he wholeheartedly believed that every dollar spent in their support was money withdrawn from anti-slavery endeavors requiring aid more desperately.[51]

By and large, however, American reformers rejected these critiques. On the first count, Wilson's work in Canada continued to strike many as directly relevant to the fight against slavery in the United States. Not everyone agreed on whether American contributions should support men and women under the protection of the (wealthy) British flag, but many vocal proponents wholeheartedly believed that the ability to showcase the welfare of African Americans in freedom was an important extension of supporting their initial exodus from slavery.[52] Moreover, Wilson's efforts on behalf of education in Canada seemed relevant to racial uplift projects in the United States. For example, the Ladies' Central Committee of Ohio for the Education of Colored People invited Wilson to lecture about the schools and the black emigrants in Upper Canada because they recognized that their own activities might benefit from his expertise and experience.[53] Although British philanthropists remained the primary funders of Wilson's missionary work in the 1840s, American reformers continued to support him both financially and ideologically throughout the antebellum period.

On the second count, Peter Gallego's argument that there was no justification for fundraising on behalf of black children's education passed over quite quickly. Initially, it seemed that Gallego's views might find purchase. Charles B. Ray, the editor of *The Colored American*, asserted his doubts about the necessity and method of Wilson's educational work shortly after reading Gallego's criticism in the *National Anti-Slavery Standard*.[54] However, Ray quickly offered a public retraction after being corrected on all points by evidence provided by the well-known and respected reformer, Samuel Ringgold Ward. Ward had traveled in

Upper Canada himself and conversed regularly with British philanthropists. Feeling himself to be well acquainted with the true state of things in
the province, he was determined to set the record straight for an African
American newspaper editor of Charles B. Ray's stature. "That colored
children are denied access to the schools, is a fact so notorious," Ward
wrote incredulously, "that I can but wonder that the editor of the Colored
American should state to the contrary."[55]

Although Peter Gallego received some validation when Hiram Wilson
noted that children in Toronto (where Gallego resided) could enroll in
public school with much less difficulty than elsewhere in Upper Canada,
his misrepresentation of a province-wide issue ultimately earned him
substantial criticism in American anti-slavery circles.[56] Gallego likely
saw his letter to the *National Anti-Slavery Standard* as a defense of black
emigrants' reputation and as an accurate portrayal of his own experience, but his depiction of black emigrants' perfect social equality in
Upper Canada, simply put, strained credulity.

The fact that this brief exchange received widespread coverage
in the American anti-slavery press reflected reformers' high level of
ongoing investment in learning about the status and conditions of
black emigrants in Canada. But it also reflected a sea change in *what*
American observers were learning. By the 1840s, it was increasingly
clear that British Canada was unable to provide the full social equality
that African Americans and white reformers had so ardently hoped it
could when free black emigrants had first started to make their way
across the border in 1830. Legal equality, yes; protection for self-
emancipated men and women, certainly. But more and more, emigrants, travelers, and close observers agreed that racial prejudice was
on the rise.

In the end, even Peter Gallego was not immune. Although he had
never denied the existence of racial prejudice in Upper Canada, he had
always firmly believed that black men could use their legal equality and
civic standing to successfully combat its pernicious effects. Yet shortly
after publishing his letter against the Canada Mission, he embarked on
a tour of the province that proved color prejudice outside Toronto was
far more toxic than he had previously realized. In a letter to the long-time
British advocate for black residents in Canada, Dr. Thomas Rolph,

Gallego described a nightmarish series of events that shook him to his core. Aboard a steamship from Toronto to Hamilton, he was asked by the captain to leave the table in the dining area so as not to offend white diners. Then, after paying his fare for a stagecoach from Hamilton to Brantford, he walked the entire distance after being informed that the white riders had "clubbed together" and refused to ride unless he took the outside seat.

His torment did not end there. On his next stop, he was dragged from his breakfast at the local inn and beaten by a man who objected to dining with "n—s." When Gallego fought back in self-defense, he was tossed onto the street by the innkeeper himself. As the final straw, when Gallego applied to the local magistrate for redress against the perpetrators, the magistrate not only refused to mete out justice, he subjected Gallego to a tirade against "amalgamation" – an anti-black term used to describe the mixing of races. Adding one last insult to injury, the magistrate then penalized *Gallego* for the blows he had struck in self-defense.[57] As British abolitionist James C. Fuller put it, "The refugee is not wanted in Canada. Were he, he would be treated differently by the people generally."[58]

Just as alarming to emigrants and observers alike was the fact that Canadian prejudice seemed to be a product of American influence. Hiram Wilson had long believed this to be the case, and Gallego now agreed, blaming his experience on the willingness of white Canadians to accommodate traveling Americans' racist attitudes.[59] Indeed, steam-ship owners and captains often pandered to white Americans' racism for simple economic reasons, insisting on segregated spaces to ensure the continued patronage of their American clientele.[60] The presence of this sort of discrimination was worthy of close scrutiny. As historian Elizabeth Stordeur Pryor has shown, access to public transportation was a key symbol of freedom and equal rights among African Americans in the antebellum era. Public conveyances like stagecoaches and steamships were important spaces for establishing and affirming social standing and equality. And, as Peter Gallego's story highlights, segregation in these spaces was also frequently dangerous, as it typically meant traveling in ways that risked exposure and bodily harm.[61] It is small wonder, then, that it was so galling for Gallego to discover that white Canadians were as committed as white Americans to customary segregation.

Even in comparatively tolerant Toronto, no fewer than eighty-five men of color agreed that the practice of American racism on Canadian soil led directly to anti-black disturbances. In a series of three petitions to the city mayor in the early 1840s, the black community expressed its hope that American entertainment troupes would be prevented from staging racist performances in the city. According to a petition submitted in 1840 (whose signatories included the ubiquitous James C. Brown), American actors visiting Toronto "invariably select[ed] for performance plays and characters which, by turning into ridicule and holding up to contempt the coloured population, cause them much heart-burning and lead occasionally to violence."[62]

Unheard, the petitioners reiterated their concern the following year, asserting that the American performers mean-spiritedly selected plays and songs to "make the Coloured man appear ridiculous and contemptible in the eyes of their audience."[63] Although the petitioners did not believe that the majority of Torontonians approved of these insulting exhibitions, it is clear that the performances had an ugly track record of contributing to "broils and suits between the white and colored inhabitants."[64] The mayor eventually declared that the circus would be allowed only "on condition of their not singing negro songs," but it took three years of sustained self-advocacy by the black community to block just one iteration of American racial prejudice from crossing the border.[65]

Clearly, while Upper Canadian communities had initially welcomed African American migrants, white Canada's response to the growing black population had soured by the late 1830s and early 1840s.[66] While the province had initially nursed a self-righteous anti-Americanism through its reception of "refugees," unnamed sources suggested to Charles B. Ray in 1837 that white Canadians had changed their tune due to fear that every African American in the United States would relocate to Canada if given the freedom and the chance.[67]

Although there was rhetorical value in simply blaming the contagion of American racism or the influx of black emigrants, the reasons for growing prejudice in Upper Canada were somewhat more complex. One significant source of anti-black sentiment was the failure of the

Wilberforce settlement (see Chapter 3). Allegations of financial mismanagement and endemic leadership problems persisted throughout the
1830s, bedeviling what should have been a promising, self-sustaining
black settlement. With its decline and ultimate failure, many white
Canadians began to see African Americans as public burdens.

Moreover, African Americans in Upper Canada drew the ire of the
province's popular Reform membership. This was critical in 1837, as
reformist political insurgents launched a rebellion against the standing
government in December of that year, in what is now known as the Upper
Canada Rebellion. African American emigrants generally became loyal
conservatives and faithful supporters of the standing government in
Upper Canada due to its role in freeing and protecting members of their
community. By contrast, the reformers were associated with republicanism
and pro-American sentiment – positions that had the potential to overturn
Upper Canada's longstanding history of rejecting U.S. diplomatic overtures on the issue of runaway slaves. During the rebellion of 1837, many
African Americans in Upper Canada readily took up arms against reformist insurgents when political hostilities broke out.[68] Needless to say, this
did not endear them to their reformist neighbors.

And, finally, economic changes within Upper Canada contributed to
the rising tenor of white prejudice around the issue of black immigration.
The availability of cheap land dwindled, leading new arrivals to concen-
trate more visibly in urban areas like Toronto. At the same time, the rise
of Irish immigration during this period presented labor competition that
enabled white Canadians to act on anti-black prejudice should they so
choose. As historian Robin Winks noted in his path-breaking study of
black Canada, "white Canadians wished to see the Negro free, and if the
Negro so wished it, resettled; but if resettlement were to be carried out on
a massive scale in British North America itself, they were less certain of
their liberal sentiments."[69]

With growing evidence of white Canadians' dwindling tolerance for
their new black neighbors, it is not surprising that some anti-slavery observers – even those who, in principle, supported emigration projects – felt
disheartened about the likelihood that emigrants in Upper Canada would
actually experience the equality they expected to find. Charles B. Ray, for
one, expressed concern that emigrants would wind up regretting their

choice to resettle in Canada – a concern he echoed in his mistrust of Trinidadian emigration. Noting that potential emigrants were "most invariably" interested in moving to Canada due to the "equal laws existing there," he asserted that there were other "disadvantages" that outweighed the benefits. He was worried by reports that there was a lack of "internal improvements" and dwindling labor opportunities, but his greatest concern of all was that legal equality in Canada did not seem to eliminate the substantial burden of racism. Although Ray was not opposed to emigration in principle – he was, in fact, a vocal proponent of western migration into the farmland of Wisconsin territory – he worried that African Americans' expectations of finding social equality in Canada would not be met.[70]

Proponents of African colonization helped to spread the growing pessimism. It was no favor, asserted the *New York Journal of Commerce* in 1843, to assist American slaves on their way to the "cold dominions of Victoria," where a black man remains "a negro, marked for degradation." While Liberia offered colonists the opportunity to be "as good as any body," the author wrote, Canada provided nothing more than the "slavery of prejudice, about which so much complaint is made."[71]

And yet, in spite of concerning reports that life in Canada did not fully match the hopes and expectations of black migrants looking for a better life, the number of African Americans crossing the U.S.–Canada border did not decrease. The black population of Upper Canada had increased notably in the later 1830s, and it increased dramatically throughout the 1840s. But something significant had shifted in terms of *who* was crossing the border. In the early to mid-1830s, it was largely free African Americans looking for legal equality and economic opportunity. From the late 1830s onward, it was almost entirely runaway slaves. Canada had remained consistent in its protection of self-liberated men and women, and its reputation for doing so only grew. And for those running from slavery and the ever-present threat of recapture in the U.S. North, reports that black life in Upper Canada was not all it was cracked up to be did not mean much. In the words of a man who had liberated himself from slavery and settled in the Canadian town of St. Catharines, "Salt and potatoes in Canada, were better than pound-cake and chickens in a state of suspense and anxiety in the United States."[72]

CHAPTER 6

Escape and Escalation: Self-Emancipation and the Geopolitics of Freedom

There is a country far away,
Friend Hopper says 't is Canada,
And if we reach Victoria's shore,
He says that we are slaves no more.

>   Chorus. *Now hasten all bondmen, let us go,*
>   *And leave this* Christian *country O;*
>   *Haste to the land of the British Queen,*
>   *Where whips for negroes are not seen.*

Now if we go, we must take the night –
We're sure to die if we come in sight –
The blood-hounds will be on our track,
And wo to us if they fetch us back.

>   Chorus. *Now haste all bondmen, let us go,*
>   *And leave this* Christian *country O;*
>   *God help us to Victoria's shore,*
>   *Where we are free and slaves no more.*

>   ~ From "A Song for Freedom," in William Wells Brown,
>   *Anti-Slavery Harp: A Collection of Songs for*
>   *Anti-Slavery Meetings* (1847)[1]

1837 was a big year for high-profile cases of self-emancipation across the U.S.–Canada border. On June 28, 1837, an enslaved Baltimorean named John Roberts managed to escape from his enslaver, Richard C. Stockton, while the two men were traveling in western New York State. With the assistance of renowned abolitionist Gerrit Smith, Roberts fled Rochester and made his way to Toronto, sparking an exchange between runaway slave and disgruntled enslaver that unfolded in the pages of newspapers on both sides of the international border.

Unwilling to cut his losses without a fight, Stockton published an open letter to Roberts in the *Rochester Daily Democrat*. His letter was dated July 4, 1837. Unlike a typical runaway slave ad, Stockton's letter appealed to the self-liberated man himself and framed the escape as a result of meddling abolitionists. Describing Roberts as a husband and father who had demonstrated an "excellent character of integrity, stability, and sobriety" during more than twenty years of service, Stockton suggested that Roberts had been "seduced" into leaving. He felt sure that Roberts would not have abandoned his life and family in the United States were it not for the interference of northern abolitionists – those "supposed friends" who encouraged slaves to run away against their own best interests. Stockton assured Roberts, therefore, that he would be "kindly received and treated as heretofore" should he decide to return to Baltimore and to slavery.[2]

John Roberts roundly rejected Stockton's offer in an open letter of his own. "Can you think," he asked, "that I would voluntarily relinquish freedom, fully secured to me by the British Government, to return to American slavery, the vilest that now crushes man and defies God?" Emphasizing the ugly irony that Stockton's letter was published on the Fourth of July, Roberts asserted that *he* clearly valued liberty more highly than his former enslaver. In fact, Roberts turned Stockton's description of his long-term enslavement entirely on its ear. Rather than seeing more than twenty years of "service" as a reason to return, Roberts argued that it should entitle him to reward. He therefore invited Stockton to reunite him with his wife and child by sending them from Baltimore to Canada, where they would join him under the British flag. Reframing Stockton's fundamental understanding of who had been wronged when he escaped to Canada, Roberts asserted that sending his family would constitute Stockton's "full acquittance" for keeping him enslaved so long. "Disproportioned as would be the cost of doing this, to the value of the services I have rendered you," Roberts noted with rhetorical flourish, "'tis all I ask."[3]

That same year, another highly politicized episode erupted at the border when David Castleman, the legal owner of a self-emancipated man named Solomon Moseby, attempted to have Moseby extradited back to Kentucky from Canada. Since Upper Canada first passed its gradual emancipation laws in 1793, the province had never recognized the act of running across the border to escape U.S. slavery as a crime. David Castleman, like Richard Stockton, knew full well that any effort to secure the extradition based on his slave's "fugitive" status would be a non-starter. But Castleman was not prepared to just let Moseby go. Instead, he sought Moseby's extradition based on the fact that he had stolen a horse in order to make his escape. At the time, there was no precedent governing extradition requests based on the theft of property during an escape from bondage. So, seeking to exploit this loophole, the Kentucky slaveholder argued that the horse Moseby had stolen to carry him to freedom should also be the cause of his unwilling return.

Because the strategy would have gained slaveholders some legal ground for battling Britain's protection of border-crossing slaves, the issue became something of a cause célèbre. Advocates of freedom rallied to Moseby's side. When the charges of horse-theft were laid, both the black and white communities of Niagara, Upper Canada, made a concerted effort to prevent the extradition. They appointed Moseby legal representation and petitioned the British government to recognize the criminal charge as a thinly veiled claim to extradite Moseby for being a runaway slave. As Moseby's lawyers were quick to argue, it seemed quite illogical that Moseby's former owner would travel at great expense to Upper Canada to recover a "thief" guilty of taking a horse worth only $150.[4]

From an official standpoint, Castleman prevailed with his creative legal strategy. The Lieutenant Governor of Upper Canada felt compelled to exact the extradition order based on the letter of the law, despite acknowledging the Niagara petitioners' fears that it would set a worrying precedent.[5] But Moseby's supporters were unwilling to abandon him. Even before the decision was made, African Americans from across the province had gathered around Moseby's jailhouse, "resolving to perish in their resistance to the law, rather than behold their fellow-man delivered up again to slavery." Knowing this, the deputy sheriff arrived to execute the extradition order armed with a contingent of British soldiers.

The extradition order ignited large-scale opposition despite the show of force. Moseby's allies rushed to help him escape, and the toll was high.

Although Moseby was able to make a successful getaway in the back of a wagon, the soldiers fired into the crowd during the confusion, leaving two of Moseby's protectors dead and several more wounded.[6] But the sacrifice of these staunch defenders of liberty secured more than just Moseby's escape. Niagara's fierce opposition to Moseby's extradition echoed in British officials' subsequent efforts to prevent loophole applications of extradition policies from being applied to runaway slaves. In 1842, when the Webster–Ashburton Treaty was finalized between the United States and Britain, anti-slavery lobbyists were able to convince the British government to remove horse theft and robbery from the list of extraditable crimes.[7]

These two protracted episodes illuminate the growing significance of the U.S.–Canada border at a moment when American slavery and anti-slavery were becoming increasingly pressing topics in national politics. Martin Van Buren had just won the 1836 election to replace Andrew Jackson as President of the United States, in part by guaranteeing southern voters that he was committed to maintaining slavery in states where it already existed. Yet episodes of international border-crossing escapes from slavery affirmed what many enslaved people and their anti-slavery allies already knew: the U.S.–Canada border was not only a boundary demarcating the former slaves' de facto attainment of freedom, it was also a secure barrier protecting runaways from recapture through multiple layers of emancipation policy and grassroots activism.

Self-emancipation was becoming collective action. In the case of John Roberts, his knowledge that Richard Stockton could not forcibly reclaim him into American slavery allowed him to boldly and publicly celebrate his new freedom. And anti-slavery advocates on both sides of the border took note. Both Stockton's letter and Roberts's response (originally published in Toronto's *Christian Guardian*) were reprinted in widely circulating anti-slavery newspapers.[8]

In Moseby's case, the Niagara community deputized itself to maintain the integrity of Upper Canada as a sanctuary for self-emancipated slaves, achieving what the law did not yet fully guarantee despite more than a decade of successful rebuffs scuttling U.S. diplomatic efforts. Through their petition drive, black and white Niagara residents indicated their investment in establishing the legal sanctity of the U.S.–Canada border as a boundary between American slavery and British freedom; through their mob tactics, they proved that they would forcibly protect the border until the law caught up. The success of Niagara's organization on a runaway's behalf was so memorable, in fact, that when noted Torontonian doctor (and son of a runaway slave) Anderson Ruffin Abbott sat down over sixty years later to pen his recollections of Toronto's black history, he cited the Moseby incident as the first time he could recall a runaway slave inciting "international complications."[9]

Yet these border episodes tell a different tale when seen through the perspective of slaveholders. They illuminate the creative lengths to which enslavers felt they had to go in order to circumvent the seemingly unassailable border protecting runaway "property" in British territory. In each case, too, the enslavers trying to recapture the self-liberated men seemed highly aware that their efforts could make an impact beyond their own immediate recovery attempts. For example, Richard Stockton's public letter "inviting" John Roberts to return to slavery was essentially a pro-slavery public relations stunt with an embedded indictment against abolitionist meddling and a defense of slavery's "paternalistic" benefits. Placing his letter in the local paper of Rochester, New York, Stockton perhaps hoped to encourage onlookers to intervene on behalf of slaveholders (for the slaves' own good, he would argue) before they reached Upper Canada.

Meanwhile, David Castleman, the Kentucky slaveholder attempting to reclaim Solomon Moseby, knew that his identification of an extradition loophole could potentially facilitate the forced return of more runaways back across the border. Within days of bringing the Moseby case before the Upper Canadian courts, Castleman filed an extradition request for yet another runaway man, Jesse Happy, who had also escaped from Kentucky to Canada by stealing a horse. Although the Happy case was thrown out because the horse itself had not crossed the border and because of the time elapsed between the escape and the extradition request (Happy had run away four years earlier), the simultaneous requests indicate that Castleman may have been attempting to establish legal grounds for the otherwise unacceptable practice of slave-catching in Canada.[10]

Whether read through the eyes of anti-slavery advocates or their slaveholding antagonists, widely publicized escapes of this sort exacerbated the sense that more and more runaways from U.S. slavery were finding sanctuary across the international border. Not only did anti-

slavery publications promote the impression that a significant and growing stream of African American migrants were arriving in Upper Canada,
they celebrated stories of danger-filled escape.[11] Indeed, regular press
coverage contributed to the public perception that a so-called
Underground Railroad of safe harbors and vigilant allies was busily
whisking runaway slaves through the northern states on their way to the
border.[12] The small town of Oswego, New York, for example, was
reported to be "almost weekly visited by colored fugitives" making their
way to Canada.[13]

While the U.S. North still remained the terminus for the vast majority
of self-liberated men and women, anti-slavery advocates in the late 1830s
and 1840s increasingly identified Canada as the more secure escape.
Moreover, as it became increasingly clear that emigrants were as likely
to experience social oppression in Canada as they were in the American
North, anti-slavery and African American newspapers shifted their attention from the prospect of free emigration to focus almost exclusively on
Canada's value as an escape from slavery.[14] As a result, Canada became so
closely correlated with self-emancipation that abolitionists in the 1840s
might readily assume all fugitive slaves were headed there. The well-
known abolitionist and judge William Jay, for example, related a story
in which he had presumed to direct a fugitive slave straight toward
Canada, only to be surprised upon discovering that the man's intended
destination was Massachusetts![15] But while a runaway slave in Boston
might forever be looking over their shoulder, a runaway slave in
Canada could rest in relative safety. The *Anti-Slavery Alphabet* for "little
readers" printed for the 1846 Anti-Slavery Fair memorialized this
distinction:

> U is for Upper Canada
> Where the poor slave has found
> Rest after all his wanderings,
> For it is British Ground![16]

Abolitionists also contributed to Upper Canada's growing reputation
as a safe haven by sharing and celebrating successful escape tales at their
organized meetings. This was the effect, for example, when well-known
New York abolitionist Alvin Stewart told the story of a runaway family

from Georgia. It was a thrilling tale. Rising from his seat in the final few minutes of the American Anti-Slavery Society's annual meeting in 1836, Stewart declared that the family had "heard of Canada, as a place where the laws made every man free, and protected him in his freedom." Yet they had no sense of how to get there. Luckily, a sympathetic Quaker pointed them in the right direction, and they made their way north. Traveling by night, they trekked through woods and over rivers until – at last – they found refuge with a "tribe of Indians" near the town of Buffalo, New York. From there, a local network of sympathizers – including a man with a stable and a local ferryman – transported the runaways into Canada across the Niagara River. They were just in the nick of time, for the Georgian slaveholder had caught up with his quarry. He sat astride his "foaming horse," pistol in hand, as the ferry "darted into the deep and rapid stream."[17] Unsurprisingly, the sympathy of Alvin Stewart's enthusiastic audience was "decidedly with the fugitive."[18]

Whether apocryphal or true, many of the runaway slave stories circulated by anti-slavery advocates during the late 1830s shared key narrative elements with Stewart's tale. Heart-stopping pursuit, an ally appearing at the critical moment, and a sense of overwhelming relief upon reaching Canadian soil – these became such recognizable tropes, in fact, that they were easily adapted into other creative formats for popular consumption. One contributor to the *Journal of Reform* was so filled with joy by the sheer number of "thrilling" slave escape stories that he felt inspired to write a poem. Titled "The Fugitive," it was a poignant homage composed of little more than a laundry list of the typical narrative elements found in most escape tales. Fleeing from slavery, an unnamed man runs by night and sleeps by day. He climbs steep mountains, crosses rapid streams, and leaps great chasms. Desperate to escape the chains of American slavery, he follows the North Star, which leads him like a beacon of liberty toward Canada.[19]

Such plot devices were so familiar that they could be "read" into visual representations as well. Any reader of the 1839 *Anti-Slavery Almanac* would have readily recognized the scene depicted in an image titled "John Bull's Monarchy a Refuge from Brother Jonathan's Slavery" (Figure 2). Representing the British-Canadian government's stalwart protection of self-emancipated men and women, the robust figure of "John Bull" stands in a boat, bodily protecting a black man who has

2 "John Bull's Monarchy a Refuge from Brother Jonathan's Slavery" in *The American Anti-Slavery Almanac for 1839* (New York and Boston, MA: S. W. Benedict and Isaac Knapp for the American Anti-Slavery Society, 1839), 9. Courtesy of the Library Company of Philadelphia.

narrowly escaped the clutches of a greedy, desperate slaveholder in hot pursuit.[20] A reader would have a stock narrative in mind to explain the scene, from the runaway's danger-filled flight from slavery to his profound joy and relief upon reaching the protection of Canadian soil. The ability to riff on the familiarity of these characters and escape narratives in creative formats not only raised the political relevance of slave flight beyond any individual anecdote, it reiterated and reproduced Upper Canada's symbolic importance as a haven for runaway slaves.

Anti-slavery advocates were determined to make the most of slave escapes in order to crack the bulwark of the southern slave system. When enslaved people ran, they did so in desperate circumstances. They faced obstacles at every turn. Weather, slave-catchers, bloodhounds, hunger, betrayal, and death all threatened fugitive slaves on the run.[21] Yet run they did. And throughout the 1840s, self-emancipation was increasingly encouraged by radical leaders of the abolitionist movement. William Lloyd Garrison, Gerrit Smith, and Henry Highland Garnet were three well-known radicals, in particular, who publicly encouraged slaves to liberate themselves whenever possible.[22]

From a political perspective, the impact of self-emancipation was enormous. But the financial impact was smaller than enslavers made it seem. By the end of the 1840s, slaveholders reported losing as much as $200,000 every year in the border slave states from men and women fleeing for freedom.[23] In pure dollars and cents, this amount paled in comparison with the value of people still enslaved and to the revenue their labor created for enslavers. Moreover, the amount of money that went into slaveholders' and slave-traders' pockets from free black people kidnapped into slavery exceeded the financial losses from people escaping it.[24] Yet the publication of high population estimates in Upper Canada by the anti-slavery press promoted the perception that a truly alarming number of southern slaves were being siphoned across the international border beyond the realm of recapture – and that their numbers were growing. Individual escapes, the encouragement of abolitionist leaders, and the growing population of a well-known free-soil haven all contributed to slaveholders' sense that they were under siege.

Slave flight also struck a major blow at the carefully constructed and religiously maintained story that slaveholders upheld at all costs: that southern slaves were happy in bondage and likely to fail in freedom. In 1846, a man named Lewis Richardson took aim at the myth of benevolence and one of its most famous promoters, the famed Kentucky statesman Henry Clay. Having spent nine of his fifty-three years of enslavement on Henry Clay's plantation, Ashland, Richardson regularly attracted large audiences anxious to hear him dispel the notion that slaveholders adequately cared for slaves' well-being.

It was no different on March 13, 1846. That evening, standing in front of a large interracial audience at Union Chapel in Amherstburg, Canada West (Upper Canada), Richardson spared no detail about his life at Ashland. He described having been stripped, tied up, and given 150 lashes on his naked back for the crime of visiting his wife at a neighboring property. He also described living on little food and without a stitch of bed-clothing beyond a coarse blanket. In his old age, he had no doubt that he would have died due to the floggings and abuse of Clay's "cruel overseer" had he not decided to risk all by running. "It has been said by some," he shared, "that Clay's slaves had rather live with him than be free." Amidst the plentiful cheers of his eager crowd, he declared it was not so. He thanked heaven he was now in Canada and declared, "If I don't live but one night, I am determined to die on free soil. Let my days be few or many, let me die sooner or later, my grave shall be made in free soil."[25]

Abolitionists relished every opportunity to point out that runaway slaves "weaken[ed] the hands and terrif[ied] the minds of southern slaveholders," robbing them of both their property and their ideological security.[26] And the growing fugitive slave population of Canada bolstered this effort significantly. Tongue in cheek, Hiram Wilson once even recommended that slaveholders organize an "Anti-Locomotive Chattelship Insurance Company" to fortify themselves against the financial losses incurred from the "wonderfully migratory tendency of human chattels northward."[27]

Radical abolitionists' increasingly vocal encouragement of runaway slaves quickly grew to encompass the support and commemoration of abolitionists bold enough to cross into the South to assist slaves' escapes to Canada. In an 1842 address to the New York State Anti-Slavery Convention, white radical Gerrit Smith declared that "the abolitionist has a perfect moral right to go into the South, and use his intelligence to promote the escape of ignorant, and imbruted slaves from their prison-house."[28] When they did so, of course, slaveholders saw it as a blatant attempt to woo away otherwise contented slaves.

Indeed, abolitionist incursions into the South made slaveholders as angry and reactionary as they made abolitionists proud. This equal and opposite reaction is well illustrated by the high-profile legal case of Underground Railroad activist Charles Torrey. In 1844, Torrey was arrested and jailed in Baltimore, Maryland, for his participation in the escape of three runaway slaves to Canada.[29] The *New York Journal of Commerce* expressed sympathy for the slaveholders, explaining, "If the abolition reports say truly, *many hundreds* of slaves have been smuggled off to Canada within the last two or three years, and the act is gloried in as a victorious achievement. It is not strange that the southern people are exasperated by such extensive schemes, and disposed to apply the needful remedies."[30] In this case, the "needful remedy" wound up including tuberculosis. Torrey was sentenced to six years in prison, but died of the disease while incarcerated.[31]

But the *New York Journal of Commerce* was right: abolitionists *did* glory in Torrey's activities as a victorious achievement. Among the more radical ranks of the anti-slavery movement, Torrey was celebrated as a martyr, and his deeds were exaggerated for political effect. In one 1846 article commemorating his life, it was reported that he had been instrumental in the flight of "THREEE [sic] TO FOUR HUNDRED slaves" who were "now on the *free* side of Niagara river."[32] Both the hyperbole and the added emphasis of strategic capitalization bolstered the sense that abolitionists were contributing to massive slave escapes and that the South was experiencing sustained challenges below the Mason–Dixon Line.[33] While slaveholders could rely on slave-catchers and vigilance patrols to retrieve their "property" from northern states, abolitionists' celebration of successful escapes to Canada particularly aggravated enslavers by underscoring their inability to pursue escapees across the international border.

However, white abolitionists were not the only ones responsible for helping enslaved people to escape from southern bondage. In some cases, individuals who had already made their way to freedom returned to the South, carrying with them critical information about freedom in Canada – as well as how to get there. Like Harriet Tubman, famous for her repeated returns to guide others to freedom, prominent self-emancipated men like Josiah Henson and Henry Bibb also helped those in bondage free themselves. In a narrative of his escape published in 1849, Henry Bibb recalled having no map or direction to Canada and having to rely on the assistance he received along the way. Once he had made it, he was eager to share his knowledge and encouragement with others. Returning to Kentucky in an effort to liberate his wife, Melinda, Bibb suffered through repeated recaptures and escapes. In one episode, a field slave snuck him a bite to eat. To thank the man for his kindness, Bibb "instructed him with regard to liberty, Canada, the way of escape, and the facilities by the way." The man, in turn, "pledged his word that himself and others would be in Canada, in less than six months from that day."[34]

Meanwhile, Josiah Henson made more than one trip back from Canada to Maryland and Kentucky in order to help others escape, expressing pleasure that he was able to assist those with "the spirit to make the attempt." "I knew the route pretty well," he recalled in 1849, "and had much greater facilities for travelling than when I came out of that Egypt for the first time."[35]

The return and assistance of self-emancipated individuals like Henson and Bibb contributed to what historian Phillip Troutman has called "geopolitical literacy," an understanding of the world beyond the plantation that allowed enslaved people to dream of places as far away as Canada. They often had enough information about the wider world to create "conceptual maps of slavery and freedom," which shaped how runaways determined where to go and what they hoped to find.[36] Unsurprisingly, widely read anecdotes such as those shared by Josiah Henson and Henry Bibb unsettled slaveholders, as they proved that many enslaved people dreamed of freedom long before executing an escape plan – and that they were ready to help other slaves do the same. Each successful escape to Canada could easily lead to more.

Hoping to discredit slaves' belief that Canada was a destination worth running to, many enslavers fabricated lies about it. Black emigrants reported that slaveholders and "others of kindred spirit" had "industriously circulated" misinformation in the late 1830s.[37] One self-emancipated man from Virginia reported that slaves were led to believe that no crop but rice would grow there and that "the wild geese were so numerous in Canada, and so bad, that they would scratch a man's eyes out."[38]

More insidiously, slaveholders played on enslaved people's fears in an effort to dismantle any dreams they had of finding freedom across the international border. A self-emancipated man named Lewis Clarke recalled the visceral fear that slaveholders were able to instill. He had been told that abolitionists waylaid slaves on their way to Canada in order to sell them to Louisiana or Mississippi. He had heard that when Canadians got hold of runaway slaves, they skinned their heads "and wear the wool on their coat collars." If caught in Canada, the British put out slaves' eyes and put them to work in mines for life. They ate young slaves. Red Coats (the symbol of the British armed forces) signaled "sure death."

Recognizing that these ideas likely sounded "ridiculous to a well-informed person," Clarke reminded readers that slaves, no matter what they hoped to find, had no way of knowing for sure what awaited them beyond the international border. "How does he know," Clarke asked, "what or whom to believe?"[39] For some, it seemed the slaveholders' propensity to go overboard in their descriptions was answer enough:

one ex-slave autobiographer reported that enslaved people "knew Canada was a good country ... because master was so anxious that we should not go there."[40] Yet for many, like Lewis Clarke himself, enslavers' "horrid stories" stuck with them well after they had made it. Clarke described traveling in a state of near-debilitating fear until he ran into two black soldiers outside the town of Chatham in Upper Canada.[41]

Even as Canada became a powerful and unmistakable symbol of freedom within the anti-slavery movement, however, enslaved people's geopolitical literacy was not restricted to the U.S.–Canada border. After all, as historian Sean Kelley suggests, "slaves were among the world's most persistent border crossers."[42] In the 1830s and 1840s, slaves, slaveholders, and anti-slavery advocates were all very much aware that there were a growing number of international free-soil borders for runaways to cross in a bid for freedom.

The British West Indies had proven to be a major thorn in slaveholders' sides. New Providence (the Bahamas), Bermuda, and Jamaica were within spitting distance of the Atlantic sea route taken by American slave-traders who regularly ferried enslaved African Americans from the Upper South to the Lower South as part of the booming domestic slave trade. Even before the British Act of Abolition, anti-slavery sentiment and tense international relations made this proximity perilous for enslavers. In 1831, for example, when the brig *Comet* ran aground off Abaco, in the Bahamas, 146 of the 164 enslaved men, women, and children held captive on board were freed by a British customs-house officer who believed the landing violated the ban on the transatlantic slave trade.[43] After Britain had abolished slavery, several more high-profile incidents on the high seas proved in no uncertain terms to slaveholders that British policy posed a direct threat to Americans' ability to safely conduct the business of slavery.[44]

The first incident took place in February 1834, when thirty-three American slaves were liberated in the Bahamas from a disabled brig, the *Encomium*. Carrying forty-five enslaved people in total, twelve elected to return to the United States, where their fate is unclear.[45] Then, on February 11, 1835, the brig *Enterprise* was forced by a hurricane to seek shelter and provisions in Bermuda. Carrying seventy-eight enslaved people from Alexandria's bustling slave market to Charleston, South

Carolina, the *Enterprise*'s crew did not receive the aid they hoped for from the island's British government. Rather, British customs officials immediately declared those enslaved aboard the vessel free. Supporting this decision, the colonial Chief Justice served a writ of *habeas corpus* commanding the enslaved men, women, and children to appear in court to state whether they wanted to remain in freedom in Bermuda or continue, as planned, to Charleston as slaves. With the intriguing exception of one woman and her five children, those liberated from the *Enterprise* asserted their preference to remain free in Bermuda. After the Chief Justice freed the seventy-two who chose to stay, the Attorney General then took up a general subscription to help support the new residents "until they began to feel their way, and had obtained employment."[46]

Both in the act of freeing the enslaved passengers and in helping to ease their transition into a new society, the colonial agents in the Bahamas and Bermuda made it clear that the British government would not hesitate to apply the spirit of its act of emancipation to all who crossed their West Indian colonial borders. The British islands were free soil.

American slaveholders and their political champions were incensed. Although Secretary of State John Forsyth and three separate ambassadors to Britain had been quietly (and unsuccessfully) attempting to achieve restitution for the liberated *Comet* and *Encomium* slaves since the incidents took place, the *Enterprise* brought the issue of Britain seizing American slaves into the limelight of national pro-slavery politics. The North Carolina legislature, for one, passed resolutions excoriating the British for freeing enslaved American "property," considering the act "nothing less than legalized robbery."[47]

Upon discovering that the British had failed to respond to diplomatic overtures regarding the recent cases, pro-slavery senator John C. Calhoun of South Carolina issued a fiery repudiation of what he saw as a clear offense against the law of nations. It was abundantly clear to Calhoun that the ships – sailing from one American port to another – were under the protection of the United States even when they were forced by "stress of weather" into foreign ports. By refusing to offer financial and diplomatic redress, he believed the British were blatantly applying their own anti-slavery principles to the United States and its citizens. He could countenance the fact that the British would violate both the law of nations and the "rights which the laws of humanity extend to the unfortunate in their situation" only by assuming that the British government was unwilling to offend the anti-slavery feelings of its subjects ("blind and misguided as they are") at the expense of American property rights. Characterizing these cases as an outright attack on American slavery, he vowed to bring the case before Congress on an annual basis as long as he held a seat in the Senate.[48]

Eventually, the British did capitulate to American diplomacy, but in such a way that covered the nick but left the wound. In 1839, the British government agreed to pay the aggrieved slaveholders compensation for the loss of the liberated individuals in each of the episodes that preceded August 1, 1834. Noting that the seizure of the slaves was, perhaps, "wrongful[ly] and prejudicial[ly]" conducted by a "functionary of the British Government," the British government agreed to pay $477 for each slave freed from the brigs *Comet* and *Encomium*.[49]

However, when the *Enterprise* was forced into a Bermudan harbor in 1835, British emancipation had already been enacted. Pursuant to the opinions that the Law Officers of the Crown first expressed in December 1836, the British government refused to compensate American slaveholders for the seventy-two individuals freed from the *Enterprise*. As soon as the ship crossed into British territory, the Law Officers stated, the slaveholders were not in lawful possession of the slaves, and the enslaved individuals themselves had "acquired rights which the Courts [in Bermuda] were bound to recognize and protect."[50]

Just as the *New York Journal of Commerce* forewarned when the incident first occurred, it seemed that the British liberation of American slaves in the West Indies would "doubtless continue to be repeated as often as [they] shall by accident or otherwise, be found in British ports."[51]

The case of Madison Washington and the brig *Creole* brought Britain's commitment to maintaining its free-soil policy in the West Indies straight to the fore of the American anti-slavery struggle. On November 9, 1841, Madison Washington and eighteen other enslaved men violently rebelled against the crew of the *Creole* while en route from Virginia to New Orleans. They directed the ship (carrying 135 enslaved individuals in total) directly to Nassau, where they knew they would be legally freed and protected.[52] But the incident did not end there. The case quickly turned into a protracted diplomatic crisis in which Secretary of State Daniel Webster repeatedly tried to demand redress from the British government on behalf of the slaveholders. As in the earlier cases, such efforts were ultimately unsuccessful.

American slaveholders were furious that the British had once again freed a ship full of slaves in the West Indies and that it seemed, yet again, there was nothing they could do about it. And the case of the *Creole* was the result of a shipboard slave uprising, not inclement weather, so the actions of the British infuriated American slaveholders exponentially more. As the *Mobile Journal* of Alabama worried, the result would be the opening of a "harbor ... where runaways, mutineers and murderers will be received and protected by an alien sovereign."[53] Not only did the officials' decision tacitly condone the use of violence by runaway slaves in their efforts to cross British free-soil borders, abolitionists' support of the "Immortal Nineteen," as Madison Washington and his compatriots became known, was an ominous indication of increasing abolitionist comfort with violence as a legitimate anti-slavery tactic.[54]

As much as the *Creole* rebellion highlighted the significance of maritime borders in free-soil politics, it was also another troubling example of the threat posed by runaway slaves' geopolitical literacy. Prior to leading the shipboard rebellion, Madison Washington had already liberated himself from slavery in Virginia and made his way to Canada. There, he had lived for a time with the renowned Hiram Wilson in early 1840. He had then returned to the United States in an ill-fated attempt to liberate his wife. When he was recaptured and placed aboard the *Creole*, abolitionists understood quite well why he had been sent via the domestic slave trade to New Orleans: "It is the custom with slaveholders in the more northern States," explained *The Friend of Man*, "to send the fugitive when secured by them to the extreme South – lest he escape again – lest he communicate to other slaves the incidents of his day of freedom." Selling a recaptured runaway into the slave market of the lethal Deep South was supposed to serve as "an example that shall strike terror to the breast of his fellows" – and prevent the individual from spreading information about their flight to free soil.[55] When slaveholders' efforts to isolate

Madison Washington and his knowledge of British free soil backfired so spectacularly, it only underscored the danger of having multiple free-soil borders adjacent to the United States.

While the *Creole* rebellion remained a touchstone episode for both anti-slavery and pro-slavery advocates for the duration of the antebellum period, it was certainly not the only successful maritime escape to the British West Indies. In 1843, seven enslaved crew members of an ocean-going vessel were able to steal themselves a boat and sail 100 miles from St. Augustine, Florida, to Nassau in the Bahamas. They instigated yet another cause célèbre for slaveholders incensed by international free-soil border crossings.[56] And just one year later, at the very same time that Charles Torrey sat in a Baltimore jail in 1844 for helping runaway slaves escape to Canada, a ship captain named Jonathan Walker awaited trial in Pensacola, Florida, for bringing escaped slaves to the West Indies.[57]

This "saltwater railroad," as scholars Irvin Winsboro and Joe Knetsch have dubbed it,[58] remained insignificant in terms of how many enslaved people actually liberated themselves by escaping to the British Caribbean. However, each episode loomed large in the United States because of the high-profile diplomatic cases that unfolded around them and the sense of crisis they inspired among southern slaveholders. Remembering when he was shipped along the Atlantic coast to New Orleans, a self-emancipated man named William Grose recalled that the ship's captain ordered all seventy slaves below deck with the hatches battened when foul weather blew the ship "near an English island." The captain wanted to ensure that no slave would get the notion to abandon ship and swim for their freedom.[59] With the maritime borders of the West Indies beckoning, Britain was officially protecting American slaves along two distinct borders of the United States – a fact that enraged slaveholders to no end.

Fugitive slaves also regularly ran across the southwest border to Mexico throughout the 1830s and 1840s. There, however, they exacerbated tensions regarding another controversial space: Texas. Although no organized settlement or emigration plans for free African Americans had been pursued after Benjamin Lundy's failed attempts in the 1830s (see Chapter 3), Mexico's free-soil reputation had only grown among enslaved people in the Lower South and Southwest.[60] Since abolishing slavery in all territories except Texas in 1829, Mexico's anti-slavery politics made the international border a beacon of liberty.

Before the Texas Revolution, self-emancipated people ran to Mexican Texas from Louisiana and away from the control of American colonists in Texas by slipping into Mexican towns and cities further to the south. Although Mexico did not institute an official free-soil policy until 1857, officials did offer aid in many cases – in part to support their own geopolitical agenda. In 1834, for example, the Mexican Secretary of State sent classified instructions to Mexico's U.S. ambassador indicating that the president hoped to recruit African Americans to help contain the ongoing threat of Comanche raiders in northern Mexico. In exchange, Mexico would offer equal rights, land, and protection.[61]

Then, when armed conflict erupted against American colonists in Texas, Mexico encouraged enslaved people to make their way to the Mexican army in exchange for freedom. While there was no consistent military policy guaranteeing liberation – a fact that resulted in some runaways being returned to Anglo slaveholders as the Mexican army retreated – runaway men and women fought and spied for the Mexican army during the Texas Revolution and joined the lines of Mexican soldiers when they eventually retreated to the south.[62]

After Texas became an independent republic in 1836, runaway slaves had further to go. From San Antonio, self-liberated slaves could make it to the Mexican state of Coahuila to the southwest if they successfully navigated through the dangerous Nueces Strip, a stretch of land between the Nueces River and the Rio Grande known for its rough-and-tumble lawlessness.[63] Or, traveling several hundred miles south along the eastern coast of the Gulf of Mexico, they might make it to the state of Tamaulipas. But even when they made it into Mexican territory, the border between the United States and Mexico was not the impermeable boundary between slavery and freedom that the U.S.–Canada border represented. Without any affirmative free-soil policy prior to 1857, slave-hunters regularly made forays beyond the border of the Republic of Texas to reclaim fugitives from bondage.

Self-emancipated men and women in the disputed borderland between the Republic of Texas and Mexico lived a perilous existence with neither state protection nor philanthropic intervention of the sort found in Canada. Those who were able to make it across the dangerous Rio Grande to places like the Mexican town of Matamoros or further south to Tampico (both in the state of Tamaulipas) could blend into the region's sizeable black population and live in relative safety. But those who remained in border towns like Piedras Negras (a major point of entry for runaways into the state of Coahuila) faced hard lives of uncertainty and, often, poverty.[64]

Nevertheless, the Texas revolt only strengthened abolitionist sentiment in Mexico, and at least 2,000 self-emancipated slaves took refuge there in the 1840s. There was no organized network of sympathetic allies to help guide runaways through unfamiliar and hostile territory, but those who risked the many perils of running through Texas to Mexico helped to spread geographical information about how to navigate the dangerous borderlands to liberty. As a result, self-emancipation across the southwestern border became such a problem for slaveholders that by 1839 the Texas Congress legislated fines to the tune of $500–$1,000 for helping runaway slaves. In 1844, the legislature allowed anyone who captured a runaway slave west of the San Antonio River (between the San Antonio and the Rio Grande) to charge $50 as a reward.[65]

By the time tension with U.S. slaveholders erupted in conflict yet again in the mid-1840s, the issue of slavery and anti-slavery in the Southwest had escalated to become a major geopolitical issue in North America. For several years, pro-slavery politicians had been advocating for the annexation of Texas to the United States as a way to protect slaveholders' interests and what they saw as the future of the U.S. agricultural economy (cotton). They feared, and not without reason, that encroaching Mexican and British abolitionism would take hold in Texas if something was not done to prevent it. Pro-slavery men like John C. Calhoun were convinced that British abolition, in particular, was part of a grand conspiracy to weaken the United States, and they were enraged to discover that the British were pressuring Mexico to leverage diplomatic recognition in exchange for the abolition of slavery in the new Republic of Texas.[66]

In a scathing letter to British envoy Richard Packenham, Calhoun declared it the sacred duty of the United States to annex Texas in order to halt the spread of abolitionism. Launching an impassioned comparison between slave states and free, he argued that former slaves had suffered as a consequence in every state where slavery had been abolished. "What is called slavery," he concluded, "is in reality a political institution, essential to the peace, safety, and prosperity of those states of the Union in which it exists." He declared that if the British refused to confine their abolitionism to their own territory, the United States had no choice but to annex Texas for their own protection.[67]

Slaveholders like Calhoun were right to recognize that they were in imminent danger of being surrounded by anti-slavery governments. As a Texan diplomatic representative in London worried, it seemed that Britain wanted to "make Texas a refuge for runaway slaves from the United States and eventually a Negro nation, a sort of Hayti on the continent."[68] Ceaselessly antagonized by adjacent British free-soil borders to the north and maritime east, the possibility of encirclement should Texas fall prey to anti-slavery maneuvering felt real and deeply threatening. And Mexico, for its part, did view abolitionism favorably as a way to weaken Texas after losing the territory in the recent revolution. To protect their interests, enslavers recognized, Texas could not become another Canada. The fear of anti-slavery intervention from all sides – which would amount to a protracted attack on the slaveholding economy of the United States – thus moved pro-slavery activists to support a geopolitical gambit that embroiled the United States in a war with Mexico over the annexation of Texas.[69]

Abolitionists, of course, fully understood why pro-slavery politicians saw the annexation of Texas as a bulwark against the encroachment of abolitionism: shoring up slavery in Texas would strengthen the institution throughout the southwest.[70] But they were of two minds on whether or not the possibility of annexation was necessarily opposed to their own interests. Some, like abolitionist Charles Lenox Remond, relished in slaveholders' increasing sense of isolation:

> To whom should the slaveholders look for sympathy, co-operation, and support, in their endeavors to keep these wretches in bondage? Will they look to the free states? Certainly not, for the very deed of dissolution precludes the possibility of that. Will they look to Mexico? No; for the Mexicans regard them with an eye of the rankest jealousy. Will they look to

Canada? The thought is absurd. Will they look to the West Indies? What! ask men who are themselves but just liberated to aid in forging chains for other wretches![71]

Activists of Remond's ilk opposed Texas annexation. They saw the idea as an obnoxious final act of slaveholder defiance in the face of the anti-slavery sentiment and policies making rapid headway throughout the Atlantic.

However, many conservative anti-slavery reformers saw things differently. Applying the same logic that kept them in favor of moderate anti-slavery measures and institutions like the American Colonization Society, conservative reformers construed the annexation of Texas as a long-term, gradual move toward the end of slavery. At an 1846 government convention held in Hillsborough, New Hampshire, for example, the attendees agreed among themselves that annexation would result in the transfer to Texas of "a considerable portion of the slaves in Maryland, Virginia, North Carolina, Kentucky, and Tennessee." They expected that this dispersal would "prepare the way" for abolition in the states sending their slaves to Texas, and that it would eventually create more free states within the union. Never addressing the haunting specter of mass sale and forced migration that such a transfer would entail, they simply hoped it would "render voluntary emancipation less objectionable" because slaves would be scattered over a larger swath of territory and less likely to form a large community of black people in any given area once freed.[72]

In one regard, they were right. The annexation of Texas in the aftermath of the U.S.–Mexican War (1846–1848) *did* lead to the transfer of slaves into Texas territory. Between 1850 and 1860, the enslaved population of Texas increased from 58,161 to 182,566.[73] This movement did not, however, inspire slaveholders from other states to relinquish their slave "property" or feel any kindlier toward the addition of more free states into the union.

Whether they supported annexation or not, it was clear to Americans that slavery in Texas, the future of slavery in the United States, and the issue of runaway slaves crossing adjacent international free-soil borders were all at stake when tensions between the United States and Mexico devolved into war from 1846 to 1848. For abolitionists, in particular, the

U.S.–Mexican War and the bid for the annexation of Texas seemed like the culmination of several decades' worth of the national government operating on behalf of sectional slavery. Only a few years earlier, during the diplomatic fallout of the *Enterprise* and *Creole* affairs, leading abolitionists had begun to reflect at length on what they saw as the U.S. government's increasing willingness to "spread a shield over American slavery abroad as well as at home."[74] As William Lloyd Garrison lamented, "Even American diplomacy must be made subservient to the interests of the slaveholders, and republican ambassadors must bear to foreign courts the wailings of our government for the escape of human property."[75]

Abolitionists were enraged that the American federal government consistently threw its weight behind the slaveholders during diplomatic crises. As tensions heightened, publications by individuals like Congressman Joshua R. Giddings, Bostonian Loring Moody, and New York State judge William Jay all began in earnest to explore the connections between the federal government's efforts on behalf of slaveholders, its efforts to force free states to assist in the recapture of fugitive slaves, and the brewing conflict with Mexico.[76] The most widely read among these indictments of the federal government's pro-slavery history was William Jay's 1839 *A View of the Action of the Federal Government in Behalf of Slavery*. It proved so popular that it was reprinted at length in the anti-slavery press and republished in 1844 with up-to-date additions.[77] Bringing together diplomatic correspondence, congressional records, legal codes, and statistical data, Jay showed in no uncertain terms that American foreign policy throughout the first decades of the nineteenth century had been decidedly and unremittingly pro-slavery.

Jay left no stone unturned. He deftly illuminated how significantly slaveholders' fears regarding self-emancipation and free soil had directed the federal government's defense of slavery at home and abroad. His evidence was wide-ranging and disturbing. He narrated the proceedings of Henry Clay and Albert Gallatin's failed diplomatic efforts to secure a treaty for the return of fugitive slaves from Canada in the late 1820s (see Chapter 2); he related a story from 1816 of the American military massacring over 200 runaway slaves in a fort where they had found sanctuary in Spanish Florida; he documented the federal government's efforts to negotiate compensation for American slaves freed by the British in the West Indies; he exposed evidence that the U.S. government had threatened to go to war with Mexico and Colombia in defense of Cuban slavery during the Spanish–American independence wars; and he elucidated the pro-slavery reasoning for the United States' quick recognition of Texan independence in 1836 relative to its longstanding refusal to formally recognize the nation of Haiti.

In drawing a clear connection between these episodes and the growing tension at the U.S.–Mexico border, Jay reminded readers that the fear of black freedom and self-emancipation abroad had long influenced the U.S. government's actions. In this context, the annexation of Texas was simply a culmination of foreign policy agendas well established at other international free-soil borders.

When the U.S.–Mexican War came to a close in 1848 with the Treaty of Guadalupe Hidalgo, Mexico acknowledged its loss of Texas and the United States acquired vast new territories in the west and southwest. In turn, however, these new acquisitions sent the federal government scrambling to establish some sort of sectional balance in relation to slavery and political power in the United States. In short order, slaveholders' multifaceted fears regarding the political and economic implications of the United States' southwest border in Texas morphed into a domestic crisis over the expansion of slavery and the growing influence of the so-called "Slave Power." Fierce congressional debate eventually led to the Compromise of 1850, a package of legislative bills intended to craft a balance between the competing – and increasingly hostile – interests of pro-slavery and anti-slavery advocates.

Yet even as politicians, lobbyists, and a passionate citizenry undertook the protracted negotiations that eventually led to the entry of Texas, California, Utah, and New Mexico into the United States, runaway slaves continued to flee across the United States' free-soil borders. Slavery had been fortified in Texas, but there was a steady leak. Canada continued to open its arms to hundreds of self-emancipated men and women each year. Although the vast majority of those who liberated themselves from bondage ultimately ended their journeys in the northern states, Canada remained a dominant international destination for escaped slaves. Its importance as a haven beyond the power of slaveholders had taken on a life of its own – and it was only growing.

As self-emancipation increasingly radicalized enslavers by the end of the decade, it is no surprise that southern congressmen fought tooth and nail for a draconian new Fugitive Slave Act to be included in the Compromise of 1850. War with Mexico had bought slaveholders time, but Canada was still a constant reminder that abolitionist sentiment was closing in.

CHAPTER 7

Free Soil, Fiction, and the Fugitive Slave Act

Yes, Melina, it was a leap for freedom. I've said "master" for the last time. I'm free; I'm bound for Canada.

~ Glen, from *The Escape; or, A Leap for Freedom*, a play
by William Wells Brown (1858)[1]

* * *

There is no country in the world so much hated by slaveholders, as Canada; nor is there any country so much beloved and sought for, by the slaves. These two feel thus oppositely towards our fair province for the same reason – IT IS A FREE COUNTRY.

~ Samuel Ringgold Ward, *Autobiography of a Fugitive Negro* (1855)[2]

In the summer of 1851, a white northerner by the name of Harriet Beecher Stowe took the American anti-slavery scene by storm with a serialized novel titled *Uncle Tom's Cabin, or Life Among the Lowly*. Published in the anti-slavery newspaper *The National Era*, the highly successful melodrama spanned thirty-six installments, capturing the nation's imagination clear through April 1852. On the heels of this literary triumph, Stowe published the story in two bound volumes. She sold 50,000 copies of her book in just eight weeks, and 1 million copies sold in the first year alone.[3]

No contribution to American anti-slavery was more widely read or influential than *Uncle Tom's Cabin*. As Joshua R. Giddings, the well-known abolitionist statesman from Ohio, declared on the floor of the U.S. House of Representatives in 1852, "a lady with her pen, has done more for the cause of freedom, during the last year, than any savant, statesman, or politician of our land." A decade later, Abraham Lincoln allegedly greeted her by asking if she was "the little woman" who had made the Civil War.[4]

In addition to bringing the anti-slavery cause into homes and hearts across the United States, *Uncle Tom's Cabin* became the touchstone of the anti-slavery cause across the English-speaking Atlantic. Millions of readers in North America and Great Britain cried at the death of little Eva, the young, terminally ill white child who touched the hearts of slaves and slaveholders alike. They held their breath for runaway slave Eliza as she was pursued by a merciless slave-catcher across the frozen Ohio River with her son in her arms. They cheered when she finally reunited with her husband, George. And they celebrated when this brave, self-liberated family crossed Lake Erie into Canada, recognizing that their passage across the international border meant freedom, reunion, and sanctuary. As George so aptly wondered, "What is freedom to a nation, but freedom to the individuals in it?"[5]

Timing is everything. Harriet Beecher Stowe wrote her classic drama of slavery and escape just one year after Congress passed a highly controversial new Fugitive Slave Act. Part of the Compromise of 1850, the law revamped the 1793 Fugitive Slave Clause in the U.S. Constitution. It deputized every American citizen to assist slave-catchers in the recapture of fugitive slaves or risk facing criminal punishment themselves. The law also denied fugitive slaves the right to a trial by jury and suspended their right to *habeas corpus*. These features were particularly ominous for free black people because they stripped them of any means to prove their free status if they were accused of being fugitive slaves.

The Fugitive Slave Act of 1850 was a disaster. In effect, it made the fragile freedom found by self-emancipated men and women in the northern states more perilous, it compounded free black northerners' vulnerability to being kidnapped into southern slavery, and it generally heightened sectional tensions between North and South over the expanding national influence of the so-called "Slave Power" of the southern states.[6] For anti-slavery advocates, the law proved once again that the U.S. federal government was committed to prioritizing the interests of slaveholders at the expense of the nation's moral integrity. It was a lightning rod of controversy, fear, and anger that galvanized new forms of action and activism within the anti-slavery movement.

The Fugitive Slave Act immediately made international free-soil havens more important than ever, both as symbols of freedom and as practical destinations where African Americans could flee. The U.S. North, where the vast majority of self-emancipated people had long ended their journeys from bondage, no longer offered a veneer of safety. Helping runaway men and women cross beyond the borders of the United States became a high priority for black activists and white anti-slavery advocates. So, too, did assessing and contributing to their welfare abroad, as they increasingly became viewed as "refugees" from the American slave system and its twin pillar, racism.

Emigrationist fervor of the sort previously expressed in the 1820s and 1830s also re-emerged among free African American communities. Many felt that the Fugitive Slave Act signaled the death knell for any hope they had of achieving social equality and recognition as citizens. African American communities resurrected the longstanding debate over Liberian colonization and resuscitated enthusiasm for free black emigration to Canada. The British West Indies suddenly also found prominent black champions willing to promote emigration to the islands, and free northerners once again found themselves publicly discussing Mexico and Haiti as emigration destinations.

It was right at this fraught socio-political moment that Harriet Beecher Stowe introduced *Uncle Tom's Cabin*, inviting readers to recognize in her beloved characters' harrowing escapes from slavery that freedom could never truly be attained within the United States while the Fugitive Slave Act existed. Not only did her story inaugurate the novel as a new, powerful form of anti-slavery print advocacy, it became a cornerstone feature of transatlantic popular culture in the mid-nineteenth century.[7] The popularity of *Uncle Tom's Cabin* built such momentum that a London newspaper described the phenomenon at the time as "Tom-Mania." It was dramatized for the stage, turned into songs, merchandized as collectible commodities, and re-written as derivative new novels seeking to capitalize on the original's success.[8]

Stowe's influence was remarkable. At the 1853 National Colored Convention, black leaders recognized *Uncle Tom's Cabin*'s astronomical popularity for instigating a "propitious awakening to the fact of our condition at home and abroad." Literary historian Sarah Meer credits the book for having "made the slavery question marketable."[9] Its success even inspired impassioned literary responses from pro-slavery writers. Determined to refute Stowe's depiction of slaveholders' cruelty and disregard for those they enslaved, southern writers produced a canon of books known collectively as "Anti-Tom" literature.[10] Both *Uncle Tom's Cabin*'s popularity and the vehemence of its detractors ensured that Stowe's book remained at the forefront of American ideas regarding slavery and freedom throughout the 1850s.

As it was a guiding light in the anti-slavery movement at mid-century, it is unsurprising – though often overlooked – that international free-soil havens played a critical role in Harriet Beecher Stowe's story. While most of the narrative unfolds in the plantation South, several of its main characters end their journeys by traveling abroad. They also spend substantial time considering where outside the United States might offer them a promising future. In *Uncle Tom's Cabin*, Stowe echoed white and black northerners' concern that neither free nor self-liberated black people were safe in the free states after the 1850 Fugitive Slave Act, and her story provides an illuminating snapshot of how free-soil options outside the United States informed anti-slavery responses to the law.

In Stowe's tale, Eliza and George's family follows in the footsteps of the thousands of real runaway slaves known to have crossed Lake Erie into Upper Canada both before and after the passage of the Fugitive Slave Act.[11] However, while two decades of Upper Canada's prominence within the anti-slavery movement made the far side of the U.S.–Canada border a logical destination for Stowe's characters, they do not remain there. Instead, their fictionalized journey ultimately guides them through a far broader geography of black mobility and emigration. In the kind of coincidence that regularly pushes the novel's plot forward, the reader discovers that George has a sister, Emily, who had been sold south when they were children. Now an adult with a young child of her own, it turns out that "a good and generous man" had purchased her, brought her to the French West Indies (Guadeloupe and Martinique), freed her, and married her. When her husband died, he left Emily with his French surname and a sizeable fortune. So, in the final chapters of the book, Emily decides to track down George and his family. With her daughter, she follows them to Canada, only to discover that they have recently relocated. The family is finally reunited in Montreal.

But the story does not end there. Once together, the whole family decides to relocate yet again, this time to France. This move allows George to attend university, where he obtains "a very thorough education." However, French political strife (likely the 1848 February Revolution) drives the family away from Europe and back to American shores. Once again, they take stock of their options. Despite the fact that their light skin could allow them to pass as white, they have no desire to live as Americans in a land marred by the institution of slavery and the blight of racism. Instead, George wants to cast his lot with "the oppressed, enslaved African race" and search out "an African *nationality*." In a letter to his friend, he considers Haiti, but he ultimately rejects the island republic in favor of relocating to Liberia. At the end of the story, *Uncle Tom's Cabin*'s protagonists embark for a new life in West Africa.[12]

With her characters' mobility and their ability to make considered choices about where they wanted to live, Stowe brought her up-to-date understanding of free-soil geopolitics to millions of readers in the early 1850s. When she reunited George and Eliza's family in Amherstburg, Upper Canada, for example, Stowe drew on the familiar route to freedom symbolized by the Underground Railroad – a concept whose influence on the anti-slavery movement had steadily increased through the 1840s. When they subsequently relocated to Montreal, her characters reflected the fact that new infrastructural changes were leading self-emancipated individuals to new destinations *within* Canada. By 1851, the Vermont Central Railroad connected northern Vermont to Montreal, making it easier for people to make their way to Lower Canada (present-day southern Quebec). At the time, there were only three or four self-emancipated individuals known definitively to live in the city of Montreal, and there were never enough to form the sort of communities and networks that developed in Upper Canada (southern Ontario). Yet Stowe's inclusion of Montreal in her story affirmed for readers that Upper Canada's reputation for protecting runaway slaves was beginning to extend into its neighboring territories.[13]

Furthermore, Stowe's story reflects the fact that France had just enacted universal emancipation in 1848, marking its second (and final) effort to abolish slavery in all its territories. In the story, George values the time his family spent living and learning in France itself, and it was in the French West Indies that his sister was freed and given a substantial inheritance. Through her characters' eyes, Stowe notes that France had recently become an anti-slavery ally akin to Britain, as well as an empire where the humanity of former slaves was universally recognized.[14]

The final leg of her characters' journey, which brought them to Liberia, linked Stowe's transnational exploration of black freedom to one of the most controversial and longstanding free-soil projects in the anti-slavery movement: African colonization. At the time, African colonization was experiencing a mid-century spike in popularity that had begun in the late 1840s due to recent shifts both in the United States and in Liberia itself. In the wake of the U.S.–Mexican War (1846–1848), territorial expansion and increasing westward migration redrew the map of the United States and heightened national anxiety over the future of American slavery. In addition, poor and working-class whites in the late 1840s began to see the American Colonization Society as a viable way to reduce competition for jobs and land. But one of the most notable shifts was that some free African Americans began to express their willingness to reconsider the prospects of Liberian colonization.[15] As of 1847, Liberia was no longer a U.S. colony administered by the ACS. It had become an independent African American republic with African American leadership, and this change encouraged some black leaders to revise their long-held antagonism toward the idea and embrace colonization.[16]

While most black Americans and staunch abolitionists continued to remain firmly opposed to Liberian colonization throughout the antebellum period, the support of even a few vocal black leaders contributed to a general surge of approval toward Liberian colonization at the end of the 1840s. Then, with the passage of the Fugitive Slave Act, the ACS experienced more widespread support and success than it had at any other point in its long history. In 1848, it sent 441 people to Liberia; between 1848 and 1854, it sent a total of 4,010. By comparison, the ACS had only sent a combined 5,829 people to Liberia during the entirety of the previous thirty years.[17] This precipitous rise in support for the ACS, especially among white anti-slavery advocates, was even reflected in the highest echelons of the U.S. government. In 1858, Abraham Lincoln himself asserted that his "first impulse" regarding slavery in the United States would be to free all slaves and send them to Liberia, "their own native land."[18]

Harriet Beecher Stowe's embrace of colonization in *Uncle Tom's Cabin* not only emerged during this widespread renewal of the ACS's popularity, it promoted a specific set of nineteenth-century ideas about black people and black freedom that made Liberian colonization particularly appealing to the white moderates who supported the anti-slavery cause. Through the eyes of her character George, Stowe explores the idea that the "African race has peculiarities, yet to be unfolded," that might never reveal themselves while African Americans remained surrounded by people of European descent. George believes that these "peculiarities" might, in fact, prove to be of a higher moral caliber than those possessed by "Anglo-Saxons," so he expresses his desire to reside in a country composed of black people, where he expects he could reach his full potential.[19] While moderate abolitionists like Stowe saw only the benefits of unfettering African Americans from the pernicious effects of racism by sending them to Africa, the underlying assumption was that African Americans in the United States *were* inferior – although due to circumstance rather than nature.

Moreover, reflecting the deeply embedded racism that many white abolitionists left unexamined, Stowe clarified in her novel that African Americans' racial potential could not be fulfilled just anywhere with a predominantly black population. While considering where he might go, George quickly and disparagingly rejects Haiti as a possible destination. "The race that formed the Haytians was a worn-out and effeminate one," he explains, "that would take centuries to amount to anything."[20] Only in Africa, he believed, could people of African descent achieve their racial potential. Through George and his enthusiastic embrace of Liberia as the future of the black race, Stowe voiced the perspective of many white colonizationists: racial segregation would benefit black people, and it should happen in Africa.[21]

The final idea about black people and black freedom that Harriet Beecher Stowe promoted through her novel was that African Americans in Liberia could be the vanguard of civilizing, republicanizing, and Christianizing Africa. The anti-slavery community – white and black alike – was largely comprised of Christian reformers, and the idea that black people could form a successful colony and bring American values to an "uncivilized" region had appealed to supporters of the ACS from its founding.[22] In fact, Stowe's husband had similarly linked the project of colonization to the project of Christianizing Africa when he had publicly endorsed the ACS in 1834.[23]

The link between colonization and the objectives of spreading Christianity and republicanism had only become stronger over time, and it was readily apparent in Americans' reactions to Liberian independence in 1847. When Liberia's black leaders transformed Liberia into an independent African American nation, it signaled to many observers that the colony had reached its full potential. It seemed that the new nation was now a black counterpart to the United States, and that it was prepared to stand on its own while extending Christianity and republican values throughout Africa. While many African Americans on both sides of the Atlantic remained ambivalent about whether Liberia should, in fact, act as an independent extension of the United States, the prospect of bringing Christian values to Africa was a major consideration for many prominent colonists who decided to relocate in the nineteenth century.[24]

For some, however, the idea that colonization could bolster Christianity and republicanism in Africa served an additional purpose. It dovetailed with the particular interests of religious white reformers who opposed slavery but abhorred the notion of living intermixed with a free black population. In a strikingly ambivalent caption for an illustration in the 1853 edition of *Uncle Tom's Cabin*, an artist named Hammatt Billings captured the colonizationist impulse with the title "Freedom to Africa" (Figure 3). For some anti-slavery advocates, Liberian colonization was a way to *bring* the freedom of Christian faith and republican values to an "uncivilized" continent. Like George, they saw colonization as a way to "roll the tide of civilization and Christianity along [Africa's] shores and plant there mighty republics."[25] For more conservative anti-slavery advocates, however, colonization offered the added benefit of providing a place to *send* freed black people so as to remove them permanently from the United States. "Freedom to Africa" could easily be read as both a liberationist theology for uplifting Africa and a call to action for relocating free black people.

3 "Freedom to Africa." Headpiece illustration by Hammatt Billings. *Uncle Tom's Cabin; or, Life Among the Lowly*, Illustrated Edition (Boston, MA: John P. Jewett, 1853). Courtesy of the William L. Clements Library, University of Michigan.

Stowe took pride in her moderate approach to such topics. Among *Uncle Tom's Cabin*'s achievements, she appreciated that it "soften[ed] and moderate[d] the bitterness of feeling in *extreme abolitionists*." She liked that it converted people to anti-slavery who had previously been repelled by the passion and radicalism of those who demanded immediate emancipation.[26] However, while her novel certainly bolstered the anti-slavery cause immensely, Stowe's advocacy of Liberian colonization – a project long associated with moderate anti-slavery sentiment – provoked criticism from some of her more radical counterparts. Although history remembers *Uncle Tom's Cabin* as one of the most important publications of the anti-slavery movement, many abolitionists at the time questioned whether the anti-slavery community should endorse her work at all.

The stakes were high. While abolitionists largely embraced the novel for its resounding indictment of American slavery, many accused Stowe of directly and substantially contributing to the growth of colonization-ism.[27] In a public exchange of letters between Frederick Douglass and his more radical colleague, Martin Delany, Delany questioned whether Stowe actually felt sympathy for black people at all beyond the injustice of their enslavement in the South. Delany pointed out that Stowe "sneer[ed] at Hayti – the only truly free and independent civilized black nation" and held the "little dependent colonization settlement of Liberia in high estimation." It was hypocritical, he declared, that black Americans and their white allies would overlook her advocacy of coloni-zation after spending decades fighting the white-led ACS. Delany, for his part, refused to do so. Stowe's "world-renowned and widely circulated work," in his estimation, reflected an anti-slavery ideology heavily invested in maintaining "white men's power."[28]

Meanwhile, prominent white abolitionist Henry C. Wright publicly denounced *Uncle Tom's Cabin* and Harriet Beecher Stowe for being just as blameworthy as Henry Clay, the architect of the Compromise of 1850, and Daniel Webster, the famed Massachusetts statesman who had turned his back on his anti-slavery constituents by endorsing the legislation. Stowe, Wright opined, "could paint the horrors of a slave auction and a slave plantation," but her support of colonization made her "but a counterpart of Henry Clay and Daniel Webster, whose names, on the records of eternity, will stand first on the list of unscrupulous tyrants, of despisers of humanity, and blasphemers against God."[29]

Other abolitionists defended Stowe's novel, however, believing that it brought much-needed support for the abolitionist cause. In responding to Henry C. Wright's critique, a writer who went by the moniker "Fair Play" noted that he did not believe Stowe's "error" in advocating colonization was a damning one. Fair Play pointed to African Americans' general approbation of *Uncle Tom's Cabin* to prove that the book's views on colonization could easily be dismissed as inconsequential.[30] Frederick Douglass – himself an avowed anti-emigrationist and anti-colonizationist – agreed. In his response to Martin Delany's letter about Harriet Beecher Stowe's embrace of colo-nization, Douglass expressed his wholehearted embrace of Stowe's anti-slavery activism. "Whoever will bring a straw's weight of influence to break the chains of our brother bondmen, or whisper one word of encouragement and sympathy to our proscribed race in the North," he wrote, "shall be welcomed by us to that philanthropic field of labor." Douglass saw strategic value in overlooking the contents of George's "brief letter" endorsing Liberia at the end of *Uncle Tom's Cabin*. It was much wiser, he averred, to capitalize on Stowe's unparalleled potential to build American support for the anti-slavery cause.[31]

In the end, Douglass's view predominated and the debate over *Uncle Tom's Cabin*'s Liberian finale lost steam. By contrast, however, public interest in and support for Stowe's characters' *first* stop – Canada – continued to thrive throughout the decade. In light of the controversy surrounding Stowe's embrace of colonization, one observer even wondered why George could not have simply remained there.[32]

Stowe's best-selling novel immortalized Canada in the imagination of readers already steeped in slave escape stories across the northern border. When George, Eliza, and their family crossed Lake Erie to find freedom in Upper Canada, they embodied the Canadian province's longstanding reputation for providing freedom and protection to runaway American slaves.[33] Readers understood perfectly when Stowe described English territory as being "charmed by a mighty spell" that could "dissolve every incantation of slavery." Her characters knew what any northerner and many slaves would have known: Canada's "blessed English shores" promised freedom for those who reached them (Figure 4).[34]

Stowe was deeply indebted to the self-emancipation stories that abounded in the anti-slavery press and drew some of her central source material from it. Perhaps her greatest inspiration came from ex-slave narratives, a powerful genre of nineteenth-century anti-slavery print culture that had become quite popular in the 1840s. Widely circulated in the American North and the broader Anglo-Atlantic among readers sympathetic to anti-slavery views, slave narratives in the 1840s had created, in the words of literary scholar William Andrews, "a growing international literary sensation."[35] But they were not new. Narratives such as Olaudah Equiano's 1789 *Interesting Narrative of the Life of Olaudah Equiano* had captivated readers during Britain's anti-slave trade initiatives of the later eighteenth century. And individuals like Boston King, Venture

4 "The Fugitives Are Safe in a Free Land." Illustration by Hammatt Billings. *Uncle Tom's Cabin*, 1st ed. (Boston, MA: John P. Jewett, 1852). Courtesy of the Newberry Library, Chicago.

Smith, Robert Voorhis, Mary Prince, and Richard Allen had all made similar contributions to the anti-slavery literary landscape between the late eighteenth century and the late 1830s.

In the 1840s, however, the production and circulation of slave narratives had increased dramatically. Whereas seventeen slave autobiographies were published in total between 1800 and 1839, twenty-five were published in the 1840s alone. In fact, genre production rose by nearly 300 percent just from the previous decade.[36] Harnessing the potential to illuminate the deeply personal experience of slavery through the eyes of those most intimately familiar with it, slave narratives in the 1840s were powerful anti-slavery weapons that had a "mass impact on the conscience of antebellum Americans."[37]

Stowe turned to these narratives when writing *Uncle Tom's Cabin* to help keep her dramatization of slavery and escape within the bounds of probability.[38] It was no stretch of the imagination, therefore, when her characters crossed the U.S.–Canada border to make their escape, as several famous producers of ex-slave narratives depicted Canada as a pivotal feature of their journeys from slavery to freedom.[39] As a physical destination and as a symbol of freedom, for example, it was a recurring theme in William Wells Brown's enormously popular 1847 autobiography. William Wells Brown was a runaway slave who rose to prominence in the 1840s with the publication of several editions of his autobiography, as well as a collection of songs and poetry intended for use in anti-slavery meetings. A skilled writer, Brown used his narrative to recount his persistent efforts to escape American slavery in the 1830s. Likely learning about the destination while hired out as a slave on a riverboat plying the Mississippi River, Brown depicted the British province as his inspiration for escaping. He had "heard much about [it] as a place where the slave might live, be free, and be protected."[40]

Throughout his narrative, it was the vision of freedom and protection that drew Brown's gaze northward. "The anxiety to be a freeman would not let me rest day or night," he wrote. "I would dream at night that I was in Canada, a freeman, and on waking in the morning, weep to find myself so sadly mistaken."[41] He hoped to find employment as soon as he arrived, so that he could buy a little farm and earn enough to purchase his sister and brothers out of bondage so they could join him in his "FREE HOME."[42] Brown reminded his readers that the people of the United States boasted of their "freedom" while keeping 3 million of their own citizens in chains. It should come as no surprise, therefore, that an "American citizen was fleeing from a Democratic, Republican, Christian government . . . to receive protection under the monarchy of Great Britain."[43]

Despite his dreams of Canada, however, Brown's narrative actually ends with him resettling in Ohio. Having arrived in Cleveland in the dead of winter, he found Lake Erie too frozen to cross by boat. Without the money to travel to the border crossing at Buffalo, New York, he took temporary employment for the duration of the season. By the time spring came, he felt himself to be "somewhat out of danger" in Cleveland, so he decided to stay and take a job on a lake steamboat. And yet, despite his own escape ending on the U.S. side of Lake Erie, Brown's story remained tethered to Canada. As a steamboat worker on the lake, he ferried sixty-nine self-emancipated individuals to the British free-soil haven between May and December of 1842 alone.[44]

As an autobiographer, Brown's national fame was second only to Frederick Douglass, whose bestselling *Narrative of the Life of Frederick*

Douglass had been published the year before.[45] Brown's was similarly well received. He sold 8,000 copies of his narrative in its first eighteen months, and, two years later (1849), he published a fourth edition replete with runaway slave advertisements, news clippings, and other items that linked his personal story to the broader narrative of fugitive slaves trying to forge a meaningful freedom for themselves in North America.[46] Due to his high profile as an anti-slavery writer, orator, and activist, Americans listened when Brown pointed to Canada as the country "where we are free and slaves no more."[47]

The British province was similarly prominent in the narrative of Henry Bibb, a self-emancipated man who, in 1849, published an account of his escape to Canada.[48] Bibb had been closely aligned in the 1840s with the politics and anti-slavery efforts of the Liberty Party and the Free Soil Party. His political activism had already stirred substantial interest in his narrative well before he put pen to paper. He had first begun narrating the facts of his escape while touring on the anti-slavery lecture circuit in 1845, but the drama of his account strained the credulity of prominent men like the white abolitionist James G. Birney. Describing himself as a "notorious runaway," Bibb's unquenchable desire to live free in Canada – and help others do the same – resulted in perilous adventure after perilous adventure. Concerned about the veracity of his story, a committee of anti-slavery advocates was formed to interrogate Bibb and solicit information from people who could corroborate his tale. Eventually, the committee offered its endorsement of Bibb's story, and when Bibb wrote his autobiography in 1849, the narrative of his odyssey from slavery to freedom in Canada was widely read and published internationally in multiple editions.[49]

But the slave narrative that received the most widespread credit for having inspired *Uncle Tom's Cabin* was produced by Josiah Henson, who dictated his story to abolitionist Arthur Phelps from his home in Upper Canada. From his narrative, readers learned of Henson's escape from slavery in 1830, the years he spent working side by side with Hiram Wilson for the uplift of black emigrants in Canada, and the fact that he was among the earliest individuals to settle at Dawn when the British American Institute opened in 1842. In one memorable passage,

Henson recalled his relief upon crossing the border at Buffalo. He felt such jubilation at having achieved his dream of reaching Canada that he threw himself to the ground and gave in to a "riotous exultation of [his] feelings." His "sundry antics" quite astonished onlookers.[50] Replete with high-stakes drama and passion, Henson's narrative sold 6,000 copies to northern readers within three years of its publication in 1849. It quickly achieved international fame when it was suggested that his narrative inspired Stowe.[51]

Although Stowe staunchly maintained that her characters were not intended as portraits of any particular individuals, notable plot developments closely resembled the widely circulated narratives, and anti-slavery readers easily recognized parallels between *Uncle Tom's Cabin* and the stories of men like Josiah Henson. Stowe even acknowledged her debt to him and other famous runaway slaves in her 1853 companion publication, *The Key to Uncle Tom's Cabin*.[52] Their heart-stopping narratives of self-emancipation anchored her moving, moralizing tale in the real-life experience of slavery, escape, and the desire to live in freedom and safety away from the reach of slave-catchers.

The 1850 Fugitive Slave Act immediately made the difference between liminal freedom in the northern free states and full, protected freedom under the British flag more significant than ever. In its wake, African Americans relocated to Canada in greater numbers and at a substantially higher rate than they went anywhere else outside the United States. In the late 1840s, an estimated 20,000 black emigrants lived in Upper Canada (which was officially redesignated Canada West from 1841 to 1861). By 1852, the estimate had risen to 30,000. By 1855, estimates suggested there were 35,000–40,000 black emigrants living in the province, and the population by the end of the decade may have been as high as 60,000. The vast majority of these emigrants were self-emancipated slaves. In fact, one estimate suggested that free-born individuals in the entire province of Canada West numbered no more than 3,000, not including children.[53]

Of course, the number of self-emancipated individuals making successful crossings to Canada should not overshadow the fact that approximately 3 million remained enslaved in the United States or the fact that the crossing itself was filled with peril. In his 1855 autobiography, the well-known ex-slave Samuel Ringgold Ward reminded readers of the "thousands of obstacles" facing every fugitive slave on their journey northward: cold, wet, hunger, betrayal, and bloodhounds were just a few of the possible threats that could doom a person on the run.[54] While overall numbers of escapees, as well as abolitionists' celebration of each triumphant escape, promoted the image of a robust and regular Underground Railroad across the U.S.–Canada border, enslaved people themselves never forgot the enormous dangers risked by self-emancipation.

Moreover, Canada was not the only place that people ran in the wake of the Fugitive Slave Act. In the southwest, for example, as many as 4,000 people emancipated themselves by crossing into Mexico between 1850 and 1855.[55] An official report indicated that in just the one border town of Matamoros, where Benjamin Lundy had been so favorably impressed by the small-but-thriving black community in the 1830s, there were at least 201 "negroes" and 250 "mulattoes" by 1853.[56] In the wake of Mexico's massive territorial loss to the United States after the Mexican–American War, many Mexican officials and inhabitants were only too happy – when they could – to protect runaways from American slave-catchers.[57]

Free and self-emancipated men and women also made the transatlantic journey to England in order to escape the threat of the Fugitive Slave Act. Whereas few had previously left for Great Britain, what historian R. J. M. Blackett describes as a flood made their way there after 1850 – enough to warrant the formation of a society in London to help them find jobs and ease resettlement.[58] Perhaps most famous among them were William and Ellen Craft, who, two years earlier, had escaped to Philadelphia from a Georgia plantation. Because Ellen was able to pass as white, they dressed her as a slave owner and William as her valet in a bold four-day journey to freedom. Now, imperiled by the Fugitive Slave Act, they left by steamship for England, where they remained for nineteen years.[59]

Nonetheless, the numbers of people going to Mexico and Great Britain paled in comparison with those going to Canada, even if one accounts for inevitable number inflation in population estimates for such a highly politicized group of people. Unless one lived in the deep southwest, Canada seemed to be the most clear-cut destination for those seeking to escape the reach of the Fugitive Slave Act. "Here men of families with limited means can come, when it would be out of the question for them to go to a more distant abode," suggested a report on emigration. "Here the panting fugitive has come, is coming, and will come, by means of the Underground Railroad, for they all know the way."[60]

For many of the self-liberated men and women who fled to Canada in the wake of the Fugitive Slave Act, this was not their first journey. They had already made their way out of slavery and had been living in the northern free states – which had long been the terminus for the vast majority of self-emancipated people escaping slavery. Many had been there for years, having built homes, made families, and established themselves among neighbors. While many of these northern communities had previously provided a sense of safety and protection, the Fugitive Slave Act now placed residents at a substantially higher risk of recapture. The famous abolitionist newspaper *The Liberator* reported that while "colored citizens" were meeting in groups across the North to commit themselves to "maintain[ing] their rights at all hazards," runaway slaves were "very naturally getting wrought up to the highest pitch of desperation."[61]

Self-emancipated people living in the North were faced with the terrible choice of staying put, potentially at risk of recapture, or leaving their homes. For many, the choice was clear. In just one issue of his paper from late 1850, William Lloyd Garrison included two statements from Pittsburgh about the exodus of fugitive slaves from the North. The first reported that "nearly all the waiters in the hotels have fled to Canada." The second indicated that sixteen "well armed" individuals had passed through Utica en route across the international border.[62] Oftentimes, these were long-time community members who were sorely missed. Such was the case for a Baptist church in Buffalo, New York, that reported the loss of 130 communicants to Canada between 1850 and 1852. Although one voice from within the congregation disputed the claim, suggesting that the loss of only two or three members was nearer the mark, the overwhelming sense was one of loss and social rupture.[63]

The emigration of family and community members inevitably led to further migration when it seemed that the destination presented a marked improvement for new arrivals. When a laundress from New

York named Mary Jane Robinson arrived in Canada, for example, she could not help but encourage her friend, Sarah Ann Harris, to follow in her footsteps. In a letter to Harris, a fellow laundress, Robinson wrote, "I do wish you would try and come to Buxton, Canada West ... Come to a land of liberty and freedom, where the coloured man is not despised nor a deaf ear turned to them. This is the place to live in peace and to enjoy the comforts of life."[64] While it is unclear whether Harris ever joined her friend over the border, this private letter was published with permission in the anti-slavery press so that other potential migrants might be encouraged by Robinson's success.

Similar letters from self-liberated men and women were frequently shared, as new migrants were often keen to encourage loved ones and strangers alike to make their way to a land of safety and opportunity. After John Henry Hill escaped from Virginia to Canada in 1853 with the aid of well-known Philadelphia abolitionist William Still, he regularly wrote to Still of his positive impressions of Canada in the hope that others would follow. "While we sit beneath the Silken folds of her flag of Perfect Liberty, we are secure," he wrote, "beyond the reach of the aggressions of the Blood hounds and free from the despotism that would wrap around our limbs by the damable [sic] Slaveholder." Believing that African Americans should "agitate the emigration to Canada," he often solicited William Still to help his acquaintances and family members in their efforts to cross the U.S.–Canada border. And thanks to these efforts, by 1861, Hill had been joined in Canada by his uncle and brother.[65]

With so much cross-border migration, Canada's paramount importance as an international free-soil haven after 1850 refracted well beyond *Uncle Tom's Cabin* in the anti-slavery movement's print culture. Ex-slave narratives, which continued to sell like hotcakes in the 1850s, depicted runaway protagonists making their way to Canada with even more frequency than they had before the Fugitive Slave Act.[66] One particularly memorable moment comes from the 1851 autobiography of Thomas Smallwood, who escaped from Washington, DC, to Toronto, Canada West, nearly a decade prior to publishing his story. He had left the city in the nick of time. Alongside his friend and compatriot, the white abolitionist martyr Charles T. Torrey, Smallwood had established

Underground Railroad operations in Washington, DC, to assist fugitive slaves making their way to Canada. After a betrayal, however, Smallwood was forced to flee just ahead of being arrested. Describing Washington, DC, as a "mock metropolis of freedom," Smallwood made his way quickly northward, stopping only in Philadelphia and Albany before crossing the border.[67] Arriving in Toronto on July 4, 1843, he could not help but note the irony of the date:

> [In the United States] I would have been compelled painfully to witness as I had done for many years their hypocritical demonstrations in honour of a day, which they say, brought to them freedom; but I sorrowfully knew that it was in honour of a day that brought to me, and my race among them, the most degrading, tyrannical and soul-withering bondage that ever disgraced the world or a nation. But here, I was on Canada's free soil, and I may rejoice and give thanks to God in honour of that day, it being the day on which I first put my feet in a land of true freedom, and equal laws.[68]

Plays, poetry, and music were not immune to this "Canada Culture," either. William Wells Brown, whose autobiographies had been so widely read in the 1840s, wrote a play in 1858 titled, "The Escape; or, A Leap for Freedom." Glorifying the U.S.–Canada border as a means of escape for two slaves who had secretly been married while enslaved in the South, his dramatic story drew its character inspiration from real self-emancipated individuals living in Canada.[69] Glen, one of the play's protagonists, decides to take "a leap for freedom" by running away. "I've said 'master' for the last time," he declares to his wife, Melina. "I'm free; I'm bound for Canada."[70]

Glen's sentiment reverberated in a popular song titled "Away to Canada" by African American poet Joshua McCarter Simpson. The song proved catchy enough in Simpson's 1852 collection of "Anti-Slavery Songs" that it was republished as poetry in the abolitionist press (Figure 5).[71] Sung to the tune of "Oh, Susannah," it cleverly reimagines the original song, which had first been popularized by Stephen Foster in the tradition of blackface minstrelsy.[72] Unlike the original lyrics of "Oh, Susannah," which follow the path of a highly caricaturized black man from Alabama to Louisiana, Simpson's lyrics pay homage to the

Underground Railroad. They celebrate Canadian legal equality, reflect the grief of separating from family in a bid for freedom, and capture the joy of living free from the fear of the auction block. Each stanza ends with a play on two lines that perfectly encapsulate the Canada Culture embraced by the anti-slavery movement after the enactment of the 1850 Fugitive Slave Act: "I'm going straight to Canada,/Where colored men are free."[73]

As self-emancipated men and women, free people, and anti-slavery advocates turned northward to Canada in the wake of the Fugitive Slave Act, they rejoiced in the fact that Canada offered a powerful escape hatch for those fleeing U.S. slavery. Building on a reputation that began when James C. Brown and his fellow Cincinnatians first crossed the border in late 1829, the British province of freedom was now, more than ever, a recognizable refuge from persecution in the United States.

Yet even as a full-fledged Canada Culture took root within the anti-slavery movement's robust print culture, the celebration of British liberty remained an extension of the deep despair that many felt regarding the lengths to which enslavers would go in defense of their institution. As famous ex-slaves, prominent black leaders, and white anti-slavery observers weighed in from across the border on thorny questions about the future of the anti-slavery movement, dramatic controversies and new ideas pushed emigrants and anti-slavery advocates in unexpected directions – and ultimately helped propel the nation toward a sectional civil war.

AWAY TO CANADA
Joshua McCarter Simpson

I'm on my way to Canada,

 That cold and dreary land;

The dire effects of slavery

 I can no longer stand.

My soul is vexed within me so,

 To think that I'm a slave,

I've now resolved to strike the blow

 For freedom or the grave.

  O! righteous Father,

   Wilt thou not pity me,

  And aid me on to Canada,

   Where colored men are free?

I heard good Queen Victoria say,

 If we would all forsake

Our native land of slavery,

 And come across the Lake,

That she was standing on the
  shore,

 With arms extended wide,

To give us all a peaceful home,

 Beyond the rolling tide.

  Farewell, old master!

   That's enough for me –

  I'm going straight to Canada,

   Where colored men are free.

I heard the old soul-driver say,

 As he was passing by,

"That darkey's bound to run away,

 I see it in his eye!"

My heart responded to the
  charge,

And thought it was no crime,

And something seemed my mind to urge,

 That now's the very time!

  O! old driver,

   Don't you cry for me –

  I'm going up to Canada,

   Where colored men are free.

Grieve not, my wife, grieve not for me,

  O! do not break my heart;

For nought but cruel slavery

 Would cause me to depart.

If I should stay to quell your grief,

 Your grief I would augment;

For no one knows the day that we

 Asunder might be rent.

  O! Susannah,

   Don't you cry for me –

  I'm going up to Canada,

   Where colored men are free.

I heard old Master pray last night –

 I heard him pray for me,

That God would come, and in his might

 From Satan set me free;

So I from Satan would escape,

 And flee the wrath to come –

If there's a fiend in human shape,

 Old Master must be one.

  O! old master,

   While you pray for me,

  I'm doing all I can to reach

   The land of Liberty!

Ohio's not the place for me;
  For I was much surprised,
So many of her sons to see,
  In garments so disguised.
Her name has gone out through the world,
  Free Labor – Soil – and Men; –
But slaves had better far be hurled
  Into the Lion's Den.
    Farewell, Ohio!
      I am not safe in thee;
    I'll travel on to Canada,
      Where colored men are free.

I've now embarked for yonder shore,
  Where man's a man by law,
The vessel soon will bear me o'er,
  To shake the Lion's paw.
I no more dread the Auctioneer,
  Nor fear the master's frowns,

I no more tremble when I hear
  The baying Negro-hounds.
    O! old Master!
      Don't think hard of me –
    I'm just in sight of Canada,
      Where colored men are free.

I've landed safe upon the shore,
  Both soul and body free;
My blood, and brain, and tears no more
  Will drench old Tennessee:
But I behold the scalding tear
  Now stealing from my eye,
To think my wife – my only dear,
  A slave must live and die.
    O! Susannah,
      Don't grieve after me –
    Forever at a Throne of Grace,
      I will remember thee.

5 "Away to Canada" by Joshua McCarter Simpson, "Poetry," *The Liberator* (Boston, MA), December 10, 1852.

CHAPTER 8

Emigration and Enmity: The Meaning of Free Soil in a Nation Divided

A thought on the emigration, en masse, of the colored people of the United States to the Canadas, Central or South America, or to Africa, may not be amiss, as it is now the theme of all others among the intelligent colored men of this country.

~ A letter to the *Provincial Freeman* from "Gaines," published January 20, 1854[1]

From September 11 to 13, 1851, fifty-three delegates from the United States, Upper Canada, and Jamaica met in Toronto to discuss emigration as a response to the Fugitive Slave Act. After substantial debate, this "North American Convention" resolved that attendees were truly grateful for the protection afforded by Great Britain's "powerful Government" and that they were fully persuaded that Upper Canada was, "by far, the most desirable place of resort for colored people, to be found on the American continent."

Not only did they believe that Canadian emigration would allow African Americans the opportunity to become "independent tillers of a free soil," they noted that emigrants in Canada could further assist in anti-slavery activism. Although they listened to "able and eloquent addresses in favor of emigration to Jamaica" – where emigrants would also enjoy the benefits of living under the British flag – the delegates ultimately resolved to endorse Canada over the British West Indies so that emigrants could be better situated to aid the fugitive slaves "daily flying from American slavery."[2]

Similar conversations unfolded across the United States and Upper Canada in the wake of the 1850 Fugitive Slave Act. Emigration was a difficult and tense topic. The U.S. North could no longer be considered free soil, so helping self-liberated men and women reach safety outside the United States became a high priority for black activists and white abolitionists. At the same time, free African Americans felt they had as much to lose as fugitive slaves. Beyond fearing for their own safety in a new legal environment where they had little recourse if they were kidnapped into slavery, many felt that the Fugitive Slave Act signaled the death knell for any hope they had of being recognized as citizens in the predominantly white United States. More than ever, international free-soil havens resonated as potent symbols of liberty, equality, uplift, and independence.

While most northern black people were committed to remaining in the United States to fight for freedom and citizenship, emigrationism dramatically re-emerged among free African Americans and self-emancipated ex-slaves. Not only did African American communities resurrect the longstanding and spirited debate over Liberian colonization and resuscitate enthusiasm for free black emigration to Canada, the British West Indies suddenly found prominent black champions willing to promote emigration to the islands. Free northerners even publicly discussed Mexico as an emigration destination for the first time since the 1820s. Interest was even greater among those living in the South. With the future of slavery in the United States becoming a key political issue, thousands of fugitive and free African Americans crossed free-soil borders by land and sea.

Even as the despised law revived interest in every Atlantic free-soil alternative, however, Canada not only remained the preeminent site of international migration, it emerged as the most important free-soil space for anti-slavery advocates specifically hoping to continue to fight slavery and racial injustice in the United States following the passage of the Fugitive Slave Act. Abolitionists with such diverse anti-slavery strategies as newspaper editor Mary Ann Shadd and armed militant John Brown used Canada as a base of operations over the course of the decade. At a time of profound disappointment for African Americans and their anti-slavery allies, many emigrants and activists began to see emigration to Upper Canada as the best last hope for black Americans who wanted to flee racial persecution in the United States but still fight against American slavery.[3]

Nevertheless, Canada was not necessarily the obvious choice for people who had already experienced a degree of freedom in the northern states – either because they were born free or because they lived in communities comparatively safe from slave-catchers. With a landscape of free-soil alternatives larger than it had ever been, emigration proponents debated at length where they thought African Americans should go and why.

In the early 1850s, no two writers more effectively captured the complexities of black emigrationism than Martin Delany and Mary Ann Shadd. Although both were well-known black activists who relocated to Canada for a number of years, they were each leading proponents of very distinct views on free-soil emigration. Delany believed that people of color should remove themselves entirely from the toxic influence of white prejudice. Shadd, a stalwart proponent of integration, repudiated the idea that people of color should separate themselves from white society.[4] Within months of the publication of *Uncle Tom's Cabin* in 1852, both had produced extensive assessments of emigration, free-soil alternatives, and what they saw as the best path for racial uplift in the wake of the Fugitive Slave Act. Read together, they illuminate a great deal about how potential emigrants measured their free-soil alternatives.

Martin Robison Delany was born in Charles Town, Virginia (now West Virginia) in 1812. The son of a free mother and an enslaved father, he learned the value of literacy early in life: his mother taught all her children to read and write, although the family was forced to flee to western Pennsylvania after authorities threatened to jail her for it. After moving to Pittsburgh in 1831, Delany became an active participant in racial uplift projects. In the 1830s and 1840s, he attended and organized Colored Conventions, the state and national political gatherings that brought African Americans together to discuss how to achieve racial justice in the United States.[5] In 1843, he launched both a medical practice and the first African American newspaper west of the Alleghenies (*The Mystery*), and from 1847 to 1849 he co-edited *The North Star* alongside Frederick Douglass. He was well known during his life for his activism and for his professional achievements as doctor, newspaper editor, author, and explorer. One of the most famous black thinkers and leaders of the nineteenth century, he was dedicated to anti-slavery activism and improving the conditions of free and freed African Americans.[6]

After a long career committed to racial justice in the United States, Delany radically shifted his views toward emigrationism at mid-century due to mounting evidence that white Americans would never be willing to recognize the social or legal equality of black people. Delany's change of heart stemmed as much from his dismissal from Harvard Medical School on account of his color in 1849 as it did from the passage of the Fugitive Slave Act.[7] He began to believe that African Americans had relied on white allies for too long and with no discernible results. After the Fugitive Slave Act was passed, he asserted that it was high time for black Americans to start "thinking for [them]selves."[8]

In 1850, Delany began considering at length where African Americans could go outside the United States to achieve "political elevation." Despite his critique of colonizationism in Harriet Beecher Stowe's *Uncle Tom's Cabin*, Delany was not at all opposed to emigration in principle – he was just fundamentally opposed to the white-led ACS and the conservative views that promoted it. Indeed, Delany came to believe that African Americans could fulfill their social and political destiny *only* by moving away from the controlling influence of white people.[9] Self-publishing his views in *The Condition, Elevation, Emigration and Destiny of the Colored People of the United States* – released just one month after the publication of *Uncle Tom's Cabin* in 1852 – Delany is now widely regarded as the father of black nationalism.[10]

Mary Ann Shadd was born free in 1823 to a family of anti-slavery activists in Delaware. Well educated, she was raised to be a vocal proponent of black freedom and equality.[11] Her father, Abraham, had been an active participant in the Colored Conventions movement since the very first meeting convened in 1830 to discuss the idea of emigrating to Upper Canada after the Ohio Black Laws were enacted.[12] A passionate advocate of black education and equality, Shadd first addressed the issue of racial uplift in the pages of Frederick Douglass's *North Star* in a letter published on March 23, 1849. She bemoaned the fact that years of holding conventions had done little to actually improve black Americans' circumstances. It was time, she believed, "to do more, and talk less."[13]

Inspired by the resolutions of the "North American Convention" held in Toronto, Shadd decided to move to Upper Canada, now Canada West, in 1851.[14] She believed that Canada would provide sanctuary from the danger in which the Fugitive Slave Act had placed every person of color in the United States.[15] Comparing the alternatives within an expanding free-soil landscape, she first published her endorsement of Canadian emigration in an 1852 pamphlet titled, *A Plea for Emigration; or, Notes from Canada West, in its Moral, Social, and Political Aspect: with Suggestions Respecting Mexico, West Indies, and Vancouver Island* (Figure 6).[16] In 1854, Shadd then became the first black woman to helm a newspaper, the *Provincial Freeman,* which she used to promote Canada and Canadian emigration until 1857.[17]

Although Shadd remains less well known in the United States today than her contemporary and friend, Frederick Douglass, her advocacy of Canada and her editorship of the widely circulated *Provincial Freeman* made her a well-known figure among anti-slavery communities throughout North America. One correspondent to *Frederick Douglass' Paper* named the *Provincial Freeman* as one of four essential newspapers for abolitionists, recommending it to anyone "wishing to become informed in regard to Canada, its laws, government, and general resources of the country." In addition, Shadd conducted a well-received lecture tour on the topic in 1856.[18]

Like many black activists of the nineteenth century, both Shadd and Delany repudiated the ACS and the idea of relocating to Liberia. They agreed that the unhealthy climate alone should deter migrants from choosing Liberia, and they each articulated doubts regarding the ACS's ideology and the Republic of Liberia's independence from it.[19] Shadd viewed the ACS's expression of its Christianity and philanthropic mission as mere window dressing, denouncing it as the puppet of slaveholders and of President Millard Fillmore's pro-slavery administration.[20] Delany regarded the ACS's ongoing political influence on the Republic of Liberia as reason to emigrate elsewhere:

> What would be thought of the people of Hayti, and their heads of government, if their instructions emanated from the American Anti-Slavery Society, or the British Foreign Missionary Board? Should they be respected at

A PLEA FOR EMIGRATION;

OR,

NOTES OF CANADA WEST,

IN ITS

MORAL, SOCIAL, AND POLITICAL ASPECT:

WITH

SUGGESTIONS RESPECTING MEXICO, WEST INDIES, AND VANCOUVER'S ISLAND,

FOR THE

INFORMATION OF COLORED EMIGRANTS.

BY MARY A. SHADD.

DETROIT:
PRINTED BY GEORGE W. PATTISON.
1852.

6 Mary Ann Shadd, *A Plea for Emigration; or, Notes from Canada West, in its Moral, Social, and Political Aspect: with Suggestions Respecting Mexico, West Indies, and Vancouver Island* (Detroit, MI: George W. Pattison, 1852).

all as a nation? Would they be worthy of it? Certainly not. We do not expect
Liberia to be all that Hayti is; but we ask and expect of her, to have a decent
respect for herself – to endeavor to be freemen instead of voluntary slaves.
Liberia is no place for the colored freemen of the United States.[21]

Both authors, in fact, believed Liberia to be so unworthy of consideration
that it was merely a point of departure for their analyses of other, more
plausible, emigration destinations.

What sets these authors apart is that they disagreed on where to go and
why. For both, ultimately, it was a question of power and influence. For his
part, Delany was loathe to leave the hemisphere. He considered Canada.
He found it "equal to any portion of the Northern States" and in possession of the very best kinds of grains, fruits, vegetables, and cattle. But he
quickly dismissed the British province due to a serious "political objec-
tion." He had no doubt whatsoever that Canada, in not too long a time,
would be willingly overtaken by the United States in a "bloodless victory"
of annexation. Should that happen, he believed that the Fugitive Slave Act
would then be "in full force" throughout Canada. In fact, he believed that
the law had been passed in 1850 with this eventuality in mind.[22] He was
not the only anti-slavery advocate to express this fear, which stemmed in
large part from the reports of the 1840s that white Canadians had been
growing increasingly sympathetic to American racism.[23]

Instead, Delany determined that "the ultimate destination and future
home of the colored race on this continent" was in Central America,
South America, or the West Indies. Of these, Central and South America
captured his attention because neither had a history of enacting policies
that codified racial inequity, and he estimated that whites (or, as he
clarified, people of "pure European descent") accounted for no more
than one-seventh of the population in these regions. Believing that racial
uplift could only be achieved away from the toxic influence of white
dominance, he cited New Granada and the northern part of South
America just south of Nicaragua as the most favorable sites for black
relocation.[24]

Although Delany's settlement plan was never as widely regarded as
those praising Canada, his activism on its behalf proved to be quite
influential among emigrationists. Two years after publishing his views

in *The Condition, Elevation, Emigration and Destiny of the Colored People of the United States,* Delany and twenty-five of his black activist allies organized a national convention to discuss "the great and important subject of emigration from the United States." Notably, advocates of African colonization and the ACS were explicitly uninvited from attending.[25] Held in Cleveland on August 24–26, 1854, this National Emigration Convention was attended by approximately 150 men and women, including delegates from Canada. To this audience, Delany delivered a powerful essay on "The Political Destiny of the Colored Race on the American Continent." Arguing that neither freedom nor safety could exist where black people remained disenfranchised, his essay moved the convention delegates to endorse his preference for resettling in Central America, South America, or the West Indies.[26]

At the time, the idea of establishing "an independent and free Republic of colored men" in any of these regions failed to elicit much interest beyond the convention.[27] Yet Delany's words still resonated eight years later among another demographic of anti-slavery thinkers: when Abraham Lincoln and other Republicans considered black relocation ideas during the American Civil War, they turned to the pamphlet of Delany's convention speech. A copy was reprinted as an appendix to the House of Representatives' *Report of the Select Committee on Emancipation and Colonization.*[28]

When Delany's hopes for a mass removal to Central or South America did not materialize, he eventually elected to become one of the thousands to cross the U.S.–Canada border. He emigrated to Upper Canada in 1856, where he established a medical practice and became a writer for Mary Ann Shadd's newspaper, the *Provincial Freeman.* At first glance, Delany's embrace of Canada certainly seems incongruous with the ideas he professed in both his book and oratory, but it did not signal a wholesale reversal of sentiment. Rather, in his speech on political destiny, Delany had actually tempered his concern regarding Canada's susceptibility to American influence with one important caveat: were a successful mass emigration to Central America, South America, or the West Indies *prevented,* he felt that "the great body of our people" should elect to remove to Upper Canada despite its pitfalls. And that is what had happened. So, recognizing that it provided political equality to people of color, he was willing to hope that Canada's proximity to the United States could provide unity and strength among African Americans if "worse [came] to worse."[29]

By contrast, Mary Ann Shadd adamantly believed from the outset that Canada was the best destination for African American emigrants. In principle, she maintained that anywhere in Britain's western empire would do as well; in practice, she spent the entirety of her pamphlet specifically promoting Canada. As Delany had done with Central and South America, Shadd endorsed Canada because it was a place where people of color were the legal equals of anyone else: "There is no legal discrimination whatever effecting colored emigrants in Canada," she informed her readers, "nor from any cause whatever are their privileges sought to be abridged."[30]

What set Canada apart from places like Mexico or South America, in Shadd's view, was Britain's firm commitment to anti-slavery and to using its power to enforce the full equality of all British subjects. Possibly inspired by the North American Convention of 1851, whose agenda included the idea that African Americans should only pledge themselves to the defense of a government that protects their liberty, Shadd was more concerned about the issue of power than she was about the influence of whites.[31] Like Delany, she was suspicious of U.S. pro-slavery imperialism. But where Delany feared that Canada would soon be overtaken by the United States, Shadd was convinced that the Mexican government's anti-slavery sentiment was not strong enough to overcome the political weakness that left it vulnerable to American pro-slavery interests. She believed that the more powerful state governments of the southern United States had "marked [Mexico] for their prey," with the result that the region would long remain embroiled in a "contest for the supremacy of slavery."[32]

Notably, her feelings were not necessarily shared by those living in the southwest. In 1857, free people of color from New Orleans and its surrounding parishes had spearheaded the creation of a black colony, Eureka, near Tampico in the state of Tamaulipas. Driven from their homes by escalating threats of violence, especially in rural areas, they were likely drawn to the area for several reasons: Mexico's president, Ignacio Comonfort, personally welcomed them with promises of legal equality, there were already strong trade links between New Orleans and nearby Veracruz, and the region was home to a relatively large population of people of African descent. As historian Mary Niall Mitchell has shown, even the *idea* of the colony was potent enough to fuel the imaginations of schoolchildren, who dreamed of emigrating to Mexico to become traders and tradesmen. Emigrants wrote back from Eureka that agricultural work was really all that was available, but, rather than feeling disappointed in the lack of more economic opportunities, it seems that most appreciated their new life.[33]

In one way, in fact, Shadd had been quite wrong. Mexico's commitment to emancipation only grew through the decade. In April 1857, Mexico ratified the abolition of slavery throughout its territory and enshrined a free-soil policy into its new Constitution. Rather than being brow-beaten by Texas, whose slaveholders continued to send slave-hunters across Mexican borders in search of runaways, Mexico not only doubled down on its anti-slavery position, it guaranteed equal rights and protection to all African Americans. Until that point, fugitive slaves in Mexico had been subject to slave-hunters from the United States as well as the insecurity of non-citizenship.[34]

Yet in one key respect the events of the 1850s eventually proved Shadd right. Within just a few short years, the Mexican government reported that the black settlement of Eureka had failed. Although the circumstances of its failure are not entirely clear, it was most likely the result of the Mexican Civil War in 1858. The colonists all left – though the government's report did not specify to where – leaving the town of Eureka the victim of an unstable government.[35] Political reform, peasant rebellions, and incessant raids by Comanches and Apaches in the northeast were just some of the challenges that contributed to endemic instability in the 1850s. "People who love liberty do not emigrate to weak governments," Shadd concluded in her pamphlet. She encouraged black Americans to join strong ones, "to add to their strength and better their own condition."[36]

The power and the (assumed) desire of the British government to protect its "colored subjects" was particularly important to Shadd when it came to African Americans' legal equality. She was not blind to the kinds of prejudice and mistreatment that had been so regularly reported in the

1840s. Reflecting the same viewpoint that Peter Gallego had expressed ten years earlier, Shadd noted that prejudice easily spread into Upper Canada via Yankees visiting the province. Echoing Gallego's earlier optimism, as well, she noted that "the most ample redress [could] be obtained" upon "taking proper [legal] measures."[37] When tavern-keepers and other "public characters" persisted in refusing service to people of color, for example, she argued that it was possible to "get redress at law." She also specified that if black emigrants familiarized themselves with "the school law that relates to them," they would know that they could demand admission to any school under government patronage, regardless of white parents' prejudice.[38]

They regularly did so. Petitions from black individuals and communities to the Superintendent of the Canadian school system in 1851, 1852, 1856, and 1859 all indicate the persistence of white efforts to keep black neighbors out of Upper Canada's "Common Schools."[39] They also bear out Shadd's assertion that black residents could and would use the law to demand access. The "colored inhabitants" of Simcoe, for example, wrote that their understanding of Article 19 of the School Act assured them that they, as Protestants, should have equal access to Common Schools. They asked only for the superintendent's aid to ensure that local whites complied with the law.[40]

In Shadd's view, Great Britain's power and its commitment to protecting black equality also ensured that Canadian emigration would serve an even higher purpose than providing African Americans with a better life than the northern states. Ending her pamphlet on "the question whether or not an extensive emigration by the free colored people of the United States would affect the institution of slavery," Shadd assured her readers that it would. She chastised black northerners for continuing to stay in the United States, nursing the hope that some "powerful miracle" would overthrow slavery despite the institution's steady expansion and the passage of the Fugitive Slave Act. She felt convinced that "there would be more of the right spirit, and infinitely more of real manliness," were African Americans to launch a "decided demand for freedom" from a secure place rather than "miserab[ly] scampering from state to state, in a vain endeavor to gather the crumbs" of it.[41]

She continued to defend and promote the premise of demanding freedom from a secure place when she began overseeing the *Provincial Freeman* two years later. In an editorial on emigration, she declared that African Americans in Canada had chosen "the only ground on which they can make despots feel the force of their words and actions."[42] When news of Delany's 1854 convention on emigration reached Upper Canada, she published a response from a local black doctor suggesting that Canada provided anti-slavery advocates the best vantage point from which to observe "the movements of [their] enemies." The doctor agreed that Canadian emigration could be a "thorn" in the "bosoms of the oppressors."[43]

Shadd's belief that black emigrants in Canada could undermine the power of American slaveholders was also shared by a man named Benjamin Drew. A prominent white abolitionist from Boston, Drew's belief that fugitive slaves could provide the most powerful indictment against slavery's cruelty brought him across the border in 1854. Donning the hat of an anti-slavery investigator, Drew spent several months traveling through towns and cities in Canada West, committed to having the American public "hear from the refugees themselves."[44] He collected interviews with black emigrants, largely conducted in their own homes, eliciting as much information as he could related to "the weighty subjects of oppression and freedom." The views of men and women who had experienced both American slavery and British freedom, he believed, would not only undermine the southern myth of slaveholders' benevolence, it would excite anti-slavery sentiment throughout the United States. He declared that the black emigrants in Canada would inspire Americans to fight slavery more energetically than ever at the regional, state, and federal levels.[45]

Including 114 stories and anecdotes from individuals living in fourteen different Canadian towns and cities, Drew's compilation of interviews was ultimately published in 1856 as a book titled *A North-Side View of Slavery*. Among the voices he incorporated were those of James C. Brown and the now famous Harriet Tubman.[46] His book was well received – even Hiram Wilson endorsed it, attesting that he personally knew many of the interviewees. Advertised in anti-slavery newspapers alongside another investigative work, Dr. C. G. Parsons' *An Inside View of Slavery: A Tour among the Planters,* Drew's interviews hit their mark: they were lauded for presenting readers with important "arguments for Freedom."[47]

Indeed, the rising tide of black migration into Canada after 1850 only fed the American public's well-developed appetite for information. How were self-emancipated slaves faring in Canada? What could be gleaned from their experiences, having transitioned from American slavery to British freedom? They were the same old questions, but they felt more pressing than ever. As Mary Ann Shadd summed it up, "Persons abroad want reliable information of Canada, from Canada."[48]

At this critical juncture, public perception was paramount. Benjamin Drew, for one, did not hesitate to advise emigrants that their "good conduct and success in life may have an important bearing on the destinies of millions of their brethren."[49] For her part, Mary Ann Shadd was also a passionate believer in what historian Ibram X. Kendi has termed "uplift suasion" – in this case proving that industriousness and success in Canada would lead to the end of slavery in the United States.[50] However, from her home in Chatham, Canada West, the question of how this success should be demonstrated was complicated by the practicalities involved with a rapidly growing population of emigrants who arrived in a wide variety of material conditions. Before long, her views on the matter pitted her against another influential black community leader and kicked off an ideological battle that struck right at the heart of the emigrant experience in Canada.

Henry Bibb, the well-known ex-slave narrator, had relocated with his wife, Mary, from Michigan to Chatham, Canada West, in the wake of the Fugitive Slave Act. Like Mary Ann Shadd, he arrived in 1851. From their new home, the Bibbs became indefatigable allies of the fugitive slaves regularly crossing into Canada with few or no resources. They opened a day school, helped to build a Methodist church for the community, and established Canada's first African American newspaper, the *Voice of the Fugitive,* which they published from 1851 to 1852.[51] Notably, historian Afua Cooper credits the *Voice of the Fugitive* with establishing the tradition of producing anti-slavery publications in Canada for a transnational audience.[52]

Like Mary Ann Shadd, Henry Bibb believed that how black emigrants were perceived by white Americans would prove critical in the battle against American slavery and racism. In an address delivered before the North American Convention in 1851, he offered a stirring articulation of every single emigrant's responsibility in the future of the anti-slavery movement:

> Every refugee in Canada is a representative of the millions of our brethren who are still held in bondage; and the eye of the civilized world is looking down upon us to see whether we can take care of ourselves or not. If our conduct is moral and upright, in spite of all the bad training we have had, it will reflect credit on ourselves, and encourage our friends in what they are doing for our elevation. But if, on the other hand, it should be seen, that under a free Government, where we have all our political and social rights, without regard to our color, and where we are permitted to sit under the sanctuary of God, "where there is none daring to molest us or make us afraid," and where we are supported by the prayers and sympathies of all good men, we should prove ourselves to be incapable of self-government, it would bring down reproach and disgrace upon the whole race with which we are connected, and would be used as an argument against emancipation. The slave-holders' predictions would be pronounced true, and society would consider the whole of us unfit for the enjoyment of liberty. How important it is, then, that we should each and all feel our responsibility and conduct ourselves accordingly.[53]

Yet while Henry Bibb and Mary Ann Shadd both understood the enormous pressure on emigrant communities to demonstrate their success, they fundamentally disagreed on what steps should be taken within their communities to ensure that black freedom was "modeled" effectively. For Shadd, it seemed imperative that new arrivals, no matter their circumstances, should integrate into Canadian society to show that free people could readily improve their conditions once they were out from under the heel of a white, pro-slavery government. Though neither her pamphlet nor her newspaper shied away from the truth of white Canadian prejudice – she once referred to it as "one of the strongest pro-slavery influences" in Canada – she passionately believed that the legal arm of the British government would guarantee emigrants' access to the institutions that would promote their elevation.[54] Furthermore, she trusted that their integration into Canadian society (as full British subjects) would speed the demise of prejudice among white neighbors by daily exposing whites to black emigrants' moral and intellectual culture.[55]

For his part, Bibb believed that the charitable provision of land, homes, and assistance to fugitive slaves was the best way of ensuring that their destitute condition upon arrival did not contribute to a negative perception of their ability to succeed in freedom.[56] Along with Josiah Henson, the self-liberated man whose well-read narrative had inspired elements of *Uncle Tom's Cabin*, Henry Bibb formed the Refugee Home Society (RHS) to purchase 50,000 acres of arable land in Upper Canada. In a plan similar to the one formulated by James C. Brown at the Wilberforce settlement in the 1830s, the idea was for black settlers to work the land in 25-acre plots, paying off toward their eventual ownership of it in small increments. As they paid for their land, the money would be used to support schools and churches, as well as to purchase more land for the settlement.[57]

As these two high-profile public figures promoted opposing strategies for emigrant success – integration and intervention – they found themselves embroiled in a longstanding public feud during Shadd's first years in Canada. For Bibb and the supporters of black settlements, the philanthropic work of the RHS seemed like a sound plan for ensuring the well-being of those newly arrived after escaping slavery. After all, American anti-slavery advocates had regularly financed black settlements in Canada for the previous two decades, and many seemed particularly keen to do so after 1850. White anti-slavery allies who lamented their inability to free slaves from bondage in the South could, with financial support, commit themselves to assisting the thousands "who have escaped and are now on free soil." One promoter, for example, found northerners' "sympathies fairly roused on the subject of slavery" after the recent publication of *Uncle Tom's Cabin* and noted their enthusiasm for assisting the "refugees" fleeing the reach of the Fugitive Slave Act.[58]

For Shadd and those who shared her integrationist perspective, however, Bibb's plan was an ideological minefield. Not only did Shadd abhor the notion of separate black settlements, she strongly opposed the solicitation of philanthropic aid directed toward assisting those who had just recently crossed the border. Antagonists of the RHS believed that the organization was complicit in a widespread "begging system" that materially compromised the reputation of black freedom by "representing [emigrants] as objects of charity."[59]

The question of whether or not the RHS should be supported spilled into the pages of the American anti-slavery press. Opponents insisted that it provided unnecessary intervention, suggested that it was no more than a land scheme, lamented that it separated fugitive slaves from the general population, and argued that its depiction of destitute ex-slaves did a disservice to the anti-slavery cause. Proving their point with good intentions, Charles C. Foote, one of the RHS's main financial backers, was so incensed by *The Liberator*'s publication of an article criticizing the RHS that he penned a lengthy response detailing just how very much in need he believed the fugitives to be: "If these people are not poor," he wrote, "then *none are poorer*. If charity should not be extended *to these*, then *there should be an end of charity*."[60]

Supporters of the RHS sniped that opponents were largely free-born or self-liberated African Americans who had already acquired property. They were therefore out of touch with the needs and conditions of those newly arrived from slavery. Furthermore, supporters of the RHS believed that their antagonists were irresponsibly preventing new arrivals from accepting the assistance they so desperately needed. James Theodore Holly, a prominent black emigrant in Canada who eventually became the leading figure in a revitalized Haitian emigration movement, articulated this viewpoint when he argued that new arrivals were only "harangued" into rejecting the RHS's aid by the "browbeating" of a "clique of inveterate opposers."[61]

However, it was not just the prospects of fugitive slaves that were at stake in these debates. In opposing the RHS, critics also saw the need to publicly vindicate the Canadian government's ability to ensure black emigrants could thrive in a free, white-dominant society. Formulating their perspectives for an American audience, RHS critics emphasized their belief that the Canadian government embodied everything fugitive slaves needed to succeed in freedom: it was a strong government, it provided legal equality, and it offered "impartial" (color-blind) avenues to affordable land ownership. At an opposition meeting held in Windsor, Canada West, attendees expressed their certainty that "the impartial character and administration of [Canada's] laws" made it possible for African Americans to support themselves without the need for charity or self-segregation.[62] To their mind, this argument emphasized the critical importance of legal equality as a tenet of freedom, and it also signaled to American observers that former slaves would not become the burden on white society that anti-abolitionists feared.

Moreover, the well-known black activist and Canada emigrant Samuel Ringgold Ward argued that the Canadian government's generous and equitable opportunities for land purchase provided all the necessary infrastructural support for emigrants to achieve self-sufficient success. In a letter published in the *National Anti-Slavery Standard*, Ward's major critique of the RHS was that there was no need for a land-buying organization to benefit fugitive slaves in Canada because the government itself already sold land at less expense and "without distinction of colour." A government that was willing to promote independent landownership would support destitute emigrants more ably, consistently, and justly, he argued, than a philanthropic organization that forced land purchasers to sign "tyrannical" contracts.[63] By suggesting that the Canadian government obviated the need for charitable schemes and self-segregation, the integrationists simultaneously hoped to resuscitate the image of the fugitive slave and articulate what kind of government policy they thought promoted the success of liberated people.

Critics like Ward and Shadd reflected the longstanding tradition of pointing out the United States' shortcomings as a pro-slavery republic by highlighting Great Britain's commitment to providing liberty and equality to all subjects, regardless of color. In Ward's case, it also reflected his values as an early member of the Liberty Party in the United States, which was committed to developing political strategies in pursuit of freedom and equality for African Americans. In 1840, American abolitionists had famously split into two factions: those who believed in moral suasion and those who believed in pursuing political anti-slavery strategies. Ward had sided with the latter position.

By the time he decided to emigrate to Upper Canada in 1851, Ward had already secured himself an anti-slavery reputation of "gigantic proportions."[64] He had been born a slave on the Eastern Shore of Maryland in 1817, but his parents escaped with him to New Jersey when he was still too young to remember. From the age of nine, he had been raised and educated in New York, where he did not, in fact, discover that he was technically a fugitive slave until he was twenty-four years old.[65] As a black activist, he was heavily invested in the idea that racial uplift began with legal equality and political intervention rather than moral suasion or social engineering. While he readily admitted in an 1852 editorial in Bibbs' *Voice of the Fugitive* that Canadian prejudice was "incomparably MEANER" and more "gratuitous" than "Yankee Negro Hate," he firmly believed that it would come to an end because it had "neither the current religion, nor the civil law, to uphold it." By contrast, he pointed out, African Americans in "Yankeedom" had "no legal protection against such outrages."[66]

Within three years of participating so vocally in the RHS debate, however, Samuel Ringgold Ward underwent a profound modification in his thinking that is representative of a broader trend relating to emigrationism and anti-slavery in the mid- to late 1850s. After an extended journey in Great Britain, Ward decided to emigrate again in 1855, this time to Jamaica. Reflecting the importance that he had ascribed to the notion of independent land ownership in Canada, he was, in part, wooed to Jamaica by the offer of a 50-acre plot of land in St. George's Parish.[67] In greater part, however, shifting ideas regarding the relative anti-slavery potential of Canadian and West Indian free soil prompted him to move.

Ward had spent his years in Canada West promoting the province as an asylum from American slavery and as a model of legal equality, but he eventually lost his faith in black emigrants' ability to overcome the pernicious effects of prejudice in the white-majority province. He did not, however, lose his faith in legal equality or the value of liberty under the British flag. So, when he was introduced to an anti-slavery approach known as the "free-produce movement" while traveling in Great Britain on behalf of the Canadian Anti-Slavery Society, he was soon convinced that becoming an agricultural producer in Jamaica would simultaneously provide a more satisfying experience of British subject-hood and furnish a different means of undermining American slavery.[68]

Originating among British Quakers in the 1790s, the free-produce movement was a radical anti-slavery concept whose aim was to undermine consumers' reliance on slave-produced products like sugar and cotton. Revitalized in Great Britain by reformers hoping to keep the universal anti-slavery spirit alive after the abolition of slavery in British colonies, the movement spread to the United States in the late 1840s and early 1850s. Gaining substantial support among prominent American activists like Frederick Douglass, Harriet Beecher Stowe, and Gerrit Smith, the practical implementation of developing alternative economies had long been influential among leading African Americans.[69] It had been the driving motivation for Paul Cuffe's interest in Sierra Leone in the early 1810s, it had played a significant role in early efforts to promote emigration to Haiti, and, most recently, it had led to the connection between J. W. C. Pennington and the Jamaica Hamic Association in the 1840s.

Now, once again, the idea circulated among African Americans considering emigrating to the British West Indies. At the North American Convention held in Toronto in 1851, two black emigrants living in Jamaica spoke to the delegates of the island's agricultural potential as a major enticement. While the convention ultimately resolved, as a body, to endorse Canada instead, Henry Bibb and the other convention leaders were inspired by the idea of forming an agricultural union between Canada and Jamaica. John T. Fisher, in particular, a black saloon-keeper in Toronto, desired to organize a "North American and West India Federal Agricultural Union." He believed it would "afford facilities of escape and the means of subsistence to negroes in the United States" and allow them to grow produce "in competition with slave labor."[70]

Although Fisher's scheme never got off the ground, the link between Jamaican emigration, free produce, and anti-slavery activism continued to intrigue black emigrants looking for an alternative to the United States. In addition to Samuel Ringgold Ward, the well-known black radical Henry Highland Garnet also moved to Jamaica in early 1853 after having worked as an agent for the free-produce movement in Great Britain for several years. Although he labored in Jamaica as a missionary, not a farmer, he encouraged Jamaican emigration as a means of increasing the island's agricultural output. The roads may have been bad and laborers' social conditions generally inferior, he admitted, but the land was fertile and well-compensated work abounded for the industrious emigrant.[71]

Yet, in spite of the brief and prominent spike in Jamaican emigrationism inspired by the free-produce movement at mid-century, fewer African Americans wound up relocating to the British West Indies than left for either Liberia or Haiti, and the migration stream was simply dwarfed by the flow toward Canada. As historian Gale Kenny points out, Jamaica never overcame the negative reputation that it developed in the wake of British emancipation.[72]

Interest in the free-produce concept was not restricted to the West Indies, however. Perhaps the most surprising scheme it inspired was one developed by Martin Delany to bring African American emigrants to West Africa in the late 1850s. After a long career of vocal opposition to the ACS, the inveterate emigrationist worked tirelessly from 1858 to 1863 to design a settlement plan that would undercut the U.S. South's cotton monopoly. Developed while living in Chatham, Canada West, Delany's plan also reflected a new iteration of his belief that African Americans needed to establish their own nationality removed from the racist influence of whites in order to fulfill their political potential. Abandoning his argument that Central or South America offered the best free-soil alternative, he turned his attention to Africa in late 1857 or early 1858.

At the 1858 National Emigration Convention, held in Chatham, Delany presented a proposal for an "exploration party" to investigate West Africa's settlement potential. He was so committed to his new plan that when the convention responded with only tepid support for his Niger Valley Exploring Party, he actually turned to his old nemesis, the ACS, to secure funding. Between April 1859 and May 1860, Delany explored West Africa and secured a treaty for land from the king of Abeokuta in the Yoruba region, present-day Nigeria. Returning to England after his travels, he produced an "official report" exhaustively detailing the region's characteristics, settlement prospects, and economic potential, and he successfully secured financial support for his free-produce plan from anti-slavery allies and manufacturing interests. In the end, his remarkable scheme was only scuttled by the outbreak of civil war in the United States and his decision to return to fight for black freedom in the land of his birth.[73]

While Delany's Niger Valley project was heavily inspired by the free-produce concept, changing political circumstances in the United States no doubt also fueled his ongoing interest in establishing a black nation for African Americans away from white influence. While the 1850 Fugitive Slave Act had led Delany to reverse his previously held belief that black Americans should fight for their political equality in the United States, his subsequent conviction that black people would never be able to achieve their potential under the thumb of white oppression seemed more true than ever by the end of the decade. Compounding the chilling effects of the Fugitive Slave Act, the 1857 Supreme Court ruling in *Dred Scott* v. *Sandford* established a legal precedent in the highest court that African Americans were not U.S. citizens.

The ruling against Dred Scott, who had sued for his freedom because his owner had brought him into territory where the Missouri Compromise had prohibited slavery, held that Scott was a non-citizen and therefore lacked legal standing to bring his case to court. The decision, written by Chief Justice Roger Taney, specifically declared that the U.S. Constitution did not, and had not intended to, provide a basis for citizenship to people whose ancestors had been imported into the country and sold as slaves.[74] With this demoralizing decision, the Supreme Court simultaneously undermined the basis for African American citizenship and reiterated once again the federal government's ongoing commitment to protecting white slave owners' property claims throughout the entire nation.

Delany was not alone in deepening his commitment to finding a new home for African Americans outside the United States in the wake of the *Dred Scott* decision. Nor was he alone among more prominent emigrationists in feeling that racial prejudice prevented white-majority Canada from representing more than a temporary alternative. While Delany looked for a new settlement in West Africa and Samuel Ringgold Ward left for the Caribbean, black activist and emigrationist James Theodore Holly breathed new life into the idea of Haitian emigration for the first time since the 1820s.

Like Ward and Mary Ann Shadd, Holly had moved to Upper Canada in 1851 after the passage of the Fugitive Slave Act. He worked closely with Henry Bibb and the RHS, and spent several years endorsing Upper

Canada as an asylum for refugees of American slavery. Yet as early as 1853, he began promoting the idea of Haitian emigration. Along with two other members of a "Committee on Emigration" reporting to an 1853 meeting held in Amherstburg, Canada West, Holly asserted that "emigration [to Haiti] in large numbers on the part of the colored Americans would do much to strengthen the hands of that Government, and forward in an incalculable degree the cause of our elevation in America."[75] By the time the National Emigration Convention was held in Cleveland, Ohio, in August 1854, Holly had moved back to the United States to promote Haitian emigration.

During the mid-1850s, Holly expanded on his ideas regarding Haiti's significance as a site of international free-soil emigration and became the foremost advocate of what historian Floyd J. Miller has termed "missionary-nationalism."[76] Having joined the Protestant Episcopal Church in 1851, Holly became intensely interested both in establishing an Episcopal mission in Haiti and in promoting Haitian emigration as a means of strengthening the island nation, uplifting the entirety of the black race, and eventually rejuvenating Africa itself. He endorsed Haiti at the 1854 National Emigration Convention and visited the island as the Convention's "official commissioner" to assess its prospects in 1855.

While investigatory free-soil travelers typically focused on producing specific information regarding the land, laws, and society of a particular free-soil locale, Holly arrived already convinced that the island was the ideal choice for prospective emigrants. So, instead, he focused his time in Haiti on his two biggest concerns regarding the emigration project. First, he hoped to ascertain the potential of establishing a mission in Haiti. Second, he was determined to acquire assurances from the Haitian government that the pitfalls of the 1820s emigration movement would not be repeated. He sought guarantees that black emigrants would receive "encouragements" to establish themselves as cultivators and industrial manufacturers on the island, that they would be granted full political and civil rights equal to native-born Haitians, that they would become full citizens after one year of residence, and that they could enjoy complete freedom of religion.

Although he was ultimately unable to extract any promises from the Haitian government whatsoever, he was undeterred. After returning to the United States, he advocated for Haitian emigration at both the 1856 and 1858 National Emigration Conventions and lectured on the history of Haiti and the Haitian Revolution. In 1857, he published a pamphlet version of his lecture stressing the political importance of African American emigration to the island, and in 1859 he reiterated his ideas in a seven-part series published in the new black literary periodical *The Anglo-African Magazine*.[77] If black emigrants carried with them from the United States "the arts, sciences and genius of modern civilization," Holly believed, they would "contribute to the continued advancement of this negro nationality of the New World [Haiti] until its glory and renown shall overspread and cover the whole earth, and redeem and regenerate by its influence in the future, the benighted Fatherland of the race in Africa."[78]

In 1859, Holly's indefatigable efforts finally bore fruit. In large part, the success of his advocacy was propelled by the fact that the Haitian government itself came on board. It sent two commissioners to the United States in 1858 with an official invitation for African American emigration. Although, as *The Liberator* reported, the commissioners were "not prepared to specify the inducements which the Emperor may offer to attract immigration to his island," the presence of the commissioners signified that Haiti was eager to encourage black Americans to emigrate, just as they had in the 1820s.[79]

In addition, Haitian emigrationism garnered the support of a white abolitionist, James Redpath, who soon became the movement's foremost representative. He helped to establish an official Haitian Bureau of Emigration and helped to woo the support of prominent black individuals like William Wells Brown to act as agents on the bureau's behalf.[80] Although many black activists, including both Martin Delany and Mary Ann Shadd (now Mary Ann Shadd Cary), were highly critical of the fact that Redpath was white, the Haitian emigration project nevertheless took off under his leadership.[81] Between 1859 and 1862, 2,000 black settlers emigrated to Haiti, including several hundred from Louisiana. While these migrants accounted for less than 1 percent of the combined free black populations of Louisiana, the Midwest, and the northeastern United States, their decision to leave for the black republic was momentous.[82]

Notably, the Haitian emigration project proved to be successful even among the black communities in Canada, underscoring the fact that James Theodore Holly's dissatisfaction with Canadian racial prejudice was widely shared. In August 1861, Mary Ann Shadd Cary's brother-in-law, George Cary, organized a group of "twelve or fifteen good, reliable men" to move from Upper Canada to Haiti. Writing to James Redpath of his intention for the group to cultivate cotton on the island, Cary lamented the circumstances of his departure from British soil: "Most of us have comfortable homes in this country, where the laws are equal; but we have damning prejudice to contend against." Canadian racism, in his view, was "preventative to a just and equal administration of the British Constitution."[83]

Noting that emigrants in Canada were interested in relocating once again, William Wells Brown, now an agent of the Haitian Bureau of Emigration, toured Upper Canada to promote interest. He spoke at town halls in Colchester, Amherstburg, Windsor, London, Hamilton, and Toronto, and met with audiences he described as "large" and "much interested in the past history and the present condition of the Republic of Hayti." Only twice did he turn away interested emigrants: once because he suspected alcoholism, and once because the prospective migrant was a fiddler who "could do nothing but *fiddle*" – and would thus have no profitable skills with which to succeed in Haiti.[84] Though Brown's reports from the field painted a highly complimentary portrait of the relative comfort, prosperity, morality, and education of black life in Canada, it was clear that many, like George Cary, still felt the sting of color prejudice in their daily lives.[85] Between the fall and winter of 1861–1862, several hundred African Americans left the British province and resettled in Haiti.[86]

As historian Chris Dixon points out, the appeal of the Haitian scheme during these years represented a significant climax to antebellum emigrationism.[87] In sheer numbers, it certainly outpaced Henry Highland Garnet's efforts to entice emigrants to Jamaica and Martin Delany's aborted plan to establish a settlement of black emigrants in West Africa. The Haitian government also proved to be more successful in luring African American settlers than did the Mexican government, which attempted to attract black emigrants with offers of subsidized land in 1857.[88]

While the "stay-and-fight" doctrine remained a more dominant ideology among African Americans than emigrationism, the success of the Haitian emigration scheme at the end of the 1850s reflects the diminishing confidence of many black Americans that they would ever win the fight for freedom and equality in the United States. Even the most prominent and longstanding anti-emigrationist, Frederick Douglass, began to change his tune as the Haitian emigration project continued into the 1860s. "Never, we think, has the feeling in favor of emigration been so strong as now," wrote Douglass in January 1861 to readers of his *Douglass' Monthly.* In his estimation, Haiti in the early 1860s offered "the strongest inducements to emigration to her shores." More important than the offer of "generous terms" to "the industrious and upright colored man and his family" was the fact that the "cry from [Haiti] is for light, labor, enterprise, order, and all the arts of an advanced civilization." By contrast, the United States offered only "slavery, vengeance and settled hate."[89]

According to Douglass, even potential allies were proving inconsistent and disappointing. "Whatever the future may have in store for us," Douglass wrote, "it seems plain that the inducements offered to the colored man to remain here are few, feeble and very uncertain." For the first time, he seriously considered the merits of emigration:

> While we have never favored any plan of emigration, and have never been willing to concede that this is a doomed country, and that we are a doomed race in it, we can raise no objection to the present, movement towards Hayti. For years we have looked to such emigration as a possible necessity to our people; and though we do not think that necessity has yet fully come, we can no longer throw our little influence against a measure which may prove highly advantageous to many families, and of much service to the Haytian Republic.[90]

The resurgence of Haiti as a popular destination was a dynamic conclusion to antebellum emigrationism, and noteworthy for the way it diverged from both the Haitian emigration project of the 1820s and the ongoing movement of African Americans across the U.S.–Canada border. As Frederick Douglass's surprising endorsement highlights, the resurgence of Haitian emigrationism at the end of the 1850s was ulti-mately more about leaving behind the disappointments of the United States than it was about fighting American slavery from abroad. Whereas the Haitian emigration movement of the 1820s held that the model of black men's success in a republican nation would positively affect anti-slavery reformism in the United States, the movement inspired by James T. Holly emphasized the importance of developing a black nationality outside the United States in order to contribute to the *global* uplift of the "African race." Haiti continued to resonate as a symbol of black revolution in the fight against slavery, but its significance as a site of African American emigration in the late 1850s was less about disman-tling American slavery than it was about cultivating a strong, global black community.

By contrast, Canada during the 1850s continued to be a base of anti-slavery action where the focus remained on achieving racial justice for African Americans in the United States. James T. Holly himself perfectly summed it up while working with Henry Bibb in Chatham, Canada West: "Here we can literally hang as a threatening *black* cloud over the American Union, waiting and praying for the Lord's day of vengeance, when we may be the humble instruments in his hands, to do the terrible work, of his settling, for centuries of oppression, wrong and blasphemy."[91] Notably, prominent black activists who never emigrated also shared this regard for the British province. Well-known Pennsylvanian William Whipper, for example, identified Upper Canada as a place where African Americans were able to perform more "practical antislavery work" than they could in the United States.[92]

By providing a protected asylum for fugitive slaves, Canada encour-aged a form of anti-slavery activism (self-emancipation) that was singu-larly galling to American slaveholders. By offering a venue for African Americans and their anti-slavery allies to model and contribute to the success of black freedom, Canada undermined pro-slavery arguments regarding the natural inferiority of black people and their unsuitability for freedom and independence. By supplying anti-slavery activists with a secure location from which they could raise their pens and their voices,

Canada provided a powerful platform from which to agitate for the legal equality and citizenship denied African Americans in the United States. In very practical ways, Canada was both an alternative to and an indictment of the United States and its racist institutions.

Perhaps no event more dramatically illustrates the practical value of Canada as a staging area for anti-slavery action than John Brown's famous raid on the federal armory at Harper's Ferry, Virginia (now West Virginia). A fiery preacher and anti-slavery radical, John Brown and several of his sons had been active fighters and leaders in the bloody "border war" that had overtaken Kansas when the 1854 Kansas–Nebraska Act had legislated that each territory would be allowed to decide for itself whether or not to allow slavery. In May 1856, Brown famously led four of his sons and three other men in the murder of five pro-slavery men at Pottowatomie Creek, enacting retribution for an earlier pro-slavery attack on the anti-slavery stronghold of Lawrence, Kansas.[93]

Brown was deeply inspired in his anti-slavery activism by Toussaint Louverture, the Haitian Revolution, and the guerrilla warfare tactics used during the slave rebellion that developed into the Haitian Revolution. Yet even as Haiti's violent anti-slavery origins encouraged Brown, he did not share emigrationists' interest in the island nation's contemporary potential to foster the future of the black race.[94] Rather, he was inspired by the island's past to develop a plan for the liberation of American slaves through a large-scale slave uprising begun from the mountainous terrain of western Virginia.

When John Brown began organizing the slave uprising and anti-slavery future that he imagined would begin with his raid on Harper's Ferry, he did so from Canada. On May 8, 1858, he brought together a clandestine group of approximately fifty anti-slavery whites, free black emigrants, and fugitive slaves at Chatham, Canada West. They discussed his plan of attack and wrote a "Provisional Constitution" for an independent anti-slavery republic that would be established in the wake of his armed foray into the South. Among the group who attended the secret "Convention" on May 8 were Mary Ann Shadd Cary's new husband, Thomas Cary, her brother, Isaac, and Martin Delany, who did much of the organizational work for the meeting.[95] With this group, Brown not only delineated his plan for an attack in Virginia, he quelled concern regarding numerical support by claiming that he would attract the support of both black northerners and African Americans in Canada. He assured the delegates attending the Chatham convention that "as many of the free negroes in Canada as could accompany him, would do so."[96] Just two months before the raid, Brown sent an agent to Chatham, Buxton, and other communities in Upper Canada to form "Liberty Leagues" from which fighters might be recruited.[97]

In many respects, John Brown's raid on Harper's Ferry was a failure. When Brown descended on the federal arsenal 60 miles northwest of the U.S. capital on October 16, 1859, he had with him a force of only five black men and sixteen white. While the group was initially able to overpower the arsenal and hold it for two days, they were surrounded and captured in the early morning of October 18. Ten of the raiders were killed in the action, along with two slaves who had joined the fight. Seven, including Brown himself, were tried for murder, treason, and conspiracy to incite a slave insurrection, and all were executed. Moreover, the raid had not instigated the massive slave rebellion that Brown had anticipated. In fact, only a handful of enslaved men from the surrounding counties had elected to join his ranks. By all counts, Brown's bold gambit to release the bonds of slavery was over before it had even begun.[98]

Yet while Brown was not successful in his lifetime, the anti-slavery plan that he set in motion from Canada West helped to push a divided nation toward a national war that historian Steven Hahn has referred to as the "greatest slave rebellion in modern history."[99] John Brown's raid was a fitting capstone to Canada's decades-long history of providing anti-slavery advocates with a free-soil base of operations from which to challenge the U.S. slave system. Although it ultimately took a civil war to end slavery in the United States – rather than a planned emancipation modeled on earlier examples or a peaceful socio-political shift effected by abolitionist strategizing – free-soil alternatives had nonetheless made an indelible mark on the culture of the American anti-slavery movement. Offering freedom to fugitive slaves who could make

the perilous journey, equality to free African Americans who had lost
hope for it in the United States, and hope for a future without chattel
slavery altogether, the expanding geography of international free-soil
havens had inspired the anti-slavery movement and helped to shape
the form and substance of racial justice activism throughout the antebellum period.

Conclusion

The fact that many thousands of blacks and mulattoes, who have fled from slavery, or from social oppression in this country, are living in Upper Canada as free men, with all the rights and privileges of British subjects, is too important to be overlooked by a Commission of Inquiry into the condition and capacity of the colored population of the United States, just set free.

~ Samuel Gridley Howe, *The Refugees from Slavery in Canada West: Report to the Freedmen's Inquiry Commission* (1864)[1]

In September 1863, just nine months after Abraham Lincoln delivered his Emancipation Proclamation freeing slaves in Confederate territory, prominent northern reformer Samuel Gridley Howe packed his bags and traveled north across the U.S.–Canada border. It was not Howe's first time in Canada. A member of the "Secret Six," a group of northern abolitionists who supported John Brown's 1859 raid on Harper's Ferry, Howe had fled to Canada to lie low until the dust settled after Brown's arrest.

This time, however, he was on official business. He was one of three men appointed by Edwin Stanton, the U.S. Secretary of War, to advise Lincoln's administration regarding the men, women, and children freed by the president's wartime emancipation initiative.[2] The mandate of the American Freedmen's Inquiry Commission (AFIC) was to determine how freed African Americans could assist in the war effort, what their needs were in the transition from slavery to freedom, and what the social effects of releasing so many men and women from bondage would likely be.

Steeped in an anti-slavery culture in which American reformers had long looked across international borders in order to formulate ideas regarding freedom's potential at home, the commissioners took a distinctly transnational approach to their mandate. While the bulk of their work consisted of conducting interviews with former slaves, military officers, and civilian officials in Union-occupied southern states, the commissioners extended their inquiries to Haiti and Canada. In addition, Howe sent a friend to report back on conditions in Jamaica and Honduras.[3]

The scope of these inquiries built on almost fifty years of social investigation in free-soil havens abroad. Beginning with Paul Cuffe's Sierra Leone plan in 1813 and continuing through to the very end of the antebellum period with James T. Holly's efforts to revive enthusiasm for Haitian emigration, the expanding geography of international free soil had remained a constant feature in the fight for freedom and racial justice in the United States. Free and enslaved African Americans, white reformers, and anti-slavery advocates along a broad ideological spectrum had spent decades investing international free-soil spaces with a wide range of ideas, opinions, plans, and hopes for the future. When asked to weigh in on how the United States should move forward in the wake of the wartime Emancipation Proclamation, it made perfect sense for the AFIC to investigate the outcome of freedom in places where freedom had already been tried.

Within the constellation of international free-soil havens, it is no surprise that Howe was particularly keen to travel to Upper Canada (now Canada West) on the commission's behalf. By the outbreak of civil war in 1861, the correlation between Canada and black freedom had been steadily growing since James C. Brown and the black Cincinnatians had first reached out to Lieutenant Governor John Colborne in 1829. While self-emancipated men and women had been crossing into Upper Canada since the late eighteenth century, the black Cincinnatians laid the groundwork for the British province to become the foremost beacon of liberty in the antebellum period. Not only did Upper Canada offer freedom and protection to those who liberated themselves from U.S. slavery, black emigrants' self-advocacy encouraged Colborne to extend legal equality to all African Americans who crossed its borders. Although not always able to deliver on the socio-economic hopes of emigrants, its reputation had only grown as the northmost terminus of the Underground Railroad. It became a safe harbor, a symbol of freedom, and the top international destination for anti-slavery advocates hoping to translate free-soil activities abroad into anti-slavery action in the United States.

Following in the footsteps of reformers like Hiram Wilson, Mary Ann Shadd, and Benjamin Drew, Samuel Gridley Howe was determined to produce a comprehensive file on "the history, condition, and prospects of the colored population of Canada."[4] Recognizing that Upper Canada's black communities had long "been trying the experiment, for their race, of their capacity for self-support and self-guidance," he believed that they provided an ideal case study for evaluating black freedom and for determining how the U.S. government should proceed in the wake of the Emancipation Proclamation.[5] Could African Americans succeed in freedom? Were they willing to work and able to support themselves? Would freedom inevitably lead to racial "amalgamation"? Were former slaves morally fit for freedom?[6]

To glean all he could from across the U.S.–Canada border, Howe reproduced several familiar methods of free-soil investigation. First, he circulated among white Canadian officials and health professionals a series of questions designed to solicit information about the black population's general health and rate of reproduction, their industriousness, and their capacity for self-support. It was the same questionnaire that the AFIC commissioners had directed to cities and towns throughout the United States, and a shortened version of a questionnaire sent to officials in the Union-occupied South, where self-emancipated men and women had essentially turned the Union Army line into a moving free-soil zone.[7] Notably, the thirteen-question survey also bore a striking resemblance to the questionnaire Hiram Wilson had sent to white officials in Upper Canada twenty-six years earlier, when the American Anti-Slavery Society had commissioned him to explore the conditions of black emigrants in 1837. In recognition of Wilson's long standing as a foremost authority on the topic, Howe also solicited more specific information about Upper Canada from Wilson himself.[8]

Next, Howe departed with his stenographer, James Yerrinton, to conduct on-the-ground interviews in communities of varying sizes throughout the province. While he certainly met with well-placed white individuals like members of Canada's Provincial Parliament, the Chief

Superintendent of Education, and even a doctor at Toronto's Lunatic Asylum, the majority of Howe's time was spent interviewing African American emigrants themselves – including a woman of 108 who could recall the Revolutionary War.[9] Over the course of two separate trips, Howe collected a total of ninety-eight interviews, constituting over 300 pages of what historian Oz Frankel has characterized as "state-sponsored investigation."[10] Noting in the margins of interviewees' testimony when they touched on themes of particular interest, Howe and Yerrinton compiled an enormous resource for evaluating the results of freedom and legal equality in a white-dominant society where the existence of prejudice was well known.[11]

The result of Howe's multi-pronged investigative work in Upper Canada was a lengthy report titled *The Refugees from Slavery in Canada West*. Published as a supplemental document alongside the AFIC's final 1864 report to the U.S. government, its findings laid the foundation for the commission's overall recommendations to the Lincoln administration.[12] Helping to shape the U.S. government's approach to freed people after the Civil War – most notably in the form of the Freedmen's Bureau – Howe's inquiries and interviews in Upper Canada ensured that the experiences of African Americans in the British province would finally exert the influence on American federal policy that nineteenth-century reformers had always hoped it would.[13]

In the end, Howe's methodology and the conclusions he conveyed to the Lincoln administration reflect both the best and the worst of what international free-soil investigation had to offer in the fight for freedom and racial justice. At its best, free-soil investigation could potentially "prove" that emancipation was a safe, economically sound, and socially promising course of action – as well as what kind of policies and protections would best support freed people. But white reformers, in particular, had a tendency to see what they expected to see. Like James Thome, Joseph Kimball, and Sylvester Hovey in the British West Indies, investigatory travelers could collect similar evidence but reach very different conclusions. At its worst, therefore, free-soil investigation ran the risk of perpetuating investigators' preconceived beliefs about black people and what they thought would be the best means of assisting them in the transition from slavery to freedom.

Howe went to Canada and saw what he expected to see. And the result was a lost opportunity to craft more nuanced advice for navigating the complexities of racism in the wake of emancipation. In part, as Howe's selection of testimony shows, this was because of his *own* damaging views about black racial inferiority. A medical doctor by training, Howe was a firm believer that black bodies were naturally suited to warmer climates. While Howe's beliefs on the topic had been developed in part through his friendship with noted racial theorist Louis Agassiz, they were not uncommon in the nineteenth century. In fact, assessing black people's health in various climates had long been a cornerstone of free-soil investigation and had often shaped white reformers' perspectives on where African Americans were most likely to thrive once free. Howe, like many nineteenth-century reformers, believed that black people living in Canada (and, by extension, the northern United States) were less healthy, weaker, and less likely to reproduce naturally than black people living in the warmer climates of the South, the Caribbean, or Africa. As a result, Howe included testimony in his final report that supported these racist ideas while omitting a great deal of testimony that refuted it.[14]

In his enthusiasm to paint the long-term effects of freedom in a positive light, Howe was also predisposed to underappreciate the impact of prejudice on black emigrants' daily lives. It is clear from his collected testimony, for example, that local whites regularly charged black emigrants with shirking hard labor. Yet because he could not countenance the merit of these claims – to him, the evidence unequivocally showed that free African Americans were able and willing to work for wages and be self-sufficient members of society – he simply concluded that such assertions must have been "made thoughtlessly." Overall, he declared, "no sensible people in Canada charge the refugees with slothfulness."[15]

While certainly presenting a favorable view of black emigrants, Howe's preconceived ideas about the emigrants' industriousness prevented him from developing a more useful appraisal of *why* local whites disparaged their work ethic – and how it related to their experience of freedom. He might have identified the labor competition existing between black emigrants and immigrant Irish, for example, or introduced into his report black emigrants' *own* perspectives on the relationship between their freedom and their labor.[16] Indeed, despite the collected testimony being positively riddled with disappointment in the racism emigrants experienced in Canada, Howe simply did not consider how it might contribute to emigrants' efforts to earn a fair wage.[17] Unable to see beyond the basic premise that African Americans could be self-sufficient in freedom, Howe missed the important opportunity to consider the ongoing socio-economic ramifications of prejudice and how it might be addressed.

Nonetheless, Howe did reflect extensively on the importance of establishing and maintaining black legal equality in order to combat white racism when it reared its head – a topic that permeated the interviews. A shoemaker named F. G. Simpson was just one of many whose testimony Howe highlighted on the topic. "I must say," Simpson asserted, "that leaving the law out of the question, I find that prejudice here is equally strong as on the other side. The law is the only thing that sustains us in this country."[18] This sentiment was shared by John Shipton, who testified that "the prejudice [in Canada] would be a heap worse than in the States, if it was not that the law keeps it down."[19] Susan Boggs of St. Catharines declared that black people in Upper Canada would actually be "mobbed" if not for "the Queen's law," and that remaining in the province would be impossible without it.[20] Interviewees such as Simpson, Shipton, and Boggs clearly did not believe that legal equality could prevent social prejudice, but Howe listened when they told him in no uncertain terms that it was the fact of their legal equality in Canada that positively distinguished British territory from the United States.

It was a radical proposition. After all, a direct relationship between freedom and equality was antithetical to the very foundation of racial inequality upon which the United States was firmly settled. But the same "Canada Culture" that had propelled Howe northward in the first place was so steeped in the importance of legal equality that he was likely predisposed to appreciate his black interviewees' consistent emphasis on its importance. The British-Canadian government's provision of legal equality was a major component of why Canada had developed such a positive reputation among African Americans and their white allies in the first place. And many who felt it was the *only* feature of Canadian life setting it apart from the northern states made no bones about the fact that they would return if it were on offer in their native land.[21]

Yet even as Howe highlighted the remarkable idea that legal equality was a crucial facet of freedom, he did not fully appreciate where it still fell short. His conclusions overlooked the persistent concerns of many emigrants that legal equality was ultimately insufficient to the task of protecting black residents from the daily effects of white racism. On a day-to-day basis, black emigrants felt the effects of school segregation, the sting of being turned away from inns and taverns, and the burn of being treated as second-class citizens by their neighbors despite their equality under British law. It was the inability of legal equality on its own to protect black emigrants from the pernicious effects of prejudice that led scores of Canadian residents to relocate to Haiti in 1861–1862. Ironically, it was also a major reason that many black emigrants in Canada moved back to the United States after the Civil War, once the Thirteenth and Fourteenth Amendments guaranteed (on paper) the same freedom and legal equality for which so many had originally fled to Canada.[22]

Glossing over the profound impact of racism, Howe noted in a final section of his report that former slaves would need no more protection than poor whites. They would become, he declared, "loyal supporters of any government which ensures their freedom and rights." Since the "white man" had failed at "taking care" of African Americans, he concluded, it was time to "let the negro try to take care of himself."[23]

While the "general inferences" he drew from Canada ensured that that the radical idea of providing legal equality to freed people became a cornerstone of the AFIC's overall recommendations to the Lincoln administration in 1864, it was not enough.[24] The guarantee of legal equality for African Americans signaled a profound shift in the bedrock of race relations in the United States, but the insidious ways that racism finds a way around the law continues to bedevil the nation to this day.

And, indeed, while Howe's research in Canada concluded the antebellum practice of sending respected agents to assess the conditions of black freedom abroad, it was not the last time that American observers missed an opportunity to learn from example that legal equality alone would not prevent black oppression in places structured by white supremacy. On October 11, 1865, in the Jamaican parish of St. Thomas-in-the-East, a large-scale rebellion broke out at Morant Bay after the colonial court decided to bring black farmers to trial for "trespassing" on the land of abandoned plantation estates. Four days earlier, a black Baptist preacher named Paul Bogle had sent a petition to the court protesting the decision: "We have been imposed upon for a period of 27 years with due obeisance to the laws of our Queen and country," he wrote, "and we can no longer endure the same."[25]

As Bogle's words suggest, black Jamaicans' grievances went far beyond the circumstances of the moment. He identified a longstanding pattern of black oppression in Jamaica that dated back to 1838, the year that enslaved Jamaicans had become legally free. Not only did his anger and his warning go unheeded, however, the island's governor declared martial law when Bogle and several hundred armed black Jamaicans gathered on the courthouse steps to make themselves heard. Within three weeks, over 500 black Jamaicans had been killed and over 1,000 homes destroyed in response to their protest.[26]

As historian Nichola Clayton argues, American observers in 1865 could not help but view Jamaica's Morant Bay Rebellion in light of their own efforts to confront the aftermath of civil war.[27] After thirty years of debate, the question of whether British emancipation in the West Indies had been a promising success or an abysmal failure was suddenly more relevant than ever as Americans wondered what to expect from the emancipation of all enslaved people. In spite of abolitionists' continued efforts to frame the outcome of British emancipation as a positive step forward for human justice, by the late 1850s American opinion had largely concluded that the "Great Experiment" had been a disaster due to the seeming inability of Jamaica's sugar economy to recover to its pre-emancipation levels.[28] As one observer put it in 1856, it was "obvious to any one who will take the trouble of inquiring" that Jamaica had been irrevocably damaged by "the philanthropy of John Bull."[29]

But public opinion changed drastically during the second half of the American Civil War. Anti-slavery arguments proved to be more acceptable to mainstream political moderates as it became increasingly clear that emancipation would be the outcome of a Union victory. Moreover, as historian Chandra Manning has documented, Union soldiers themselves saw the war as a fight to end slavery. As part of this sea change, the idea that free (non-slave) labor was economically superior was suddenly resuscitated to such a degree that it seemed to be "received wisdom" within the pages of the same journals that had unambiguously rejected the idea just a few years earlier.[30] Yet just when both moderate and radical Republicans agreed to count the British example as proof positive of emancipation's economic viability, the Morant Bay Rebellion revitalized the pro-slavery narrative that emancipation would inevitably have dire social consequences. While many saw the rebellion was the inevitable result of planters' unwillingness to treat laborers fairly, planters and their northern allies closed ranks around the belief that emancipation would produce an unwilling workforce and an unsafe society.[31]

Like Howe's inability to recognize the limitations of legal equality in Canada, the inability of American observers to agree on what lessons should be learned from the Morant Bay Rebellion presaged the ongoing racial inequality that became a defining characteristic of the United States in the second half of the nineteenth century. While Reconstruction ushered in a twelve-year period of political and social gains for black southerners, many of its achievements were not long lasting. The Fourteenth and Fifteenth Amendments defined African Americans as citizens, guaranteed the right of black men to vote, and provided the same legal protections for people of color as white Americans received. Yet the meaningful practice of these legal guarantees was gradually eroded by new patterns of labor coercion, judicial evisceration, and the growth of paramilitary anti-black violence intended to reestablish white supremacy. While African Americans remained equal citizens under federal law, deeply rooted racism had undermined the social and political promises of Reconstruction even before it ended in 1877.[32]

Because racial inequality long outlasted slavery in the United States, so too did emigrationism, proving itself to be one of the final legacies of nineteenth-century free-soil culture. As white southerners increasingly targeted freed people – as well as their legal rights and protections – in the mid-1870s, many black southerners and their communities began to express interest in considering geopolitical alternatives to the post-emancipation South. Particularly in cotton-growing regions where black majorities had initially made substantial political gains under Reconstruction, African Americans in the South began looking for more promising places to resettle.

Whereas Canada had been the dominant pre-war destination for black emigrants, its antebellum reputation for protecting fugitive slaves and providing legal equality were less relevant to those living in the post-Civil War United States. Instead, new patterns of emigration emerged as black southerners considered where they might go to escape the abuses of a southern society so deeply rooted in racism and inequity. While many looked west toward Kansas and Indiana, some turned toward Liberia and the waiting arms of the American Colonization Society. As black northerners had prior to the Civil War, southerners began meeting to discuss Liberia's potential. Using rural political infrastructures to support what historian Steven Hahn has called "grassroots emigrationism," black southerners formed interest groups like the Liberia Exodus Association of Pinesville, Florida, and the Pilgrim Travelers of Robertson County, Texas.[33]

While most black northerners in the antebellum period had seen the ACS as anathema to their best interests, black southerners during the Reconstruction era and beyond were more willing to view it positively. Many saw Liberian emigration as an escape from the pervasive racism preventing them from experiencing the equality they expected as free American citizens. They viewed the ACS's financial support as a means to that end. For example, when black Mississippian A. B. Coleman wrote to the ACS in 1880, he noted both his disappointment in the current condition of his community members and his interest in Liberian emigration. Noting the poverty that characterized the lives of "the majority," he looked forward to the day when "justice will be meted out to every one, without regard to color or former condition of servitude." He wanted to "see [his] race have their rights." In the meantime, however, he believed that as many African Americans as could "conveniently go" should leave for Liberia in order to be "better off."[34]

Despite Coleman's confidence in Liberian emigration, the actual number of black Americans who relocated to West Africa remained as comparatively low as the colonization numbers had been prior to the American Civil War. Between 1877 and 1880, only 388 black southerners left for Liberia, and only 3,812 left for Liberia during the entire post-Civil War period. In comparative perspective, somewhere between 20,000 and 25,000 migrated from the southern states to Kansas between 1879 and 1880 alone.[35] But as A. B. Coleman's letter suggests, when the legal protections afforded by the Fourteenth and Fifteenth Amendments failed to ensure meaningful social equality, African Americans in the late nineteenth century continued to tap into the legacy of antebellum emigrationism to consider whether freedom might feel more "free" elsewhere.

In the end, the fact that free-soil emigration continued to resonate during and after Reconstruction underscores a central facet of nineteenth-century free-soil culture: the futures that Americans imagined by engaging with international free-soil havens were rooted in possibilities represented by "somewhere else." For decades, African Americans and their white allies had engaged with free-soil examples to ensure that black Americans were given a fair shake. International free-soil havens were inflected with the changing desires, opinions, and concerns of many different people over decades characterized by immense international and domestic changes related to slavery and freedom. Yet their significance within the American anti-slavery movement was fundamentally grounded in the fact that they offered physical and conceptual alternatives to the prevailing pro-slavery policies of the United States.

While the lessons learned in international free-soil spaces were more complex than any could have predicted – and their practical application proved to be uneven in a divided nation where emancipation had only been achieved in the aftermath of civil war – the practice of producing and sharing information about black freedom abroad was ultimately about drawing hope and inspiration from elsewhere into the ongoing struggle for racial justice at home.

Appendix

TABLE 1 *International Free-Soil Emigration Streams*

Date(s)	Free-Soil Destination	Migrant Nos. (Where noted, numbers reflect overall population rather than total migrants)
1793–1829	Upper Canada	Regular destination of fugitive slaves, numbers unknown[1]
1813–1817	Sierra Leone	38[2]
1820s–1840s	Mexico	Regular destination of hundreds of fugitive slaves, exact number unknown[3]
1821–1847	Liberia	5,829[4]
1825–1827	Haiti	~6,000[5]
1829	Upper Canada	~460–600[6]
1831	Upper Canada	1,000–2,000[7]
1831–1840	Upper Canada	~5,000–13,511(overall population)[8]
1831–1841	Bahamas	391[9]
1840–1844	Jamaica	29–480[10]
1842–1848	Upper Canada	4,167–~20,000 (overall population)[11]
1843–1850	British West Indies	Destination of fugitive slaves, number unknown[12]
1848–1854	Liberia	4,010[13]
1850–1854	Mexico	~2,000–~4,000[14]
1851–1860	Upper Canada	4,669–~60,000(?) (overall population)[15]
1853–1855	Jamaica	Small, but prominent, migration of free African Americans[16]
1857	Mexico	Small, unknown number of free emigrants, largely from New Orleans[17]
1859–1862	Haiti	~2,000[18]
1861	Upper Canada	11,223–17,053 (overall population)[19]
1877–	Liberia	4,200[20]

Acknowledgments

So many individuals, communities, and institutions have made this book possible. It is a joy to acknowledge them here and offer my sincere thanks.

My journey as a historian started at Occidental College under the mentorship of two incredible scholars, mentors, and women: Gabrielle Foreman and Sharla Fett. When they took me under their wings and offered their generous wisdom, guidance, training, and friendship, they opened my eyes to the world in new ways and helped me to think more expansively about who I want to be in it. It was also their support that set the wheels in motion for this book – although I certainly had no inkling of it at the time. Not only did they get me hooked on archives and teach me how to pose rich research questions, they were my champions as I designed my first research projects, wrote my first grant proposals, and struggled to put it all together into meaningful scholarship for the first time. My interest in many of the historical individuals, episodes, and themes discussed in this book dates back to my time learning from these two educator-scholars, and they continue to be a guiding light.

I also owe a great debt to the Occidental community as a whole. The History, English, and Critical Theory and Social Justice Departments collectively offered constant encouragement, allowed me to take my own path, and modeled the very best of intellectual engagement. Occidental College's Undergraduate Research Center provided financial support that took me to the Caribbean on my first international research trips, and through the wonderful library I met Marsha Schnirring, who taught me so much about library systems, archives, and collaboration. I would also like to thank Elmer Griffin and Nicole

Anderson Cobb, who, each in their own way, radically informed my understanding of racial justice and offered great kindness as they challenged my thinking in the classroom and beyond. The gift of receiving such widespread mentorship, rigorous hands-on training, and institutional support early on in my life has, in no small way, made this book possible.

The years I spent at Georgetown University were similarly transformative. My wonderful advisor, Adam Rothman, encouraged me to explore and experiment – even when my interests took me far afield – and he was always there to help me wrangle my ideas when the time came to move forward. Thank you for challenging me, guiding me, and supporting me – from the first day I walked into your office all the way through to the publication of this book. In graduate school, I was once again blessed with the mentorship and friendship of two incomparable women and scholars: Alison Games and Chandra Manning. This book would not exist without them. The first steps into my research were taken during a seminar with Alison Games, and her constant encouragement to consider the transatlantic connections and currents gave my work substance and shape throughout the dissertation process. The doyenne of Team Atlantic, she created a cohort that made graduate life infinitely better and full of interesting opportunities. And I could not have asked for a better neighbor. Chandra Manning, you have been a beacon. In addition to your clarion guidance, key questions, and unparalleled generosity, you have been an unending source of inspiration and friendship. Your superpower is seeing the significance of people's ideas and helping them step into their full potential. I have learned so much from you, and your stalwart support and encouragement have meant the world to me for over a decade. And, of course, a special thank you to Aidan Manning, who asked about Mexico.

There are so many at Georgetown who contributed to my thinking, writing, and life as this project came into being. Maurice Jackson and Lori Merish both provided guidance and supervision at key moments in my graduate journey. Team Atlantic – including John McNeill, Jordan Smith, Chelsea Berry, Mike Hill, Earnie Porta, Suze Zijlstra, Katherine Steir, Roz Rothwell, and Rachel Lee – was a source of enormous camaraderie and accountability. The Early Modern Global

History Seminar and the 19th-Century U.S. History Workshop – as well as the visiting scholars who shared their work in these venues – provided a wonderful opportunity to learn from so many historians at various stages of their research. They taught me to ask better questions, share my ideas, and think in community. The Glover Park Tea Group was a source of solace, laughter, and delicious baked goodies. Meredith Denning, Robynne Mellor, Jenn De Vries, Sylvia Mullins, Liz Williams, Soha El Achi, Laura Goff, Madeleine Chartrand – we were a motley crew who were rarely in town at the same time, but our afternoons together were a happy time of giggling, eating well, and learning from one another in unexpected ways. Jordan Smith, Brian Taylor, Meredith Denning, Katy Hull, your friendships have been a source of laughter, wisdom, ridiculousness, and joy throughout the research and writing that made this book possible. And to all my friends at Georgetown and beyond, thank you.

Many fellowships and awards made the research and development of this book possible, and I am honored to thank the institutions that offered such significant support and affirmation: the Georgetown University Graduate School and Georgetown History Department, the Cosmos Club Foundation, and the Omohundro Institute of Early American History and Culture. Thank you as well to the many librarians and archivists who have offered their wealth of knowledge and kind assistance at the Bahamas National Archives, the Jamaica Archives and Records Department, the National Library of Jamaica, the U.S. National Archives, the Boston Public Library, the Massachusetts Historical Society, the Toronto Public Library, and the Ontario Provincial Archives. And thank you to the incredible work of so many librarians, archivists, students, volunteers, and other individuals who have been ceaselessly engaged in the work of digitizing and making available to the public the incredibly rich archival material related to slavery, the anti-slavery movement, and racial justice in the United States. I would like to extend my particular gratitude to the collective work of the Colored Conventions Project, which has been leading the way in transcribing the minutes and records of the Colored Conventions and bringing them to life for the twenty-first century. From community engagement and scholarly enterprise to pushing the potential of digital history to make historical people and events relevant and accessible, your work has been a resource and an inspiration. Thank you.

It is also a pleasure to acknowledge the many rich and collegial conversations that deepened my analysis at key junctures. In particular, I would like to thank the organizers of the fourth annual Summer Academy of Atlantic History and the third annual Emerging Scholars Workshop at Penn State's George and Ann Richards Civil War Era Center for inviting me to share my work. Keisha N. Blain provided invaluable feedback on a session I was lucky enough to share with Caree Banton at the Emerging Scholars Workshop, and the discussions these scholars inspired pushed my thinking forward in exciting ways. At the Summer Academy, I found encouragement, companionship, and valuable feedback, all of which helped to sustain me during late nights of drafting and head banging.

I am so thankful to the wonderful people who have brought this book to life. Thank you to my tireless agent, Anne Depue, who wanted to read this book and believed that other people would want to, as well. Our conversations always inspire me to think boldly about what's next. Thank you to Debbie Gershenowitz who championed the acquisition of this book, and to my glorious editor, Cecelia Cancellero, who made sure it was the very best version of itself that it could possibly be. This work owes a great debt to Reviewers A and B, who offered kind critique and thoughtful recommendations. Their insights made this book better, and I am grateful for their generosity of time and spirit. Michelle Martinez, indexer extraordinaire, you helped me to see my work in new ways, and I appreciate you immensely. Thank you to Ruth Boyes for shepherding this book through the publication process, to Lyn Flight and Jack Webb for their close reading and eagle eyes, to David Cox for translating all my concept notes into beautiful maps, and to the design team for creating such a stunning cover. The marketing department has worked hard to bring this book into readers' hands, and I am so thankful for their vision and expertise.

Through the many years of research and writing that culminated in this book, I have been sustained by the very best people on earth. My wonderful parents read this work at various stages and boosted my spirit at every turn. Thank you for believing in my vision for my life and always being there to offer hugs. My beloved siblings: Julia, Sasha, and Arina. The three of you have been unending founts of love, wisdom, absurdity, and joy. I'm so proud to be one of you. Joe and Becky Hogan, you engaged with my writing at a critical moment when I could no longer see it. I'm so grateful for a lifetime of your love, your incredible wit, and your boundless good humor. Sierra, Theodora, Michelle, and Beth, you have been my people for so, so many years. You've cheered me on at every turn, and I love you dearly. George, Marty, Alison, and Becky, I'm so lucky to be your outlaw. Thank you all for the love and support you've given me in such abundance through the years of writing this book and beyond.

And, finally, David, my best friend and my beating heart. You have been an amazing partner from the beginning, and life with you has been endlessly joyful and adventurous. You have lived with this book for as long as I have, and our conversations have shaped it in countless ways. I am so proud to be able to dedicate this book to you.

Notes

INTRODUCTION

1. For more on the practice, scope, and culture of the American domestic slave trade, see Steven Deyle, *Carry Me Back: The Domestic Slave Trade in American Life* (Oxford: Oxford University Press, 2005).

2. On the *Creole* rebellion, see Jeffrey Kerr-Ritchie, *Rebellious Passage: The Creole Revolt and America's Coastal Slave Trade* (New York: Cambridge University Press, 2018); Arthur T. Downey, *The Creole Affair: The Slave Rebellion that Led the U.S. and Great Britain to the Brink of War* (Lanham, MD: Rowman & Littlefield, 2014); George Hendrick and Willene Hendrick, *The Creole Mutiny: A Tale of Revolt Aboard a Slave Ship* (Chicago: Ivan R. Dee, 2003); Phillip Troutman, "Grapevine in the Slave Market: African American Geopolitical Literacy and the 1841 Creole Revolt," in *The Chattel Principle: Internal Slave Trades in the Americas*, ed. Walter Johnson (New Haven: Yale University Press, 2004), 203–233.

3. Stanley Harrold, "Romanticizing Slave Revolt: Madison Washington, the Creole Mutiny, and Abolitionist Celebration of Violent Means," in *Antislavery Violence: Sectional, Racial, and Cultural Conflict in Antebellum America*, ed. John R. McKivigan and Stanley Harrold (Knoxville: University of Tennessee Press, 1999), 89–107; Edward Bartlett Rugemer, *The Problem of Emancipation: The Caribbean Roots of the American Civil War* (Baton Rouge: Louisiana State University Press, 2008), 175–176, 181, 203–204.

4. On Mary Ann Shadd's early life in the U.S. and her removal to Canada, see Jane Rhodes, *Mary Ann Shadd Cary: The Black Press and Protest in the Nineteenth Century* (Bloomington: Indiana University Press, 1999), 1–134.

5. On the intersection of black activism and national identity in Shadd's Canada years, see Benjamin Fagan, *The Black Newspaper and the Chosen Nation* (Athens, GA: University of Georgia Press, 2018), 95–118; Jane Rhodes, "The Contestation over National Identity: Nineteenth-Century Black Americans in Canada," *Canadian Review of American Studies* 30, no. 2 (January 1, 2000): 173–184. On the ideology of "racial uplift," see Kevin K. Gaines, *Uplifting the Race: Black Leadership, Politics, and Culture in the Twentieth Century* (Chapel Hill: University of North Carolina Press, 1996), 1–18. On the role of "racial uplift" in the daily lives of the nineteenth-century black middle class, see Erica Ball, *To Live an Antislavery Life: Personal Politics and the Antebellum Black Middle Class* (Athens, GA: University of Georgia Press, 2012).

6. *Provincial Freeman* (Toronto, Canada West), May 20, 1854, and May 25, 1854.

7. Sue Peabody and Keila Grinberg, "Free Soil: The Generation and Circulation of an Atlantic Legal Principle," *Slavery & Abolition* 32, no. 3 (2011): 331.

8. On the "free soil" ideology and political party of the nineteenth-century United States, see Eric Foner, *Free Soil, Free Labor, Free Men: The Ideology of the Republican Party before the Civil War* (New York: Oxford University Press, 1995); Jonathan Halperin Earle, *Jacksonian Antislavery and the Politics of Free Soil, 1824–1854* (Chapel Hill: University of North Carolina Press, 2004). Scholars of Atlantic free soil include Ada Ferrer, Martha Jones, and Richard Newman, who have illuminated specific case studies showing how enslaved men and women attempted to become legal freepersons by navigating across free-soil borders in the Caribbean and United States during the age of Atlantic revolutions. See Ada Ferrer, "Haiti, Free Soil, and Antislavery in the Revolutionary Atlantic," *American Historical Review* 117, no. 1 (February 2012): 40–66; Richard S. Newman, "'Lucky to Be Born in Pennsylvania': Free Soil, Fugitive Slaves, and the Making of Pennsylvania's Anti-Slavery Borderland," *Slavery & Abolition* 32, no. 3 (2011): 413–430; Martha S. Jones, "Time, Space, and Jurisdiction in Atlantic World Slavery: The Volunbrun Household in Gradual Emancipation New York," *Law and History Review* 29, no. 4 (2011): 1031–1060. See also, Edlie L. Wong, *Neither Fugitive nor Free: Atlantic Slavery, Freedom Suits, and the Legal Culture of Travel* (New York: New York University Press, 2009).

9. On the "geopolitical literacy" of slaves, see Troutman, "Grapevine in the Slave Market," 203–233; Sean Kelley, "'Mexico in His Head': Slavery and the Texas–Mexico Border, 1810–1860," *Journal of Social History* 37, no. 3 (2004): 709–723. On the access of enslaved people to newspapers, see Fagan, *The Black Newspaper*, 11–14. On the knowledge and information gained by riverboat slaves as they plied up and down the great western waterways, see Thomas C. Buchanan, *Black Life on the Mississippi: Slaves, Free Blacks, and the Western Steamboat World* (Chapel Hill: University of North Carolina Press, 2004), 19–52, 101–122.

10. On self-emancipated (fugitive) slaves and their routes to freedom within the United States, see R. J. M. Blackett, *The Captive's Quest for Freedom: Fugitive Slaves, the 1850 Fugitive Slave Law, and the Politics of Slavery* (New York: Cambridge University Press, 2018); Damian Alan Pargas, ed., *Fugitive Slaves and Spaces of Freedom in North America* (Gainesville: University Press of Florida, 2018); and Eric Foner, *Gateway to Freedom: The Hidden History of the Underground Railroad* (New York: W. W. Norton, 2016).

11. On the many ways that African Americans self-defined as citizens and fought for respect and recognition as citizens, see, for example, Martha S. Jones, *Birthright Citizens: A History of Race and Rights in Antebellum America* (New York: Cambridge University Press, 2018); Derrick R. Spires, *The Practice of Citizenship: Black Politics and Print Culture* (Philadelphia: University of Pennsylvania Press, 2019); Stephen Kantrowitz, *More Than Freedom: Fighting for Black Citizenship in a White Republic, 1829–1889* (New York: Penguin, 2012).

12. See, for example, Bronwen Everill, *Abolition and Empire in Sierra Leone and Liberia* (Hampshire: Palgrave Macmillan, 2012); Carol Faulkner, "The Root of the Evil: Free Produce and Radical Antislavery, 1820–1860," *Journal of the Early Republic* 27, no. 3

(2007): 377–405; Floyd J. Miller, *The Search for a Black Nationality: Black Emigration and Colonization, 1787–1863* (Urbana: University of Illinois Press, 1975); Chris Dixon, *African America and Haiti: Emigration and Black Nationalism in the Nineteenth Century* (Westport, CT: Greenwood Press, 2000).

13. Ibram X. Kendi, *Stamped from the Beginning: The Definitive History of Racist Ideas in America* (New York: Nation Books, 2016), 124.

14. For accounts of the Stono Rebellion, see Peter Charles Hoffer, *Cry Liberty: The Great Stono River Slave Rebellion of 1739* (New York: Oxford University Press, 2011); Peter H. Wood, *Black Majority: Negroes in Colonial South Carolina from 1670 through the Stono Rebellion* (New York: Knopf, 1974), 308–330. On the origins of British slaves escaping to Spanish Florida, as well as an examination of their experience in a sanctuary town called *Gracia Rael de Santa Teresa de Mose*, see Jane Landers, *Black Society in Spanish Florida* (Urbana: University of Illinois Press, 1999), 29–60.

15. See Alan Gilbert, *Black Patriots and Loyalists: Fighting for Emancipation in the War for Independence* (Chicago: University of Chicago Press, 2013), 1–45; Cassandra Pybus, *Epic Journeys of Freedom: Runaway Slaves of the American Revolution and Their Global Quest for Liberty* (Boston, MA: Beacon Press, 2007), 3–73.

16. For a recent historical assessment of how the issue of slavery proved the limits of U.S. support for the new South American republics when the latter began incorporating anti-slavery sentiment into their revolutionary and republican agendas, see Caitlin Fitz, *Our Sister Republics: The United States in an Age of American Revolutions* (New York: Liveright, 2016).

17. On British abolitionism in the wake of the American Revolution, see Christopher Leslie Brown, *Moral Capital: Foundations of British Abolitionism* (Chapel Hill: University of North Carolina Press, 2006). On the founding of Sierra Leone as a black colony oriented toward the diminution of the transatlantic slave trade, see Alexander X. Byrd, *Captives and Voyagers: Black Migrants Across the Eighteenth-Century British Atlantic World* (Baton Rouge: Louisiana State University Press, 2008).

18. Richard Newman and James Mueller, eds. *Antislavery and Abolition in Philadelphia: Emancipation and the Long Struggle for Racial Justice in the City of Brotherly Love* (Baton Rouge: Louisiana State University Press, 2011); David N. Gellman, *Emancipating New York: The Politics of Slavery and Freedom, 1777–1827* (Baton Rouge: Louisiana State University Press, 2006); Shane White, *Somewhat More Independent: The End of Slavery in New York City, 1770–1810* (Athens, GA: University of Georgia Press, 1991); Manisha Sinha, *The Slave's Cause: A History of Abolition* (New Haven, CT: Yale University Press, 2016), 65–96; Dana Elizabeth Weiner, *Race and Rights: Fighting Slavery and Prejudice in the Old Northwest, 1830–1870* (DeKalb, IL: Northern Illinois University Press, 2013).

19. See, for example, Newman, "Lucky to Be Born in Pennsylvania," 413–430; Jones, "Time, Space, and Jurisdiction in Atlantic World Slavery," 1031–1060; Wong, *Neither Fugitive nor Free*; Kelly M. Kennington, *In the Shadow of Dred Scott: St. Louis Freedom Suits and the Legal Culture of Slavery in Antebellum America* (Athens, GA: University of Georgia Press, 2017).

20. On the ever-present fear of kidnapping in the U.S. North, see Peter B. Hinks, "'Frequently Plunged into Slavery': Free Blacks and Kidnapping in Antebellum

Boston," *Historical Journal of Massachusetts* (Winter 1992): 16–31; Graham Russell Gao Hodges, *David Ruggles: A Radical Black Abolitionist and the Underground Railroad in New York City* (Chapel Hill: University of North Carolina Press, 2010), 63–154; Leslie M. Harris, *In the Shadow of Slavery: African Americans in New York City, 1626–1863* (Chicago: University of Chicago Press, 2003), 206–216.

21. On the fight to establish citizenship status based on being born in the United States, see Jones, *Birthright Citizens.*

22. Social scientist Albert O. Hirschman has famously categorized these choices as "exit" and "voice." He argues that one can leave an unsatisfying situation in preference for another opportunity, or one can use one's voice to make changes from within. The idea of "loyalty," he suggests, most frequently supports the use of "voice" to help promote positive changes from within, whereas "exit" is often posited as the antithesis of loyalty. Conceptualizing these alternatives as ways to respond to dissatisfaction with business firms or organizations, they are broadly applicable and certainly characterize the choice faced by nineteenth-century African Americans considering the intersection between national loyalty and emigration. Albert O. Hirschman, *Exit, Voice, and Loyalty: Responses to Decline in Firms, Organizations, and States* (Cambridge, MA: Harvard University Press, 1970).

23. On the nineteenth-century emigration and colonization debates that took place among African American communities throughout the United States, see Ousmane K. Power-Greene, *Against Wind and Tide: The African American Struggle against the Colonization Movement* (New York: New York University Press, 2014); Miller, *The Search for a Black Nationality*; Kwando Mbiassi Kinshasa, *Emigration vs. Assimilation: The Debate in the African American Press, 1827–1861* (Jefferson, NC: McFarland, 1988); Dixon, *African America and Haiti.*

24. Another terminological distinction could be drawn between "emancipationists" and "abolitionists." Those who began demanding immediate abolition in the 1830s called themselves "abolitionists," a practice continued by most historians. They set themselves apart from "gradualists" (who had previously referred to *them*selves as "abolitionists") by calling gradual anti-slavery advocates "emancipationists." Regardless of these terminological distinctions, however, they all existed along a spectrum of "anti-slavery advocacy." This book seeks to differentiate between ideological practices rather than terminological ones. See James McPherson, *The Struggle for Equality* (Princeton: Princeton University Press, 1964), 2–8; Beverly C. Tomek, *Colonization and Its Discontents: Emancipation, Emigration, and Antislavery in Antebellum Pennsylvania* (New York: New York University Press, 2012), 3; and Stanley Harrold, *American Abolitionism: Its Direct Political Impact from Colonial Times into Reconstruction* (Charlottesville: University of Virginia Press, 2019).

25. On how colonization tapped into both humanitarian and conservative political agendas, see Tomek, *Colonization and Its Discontents.*

26. A note on terminology: this book investigates the migration of African Americans who left the United States under a variety of conditions related to necessity or ideology. The term "colonist" is used to refer specifically to freed slaves who were involuntarily relocated to the American Colonization Society's Liberia colony as a condition of

their freedom. Where appropriate, it is also used in reference to free African Americans who voluntarily moved to Liberia under the auspices of the American Colonization Society. Otherwise, this book uses the term "emigrant." This choice reproduces the language used by historical actors and observers themselves, who used the term indiscriminately in the same way that most people in the twenty-first century use the term "immigrant." This choice also reflects an important definition used within contemporary migration sociology: the term *immigrant* refers to someone assimilating into a new society (an immigrant, say, who has moved *into* Canada from the United States), whereas the term *emigrant* emphasizes the connections maintained by a person *leaving* their original home society (an *American* emigrant moving into Canada). This book's use of the term "emigrant" to refer to African Americans who voluntarily moved from the United States to different free-soil havens abroad underscores the emotional, political, and interpersonal links that many black migrants maintained with the United States and its anti-slavery movement. Roger Waldinger, *The Cross-Border Connection: Immigrants, Emigrants, and Their Homelands* (Cambridge, MA: Harvard University Press, 2015), 37–56.

27. On Haitian emigration, this book builds on the work of Dixon, *African America and Haiti*, and Sara Fanning, *Caribbean Crossing: African Americans and the Haitian Emigration Movement* (New York: New York University Press, 2015). On Canadian emigration, it builds on the work of Robin W. Winks, *The Blacks in Canada: A History* (Montreal: McGill-Queen's University Press, 1997); Sharon A. Roger Hepburn, *Crossing the Border: A Free Black Community in Canada* (Urbana: University of Illinois Press, 2007); Karolyn Smardz Frost, *I've Got a Home in Glory Land: A Lost Tale of the Underground Railroad* (New York: Farrar, Straus & Giroux, 2008); Donald George Simpson, *Under the North Star: Black Communities in Upper Canada Before Confederation (1867)*, ed. Paul E. Lovejoy (Trenton, NJ: Africa World Press, 2005); and Jason H. Silverman, *Unwelcome Guests: Canada West's Response to American Fugitive Slaves, 1800–1865* (Millwood, NY: Associated Faculty Press, 1985). On the experiences of free emigrants in Mexico, it follows in the footsteps of Sarah E. Cornell, "Citizens of Nowhere: Fugitive Slaves and Free African Americans in Mexico, 1833–1857," *Journal of American History* 100, no. 2 (September 2013): 351–374; and Mekala Audain, "Mexican Canaan: Fugitive Slaves and Free Blacks on the American Frontier, 1804–1867," PhD diss., Rutgers, 2014; and James David Nichols, *The Limits of Liberty: Mobility and the Making of the Eastern U.S.–Mexico Border* (Lincoln: University of Nebraska Press, 2018).

28. For a comprehensive study on black opposition to colonization, see Power-Greene, *Against Wind and Tide*. On the ideology and actions of white colonization promoters, see P. J. Staudenraus, *The African Colonization Movement 1816–1865* (New York: Columbia University Press, 1961); Tomek, *Colonization and Its Discontents*; Eric Burin, *Slavery and the Peculiar Solution: A History of the American Colonization Society* (Gainesville: University Press of Florida, 2008). On black interest and support for colonization and their experiences as migrants, see Claude A. Clegg, *The Price of Liberty: African Americans and the Making of Liberia* (Chapel Hill: University of North Carolina Press, 2009); and Miller, *The Search for a Black Nationality*.

29. On the self-emancipation across the Mexico border, see Nichols, *The Limits of Liberty*; Cornell, "Citizens of Nowhere"; Kelley, "Mexico in His Head," 709–723; Audain, "Mexican Canaan"; Rosalie Schwartz, *Across the Rio to Freedom: U.S. Negroes in Mexico* (El Paso: Texas Western Press, 1975); and Alice Baumgartner, *South to Freedom: Runaway Slaves to Mexico and the Road to the Civil War* (New York: Basic Books, 2020, forthcoming at the time of this writing). On runaway slaves crossing to Canada, see Fergus M. Bordewich, *Bound for Canaan: The Underground Railroad and the War for the Soul of America* (New York: Amistad, 2005); Gregory Wigmore, "Before the Railroad: From Slavery to Freedom in the Canadian–American Borderland," *Journal of American History* 98, no. 2 (September 1, 2011): 437–454. On self-emancipation across maritime borders in the Caribbean, see Irvin D. S. Winsboro and Joe Knetsch, "Florida Slaves, the 'Saltwater Railroad' to the Bahamas, and Anglo-American Diplomacy," *Journal of Southern History* 79, no. 1 (February 2013): 51–78. On fugitive slaves in England, see R. J. M. Blackett, *Building an Antislavery Wall: Black Americans in the Atlantic Abolitionist Movement, 1830–1860* (Baton Rouge: Louisiana State University Press, 1983).

30. Blackett, *Building an Antislavery Wall*; W. Caleb McDaniel, *The Problem of Democracy in the Age of Slavery: Garrisonian Abolitionists and Transatlantic Reform* (Baton Rouge: Louisiana State University Press, 2013); Van Gosse, "'As a Nation, the English Are Our Friends': The Emergence of African American Politics in the British Atlantic World, 1772–1861," *American Historical Review* 113, no. 4 (October 2008): 1003–1028; Rugemer, *The Problem of Emancipation.*

31. On the Underground Railroad's ongoing significance as a symbol of freedom and escape, see David Blight, ed., *Passages to Freedom: The Underground Railroad in History and Memory* (Washington DC: Harper, 2006), 1–12. For a crucial history of and corrective to the many common misconceptions that U.S. cultural memory maintains about the Underground Railroad, see Larry Gara, *The Liberty Line: The Legend of the Underground Railroad* (Lexington: University Press of Kentucky, 1996).

32. See, for example, Jones, *Birthright Citizens*, 35–49; Patrick Rael, *Black Identity and Black Protest in the Antebellum North* (Chapel Hill: University of North Carolina Press, 2002), 82–117, 237–279; Power-Greene, *Against Wind and Tide*, 3, 13; David Brion Davis, *The Problem of Slavery in the Age of Emancipation* (New York: Knopf, 2014), 177.

33. Appadurai's study of anti-minority violence in the late twentieth century, while not precisely analogous to anti-black sentiment and colonizationism in the nineteenth century, nonetheless offers a salient analysis of how minorities are seen in situations where the majority population has successfully defined the national identity as a singular ethnicity correlating to their own. Arjun Appadurai, *Fear of Small Numbers: An Essay on the Geography of Anger* (Durham, NC: Duke University Press, 2006), 51–53.

34. On the emergence of transatlantic social inquiries as tools of reform in the nineteenth century, see Oz Frankel, *States of Inquiry: Social Investigations and Print Culture in Nineteenth-Century Britain and the United States* (Baltimore, MD: Johns Hopkins University Press, 2006). See also Amanda Claybaugh, *The Novel of Purpose: Literature and Social Reform in the Anglo-American World* (Ithaca, NY: Cornell University Press, 2007).

35. Carolyn Calloway-Thomas, "Mary Ann Shadd Cary: Crafting Black Culture Through Empirical and Moral Arguments," *Howard Journal of Communications* 24, no. 3 (July 2013): 240.

36. Meredith L. McGill, *American Literature and the Culture of Reprinting, 1834–1853* (Philadelphia: University of Pennsylvania Press, 2003); Ryan Cordell, "Reprinting, Circulation, and the Network Author in Antebellum Newspapers," *American Literary History* 27, no. 3 (September 2015): 417–445; Trish Loughran, *The Republic in Print: Print Culture in the Age of U.S. Nation Building, 1770–1870* (New York: Columbia University Press, 2007); Ronald J. Zboray, *A Fictive People: Antebellum Economic Development and the American Reading Public* (New York: Oxford University Press, 1993); Fagan, *The Black Newspaper*; Robert A. Gross and Mary Kelley, eds., *An Extensive Republic: Print, Culture, and Society in the New Nation, 1790–1840* (Chapel Hill: University of North Carolina Press, 2007); Lara Langer Cohen and Jordan Alexander Stein, eds., *Early African American Print Culture* (Philadelphia: University of Pennsylvania Press, 2012).

37. Loughran, *The Republic in Print*, 4, 303–362.

38. Jeannine Marie DeLombard, *Slavery on Trial: Law, Abolitionism, and Print Culture* (Chapel Hill: University of North Carolina Press, 2007), 1.

39. Mary Niall Mitchell, *Raising Freedom's Child: Black Children and Visions of the Future after Slavery* (New York: New York University Press, 2010), 11–50.

40. Sinha, *The Slave's Cause*, 5.

41. See Cordell, "Reprinting, Circulation, and the Network Author in Antebellum Newspapers." In addition, see Ellen Gruber Garvey, *Writing with Scissors: American Scrapbooks from the Civil War to the Harlem Renaissance* (New York: Oxford University Press, 2012), 421–444. While Garvey uses material, rather than digital sources, her approach to gleaning patterns of interconnection from within nineteenth-century print culture is similarly instructive for this project. She examines scrapbooks for patterns reflecting what readers valued in the ever-growing newspaper landscape of the nineteenth century. Her work shows that readers regularly *removed* news clippings from their original context, and that analyzing their reading and scrapbooking activities illuminates discrete cultural communities cultivated through shared print culture.

1 REFORM AND RELOCATION: WEST AFRICA AND HAITI IN THE EARLY REPUBLIC

1. "A Poem to the Free and Independent Haytiens," *Genius of Universal Emancipation* (Baltimore, MD), February 11, 1826, American Periodicals Series II.

2. James Sidbury, *Becoming African in America: Race and Nation in the Early Black Atlantic* (New York: Oxford University Press, 2009), 11, 145–147; Lamont D. Thomas, *Paul Cuffe: Black Entrepreneur and Pan-Africanist* (Urbana: University of Illinois Press, 1988), 49.

3. Byrd, *Captives and Voyagers*, 125–153. On African American interest in African colonization in the 1880s, see Davis, *The Problem of Slavery in the Age of Emancipation*, 169; James Oliver Horton and Lois E. Horton, *In Hope of Liberty: Culture, Community, and Protest among Northern Free Blacks, 1700–1860* (New York: Oxford University Press, 1997), 179–181; Gary B. Nash,

Forging Freedom: The Formation of Philadelphia's Black Community, 1720–1840 (Cambridge, MA: Harvard University Press, 1988), 101–103.

4. Richard S. Newman, *Freedom's Prophet: Bishop Richard Allen, the AME Church, and the Black Founding Fathers* (New York: New York University Press, 2008), 186–187.

5. On legitimate commerce, see Brown, *Moral Capital*, 219–230.

6. Everill, *Abolition and Empire*, 23–30; Sinha, *The Slave's Cause*, 162.

7. Thomas, *Paul Cuffe*, 75–81.

8. Paul Cuffe to U.S. Congress (June 1813) in *Captain Paul Cuffe's Logs and Letters, 1808–1817: A Black Quaker's "Voice from Within the Veil,"* ed. Rosalind Cobb Wiggins, (Washington, DC: Howard University Press, 1996), 252–253.

9. Paul Cuffe to James Forten (March 13, 1815), Paul Cuffe to Richard Allen (March 27, 1815), Paul Cuffe to Peter Williams, Jr. (March 13, 1815), Paul Cuffe to Daniel Coker (March 13, 1815), Prince Saunders to Paul Cuffe (March 21, 1815), Paul Cuffe to James Forten (March 27, 1815), in Wiggens, *Captain Paul Cuffe's Logs and Letters*, 329, 331, 321, 322, 336, 330, respectively.

10. See Wiggins, *Captain Paul Cuffe's Logs and Letters, 1808–1817*; Thomas, *Paul Cuffe*, 94–95.

11. Staudenraus, *The African Colonization Movement*, 11.

12. On the link between anti-slavery, empire, and commercial opportunity in Sierra Leone and Liberia, and in particular on the influence of Britain's Sierra Leone colony on the formation of the American Colonization Society, see Everill, *Abolition and Empire*.

13. Population figures calculated from "1810 Census" and "1820 Census," Minnesota Population Center, National Historical Geographic Information System, Version 11.0 [Database], University of Minnesota, Minneapolis, 2016, available at: http://doi.org/10.18128/D050.V11.0.

14. Richard S. Newman, *The Transformation of American Abolitionism: Fighting Slavery in the Early Republic* (Chapel Hill: University of North Carolina Press, 2001), 112.

15. Joanne Pope Melish, *Disowning Slavery: Gradual Emancipation and "Race" in New England, 1780–1860* (Ithaca, NY: Cornell University Press, 1998), 110, 117.

16. Lois E. Horton, "From Class to Race in Early America: Northern Post-Emancipation Racial Reconstruction," *Journal of the Early Republic* 19, no. 4 (December 1999): 644–645; Sara C. Fanning, "The Roots of Early Black Nationalism: Northern African Americans' Invocations of Haiti in the Early Nineteenth Century," *Slavery & Abolition* 28, no. 1 (April 2007): 63; Newman, *Freedom's Prophet*, 184, 191–194.

17. Stephen Womsley, for example, wrote to Cuffe on August 13, 1815, requesting information about emigration despite clearly never having met Cuffe in person. "Cap Cuff," he wrote, "I am a black man and want to know what condition the black are to sail upon [sic] and when the vessel is to sail. I wish if you pleas [sic] to write back as quick as possible and let me know so that I may get reddy [sic]. I am your humble Servant. Stephen Womsley," in Wiggins, *Captain Paul Cuffe's Logs and Letters, 1808–1817*, 374.

18. Robert Finley to John P. Mumford (February 14, 1816), in Isaac V. Brown, *Memoirs of the Rev. Robert Finley, D.D.* (New Brunswick, NJ: Terhune & Letson, 1819), 77.

19. Ibid.

20. Ibid.

21. Staudenraus, *The African Colonization Movement*, 29.

22. Ibid., 19; Thomas, *Paul Cuffe*, 111.

23. Paul Cuffe to Robert Finley (January 8, 1817), in Wiggins, *Captain Paul Cuffe's Logs and Letters, 1808–1817*, 492.

24. Paul Cuffe to Samuel J. Mills (January 6, 1817), ibid., 491.

25. Paul Cuffe to Samuel J. Mills (January 6, 1817), ibid., 492.

26. Staudenraus, *The African Colonization Movement*, 11.

27. See Ashli White, *Encountering Revolution: Haiti and the Making of the Early Republic* (Baltimore, MD: Johns Hopkins University Press, 2010); Alfred N. Hunt, *Haiti's Influence on Antebellum America: Slumbering Volcano in the Caribbean* (Baton Rouge: Louisiana State University Press, 1988).

28. Staudenraus, *The African Colonization Movement*, 28–29.

29. Newman, *Freedom's Prophet*, 203.

30. Power-Greene, *Against Wind and Tide*, 2–3; Newman, *The Transformation of American Abolitionism*, 103.

31. James Forten and Russell Perrott, "Address to the humane and benevolent Inhabitants of the city and county of Philadelphia" (1817), in *Minutes of the proceedings of a special meeting of the fifteenth American Convention for Promoting the Abolition of Slavery and Improving the Condition of the African Race, Assembled at Philadelphia, on the tenth day of December, 1818, and continued by adjournments until the fifteenth of the same month, inclusive* (Philadelphia: Hall & Atkinson, 1818), i–iv.

32. See Newman, *Freedom's Prophet*, 203.

33. Forten and Perrott, "Address to the humane and benevolent Inhabitants of the city and county of Philadelphia," iii.

34. Ibid., ii–iii.

35. Ibid., i–ii.

36. William J. Novak, "The Legal Transformation of Citizenship in Nineteenth-Century America," in *The Democratic Experiment*, ed. Meg Jacobs, William J. Novak, and Julian E. Zelizer (Princeton: Princeton University Press, 2003), 85–119. See also Andrew Diemer, *The Politics of Black Citizenship: Free African Americans in the Mid-Atlantic Borderland, 1817–1863* (Athens, GA: University of Georgia Press, 2016), 11–30. On the ways that ideas about citizenship took shape and hardened as black men and women made specific claims of the federal government based on their wartime service, see Chandra Manning, *Troubled Refuge: Struggling for Freedom in the Civil War* (New York: Alfred A. Knopf, 2016), 201–231.

37. Power-Greene, *Against Wind and Tide*, 20–21.

38. Winston James, *The Struggles of John Brown Russwurm: The Life and Writings of a Pan-Africanist Pioneer, 1799–1851* (New York: New York University Press, 2010), 14; Arthur O. White, "Prince Saunders: An Instance of Social Mobility Among Antebellum New England Blacks," *Journal of Negro History* 60, no. 4 (October 1975): 527.

39. Historians disagree on the impetus for Saunders's shift from Sierra Leone to Haiti. Cuffe's biographer Lamont Thomas suggests that Prince Saunders was turned off the Sierra Leone plan upon hearing the negative impressions of the African Institution's management circulating at the time, while John Brown Russwurm's recent biographer,

Winston James, follows A. O. White's earlier assertion that Saunders made such a favorable impression on Clarkson and Wilberforce that they convinced him to take the new commission. Most recently, Ousmane K. Power-Greene has argued that Wilberforce simply tapped into Saunders's pre-existing predisposition toward Haitian emigration by confirming his positive impression. See Thomas, *Paul Cuffe*; James, *The Struggles of John Brown Russwurm*, 12; White, "Prince Saunders," 528; Power-Greene, *Against Wind and Tide*, 20.

40. James, *The Struggles of John Brown Russwurm*, 12; White, "Prince Saunders," 528.

41. Prince Saunders, *Haytian Papers: A Collection of the Very Interesting Proclamations and Other Official Documents: Together with Some Account of the Rise, Progress, and Present State of the Kingdom of Hayti* (London: W. Reed, law bookseller, 1816).

42. Saunders, *Haytian Papers*, iv, vi.

43. Although it is unclear how many copies were included in the 1816 edition, there were enough to be read widely in Britain and the United States and to secure Saunders's social and political prominence in major cities like London, Boston, and Philadelphia. Unfortunately for Saunders, it also seems to have "saturated the market," as his reprinted second edition saddled him with debt rather than profit. See White, "Prince Saunders," 530.

44. Ibid., 182.

45. See, for example, Gilbert, *Black Patriots and Loyalists*; Maya Jasanoff, *Liberty's Exiles: American Loyalists in the Revolutionary World* (New York: Alfred A. Knopf, 2011).

46. Saunders, *Haytian Papers*, 192–193.

47. "People of Color," *Niles' Weekly Register*, October, 17 1818, as cited in Power-Greene, *Against Wind and Tide*, 23–24, n. 33 (p. 208).

48. James, *The Struggles of John Brown Russwurm*, 13.

49. Robert Duane Sayre, "The Evolution of Early American Abolitionism: The American Convention for Promoting the Abolition of Slavery and Improving the Condition of the African Race, 1794–1837" (PhD diss., Ohio State University, 1987, 57–58; Newman, *The Transformation of American Abolitionism*, 19; J. R. Oldfield, *Transatlantic Abolitionism in the Age of Revolution: An International History of Anti-Slavery, c. 1787–1820* (New York: Cambridge University Press, 2013), 110–113; Sinha, *The Slave's Cause*, 173–176.

50. American Convention for Promoting the Abolition of Slavery and Improving the Condition of the African Race, *Minutes of the proceedings of the Fifteenth American Convention for Promoting the Abolition of Slavery and Improving the Condition of the African Race, Assembled at Philadelphia, on the fifth day of August, 1817, and continued by adjournments until the eighth of the same month, inclusive* (Philadelphia: Merritt, 1817), 26–27, quotation on p. 30.

51. Though it was held over a year later, the December 1818 meeting was specifically a "special meeting" pursuant to 1817's fifteenth Convention rather than a commencement of the sixteenth annual gathering.

52. The examples noted by the special committee were specifically identified as colonization schemes that were intended to influence the ending of the transatlantic slave trade. They cited a year-long British colonial venture on the island of Bulama, off the

mouth of the Rio Grande, from 1792 to 1793; a settlement of an anti-slavery Swedish colony near Goree in West Africa in 1780; and a short-lived Danish colony at Aquapin on the western coast of Africa in 1788. American Convention for Promoting the Abolition of Slavery and Improving the Condition of the African Race, *Minutes of the proceedings of a special meeting of the fifteenth American Convention for Promoting the Abolition of Slavery and Improving the Condition of the African Race, Assembled at Philadelphia, on the tenth day of December, 1818, and continued by adjournments until the fifteenth of the same month, inclusive* (Philadelphia: Hall & Atkinson, 1818), 50–52, Slavery and Anti-Slavery: A Transnational Archive. For a broader historical analysis of colonizationist sentiment in the United States during the Revolutionary era, see Burin, *Slavery and the Peculiar Solution*, 8–10. Burin argues that the idea that colonization was a necessary corollary of black freedom predated any formalized efforts to relocate manumitted African Americans.

53. American Convention, *Minutes of the proceedings of a special meeting of the fifteenth American Convention* (1818), 26–27.

54. Power-Greene, *Against Wind and Tide*, 23–24.

55. Prince Saunders, *A Memoir Presented to the American Convention for Promoting the Abolition of Slavery, and Improving the Condition of the African Race, December 11th, 1818* (Philadelphia: Dennis Heartt, 1818), 8.

56. Earl Leslie Griggs and Clifford H. Prator, eds., *Henry Christophe and Thomas Clarkson: A Correspondence* (New York: Greenwood, 1968), 45–56; Johnhenry Gonzalez, "Defiant Haiti: Free-Soil Runaways, Ship Seizures and the Politics of Diplomatic Non-Recognition in the Early Nineteenth Century," *Slavery & Abolition* 36, no. 1 (2015): 125. For an account of the schism which led to the leadership of Christophe in the north and Pétion in the south, see Griggs and Prator, *Henry Christophe and Thomas Clarkson*, 38–46.

57. On the fears that the Haitian Revolution incited in the United States and around the Atlantic, see Hunt, *Haiti's Influence on Antebellum America*; David P. Geggus, ed., *The Impact of the Haitian Revolution in the Atlantic World* (Columbia: University of South Carolina Press, 2001); White, *Encountering Revolution*; Ada Ferrer, *Freedom's Mirror: Cuba and Haiti in the Age of Revolution* (New York: Cambridge University Press, 2014).

58. Ferrer, "Haiti, Free Soil, and Antislavery in the Revolutionary Atlantic," 43–44.

59. Saunders, *A Memoir*, i–ii.

60. Ibid., 12–13.

61. American Convention, *Minutes of the proceedings of a special meeting of the fifteenth American Convention* (1818), 55.

62. Ibid., 49.

63. For more on the intersection of the transatlantic "Free-Produce" anti-slavery movement and the free-labor potential of Haiti, see Fanning, *Caribbean Crossing*, 69–70, 90–91.

64. Lewis' letter, it seems, may never have been read. It was recovered from the Haitian archives in 1849 by an English merchant, after which it was printed by the *Friends' Weekly Intelligencer* as an "interesting historical document, worthy of preservation." "To Henry the First, King of Hayti," *Friends' Weekly Intelligencer* (Philadelphia), May 19, 1849, American Periodicals Series II.

65. On the relationship between Boyer's invitation to African Americans, his diplomatic mission to secure international recognition for Haiti, and his efforts to secure Haiti's political and economic sectors, see Fanning, *Caribbean Crossing.*

66. "American Convention," *Genius of Universal Emancipation* (Greenville, TN), March 1824, American Periodicals Series II.

67. Fanning, *Caribbean Crossing,* 17, 87, 89–90.

68. According to calculations drawn from the United States Census of 1820, a combined total of approximately 144,338 free black people lived in the Northeastern and Chesapeake regions from which most migrants originated. "1820 Census," Minnesota Population Center, National Historical Geographic Information System, Version 11.0.

69. To date, there has only been one full-length biographical treatment of Benjamin Lundy, see Merton L. Dillon, *Benjamin Lundy and the Struggle for Negro Freedom* (Urbana: University of Illinois Press, 1966). Previously, Thomas Earle's 1847 publication, *The Life, Travels and Opinions of Benjamin Lundy,* published eight years after Lundy's death, remained the most comprehensive treatment of Lundy's life and views. See Thomas Earle, *The Life, Travels and Opinions of Benjamin Lundy: Including His Journeys to Texas and Mexico; with a Sketch of Contemporary Events, and a Notice of the Revolution in Hayti* (Philadelphia: William D. Parrisi, 1847). Both Earle and Dillon, along with Lundy's own considerable editorial output, form the basis for contemporary studies of Lundy's role in the abolitionist movement. See, for example, Ford Risley, *Abolition and the Press: The Moral Struggle Against Slavery* (Evanston, IL: Northwestern University Press, 2008).

70. "Proposals," *Genius of Universal Emancipation* (Baltimore, MD) March 1825, American Periodicals Series II.

71. "Mission to Hayti," *Genius of Universal Emancipation* (Greenville, TN), December 1823, American Periodicals Series II.

72. In its Annual Report of 1823, the American Convention adopted a resolution to recommend that every member society promote subscriptions to the *Genius.* The Convention itself subscribed to ten copies. "American Convention," *Genius of Universal Emancipation* (Greenville, TN), March 1824, American Periodicals Series II.

73. "Emigration to Hayti – No. 1," *Genius of Universal Emancipation* (Baltimore, MD), October 1824, American Periodicals Series II.

74. Ibid.

75. Ibid.

76. "Letters From Hayti," *Genius of Universal Emancipation* (Baltimore, MD), March 1825, American Periodicals Series II.

77. "Letters From Hayti," *Genius of Universal Emancipation* (Baltimore, MD), July 1825, American Periodicals Series II.

78. Fanning, *Caribbean Crossing,* 112–116.

79. "Letter from Rev. Loring D. Dewey, now on tour in Hayti, to Daniel Raymond, Esq. of Baltimore," *Genius of Universal Emancipation* (Baltimore, MD), March 1825, American Periodicals Series II.

80. Not only did the Haitian plan out-compete the ACS for African American support (thus, in turn, tilting the white balance of favor toward Haiti as well), the ACS's

slaveholding members feared the power of the nearby black republic and worried that it would incite their own slaves to run away or rebel. Power-Greene, *Against Wind and Tide*, 29–30; Staudenraus, *The African Colonization Movement*, 84–87. See also Horton and Horton, *In Hope of Liberty*, 194.

81. "The Emigrants to Hayti," *Genius of Universal Emancipation* (Baltimore, MD), January 1825, American Periodicals Series II. See also, for example, "Hayti. – No. 1," *Genius of Universal Emancipation* (Baltimore, MD), June 17, 1826, American Periodicals Series II; "Emigration to Hayti," *Genius of Universal Emancipation* (Baltimore, MD), July 4, 1825, American Periodicals Series II.

82. Staudenraus, *The African Colonization Movement*, 82–84.

83. "Republic of Hayti," *Genius of Universal Emancipation* (Baltimore, MD), October 1824, American Periodicals Series II.

84. Dixon, *African America and Haiti*, 35; Loring D. Dewey, *Correspondence Relative to the Emigration to Hayti, of the Free People of Colour, in the United States. Together with the Instructions to the Agent Sent Out by President Boyer* (New York: Mahlon Day, 1824), 2–6.

85. Dixon, *African America and Haiti*, 41.

86. "Letter from Rev. Loring D. Dewey, now on tour in Hayti, to Daniel Raymond, Esq. of Baltimore," *Genius of Universal Emancipation* (Baltimore, MD), March 1825, American Periodicals Series II.

87. For example, see "Letters on Hayti," *Genius of Universal Emancipation* (Baltimore, MD), October 1, 1825, American Periodicals Series II; "Letter from Hayti," *Connecticut Courant* (Hartford, CT), February 22, 1825, America's Historical Newspapers; "Emigration to Hayti," *Pittsfield Sun* (Pittsfield, MA), April 7, 1825, America's Historical Newspapers; "From Hayti," *The Farmer's Cabinet* (Amherst, NH), April 9, 1825, America's Historical Newspapers; "Hayti," *Eastern Argus* (Portland, ME), June 13, 1825, America's Historical Newspapers.

88. "From the United States Gazette, Emigrants Returning," *Genius of Universal Emancipation* (Baltimore, MD), August 1825, American Periodicals Series II. This higher estimate of returnees comes from Horton and Horton, *In Hope of Liberty*, 195. In fact, the number of migrants to Haiti may have been as high as 8,000 in total throughout the 1820s.

89. No title, *Genius of Universal Emancipation* (Baltimore, MD), January 1825, American Periodicals Series II.

90. "Expedition from North Carolina to Hayti," *Genius of Universal Emancipation* (Baltimore, MD), August 12, 1826, American Periodicals Series II.

91. Dixon, *African America and Haiti*, 41–42; Power-Greene, *Against Wind and Tide*, 37.

92. "Hayti. – No. 1," *Genius of Universal Emancipation* (Baltimore, MD), June 17, 1826, American Periodicals Series II.

93. "Expedition from North Carolina to Hayti," *Genius of Universal Emancipation* (Baltimore, MD), August 12, 1826, American Periodicals Series II.

94. Dixon, *African America and Haiti*, 42–43.

95. "Expedition from North Carolina to Hayti," *Genius of Universal Emancipation* (Baltimore, MD), August 12, 1826, American Periodicals Series II.

96. Ibid.

97. On Haiti as a symbol of freedom for anti-slavery advocates in the late years of the Early Republic and through the antebellum period, see Fanning, "The Roots of Early Black Nationalism"; Charlton W. Yingling, "No One Who Reads the History of Hayti Can Doubt the Capacity of Colored Men: Racial Formation and Atlantic Rehabilitation in New York City's Early Black Press, 1827–1841," *Early American Studies: An Interdisciplinary Journal* 11, no. 2 (2013): 315–317; Mitchell A. Kachun, *Festivals of Freedom: Memory and Meaning in African American Emancipation Celebrations, 1808–1915* (Amherst: University of Massachusetts Press, 2003); Hunt, *Haiti's Influence on Antebellum America.*

98. Jacqueline Bacon, *Freedom's Journal: The First African American Newspaper* (Lanham, MD: Lexington Books, 2007), 51–52. Bacon's estimate that the journal had at least 800 subscribers is based on subscription numbers for the *Rights of All* in 1829, which was Samuel Cornish's continuation of *Freedom's Journal* by another name after Russwurm's departure from the paper. In addition, Bacon suggests that textual references penned by Russwurm himself indicate that *Freedom's Journal* was being widely shared beyond the actual subscription rates, which was a regular practice in nineteenth-century periodical culture that augmented a newspaper's reach (often at the expense of editors' revenue stream).

99. "To Our Patrons," *Freedom's Journal* (New York), March 16, 1827, Accessible Archives.

100. Ibid.

101. James, *The Struggles of John Brown Russwurm*, 6–24, 44–45.

102. For extensive analyses of how *Freedom's Journal* represented Haiti, see Bacon, *Freedom's Journal*, 165–171, and Yingling, "No One Who Reads the History of Hayti Can Doubt the Capacity of Colored Men," 328–334.

103. See, for example, "Hayti. – No. III," *Freedom's Journal* (New York), Accessible Archives; "Hayti. – No. VI," *Freedom's Journal* (New York), October 12, 1827; "Hayti. – No. V.," *Freedom's Journal* (New York), June 29, 1827, Accessible Archives; "African Free Schools in the United States," *Freedom's Journal* (New York), June 1, 1827, Accessible Archives.

104. "Haytien Revolution," *Freedom's Journal* (New York), April 6, 1827, Accessible Archives.

105. A selected extract from a study titled "America, or a General Survey," for example, cast significant doubt on how long Haiti could maintain its independence due its outstanding debt to France. Yet, the author asserted, "the example of Hayti has been upon the whole of a nature to encourage the expectations of the friends of humanity, in regards to the capacity of the black race, for self-government and the arts and habits of a civilized life." From "European Colonies in America," *Freedom's Journal* (New York), Accessible Archives.

2 EXIT AND EXPANSION: THE SEARCH FOR LEGAL EQUALITY IN A TIME OF CRISIS

1. "Extract from an Address," *Freedom's Journal* (New York), May 18, 1827, Accessible Archives.

2. "Poetry: The Fugitive," *The Friend of Man* (Utica, NY), July 28, 1836, Slavery and Anti-Slavery: A Transnational Archive.

3. Benjamin Drew, ed., "J. C. Brown," in *A North-Side View of Slavery. The Refugee: Or The Narratives of Fugitive Slaves in Canada. Related by Themselves, with an Account of the History and Condition of the Colored Population of Upper Canada* (Boston, MA: J. P. Jewett, 1856), 239–240.

4. Ibid., 241. Narrating his memories of this period in the year 1856, almost forty years later, Brown refers to the area he investigated in 1819 as "Texas." Though it was part of New Spain at the time, it would become Mexican Texas two years later after Mexican Independence in 1821. Even after Mexico's independence from the Spanish Empire, however, Texas remained highly disputed territory until the United States finally annexed it at the culmination of the Mexican–American War in 1848.

5. Ibid. It is unclear where exactly Brown visited in Spanish Texas, or from whom he received this information. He remembered the councilman's name as "Black" or "Blake," but there is no sense of what council the man sat on. Brown refers to it as the council of a colony, but there does not seem to have been an organized American colony in Texas territory at that time. According to historian Randolph Campbell, American settlers had started filtering into Texas territory in 1816, extending southeast from Miller County, Arkansas, but they had no legal right to be there. It was not until 1821 that Moses Austin received permission from the government to settle a colony in the area. However, it is no surprise that the man Brown spoke to indicated that the province would be inhospitable to a free black settlement. Even after Mexican independence in 1821, when the liberal politics of the new Mexican government threatened the institution of slavery, there was not a strong enough legal proscription against the institution to hamper American settlers' importation of enslaved people to cultivate cash crops. Potential settlers expressed concern about the effect that Mexican antislavery might have on their property rights, but those who did relocate to Texas nevertheless relocated with their enslaved laborers. Thus, from 1816 onward, American settlement in the area expanded arm-in-arm with a thriving pro-slavery culture. See, Randolph B. Campbell, *An Empire for Slavery: The Peculiar Institution in Texas, 1821–1865* (Baton Rouge: Louisiana State University Press, 1991), 13–18.

6. Drew, "J. C. Brown," 245.

7. Nikki Marie Taylor, *Frontiers of Freedom: Cincinnati's Black Community, 1802–1868* (Athens, OH: Ohio University Press, 2005), 32–35.

8. Winks, *The Blacks in Canada*, 155.

9. Taylor, *Frontiers of Freedom*, 63–64.

10. Both at the time and retrospectively over the next several decades, assessments of just how many black Ohioans emigrated from Cincinnati vary considerably. The *Genius of Universal Emancipation*, for example, reported in February 1830 that 600 Cincinnati natives had relocated to Upper Canada. This number was also echoed in a widely reprinted article from the St. Clairsville *Historian* from January of the same year. In June of the following year, the delegates of the first annual Convention of the People of Color asserted that 2,000 had crossed into Upper Canada, though it does not specify that all were from Cincinnati. In 1832, British traveler and public figure Charles Stuart asserted that the original number of emigrants to Upper Canada was 1,100. Then,

looking back from the vantage point of 1856, James C. Brown himself claimed that only 460 of 2,700 intended settlers actually moved across the U.S.–Canadian border in the exodus of 1830. This disparity has led scholars including Nikki Taylor to use the range 460–2,000. But it seems the early estimate of 600 is the most likely approximation. See "African Colony in Canada," *Genius of Universal Emancipation* (Baltimore, MD), February 5, 1830; "From the St. Clairsville (Ohio) Historian," *Norwich Courier* (Norwich, CT), January 20, 1830; Howard Holman Bell, ed., "Minutes and Proceedings of the First Annual Convention of the People of Color (1831)," in *Minutes of the Proceedings of the National Negro Conventions, 1830–1864* (New York: Arno Press, 1969), 13; Charles Stuart, *Remarks on the Colony of Liberia and the American Colonization Society, with some account of the settlement of Colored People at Wilberforce, Upper Canada* (London: J. Messeder, 1832), 9; Drew, *A North-Side View of Slavery*, 246; Taylor, *Frontiers of Freedom*, 65.

11. See, for example, Winks, *The Blacks in Canada*, 155–157; Silverman, *Unwelcome Guests*, 26–28; Taylor, *Frontiers of Freedom*, 61–63. In each of these narratives, Upper Canada is presented as the "logical" choice (see Silverman, *Unwelcome Guests*, 27) for relocation, though the story, in each, begins in 1829 without reference to other free-soil spaces or the genesis of Canada as a place where the Cincinnatians would consider.

12. Taylor, *Frontiers of Freedom*, 21.

13. "The following has appeared in several of our newspapers," *Genius of Universal Emancipation* (Greenville, TN), January 1825, American Periodicals Series II.

14. Taylor, *Frontiers of Freedom*, 60.

15. "Another View of Colonization," *Freedom's Journal* (New York), January 31, 1829, Accessible Archives.

16. See Taylor, *Frontiers of Freedom*, 60; "Another View of Colonization," *Freedom's Journal* (New York), January 31, 1829, Accessible Archives.

17. "Another View of Colonization," *Freedom's Journal* (New York), January 31, 1829, Accessible Archives.

18. Ibid.

19. Christopher Schmidt-Nowara, *Slavery, Freedom, and Abolition in Latin America and the Atlantic World* (Albuquerque: University of New Mexico Press, 2011), 112–116.

20. John Lynch, *Simón Bolívar: A Life* (New Haven, CT: Yale University Press, 2006), 97.

21. Notably, gradual anti-slavery legislation ultimately made little impact in Gran Colombia by the time the republic dissolved in 1831. Following the dissolution of Gran Colombia into separate political entities, slavery remained in place in Venezuela, Colombia, and Ecuador until the early 1850s. See Russell Lohse, "Reconciling Freedom with the Rights of Property: Slave Emancipation in Colombia, 1821–1852, with Special Reference to La Plata," *Journal of Negro History* 86, no. 3 (2001): 203–227.

22. On the shifting and complex American reactions toward the Spanish American revolutions, particularly with regard to the issue of slavery, see Fitz, *Our Sister Republics*.

23. See American Convention, *Minutes of the proceedings of a special meeting of the fifteenth American Convention* (1818), 15–17.

24. Schmidt-Nowara, *Slavery, Freedom, and Abolition in Latin America and the Atlantic World*, 115; Philip S. Foner, "Alexander Von Humboldt on Slavery in America," *Science &*

Society 47, no. 3 (October 1983): 335–338. Humboldt's *Ensayo político sobre la Isla de Cuba* was published in Paris in 1827 by J. Renouard.

25. "Extract from an Address," *Freedom's Journal* (New York), May 18, 1827, Accessible Archives.

26. Ibid.

27. Audain, "Mexican Canaan," 14–35; Eric Herschthal, "Slaves, Spaniards, and Subversion in Early Louisiana: The Persistent Fears of Black Revolt and Spanish Collusion in Territorial Louisiana, 1803–1812," *Journal of the Early Republic* 36, no. 2 (June 2016): 289–293.

28. See Campbell, *An Empire for Slavery*, 15–26; Kelley, "Mexico in His Head," 714–715.

29. Campbell, *An Empire for Slavery*, 15–26; Nichols, *The Limits of Liberty*, 57; Kelley, "Mexico in His Head," 713–715.

30. Kelley, "Mexico in His Head," 712–716; Nichols, *The Limits of Liberty*, 57.

31. "To the Editors of the St. Louis Beacon," *Richmond Enquirer* (Richmond, VA), September 11, 1829, America's Historical Newspapers.

32. Mekala Audain, "'Design His Course to Mexico': The Fugitive Slave Experience in the Texas–Mexico Borderlands, 1850–1853," in Damian Alan Pargas, (ed.), *Fugitive Slaves and Spaces of Freedom in North America* (Gainesville: University of Florida Press, 2018), 235–245.

33. James David Nichols, "Freedom Interrupted: Runaway Slaves and Insecure Borders in the Mexican Northeast," in *Fugitive Slaves and Spaces of Freedom in North America*, ed. Damian Alan Pargas (Gainesville: University of Florida Press, 2018), 251–252, 254–255.

34. See "Negotiations with Mexico," *Richmond Enquirer* (Richmond, VA), January 2, 1827, America's Historical Newspapers; "Fugitive Slaves," *Freedom's Journal* (New York), January 16, 1829, Accessible Archives; and Schwartz, *Across the Rio to Freedom*, 9–10, 12–14, 17–18.

35. "To Our Patrons," *Freedom's Journal* (New York), March 16, 1827, Accessible Archives.

36. "African Free Schools in the United States," *Freedom's Journal* (New York), June 1, 1827, Accessible Archives.

37. In his article on the topic, Lundy relies on reflections penned by Henry George Ward from Mexico, dated March 13, 1826. Ward had served as the British envoy in Mexico in 1825. "Culture of Sugar by Free Labor," *Genius of Universal Emancipation* (Baltimore, MD), December 11, 1829, American Periodicals Series II.

38. "Slavery" [reprinted from the *New York Observer*], *Haverhill Gazette and Patriot* (Haverhill, MA), July 31, 1824, America's Historical Newspapers.

39. See, for example, Walter Johnson, *River of Dark Dreams: Slavery and Empire in the Cotton Kingdom* (Cambridge, MA: Belknap Press, 2013); Edward E. Baptist, *The Half Has Never Been Told: Slavery and the Making of American Capitalism* (New York: Basic Books, 2016).

40. "To the Editors of the St. Louis Beacon," *Richmond Enquirer* (Richmond, VA), September 11, 1829.

41. See, for example, "Negotiations with Mexico," *Richmond Enquirer* (Richmond, VA), January 2, 1827, America's Historical Newspapers; "In Senate," *Richmond Enquirer*

(Richmond, VA), January 19, 1828, America's Historical Newspapers; "Mexico," *The Pittsfield Sun* (Pittsfield, MA), January 31, 1828, America's Historical Newspapers; and "Fugitive Slaves," *Genius of Universal Emancipation* (Baltimore, MD), January 3, 1829, American Periodicals Series II.

42. See "Mexican Insurrection," *Freedom's Journal* (New York), January 31, 1829, Accessible Archives.

43. Drew, "J. C. Brown," 241–244.

44. Winks, *The Blacks in Canada*, 25–26; on the public's interpretation of the *Somerset* decision in England, see Brown, *Moral Capital*, 97–98.

45. During the American Revolution, Lord Dunmore explicitly offered freedom to run-away American slaves in an effort to undermine the rebel colonists' economic base. By contrast, Vice-Admiral Cochrane offered to transport any resident of the United States to other British possessions and support their resettlement as loyal subjects elsewhere. Though he did not explicitly encourage slaves, several hundred slaves pursued their freedom by running toward British military posts. In both cases, more than 2,000 African Americans – free and formerly enslaved – left with the British after each war. See Jasanoff, *Liberty's Exiles*, 88–91; Winks, *The Blacks in Canada*, 114–116.

46. Britain's decision to transport and resettle African Americans who claimed their protection also laid the foundation for what historian Christopher Brown has called Britain's "moral capital" as it re-conceptualized itself in the wake of losing thirteen of its mainland colonies. Brown argues that Britain's organized anti-slavery efforts in the wake of the American Revolution provided the British Empire with a powerful new form of imperial legitimacy. See Brown, *Moral Capital*.

47. Silverman, *Unwelcome Guests*, 9.

48. Wigmore, "Before the Railroad," 438–439.

49. Ibid., 450–454.

50. On the word-of-mouth spread of information from the Detroit River Valley, see Wigmore, "Before the Railroad," 450. On the return of soldiers from the War of 1812, see Henry Wilson, *Rise and Fall of the Slave Power in America*, vol. 2 (Boston, MA: James R. Osgood, 1874), 63. On Great Britain's reputation for protecting black people's freedom in Nova Scotia after the American Revolution and War of 1812, see Gosse, "As a Nation, the English Are Our Friends," 1009–1011.

51. Wilson, *Rise and Fall of the Slave Power in America*, 2:63.

52. William Birney, *James G. Birney and His Times: The Genesis of the Republican Party with Some Account of Abolition Movements in the South before 1828* (New York: Appleton, 1890), 435.

53. See, for example, *Freedom's Journal* (New York), January 16, 1829, Accessible Archives.

54. Gerald Horne, *Negro Comrades of the Crown: African Americans and the British Empire Fight the U.S. Before Emancipation* (New York: New York University Press, 2012), 2–3.

55. Two Hundred Coloured Persons, "A Petition, Discovered by the Honourable William Renwick Riddell, Justice of Appeal, Ontario, Canada (June 18, 1828)," *Journal of Negro History* 15, no. 1 (January 1930): 115–116.

56. Winks, *The Blacks in Canada*, 144–145; Silverman, *Unwelcome Guests*, 22–23.

57. On the Panic of 1819, the Missouri Compromise, and the history of American section-alism, see Robert Pierce Forbes, *The Missouri Compromise and Its Aftermath: Slavery and the Meaning of America* (Chapel Hill: University of North Carolina Press, 2007); and Andrew H. Browning, *The Panic of 1819: The First Great Depression* (Columbia, MO: University of Missouri Press, 2019).

58. As quoted in Alexander Lovell Murray, "Canada and the Anglo-American Anti-Slavery Movement: A Study in International Philanthropy" (PhD diss., University of Pennsylvania, 1960), 117.

59. "Fugitive Slaves," *Annals of Congress*, 16th Congress, 2nd Session, 941.

60. See "Fugitive Slaves" [C. A. Wickliffe to Henry Clay], *Niles' Weekly Register* (Baltimore, MD), June 24, 1826, American Periodicals Series II; and "Fugitive Slaves" [Mr. Clay to Mr. Gallatin February 24, 1827], *Freedom's Journal* (New York), January 16, 1829, Accessible Archives.

61. "Fugitive Slaves (Extract … dated June 19, 1826)," *Freedom's Journal* (New York), January 16, 1829, Accessible Archives.

62. "Fugitive Slaves" [Mr. Gallatin to Mr. Clay dated Sept. 26, 1827], *Freedom's Journal* (New York), January 16, 1829, Accessible Archives.

63. "Fugitive Slaves" [Mr. Clay to Mr. Barbour June 31, 1828], *Freedom's Journal* (New York), January 16, 1829, Accessible Archives.

64. "Fugitive Slaves," *Niles' Weekly Register* (Baltimore, MD), December 27, 1828, American Periodicals Series II; "Fugitive Slaves," *Genius of Universal Emancipation* (Baltimore, MD), January 3, 1829, American Periodicals Series II; "Fugitive Slaves," *Freedom's Journal* (New York), January 16, 1829, Accessible Archives.

65. "Freedom is the Brilliant Gift of Heaven," *Freedom's Journal* (New York), January 16, 1829, Accessible Archives.

66. "Runaway Slaves," *Freedom's Journal* (New York), January 9, 1829, Accessible Archives.

67. Cornell, "Citizens of Nowhere," 353.

68. "Foreign Intelligence (New York Statesman)," *The Christian Register* (Boston, MA), September 9, 1826, American Periodicals Series II.

69. "People of Colour (Continued)," *Freedom's Journal* (New York), April 13, 1827, Accessible Archives.

70. Drew, "J. C. Brown," 244.

71. On the history of African Americans in Nova Scotia, see Harvey Amani Whitfield, *Blacks on the Border: The Black Refugees in British North America, 1815–1860* (Burlington: University of Vermont Press, 2006), and Winks, *The Blacks in Canada*, 117–129, 134–141. Regarding, many Black Loyalists decided to leave Nova Scotia for Sierra Leone due to prejudicial treatment, see Winks, *The Blacks in Canada*, 63–64, 77.

72. Two Hundred Colored Persons, "A Petition."

73. Although the British Empire as a whole was moving in the direction of political equality by 1830, no consistent, empire-wide policy was set in place until 1833. See Arnold A. Sio, "Race, Colour, and Miscegenation: The Free Coloured of Jamaica and Barbados," *Caribbean Studies* 16, no. 1 (April 1976): 8–9; Samuel J. Hurwitz and Edith F. Hurwitz,

"A Token of Freedom: Private Bill Legislation for Free Negroes in Eighteenth-Century Jamaica," *William and Mary Quarterly* 24, no. 3 (1967): 424–425.

74. John Malvin, *Autobiography of John Malvin: A Narrative, Containing an Authentic Account of His Fifty Years' Struggle in the State of Ohio in Behalf of the American Slave and the Equal Rights of All Men Before the Law Without Reference to Race or Color; Forty-Seven Years of Said Time Being Expended in the City of Cleveland* (Cleveland, OH: Leader Printing Co., 1879), 12.

75. Drew, "J. C. Brown," 244.

76. "To the Generous Public," *Daily Cincinnati Gazette* (Cincinnati, OH), July 30, 1829, vol. 3, No. 650, Library of Congress.

77. Drew, "J. C. Brown," 244–245.

78. Previous historical studies on the topic have underappreciated the significance of Colborne's letter and the way it shifted the relationship between the British government and African American emigrants. Jason Silverman, for example, argued that the Cincinnatians found Upper Canada to be "the most logical place to relocate" based on the land availability. In Silverman's narrative, Colborne's words of welcome were an encouraging sanction to a decision already made. Nikki Taylor and Robin Winks, meanwhile, make clear that the decision to relocate was made only after receiving Colborne's letter, but do not reflect on the fact that this letter and its promise of equality fundamentally altered the relationship between African American emigrants and the Upper Canadian government from what it had previously been. Silverman, *Unwelcome Guests*, 27; Taylor, *Frontiers of Freedom*, 61; Winks, *The Blacks in Canada*, 155–156.

79. Drew, "J. C. Brown," 245; "To the Generous Public," *Daily Cincinnati Gazette* (Cincinnati, OH), July 30, 1829, vol. 3, No. 650, Library of Congress.

80. "Article Six – No Title," *Genius of Universal Emancipation* (Baltimore, MD), January 15, 1830, American Periodicals Series II.

81. It is unknown if this was, indeed, the exact language of Colborne's guarantee. First found in sociologist Harriet Martineau's widely read *The Martyr Age of the United States*, it has been used ever after to capture the essence of his words. Harriet Martineau, *The Martyr Age of the United States* (Boston, MA: Weeks, Jordan & Co., 1839), 6.

3 DEPARTURE AND DEBATE: FREE BLACK EMIGRATION TO CANADA AND MEXICO

1. "Wilberforce Settlement," *The Liberator* (Boston, MA), April 7, 1832, Slavery and Anti-Slavery: A Transnational Archive.

2. "Public Notice," *Daily Cincinnati Gazette* (Cincinnati, OH), August 25, 1829, vol. 3, No. 672, American Periodicals Series II; "People of Colour," *Rights of All* (New York), August 7, 1829, America's Historical Newspapers.

3. "Colony in Canada," *Genius of Universal Emancipation* (Baltimore, MD), April 1830, American Periodicals Series II.

4. "Canada Colony," *Genius of Universal Emancipation* (Baltimore, MD), March 1831, American Periodicals Series II.

5. In their "Address to the Free People of Colour," delegates to the first annual Convention of People of Color (1830) noted that many black Ohioans instead continued to "crowd into the Atlantic cities." See "Address to the Free Persons of Color in the United States," in Howard Holman Bell, ed., "Constitution of the American Society of Free Persons of Color, for Improving Their Condition in the United States; for Purchasing Lands; and for the Establishment of a Settlement in Upper Canada," in *Minutes of the Proceedings of the National Negro Conventions, 1830–1864*, 10.

6. See Drew, "J. C. Brown," 246; "Public Notice," *Daily Cincinnati Gazette* (Cincinnati, OH), August 25, 1829, vol. 3, No. 672, Library of Congress; "To the Generous Public," *Daily Cincinnati Gazette* (Cincinnati, OH), July 30, 1829, vol. 3, No. 650, Library of Congress.

7. Drew, "J. C. Brown," 246; Austin Steward, *Twenty-Two Years a Slave and Forty Years a Freeman; Embracing a Correspondence of Several Years, While President of Wilberforce Colony, London, Canada West* (Rochester, NY: W. Alling, 1857), 179.

8. See Horne, *Negro Comrades of the Crown.*

9. "Colored Citizens of Ohio," *The North Star* (Rochester, NY), June 29, 1849, Accessible Archives.

10. Drew, "J. C. Brown," 245.

11. Stuart, *Remarks on the Colony of Liberia and the American Colonization Society*, 10.

12. "African Colony in Canada," *Genius of Universal Emancipation* (Baltimore, MD), March 5, 1830, American Periodicals Series II.

13. On the transition from gradualism to immediatism in American anti-slavery, see Newman, *The Transformation of American Abolitionism*. On the causes of the transition, see, in particular, pp 8–11 and chs. 4 and 5. See also, Harrold, *American Abolitionism*, chs. 2–3; and Sinha, *The Slave's Cause*, 198–227.

14. On Garrison's relationship with Lundy and his early abolitionist thinking, see McDaniel, *The Problem of Democracy in the Age of Slavery*, 31–37.

15. "To the Public," *The Liberator* (Boston, MA), January 1, 1831, Slavery and Anti-Slavery: A Transnational Archive.

16. See, for example, McDaniel, *The Problem of Democracy in the Age of Slavery*, 37–38; Davis, *The Problem of Slavery in the Age of Emancipation*, 188; Newman, *The Transformation of American Abolitionism*, 104.

17. David Walker, *Walker's Appeal, in Four Articles; Together with a Preamble, to the Colored Citizens of the World, but in Particular, and Very Expressly, to Those of the United States of America* (Boston, MA, 1829), 3.

18. James Brewer Stewart, *Abolitionist Politics and the Coming of the Civil War* (Amherst: University of Massachusetts Press, 2008), 13.

19. There is a long, robust historiography on American abolitionism, the motivations driving the movement and its members, and the activities they spearheaded in their fight to end slavery. For a topical overview from leading historians on the topic, see Timothy Patrick McCarthy and John Stauffer, eds., *Pamphlets of Protest: Reconsidering the History of American Abolitionism* (New York: New Press, 2006). See also Sinha, *The Slave's Cause*; Stanley, *American Abolitionism*; Andrew Delbanco, *The Abolitionist Imagination* (Cambridge, MA: Harvard

University Press, 2012); John Stauffer, *The Black Hearts of Men: Radical Abolitionists and the Transformation of Race* (Cambridge, MA: Harvard University Press, 2004).

20. Power-Greene, *Against Wind and Tide*, 50.

21. Newman, *The Transformation of American Abolitionism*, 96.

22. Staudenraus, *The African Colonization Movement*, 82–97.

23. Ibid., 82–87, 94–99; Burin, *Slavery and the Peculiar Solution*, 16; Power-Greene, *Against Wind and Tide*, 39, 45.

24. "Annual Meeting of the Colonization Society," *African Repository and Colonial Journal* (Washington, DC), March 1, 1825, Slavery and Anti-Slavery, A Transnational Archive.

25. "Liberia," *Freedom's Journal* (New York), February 21, 1829, Accessible Archives.

26. See, for example, "Take Care of Number One!" *The Colored American* (New York), January 27, 1838, Slavery and Anti-Slavery: A Transnational Archive.

27. "Colonization," *Freedom's Journal* (New York), March 14, 1829, Accessible Archives.

28. "Liberia," *Freedom's Journal* (New York), February 21, 1829, Accessible Archives.

29. "Liberia," *Freedom's Journal* (New York), February 21, 1829, Accessible Archives.

30. "Liberia Herald – John B. Russwurm," *The Liberator* (Boston, MA), February 25, 1832, Slavery and Anti-Slavery: A Transnational Archive.

31. See, for example, "A Voice from the West: Pittsburgh," *The Liberator* (Boston, MA), September 17, 1831, Slavery and Anti-Slavery: A Transnational Archive.

32. "A Voice from Columbia, PA!" *The Liberator* (Boston, MA), August 20, 1831, Slavery and Anti-Slavery: A Transnational Archive; "A Voice from Trenton!" *The Liberator* (Boston, MA), December 17, 1831, Slavery and Anti-Slavery: A Transnational Archive; "A Voice from Rochester!" *The Liberator* (Boston, MA), October 29, 1831, Slavery and Anti-Slavery: A Transnational Archive; "A Voice from Ohio!" *The Liberator* (Boston, MA), February 4, 1832, Slavery and Anti-Slavery: A Transnational Archive.

33. "A Voice from Columbia, PA!" *The Liberator* (Boston, MA), August 20, 1831, Slavery and Anti-Slavery: A Transnational Archive.

34. "American Colonization Society, No. III," *Freedom's Journal* (New York), September 28, 1827, Accessible Archives.

35. In his remarks on colonization published in the ACS's *African Repository*, for example, Professor Calvin Stowe argued that even though both Liberia and Canada were "open" to people of African descent, the latter was "too cold for blacks born in North Carolina." "Professor Stowe on Colonization," *African Repository and Colonial Journal* (Washington, DC), December 1, 1834, Slavery and Anti-Slavery: A Transnational Archive.

36. John H. Kennedy, for example, who penned a series of pro-ACS editorials in *Freedom's Journal*, argued that the high death rates of Liberian colonists were comparable to the high mortality pervasive in every early colonial endeavor, and that deaths were actually less frequent in Liberia than they were in Philadelphia in proportion to the population. See, "American Colonization Society, No. III," *Freedom's Journal* (New York), September 28, 1827, Accessible Archives.

37. "A Voice from the West: Pittsburgh," *The Liberator* (Boston, MA), September 17, 1831, Slavery and Anti-Slavery: A Transnational Archive; "Mortality in Liberia," *The Liberator* (Boston, MA), July 2, 1831, Slavery and Anti-Slavery: A Transnational Archive.

38. "Review: Address delivered before the Hawkins County Colonization Society, Tennessee, by John A. M. Kinney, Esq., July 4th, 1830," *African Repository and Colonial Journal*, October 1830, vol. 6, No. 8, Slavery and Anti-Slavery: A Transnational Archive.

39. "Review: The American Colonization Society Further Unravelled. By Charles Stuart," *The Liberator* (Boston, MA), April 19, 1834, Slavery and Anti-Slavery: A Transnational Archive.

40. "Address to the Colored Citizens of Brooklyn," *The Liberator* (Boston, MA), July 2, 1831, Slavery and Anti-Slavery: A Transnational Archive.

41. "African Colony in Canada," *Genius of Universal Emancipation* (Baltimore, MD), February 5, 1830, American Periodicals Series II.

42. "African Colony in Canada" (reprint from Ohio's *Mount Pleasant Repository*), *Genius of Universal Emancipation* (Baltimore, MD), March 5, 1830, American Periodicals Series II.

43. The most recent work on the Colored Convention Movement comes from a collective digital humanities project out of the University of Delaware, The Colored Conventions Project, see at: http://coloredconventions.org. For scholarship emerging from this collective enterprise, see P. Gabrielle Foreman, Jim C. Casey, and Sarah L. Peterson, eds., *The Colored Conventions Movement: Black Organizing in the Nineteenth Century* (Chapel Hill: University of North Carolina Press, 2021).

44. "Address to the Free People of Color," in Bell, "Constitution of the American Society of Free Persons of Color, for Improving Their Condition in the United States; for Purchasing Lands; and for the Establishment of a Settlement in Upper Canada," 9–11.

45. Bell, "Minutes and Proceedings of the First Annual Convention of the People of Color (1831)," 12–13; Steward, *Twenty-Two Years a Slave and Forty Years a Freeman*, 182.

46. Winks, *The Blacks in Canada*, 156.

47. For examples of the estimates ongoing circulation, see "Movements of the People of Color," *Genius of Universal Emancipation* (Baltimore, MD), April 1831, American Periodicals Series II; and "Wilberforce Settlement," *The Liberator* (Boston, MA), April 7, 1832, Slavery and Anti-Slavery: A Transnational Archive. For the relevant population data, see "1830 Census," Minnesota Population Center, National Historical Geographic Information System, Version 11.0.

48. "Colony in Canada," *Genius of Universal Emancipation* (Baltimore, MD), August 1830, American Periodicals Series II. On Grice's personal history, including his fight for equality and eventual emigration to Haiti in 1832, see Jones, *Birthright Citizens*, 38–49.

49. "The Canada Colony," *Genius of Universal Emancipation* (Baltimore, MD), April 1830, American Periodicals Series II. Over a year later, news of extensive migration preparation continued to make the news. In December 1831, a "gentleman of New-York" informed Benjamin Lundy that "400 colored persons have arrived in that place, from the South, on their way to the Canada Settlement." "Persecution of Free People of Color," *Genius of Universal Emancipation* (Baltimore, MD), December 1831, American Periodicals Series II.

50. "Colony in Canada," *Genius of Universal Emancipation* (Baltimore, MD), August 1830, American Periodicals Series II.

51. See, for example, "Colored People in Ohio," *Rights of All* (New York), August 7, 1829, America's Historical Newspapers; "A Voice from Trenton!" *The Liberator* (Boston, MA), December 17, 1831, Slavery and Anti-Slavery: A Transnational Archive; "A Voice from Rochester!" *The Liberator* (Boston, MA), October 29, 1831, Slavery and Anti-Slavery: A Transnational Archive.

52. See, "From the [Albany] African Sentinel," *Genius of Universal Emancipation* (Baltimore, MD), September 1831, American Periodicals Series II; "Wilberforce Settlement," *Genius of Universal Emancipation* (Baltimore, MD), March 1832, American Periodicals Series II; "Emigration," *The Liberator* (Boston, MA), May 26, 1832, Slavery and Anti-Slavery: A Transnational Archive.

53. "Wilberforce Settlement," *The Liberator* (Boston, MA), April 7, 1832, Slavery and Anti-Slavery: A Transnational Archive.

54. For examples of fundraising, see "Colony of Blacks" (reprint from the *Cincinnati Gazette*), *Genius of Universal Emancipation* (Baltimore, MD), July 1830, American Periodicals Series II; "The Canada Settlement," *Genius of Universal Emancipation* (Baltimore, MD), September 1830, American Periodicals Series II; and "Colony in Upper Canada," *The Liberator* (Boston, MA), September 17, 1831, Slavery and Anti-Slavery: A Transnational Archive.

55. Quote from "From the [Albany] African Sentinel," *Genius of Universal Emancipation* (Baltimore, MD), September 1831, American Periodicals Series II. See also "Article 6 – No Title," *Genius of Universal Emancipation* (Baltimore, MD), January 15, 1830, American Periodicals Series II.

56. See, for example, "Canada Colony," *Genius of Universal Emancipation* (Baltimore, MD), March 1831, American Periodicals Series II.

57. William Lloyd Garrison's *Liberator* was the most prominent and widely read among the newspapers that followed the scandal closely. See, as a late example, "Wilberforce Colony," *The Liberator* (Boston, MA), February 23, 1833, Slavery and Anti-Slavery: A Transnational Archive.

58. See "Wilberforce Settlement, U.C.," *The Liberator* (Boston, MA), August 25, 1832, Slavery and Anti-Slavery: A Transnational Archive; and "African Canadian Colonization," *The Liberator* (Boston, MA), February 23, 1833, Slavery and Anti-Slavery: A Transnational Archive.

59. "Beware of Impostors," *New York Observer and Chronicle* (New York), February 16, 1833, American Periodicals Series II.

60. "Wilberforce Settlement," *Genius of Universal Emancipation* (Baltimore, MD), March 1832, American Periodicals Series II.

61. See Winks, *The Blacks in Canada*, 159.

62. "Canada Colony," *Genius of Universal Emancipation* (Baltimore, MD), March 1831, American Periodicals Series II.

63. "Wilberforce Settlement," *Genius of Universal Emancipation* (Baltimore, MD), March 1832, American Periodicals Series II; "Tour in Upper Canada," *Genius of Universal Emancipation* (Baltimore, MD), April 1832, American Periodicals Series II; "Tour in

Upper Canada," *Genius of Universal Emancipation* (Baltimore, MD), May 1832, American Periodicals Series II.

64. Quote from "Wilberforce Settlement," *The Liberator* (Boston, MA), May 12, 1832, Slavery and Anti-Slavery: A Transnational Archive. See also, "Benjamin Lundy," *The Liberator* (Boston, MA), August 18, 1832, Slavery and Anti-Slavery: A Transnational Archive.

65. "Emigration," *The Liberator* (Boston, MA), May 26, 1832, Slavery and Anti-Slavery: A Transnational Archive.

66. "Tour in Upper Canada," *Genius of Universal Emancipation* (Baltimore, MD), April and May 1832, American Periodicals Series II.

67. "Emigration to Canada," *Genius of Universal Emancipation* (Baltimore, MD), May 1830, American Periodicals Series II.

68. "The Mexicans," *Genius of Universal Emancipation* (Baltimore, MD), October 1831, American Periodicals Series II.

69. Ibid.

70. See "The Mexicans, in 1830," *Genius of Universal Emancipation* (Baltimore, MD), August 1831, American Periodicals Series II; "The Mexicans," *Genius of Universal Emancipation* (Baltimore, MD), September 1831, American Periodicals Series II; "The Mexicans," *Genius of Universal Emancipation* (Baltimore, MD), October 1831, American Periodicals Series II.

71. Loughran, *The Republic in Print*, 318.

72. Benjamin Lundy, *The life, travels, and opinions of Benjamin Lundy: including his journeys to Texas and Mexico, with a sketch of contemporary events, and a notice of the revolution in Hayti* (Philadelphia: William D. Parrish, 1847), 31.

73. "Visit to Texas," *Genius of Universal Emancipation* (Baltimore, MD), November 1832, American Periodicals Series II.

74. In December 1832, a friend residing in Wilberforce congratulated Lundy on his plans for establishing a settlement in Mexico. See "Letter from Canada," *Genius of Universal Emancipation* (Baltimore, MD), December 1832, American Periodicals Series II. In December 1836, he officially announced the location of Tamaulipas. See "Mexican Colonization," *Genius of Universal Emancipation* (Baltimore, MD), December 1836, American Periodicals Series II.

75. On Lundy's time in Mexico, see Dillon, *Benjamin Lundy and the Struggle for Negro Freedom*, 184–205.

76. Lundy, *The life, travels, and opinions of Benjamin Lundy*, 42–48.

77. Ibid.

78. Ibid., 166–167.

79. "The Genius of Universal Emancipation," *Genius of Universal Emancipation* (Baltimore, MD), November 1835, American Periodicals Series II.

80. "Letter from Canada," *Genius of Universal Emancipation* (Baltimore, MD), December 1832, American Periodicals Series II.

81. "A Voice from Ohio!" *The Liberator* (Boston, MA), February 4, 1832, Slavery and Anti-Slavery: A Transnational Archive; "A Voice from Trenton!" *The Liberator* (Boston, MA), December 17, 1831, Slavery and Anti-Slavery: A Transnational Archive.

82. "Emigration to Mexico," *The Liberator* (Boston, MA), January 1832, 19th-Century U.S. Newspapers.

83. John Quincy Adams to Benjamin Lundy, May 20, 1836, vol. 6, no.19, Boston Public Library, Special Collections, Anti-Slavery Collection.

84. Nichols, *The Limits of Liberty*, 82.

85. Ibid., 57–59.

86. Audain, "Design His Course to Mexico"; Kelley, "Mexico in His Head," 714–716.

87. Audain, "Mexican Canaan," 84.

88. Nichols, *The Limits of Liberty*, 77, 143.

89. In November 1835, Lundy noted with surprise that both *The Liberator* in Boston and *The Emancipator* in New York had come out in opposition to his settlement scheme. In his estimation, however, he felt that their reactions were more indicative of a knee-jerk reaction to the word "colonization" than to any serious disapprobation of the plan itself. See, "Mexican Colonization," *Genius of Universal Emancipation* (Baltimore, MD), November 1835, American Periodicals Series II.

90. "Letter 1 – No Name," *Genius of Universal Emancipation* (Baltimore, MD), June 1833, American Periodicals Series II.

91. "Emigration to Mexico," *Genius of Universal Emancipation* (Baltimore, MD), January 1833, American Periodicals Series II.

4 ASSESSING ABOLITION: INVESTIGATING THE RESULTS OF BRITISH EMANCIPATION

1. "Hovey's Letters from the West Indies," *The Liberator* (Boston, MA), June 1, 1838, American Periodicals Series II.

2. "Emancipation," *The Philanthropist* (Cincinnati, OH), April 14, 1837, American Periodicals Series II.

3. Seymour Drescher, *The Mighty Experiment: Free Labor versus Slavery in British Emancipation* (Oxford: Oxford University Press, 2002), 121, 134; Seymour Drescher, *Abolition: A History of Slavery and Antislavery* (Cambridge: Cambridge University Press, 2009), 250, 264.

4. Davis, *The Problem of Slavery in the Age of Emancipation*, 271.

5. On the roots of this ideological defense in a national (rather than sectional) tradition of conservative thought dating back to the American Revolution, see Larry E. Tise, *Proslavery: A History of the Defense of Slavery in America, 1701–1840* (Athens: University of Georgia Press, 1987). On the ideological "domestication" of slavery through the extended metaphor of the plantation "family" presided over by a benevolent patriarch, see Willie Lee Rose, "The Domestication of Domestic Slavery," in *Slavery and Freedom*, ed. William W. Freehling (New York: Oxford University Press, 1982), 18–36; and Jeffrey Robert Young, *Domesticating Slavery: The Master Class in Georgia and South Carolina, 1670–1837* (Chapel Hill: University of North Carolina Press, 1999). For the well-known and much-debated argument that slaveholders truly believed in the concept of their paternalistic duty (rather than self-consciously using the ideology to mask and legitimize their complicity in an oppressive, violent institution), see Eugene D. Genovese, *Fatal Self-Deception: Slaveholding Paternalism in*

the Old South (New York: Cambridge University Press, 2011). On the evolution of proslavery paternalism as a cohesive ideology, see Drew Gilpin Faust, "A Southern Stewardship: The Intellectual and the Proslavery Argument," in *Proslavery Thought, Ideology, and Politics*, ed. Paul Finkelman (New York: Garland, 1989), 129–146; and Lacy Ford, "Reconfiguring the Old South: 'Solving' the Problem of Slavery, 1787–1838," *Journal of American History* 95, no. 1 (June 2008): 95–122, 14–15.

6. Thomas C. Holt, *The Problem of Freedom: Race, Labor, and Politics in Jamaica and Britain, 1832–1938* (Baltimore, MD: Johns Hopkins University Press, 1992), 55–80; Natasha Lightfoot, *Troubling Freedom: Antigua and the Aftermath of British Emancipation* (Durham, NC: Duke University Press, 2015).

7. "West Indies," *Portsmouth Journal of Literature and Politics* (Portsmouth, NH), December 13, 1834, America's Historical Newspapers.

8. "Slavery in the West Indies," *New Hampshire Patriot and State Gazette* (Concord, NH), November 30, 1835, America's Historical Newspapers.

9. "Ruin of the West Indies," *The Colored American* (New York), November 4, 1837, Slavery and Anti-Slavery: A Transnational Archive.

10. "From Jamaica," *Richmond Enquirer* (Richmond, VA), October 7, 1834, America's Historical Newspapers.

11. "Abolition of Slavery," *Portsmouth Journal of Literature and Politics* (Portsmouth, NH), October 4, 1834, America's Historical Newspapers.

12. "West Indies," *Richmond Enquirer* (Richmond, VA), December 13, 1834, America's Historical Newspapers.

13. "West Indies," *Richmond Enquirer* (Richmond, VA), December 13, 1834, America's Historical Newspapers.

14. "St. Domingo. Results of Emancipation," *American Anti-slavery Reporter* (New York), August 1834, vol. 1, no. 8, 116, Samuel J. May Anti-Slavery Collection.

15. "Effects of Abolition in Jamaica," *Richmond Enquirer* (Richmond, VA), October 2, 1835, America's Historical Newspapers.

16. "Emancipation," *Portsmouth Journal of Literature and Politics* (Portsmouth, NH), August 9, 1834, America's Historical Newspapers.

17. "First Fruits of Abolition," *Richmond Enquirer* (Richmond, VA), September 5, 1834, America's Historical Newspapers.

18. "Slavery in the West Indies," *New Hampshire Patriot and State Gazette* (Concord, NH), November 30, 1835, America's Historical Newspapers (original emphasis).

19. Rugemer, *The Problem of Emancipation*, 66–113.

20. Daniel Mallory, ed., *The Life and Speeches of the Hon. Henry Clay*, 2nd ed., 2 vols (New York: R. P. Bixby, 1843), 2:360–361.

21. Ibid., 2:360–361, 375.

22. "South Carolina, Extracts from Governor McDuffie's Message," *Richmond Enquirer* (Richmond, VA), December 4, 1835, America's Historical Newspapers.

23. Ibid.

24. "To the Members of the Society of Friends.: Some Reflections on the Subject of Slavery …," *American Anti-Slavery Reporter* (New York), August 1834, American Periodicals Series II.

25. "Abolition in the British West Indies," *New Hampshire Sentinel* (Keene, NH), April 13, 1837, America's Historical Newspapers.

26. "The West Indies," *The Liberator* (Boston, MA), August 23, 1834, American Periodicals Series II.

27. New York City Anti-Slavery Society, *Address of the New-York City Anti-Slavery Society, to the People of the City of New-York* (New York: West & Trow, 1833), 34.

28. See, for example, "Dreadful Consequences of Immediate Emancipation!!: Hear! Hear!," *The Liberator* (Boston, MA), August 30, 1834, American Periodicals Series II.

29. William Jay to Elizur Wright, July 2, 1835, Elizur Wright Papers, Library of Congress (Washington, DC), as quoted in Rugemer, *The Problem of Emancipation*, 161.

30. See, for example, "Secular Intelligence: The First of August," *New York Evangelist* (New York), September 27, 1834, American Periodicals Series II; "Secular Intelligence: From the West Indies," *New York Evangelist* (New York), March 7, 1835, American Periodicals Series II; "Secular Intelligence: From Barbadoes," *New York Evangelist* (New York), April 25, 1835, American Periodicals Series II.

31. On the nature of copyright law in the antebellum United States, see McGill, *American Literature and the Culture of Reprinting*, 45–75, esp. 71.

32. Garvey, *Writing with Scissors*, 29–30.

33. "Secular Intelligence: From the West Indies," *New York Evangelist* (New York), March 7, 1835, American Periodicals Series II.

34. Judith Adler, "Travel as Performed Art," *American Journal of Sociology* 94, no. 6 (1989): 1369.

35. *Exposition of the Object and Plans of the American Union for the Relief and Improvement of the Colored Race* (Boston, MA, 1835), 14.

36. Ibid., 16.

37. Sylvester Hovey, *Letters from the West Indies. Relating Especially to the Danish Island St. Croix, and to the British Islands Antigua, Barbados, and Jamaica* (New York: Gould & Newman, 1838), 14.

38. Ibid., 2. Quote: "New Publications: Letters from the West Indies," *Boston Recorder* (Boston, MA), June 29, 1838, American Periodicals Series II.

39. See "Hovey's Letters from the West Indies," *The Liberator* (Boston, MA), June 1, 1838, American Periodicals Series II.

40. While comparisons generally found Hovey's work shorter, cheaper, and more to the point than the report produced in 1838 by Joseph Kimball and James Thome on behalf of the American Anti-Slavery Society (*Emancipation in the West Indies*), they generally found it less "explicit" and less "detailed." See, for example, "New Publications: Letters from the West Indies," *Boston Recorder* (Boston, MA), June 29, 1838, American Periodicals Series II; and "Hovey's Letters from the West Indies," *The Liberator* (Boston, MA), June 1, 1838, American Periodicals Series II.

41. William Jay to Elizur Wright, July 2, 1835, Elizur Wright Papers, Library of Congress (Washington, DC), as quoted in Rugemer, *The Problem of Emancipation*, 161. In *An Inquiry into the Character and Tendency of the American Colonization, and American Anti-Slavery Societies,* Jay championed immediate emancipation by examining the historical precedents for abolition. In his seventh and eighth chapters, he focused on whether

emancipation was safe, drawing attention to the "fact" that gradual and full emancipation measures in South America, Mexico, and the French Caribbean had not led to bloodshed. In the case of Haiti, he reminded readers, bloodshed had led to the politically expedient act of abolition, rather than abolition leading to bloodshed. In his ninth chapter addressing the example of the British West Indies, he argued that the implementation of immediate emancipation in Antigua had achieved far better results than the system of apprenticeship. In developing each of these arguments, he cited firsthand, seemingly neutral observations either produced by government officials or reported in the mainstream U.S. press to support his viewpoint. See William Jay, *An Inquiry into the Character and Tendency of the American Colonization, and American Anti-Slavery Societies* (New York: Leavitt, Lord, 1835), 163–188, Slavery and Anti-Slavery: A Transnational Archive. For more on William Jay's refusal of Wright's suggestion he travel as agent to the West Indies on behalf of the American Anti-Slavery Society, see Rugemer, *The Problem of Emancipation*, 160–161.

42. James A. Thome and Joseph Horace Kimball, Introduction to *Emancipation in the West Indies: A Six Months' Tour in Antigua, Barbadoes, and Jamaica in the Year 1837* (New York: American Anti-Slavery Society, 1838), iii–iv, Slavery and Anti-Slavery: A Transnational Archive.

43. See, for example: "Slavery: Letter From Antigua," *New York Evangelist* (New York), March 25, 1837, American Periodicals Series II; "Emancipation," *The Philanthropist* (Cincinnati, OH), April 14, 1827, American Periodicals Series II, "Letter from Antigua," *Zion's Herald* ((Boston, MA), April 19, 1837, American Periodicals Series II; "Emancipation in the West Indies – Letter from J. H. Kimball," *The Religious Intelligencer* (New Haven, CT), May 6, 1837; "West India Emancipation – Extracts from the Statements of J. H. Kimball," *Genius of Universal Emancipation* (Baltimore, MD), July 1837, American Periodicals Series II; "Letter from J. H. Kimball," *New England Spectator* (Boston, MA), April 26, 1837, Slavery and Anti-Slavery: A Transnational Archive.

44. "Colored People in the West Indies," *The Colored American* (New York), March 18, 1837, Slavery and Anti-Slavery: A Transnational Archive; "Letters from the West-Indies," *The Colored American* (New York), March 25, 1837, April 8, 1837, April 15, 1837, Slavery and Anti-Slavery: A Transnational Archive; "Emancipation in the W. Indies," *The Colored American* (New York), May 6, 1837, Slavery and Anti-Slavery: A Transnational Archive; "The Island of Antigua," *The Colored American* (New York), July 22, 1837, Slavery and Anti-Slavery: A Transnational Archive; "Ruin of the West Indies," *The Colored American* (New York), November 4, 1837, Slavery and Anti-Slavery: A Transnational Archive.

45. "Introduction," in *Emancipation in the West Indies*, v; Rugemer, *The Problem of Emancipation*, 165–166.

46. Thome and Kimball, *Emancipation in the West Indies: A Six Months' Tour in Antigua, Barbadoes, and Jamaica in the Year 1837*.

47. William Lloyd Garrison felt the rate to be so accessible that he proclaimed that "there is no town anti-slavery society so small or poor that it cannot place this work within easy reach of every person within its limits." James A. Thome and Joseph Horace Kimball, "Emancipation in the West Indies: A Six Months' Tour in Antigua, Barbadoes, and Jamaica in the Year 1837" (Pamphlet), *The Anti-Slavery Examiner* (New York), 1838,

Slavery and Anti-Slavery: A Transnational Archive; "Miscellaneous.: To Officers of Anti-Slavery Societies, and Friends of the Slave Where Such Societies Ought to be Formed," *The Liberator* (Boston, MA), August 24, 1838, American Periodicals Series II.

48. Garrison printed testimonials from Massachusetts governor Edward Everett, Connecticut governor William W. Ellsworth, and William Ellery Channing, among others, all attesting to the value of Thome and Kimball's evidence. See "Thome and Kimball's Report: Additional Testimony," *The Liberator* (Boston, MA), July 6, 1838, American Periodicals Series II.

49. "Anti-Slavery: 'PM Convinced,'" (reprint from the *Herald of Freedom*), *The Liberator* (Boston, MA), October 5, 1838, American Periodicals Series II.

50. "Mr. Editor," *The Colored American* (New York), December 29, 1838, Slavery and Anti-Slavery: A Transnational Archive.

51. A keyword search methodology of the full runs of *The Liberator* (1831–1865, in American Periodicals database) and *The Colored American* (1837–1842, in Accessible Archives database), chosen as illustrative, widely circulated anti-slavery newspapers with publication spans long enough to assess pattern repetition, supports this assessment. Despite its diminishing visibility in the anti-slavery newspaper press after 1838, its continued use as a trusted source of information on the West Indies is evident throughout the antebellum period. See, for example, "The British West Indies," *The National Era* (Washington, DC), September 13, 1849, American Periodicals Series II; "Substance of Wm. I. Bowditch's Remarks at Worcester, on the First of August," *The Liberator* (Boston, MA), August 22, 1851, American Periodicals Series II; "The Story of West India Emancipation, by R. W. Emerson," *The Dial: A Monthly Magazine for Literature, Philosophy and Religion* (Cincinnati, OH), November 1860, vol. 1, no. 2, American Periodicals Series II; "Celebration of the First of August at Abington: Speech of Samuel J. May," *The Liberator* (Boston, MA), August 9, 1861, American Periodicals Series II.

52. On freed Antiguans' perspective on freedom and the experience of emancipation, see Lightfoot, *Troubling Freedom*.

53. See, for example, "From Jamaica," *Newport Mercury* (Newport, RI), August 23, 1834, America's Historical Newspapers; "From Jamaica," *Richmond Enquirer* (Richmond, VA), October 7, 1834, America's Historical Newspapers; "West Indies," *Portsmouth Journal of Literature and Politics* (Portsmouth, NH), December 13, 1834, America's Historical Newspapers; "Effects of Emancipation," *New-Bedford Mercury* (New Bedford, MA), July 17, 1835, America's Historical Newspapers.

54. "Abolition of Slavery," *Portsmouth Journal of Literature and Politics* (Portsmouth, NH), October 4, 1834, America's Historical Newspapers; "From the West Indies," *Richmond Enquirer* (Richmond, VA), September 9, 1834, America's Historical Newspapers; "From Barbados," *Salem Gazette* (Salem, MA), October 28, 1834, America's Historical Newspapers.

55. Hovey, *Letters from the West Indies*, 17.

56. "New Publications: Letters from the West Indies," *Boston Recorder* (Boston, MA), June 29, 1838, American Periodicals Series II.

57. The listed format of these conclusions was first introduced in the introduction to *Emancipation in the West Indies*, but were reprinted in the anti-slavery press as

representing the shared conclusions of both texts. See "Introduction," in *Emancipation in the West Indies*," vi; "New Publications: Letters from the West Indies," *Boston Recorder* (Boston, MA), June 29, 1838, American Periodicals Series II.

58. Thome and Kimball, "Emancipation in the West Indies" (Pamphlet), 83.

59. Ibid., 34, 38.

60. Hovey, *Letters from the West Indies*, 156.

61. "Literary Notices," *New York Evangelist* (New York), May 26, 1838, American Periodicals Series II.

62. "Hovey's Letters from the West Indies," *The Liberator* (Boston, MA), June 1, 1838, American Periodicals Series II.

63. Joseph Sturge and Thomas Harvey, *The West Indies in 1837; Being a Journal of a Visit to Antigua, Montserrat, Dominica, St. Lucia, Barbadoes, and Jamaica; Undertaken for the Purpose of Ascertaining the Actual Condition of the Negro Population of Those Islands*, 2nd ed. (London: Hamilton, Adams, 1838), ix, Slavery and Anti-Slavery: A Transnational Archive; On the British public's push for an early end to apprenticeship, see Drescher, *The Mighty Experiment*, 150–151.

64. Sturge and Harvey were recognized by American anti-slavery advocates as experts on the topic of emancipation and apprenticeship in the West Indies. When Thomas Harvey visited New York in 1837, he was welcomed as a knowledgeable speaker and his remarks on the West Indies were reprinted by several anti-slavery publications. Similarly, lectures given by Sturge in England were excised for publication in the United States after his return from the West Indies in 1837. But their book received almost no notice in the anti-slavery press. When Governor Edward Everett of Massachusetts famously penned his appreciation for Thome and Kimball's book, he professed no knowledge of Sturge and Harvey's publication, despite its earlier publication date and overwhelming significance to British abolitionism. Keyword searches in anti-slavery newspaper databases clearly demonstrate the point that Sturge and Harvey's work did not make its way into American newspapers, either as excised reprints or in the form of editorial recommendations. See "Emancipation. Arrival of agents from the West Indies" (reprint from the *Emancipator* (New York), *The Philanthropist* (Cincinnati, OH), July 21, 1837, American Periodicals Series II; "Emancipation in the West Indies – Working of the Apprenticeship System," *The Friend* (Philadelphia, PA), September 23, 1837, American Periodicals Series II; "Emancipation in the British Possessions: Boston, 26th April 1838," *New Hampshire Sentinel* (Keene, NH), May 24, 1838, America's Historical Newspapers.

65. Drescher, *The Mighty Experiment*, 145–147, 149. According to Drescher, West Indian sugar exports dropped by 10 percent, but the price in London rose by more than 40 percent. In Jamaica, the most important sugar island, sugar production fell more precipitously than the other islands, yet Drescher contends that both profitability and investment rose. The Antiguan sugar output rose by 1 percent during the apprenticeship period. Notably, Thomas C. Holt offers a somewhat different assessment of how the compensation money was spent by looking specifically at the Jamaican case. First, he suggests that a significant portion of it went directly to British merchants to settle outstanding debts, rather than

to the planters themselves (he cites 15 percent based on Kathleen Butler's examination of Jamaican slave compensation). In addition, he notes that the increased capital investment and money circulation in Jamaica went toward land investments alone, rather than toward technological improvements. However, for the purpose of the present analysis, Drescher's assessment of planter income relative to production is the more pertinent metric to illustrate the point that, for just the apprenticeship period, planters' overall profits did not fall even though production did. This point further corresponds with Holt's concession that there was a "brief bubble of optimism generated by the flow of compensation cash." See Holt, *The Problem of Freedom*, 130–131, quote on 131.

66. Holt, *The Problem of Freedom*, 8.
67. Ibid., 140.
68. O. Nigel Bolland, "The Politics of Freedom in the British Caribbean," in *The Meaning of Freedom: Economics, Politics, and Culture after Slavery*, ed. Frank McGlynn and Seymour Drescher (Pittsburgh, PA: University of Pittsburgh Press, 1992), 119–120.
69. C. C. Terrel, *Letters: November 01, 1847 to Brother Whipple; Fern Hill, Jamaica*, MS American Missionary Association Archives, 1839–1882, F1-1350, Amistad Research Center at Tulane University, Slavery and Anti-Slavery: A Transnational Archive.
70. Bolland, "The Politics of Freedom in the British Caribbean," 123, 126–129; Holt, *The Problem of Freedom*, 144; William A. Green, *British Slave Emancipation: The Sugar Colonies and the Great Experiment, 1830–1865* (Oxford: Oxford University Press, 1976), 171.
71. One Baptist missionary residing in Jamaica claimed that land prices in the island's interior had risen by 66 percent between 1833 and 1838. See Holt, *The Problem of Freedom*, 144.
72. "Letter from Jamaica" (C. Stewart Renshaw), *The Colored American* (New York, NY), May 23, 1840, Slavery and Anti-Slavery: A Transnational Archive.
73. James M. Phillippo, *Jamaica: Its Past and Present State* (London: John Snow, 1843), 220–222.
74. Historian Catherine Hall has shown that free villages were heavily invested in the imperialistic "civilizing" mission and largely ignored the existence of black cultural values. This imperialistic tendency is quite apparent, for example, in the reflections of famous Baptist missionary James Phillippo from his time in Jamaica. While he established a mission village to facilitate freed men and women leaving the plantation complexes, he expressed particular pride in the villages for their "progress in social taste and improvement." An illustrative example of this assertion was that the inhabitants of Sligoville dressed similarly, in his estimation, to "persons of the same class during the summer in England." See Catherine Hall, *Civilising Subjects: Metropole and Colony in the English Imagination 1830–1867* (Chicago: University of Chicago Press, 2002), 132; Phillippo, *Jamaica: Its Past and Present State*, 229–230.
75. Joseph John Gurney, *Familiar Letters to Henry Clay of Kentucky, Describing a Winter in the West Indies* (New York: Mahlon Day, 1840), 79.
76. Holt, *The Problem of Freedom*, 119–121.
77. On the history of "Liberated Africans" in Jamaica, see Monica Schuler, *"Alas, Alas, Kongo": A Social History of Indentured African Immigration into Jamaica, 1841–1865* (Baltimore, MD: Johns Hopkins University Press, 1980); Rosanne Marion Adderley,

"New Negroes from Africa": Slave Trade Abolition and Free African Settlement in the Nineteenth-Century Caribbean (Bloomington, IN: Indiana University Press, 2006).

78. "Emigration of Colored People to Jamaica," *The Liberator* (Boston, MA), September 11, 1840, American Periodicals Series II.

79. Ibid.

80. "Emigration to Jamaica," *The Liberator* (Boston, MA), August 13, 1841, American Periodicals Series II.

81. Of the fourteen aboard the *Isabella*, nine were members of one family, the Parraways, consisting of seven children belonging to Absalom Parraway, a bricklayer, and his wife Maria, a washerwoman. "Return of Immigrants," "Journals of the Council, Dec. 1840–Feb. 1844," National Archives of Jamaica, Spanish Town, JA, 1B/5/4.

82. Ibid.

83. In October 1840, for example, Charles B. Ray of *The Colored American* claimed himself unable to see why West Indian immigrationists would want to import laborers "unless it is to displace the present ones, and thus to gratify the grudge they owe them for being free," or to glut the labor market in order to monopolize labor. See "West India Emigration," *The Colored American* (New York), October 17, 1840, Slavery and Anti-Slavery: A Transnational Archive.

84. "Jamaica, West Indies," *The Colored American* (New York), March 6, 1841, Slavery and Anti-Slavery: A Transnational Archive.

85. B. W. Higman, ed., "Jamaican Census of 1844," in *The Jamaican Censuses of 1844 and 1861* (Mona, JA: Department of History, University of the West Indies, 1980), 5.

86. In the eighty issues printed between August 31, 1839 (when Ray first introduced the topic) and June 19, 1841, when Trinidadian emigration was broached for the final time in his newspaper, Ray included thirty-two articles, editorials, and letters to the editor that substantively discussed the issue. Of these, twenty-three were printed as part of the thirty-eight issues published in the first year (between August 31, 1839 and August 29, 1840). For Burnley's initial letter to the paper, see "Description of the Island of Trinidad, and the Advantages to be Derived from Emigration to that Colony," *The Colored American* (New York), August 31, 1839, Slavery and Anti-Slavery: A Transnational Archive.

87. Quote: "Trinidad," *The Colored American* (New York), August 31, 1839, Slavery and Anti-Slavery: A Transnational Archive.

88. "Emigration vs. Colonixation [sic]," *The Colored American* (New York), November 16, 1839, Slavery and Anti-Slavery: A Transnational Archive. On the potential of advancement, see "Our Prospects," *The Colored American* (New York), September 14, 1839, Slavery and Anti-Slavery: A Transnational Archive.

89. "Trinidad Emigration," *The Colored American* (New York), October 5, 1839, Slavery and Anti-Slavery: A Transnational Archive.

90. "News from Trinidad," *The Colored American* (New York), April 11, 1840, Slavery and Anti-Slavery: A Transnational Archive.

91. Jones, *Birthright Citizens*, 59–62; "Counter Statement," *The Colored American* (New York), May 16, 1840, Slavery and Anti-Slavery: A Transnational Archive.

92. "Retrospective," *The Colored American* (New York), February 27, 1841, Slavery and Anti-Slavery: A Transnational Archive. Indeed, when an "Anti-Trinidad Meeting" was held in New York City on October 29, 1840, Ray expressed surprise given that public sentiment on the matter had already been rendered the topic "about dead among us." See "Anti-Trinidad Meeting," *The Colored American* (New York), October 31, 1840, Slavery and Anti-Slavery: A Transnational Archive.

93. *The Liberator*, for example, only published seven pieces on Jamaican emigration between September 11, 1840 and February 4, 1842 (in addition to two advertisements for emigrants submitted by Edmund Grattan, the Jamaican agent, in August and September 1841).

94. "Death of Jas. G. Barbadoes," *The Liberator* (Boston, MA), August 20, 1841, American Periodicals Series II; "The Jamaican Emigration Plot," *The Liberator* (Boston, MA), June 25, 1841, American Periodicals Series II. On Samuel Whitmarsh, see "Emigration to Jamaica," *The Emancipator* (New York), September 3, 1840, 19th-Century U.S. Newspapers.

95. Nancy Prince, *The West Indies: Being a Description of the Islands, Progress of Christianity, Education, and Liberty among the Colored Population Generally* (Boston: Dow & Jackson, 1841), 12, 14–15.

96. See, for example, "Jamaica, West Indies," *The Colored American* (New York), March 6, 1841, Slavery and Anti-Slavery: A Transnational Archive. See also, "Letter from Rev. C. S. Renshaw," *The Emancipator* (New York), July 9, 1840, 19th-Century U.S. Newspapers; and "Letter from Rev. C. S. Renshaw," *The Colored American* (New York), July 18, 1840, Slavery and Anti-Slavery: A Transnational Archive. Responding to "colored friends" who requested that he "ascertain the advantages of emigration" to Jamaica, the Rev. C. S. Renshaw captured the breadth of Jamaican emigration's potential pitfalls in a letter addressed to both Charles B. Ray of *The Colored American* and Joshua Leavitt of *The Emancipator*. He addressed wages, prices, education, and religion, and determined that emigration to the island "would result most disastrously to the emigrants." In-text quotations: "Letter from Rev. C. S. Renshaw."

97. On June 25, 1841, for example, William Lloyd Garrison's *Liberator* reprinted correspondence from the prominent African American leader Richard Allen originally published in the *Freeman's Journal*. Allen's negative perception of Jamaica was formed, in part, by a letter he received from a trusted correspondent in Jamaica. "Jamaican Emigration," *The Liberator* (Boston, MA), June 25, 1841, American Periodicals Series II.

98. "Proceedings of the National Convention of Colored People and Their Friends; held in Troy, NY; on the 6th, 7th, 8th, and 9th of October, 1847," *ColoredConventions.org*, 21–25.

99. "Trinidad – An Explanation," *The Colored American* (New York), October 12, 1839, Slavery and Anti-Slavery: A Transnational Archive.

100. See Jeffrey R. Kerr-Ritchie, *Rites of August First Emancipation Day in the Black Atlantic World* (Baton Rouge: Louisiana State University Press, 2007); Kachun, *Festivals of Freedom*; Natasha L. Henry, *Emancipation Day: Celebrating Freedom in Canada* (Toronto: Dundurn Press, 2010); Rugemer, *The Problem of Emancipation*, 232–240.

5 REPUTATIONS AND EXPECTATIONS: ASSESSING MIGRANT LIFE IN UPPER CANADA

1. "The Colored Man in Canada," *The Colored American* (New York), March 4, 1837, Slavery and Anti-Slavery: A Transnational Archive.
2. "Mr. Hiram Wilson, New-York," *The Emancipator* (New York), December 22, 1836, 19th-Century U.S. Newspapers.
3. In an editorial published in the *Colored American*, for example, Samuel Cornish – the prominent former editor of *Freedom's Journal* and *The Friend of Man* – asserted that Wilson's Canada mission "must be sustained" due to the great work achieved by Wilson's "self-sacrificing, zealous efforts." See "Rev. Hiram Wilson," *The Colored American* (New York), September 29, 1838, Slavery and Anti-Slavery: A Transnational Archive. Eight months later, the paper referred to Wilson as "one of the most disinterested, sacrificing philanthropists living." See "Rev. Hiram Wilson," *The Colored American* (New York), June 1, 1839, Slavery and Anti-Slavery: A Transnational Archive. William Lloyd Garrison, meanwhile, determined in 1838 that Wilson's two years of missionary work in Upper Canada had fully established him as a "well-qualified" provider of information. See "American Exiles in Upper Canada," *The Liberator* (Boston, MA), September 21, 1838, Slavery and Anti-Slavery: A Transnational Archive.
4. Examples of violence and mob violence include anti-abolition and anti-black riots lasting several days in New York City (1834) and Cincinnati (1836); gangs disrupting abolitionist meetings and threatening black lives in cities and towns throughout the north and north-west; and abolitionist newspaper editor Elijah P. Lovejoy being killed by a pro-slavery mob in Illinois in 1837. See Stewart, *Abolitionist Politics*, 14–16. On the targeting of printers and printing presses, specifically, see Loughran, *The Republic in Print*, 348–349.
5. The change from Upper Canada to "Canada West" occurred in the wake of the 1840 Act of Union, when the legislatures of Lower Canada and Upper Canada merged to form the Province of Canada. Although the region remained "Canada West" until 1867, the year of Canadian Confederation, this chapter continues to use the designation "Upper Canada" for clarity and continuity.
6. Winks, *The Blacks in Canada*, 235.
7. "American Anti-Slavery Society: Abstract of the Fourth Annual Report," *New York Evangelist* (New York), May 13, 1837.
8. "British and Foreign Anti-Slavery Convention," *The Philanthropist* (Cincinnati, OH), August 25, 1840, Slavery and Anti-Slavery: A Transnational Archive.
9. The most conservative population estimates were drawn from the official Censuses of Upper Canada. It was by comparing the Census of 1842 with the Census of 1847 that the editor of the ACS's *African Repository and Colonial Journal* arrived at the estimate of 281 per year, although he admitted that there was "no means of judging" how many were free and how many were fugitive. Regardless of actual number, however, he noted that the rate of emigration was "large enough to attract the attention of the newspapers." See, "Colored Population of Canada, according to the Census of 1847," *African Repository and Colonial Journal* (Washington, DC), January 1849, American Periodicals Series II.

10. "Multiple News Items – Colored People in Upper Canada," *The Liberator* (Boston, MA), May 29, 1840, Slavery and Anti-Slavery: A Transnational Archive.

11. "Negroes in Canada," *African Repository and Colonial Journal* (Washington, DC), November 15, 1841, American Periodicals Series II; "Multiple News Items," *The Liberator* (Boston, MA), August 20, 1841, Slavery and Anti-Slavery: A Transnational Archive; "Letter from Hiram Wilson," *The North Star* (Rochester, NY), November 10, 1848, Slavery and Anti-Slavery: A Transnational Archive; "Colored Population of Canada, according to the Census of 1847," *African Repository and Colonial Journal* (Washington, DC), January 1849, American Periodicals Series II.

12. "Communications," *Liberty Standard* (Hallowell, ME), June 14, 1843, Slavery and Anti-Slavery: A Transnational Archive.

13. "Communications," *The Liberator* (Boston, MA), September 27, 1834, Slavery and Anti-Slavery: A Transnational Archive.

14. "For the Colored American. My dear sir," *The Colored American* (New York), September 14, 1839, Slavery and Anti-Slavery: A Transnational Archive. For further information about Jehu Jones, see C. Peter Ripley, ed, *The Black Abolitionist Papers, Vol. 2: Canada, 1830–1865* (Chapel Hill: University of North Carolina Press, 1985), 82–83.

15. "An Asylum for the Oppressed," *The Colored American* (New York), March 29, 1838, Slavery and Anti-Slavery: A Transnational Archive.

16. American Anti-Slavery Society, *Fourth Annual Report of the American Anti-Slavery Society, with the Speeches Delivered at the Anniversary Meeting Held in the City of New York on the 9th May, 1837* (New York: William S. Dorr, 1837), 33, Oberlin College Library Anti-Slavery Collection; "American Anti-Slavery Society: Abstract of the Fourth Annual Report," *New York Evangelist* (New York), May 13, 1837; "American Anti-Slavery Society," *New England Spectator* (Boston, MA), May 17, 1837; "American Anti-Slavery Society," *Philanthropist* (Cincinnati, OH), May 26, 1837.

17. "Letters from H. Wilson – Letters 1–4," *The Emancipator* (New York), February 23, 1837, 19th-Century U.S. Newspapers.

18. "During the evening on which I arrived …" *Zion's Watchman* (New York), March 24, 1838, Slavery and Anti-Slavery: A Transnational Archive.

19. On January 1, 1839, for example, Wilson wrote a letter responding to a request from Ohio's Trumbull County Anti-Slavery Society for updated information on the Wilberforce settlement in Upper Canada. Modeling his awareness of broad public interest in his observations, Wilson forwarded his response to the Rev. Warren Isham for publication in Isham's *Michigan Observer*. From there, Wilson's letter was further extracted for publication in papers such as *The Colored American*. See "Wilberforce Colony," *The Colored American* (New York), February 16, 1839, Slavery and Anti-Slavery: A Transnational Archive.

20. "Letters from H. Wilson – Letters 1–4," *The Emancipator* (New York), February 23, 1837, 19th-Century U.S. Newspapers.

21. "American Exiles in Upper Canada," *The Liberator* (Boston, MA), September 21, 1838, Slavery and Anti-Slavery: A Transnational Archive; "Letters from H. Wilson – Letters 1–4," *The Emancipator* (New York), February 23, 1837, 19th-Century U.S. Newspapers.

22. Ibid.

23. Wilson addressed the circumstances of free migrants and fugitive slaves in Toronto in the final letter of a four-part series reprinted in several anti-slavery newspapers. Notably, he states his reliance on James C. Brown for information about Toronto, rather than relying on his own eye witness. Of life in Toronto, he included the fact that African Americans were generally successful, and had built a supportive community with mutual aid societies to help their own. "Letters from H. Wilson – Letters 1–4," *The Emancipator* (New York), February 23, 1837, 19th-Century U.S. Newspapers.

24. See Lamin O. Sanneh, *Abolitionists Abroad: American Blacks and the Making of Modern West Africa* (Cambridge, MA: Harvard University Press, 1999); Clara Merritt DeBoer, *Be Jubilant My Feet: African American Abolitionists in the American Missionary Association, 1839–1861* (New York: Garland, 1994); Hall, *Civilising Subjects*; Gale L. Kenny, *Contentious Liberties: American Abolitionists in Post-Emancipation Jamaica, 1834–1866* (Athens, GA: University of Georgia Press, 2010); Mary Turner, *Slaves and Missionaries: The Disintegration of Jamaican Slave Society, 1787–1834* (Urbana: University of Illinois Press, 1982).

25. Harrold, *American Abolitionists*, 52.

26. See, for example, "Mr. Hiram Wilson, New-York," *The Emancipator* (New York), December 22, 1836; "Letters from H. Wilson – Letters 1–4," *The Emancipator* (New York), February 23, 1837, 19th-Century U.S. Newspapers.

27. "Miscellaneous," *The Liberator* (Boston, MA), August 25, 1837, Slavery and Anti-Slavery: A Transnational Archive; "Colored People in Canada," *New England Spectator* (Boston, MA), October 11, 1837, Slavery and Anti-Slavery: A Transnational Archive.

28. "Letters from H. Wilson – Letter 1," *The Emancipator* (New York), February 23, 1837, 19th-Century U.S. Newspapers.

29. "Negro Settlers," *The Banner of the Constitution* (Washington, DC), April 3, 1830, American Periodicals Series II.

30. According to abolitionist Charles Stuart, the bill was "at once" rejected by the Upper House. See "Review. The American Colonization Society Further Unravelled [sic]," *The Liberator* (Boston, MA), April 19, 1834, Slavery and Anti-Slavery: A Transnational Archive.

31. "Mr. Hiram Wilson, New-York," *The Emancipator* (New York), December 22, 1836, 19th-Century U.S. Newspapers.

32. Bruce Curtis, "Preconditions of the Canadian State: Educational Reform and the Construction of a Public in Upper Canada, 1837–1846," in *Historical Essays on Upper Canada: New Perspectives*, ed. J. K. Johnson and Bruce G. Wilson (Ottawa: Carleton University Press, 1989), 346–350.

33. Historian Sharon Hepburn, for example, has described white Canadians' racist attitudes as a "pervasive deterrent to black education." Hepburn, *Crossing the Border*, 157. See also Lyndsay Campbell, "The Northern Borderlands: Canada West," in Tony Freyer

and Lyndsay Campbell, eds., *Freedom's Conditions in the U.S.–Canadian Borderlands in the Age of Emancipation* (Durham, NC: Carolina Academic Press, 2011), 210–213.

34. Allen P. Stouffer, *The Light of Nature and the Law of God: Antislavery in Ontario, 1833–1877* (Baton Rouge: Louisiana State University Press, 1992), 59.

35. Archives Ontario (AO), Ontario Department of Education Incoming General Correspondence, RG 2-12, Container 2, The Coloured People of Hamilton to Charles Metcalf, October 15, 1843; and RG 2-12, Container 2, Reverend Brown to Charles Metcalf, October 4, 1843.

36. Archives Ontario (AO), Ontario Department of Education Incoming General Correspondence, RG 2-12, Container 2, Robert Murray to George S. Tiffany, October 19, 1843; and RG 2-12, Container 2, George S. Tiffany to Robert Murray, November 9, 1843.

37. Hepburn, *Crossing the Border*, 157.

38. "Rev. Hiram Wilson," *The Colored American* (New York), June 1, 1839, Slavery and Anti-Slavery: A Transnational Archive.

39. Historian Allen P. Stouffer, for example, argues that abolitionists saw education and religion as key factors in proving the viability of emancipation, and notes that abolitionists' view of Upper Canada's relevance to the anti-slavery struggle was based on this proof. See Stouffer, *The Light of Nature and the Law of God*, 82–83.

40. "The Star-Led Fugitives," *The Liberator* (Boston, MA), March 17, 1843, Slavery and Anti-Slavery: A Transnational Archive.

41. Ibid.

42. Davis, *The Problem of Slavery in the Age of Emancipation*, 298–300.

43. Blackett's *Building an Antislavery Wall* remains the foundational scholarly work on black abolitionists in Great Britain, as well as the political role their travels played in the American anti-slavery movement.

44. Ibid., 40–41; Davis, *The Problem of Slavery in the Age of Emancipation*, 301. See also McDaniel, *The Problem of Democracy in the Age of Slavery*.

45. On prejudice on transatlantic steamships, see Elizabeth Stordeur Pryor, *Colored Travelers: Mobility and the Fight for Citizenship before the Civil War* (Chapel Hill: University of North Carolina Press, 2016), ch. 5.

46. Ibid., 150.

47. Ibid.; Blackett, *Building an Antislavery Wall*, 41.

48. "Hiram Wilson's Settlement for Colored People in Canada," *National Anti-Slavery Standard* (New York), March 24, 1842, Slavery and Anti-Slavery: A Transnational Archive; "Selections. Sixth Annual Report of the Canada Missions," *The Liberator* (Boston, MA), March 17, 1843, Slavery and Anti-Slavery: A Transnational Archive.

49. Hiram Wilson to Hamilton Hill, Esq. April 25, 1843, The Letters of Hiram Wilson (Hiram Wilson Project).

50. Frances Drake to Maria Weston Chapman, October 31, 1843, Boston Public Library, Special Collections, Anti-Slavery Collection. See also "Fugitive Slaves in Canada," *The Liberator* (Boston, MA), November 27, 1840, Slavery and Anti-Slavery: A Transnational Archive.

51. "The Canada Mission," *National Anti-Slavery Standard* (New York), January 28, 1841, Slavery and Anti-Slavery: A Transnational Archive.

52. William Lloyd Garrison, for example, advised readers to provide Wilson with their unstinting support because "the elevation of the emancipated colored population of Canada will have a very important bearing on the total and speedy abolition of slavery in [the United States]." "The Star-Led Fugitives," *The Liberator* (Boston, MA), March 17, 1843, Slavery and Anti-Slavery: A Transnational Archive.

53. "Education of Colored People," *The Philanthropist* (Ohio), June 23, 1840, Slavery and Anti-Slavery: A Transnational Archive.

54. "Labors of Rev. Hiram Wilson," *The Colored American* (New York), February 6, 1841, Slavery and Anti-Slavery: A Transnational Archive.

55. "Labors of Rev. Hiram Wilson – A Reply," *The Colored American* (New York), March 13, 1841, Slavery and Anti-Slavery: A Transnational Archive.

56. For Wilson's assessment of Toronto schools, see "Canada Mission," *The Colored American* (New York), March 20, 1841, Slavery and Anti-Slavery: A Transnational Archive. In addition to Ward's response to Gallego (n. 47, above), James C. Fuller's letter to William Goodell, first published in Goodell's *Friend of Man* (the news organ of the New York State Anti-Slavery Society), exposed the fallacies and shortcomings of Gallego's overly optimistic assessment of black life in Upper Canada. Fuller was a British abolitionist whose fundraising efforts allowed Wilson's Canada Mission to expand and become the British American Institute and Dawn settlement in 1841. Fuller's letter is republished in the *National Anti-Slavery Reporter* (the official journal of the American Anti-Slavery Society): "Respected Friend, William Goodell," *National Anti-Slavery Reporter* (New York), April 8, 1841, Slavery and Anti-Slavery: A Transnational Archive.

57. "American Prejudice Against Colour in Canada," *The British and Foreign Anti-Slavery Reporter* (London), September 7, 1842, Slavery and Anti-Slavery: A Transnational Archive.

58. "Respected Friend, William Goodell," *National Anti-Slavery Reporter* (New York), April 8, 1841, Slavery and Anti-Slavery: A Transnational Archive.

59. "Labors of Rev. Hiram Wilson – A Reply," *The Colored American* (New York), March 13, 1841, Slavery and Anti-Slavery: A Transnational Archive; "American Prejudice Against Colour in Canada," *The British and Foreign Anti-Slavery Reporter* (London), September 7, 1842, Slavery and Anti-Slavery: A Transnational Archive.

60. Pryor, *Colored Travelers*, 132–133.

61. Ibid., 44–75.

62. "Petition of various citizens, praying that performances by American actors will be forbidden when they turn to ridicule the coloured race" (July 20, 1840), City of Toronto Archives, Fonds 200, Series 1081, Item 605. The petitioners are likely referring to blackface minstrelsy, a form of musical theater that gained widespread popularity in the 1840s. See William J. Mahar, *Behind the Burnt Cork Mask: Early Blackface Minstrelsy and Antebellum American Popular Culture* (Urbana: University of Illinois Press, 1998), 1–41.

63. "Petition of various people of colour in Toronto" (October 14, 1841), City of Toronto Archives, Fonds 200, Series 1081, Item 785.

64. Ibid.; "Petition of various coloured inhabitants of Toronto, praying that no licences will be granted to circuses, shows, etc., which have performances casting ridicule on the coloured population" (April 12, 1843), City of Toronto Archives, Fonds 200, Series 1081, Item 1006.

65. "Adam Wilson to Robert Baldwin" (July 12, 1843), Toronto Public Library Special Collections, Robert Baldwin Correspondence Papers, L5 Baldwin Papers A77, no. 53.

66. Silverman, *Unwelcome Guests*, 35; Winks, *The Blacks in Canada*, 142.

67. "Emigration of Colored People to Canada," *The Colored American* (New York), November 18, 1837, Slavery and Anti-Slavery: A Transnational Archive.

68. Silverman, *Unwelcome Guests*, 33–36; Winks, *The Blacks in Canada*, 149.

69. Winks, *The Blacks in Canada*, 143–144, quote 143.

70. "Emigration of Colored People to Canada," *The Colored American* (New York), November 18, 1837, Slavery and Anti-Slavery: A Transnational Archive.

71. "From the New-York Journal of Commerce. Emigration, or Running Away," *The Liberator* (Boston, MA), June 23, 1843, Slavery and Anti-Slavery: A Transnational Archive.

72. Drew, *North Side View of Slavery*, 39.

6 ESCAPE AND ESCALATION: SELF-EMANCIPATION AND THE GEOPOLITICS OF FREEDOM

1. William Wells Brown, "A Song for Freedom," in *The Anti-Slavery Harp: A Collection of Songs for Anti-Slavery Meetings* (Boston, MA: Bela Marsh, 1848).

2. "They Don't Know What is Good for Them," *The Liberator* (Boston, MA), August 25, 1837; see also Ripley, *The Black Abolitionist Papers*, 2:65–66.

3. "They Don't Know What is Good for Them," *The Liberator* (Boston, MA), August 25, 1837, American Periodicals Series II. Roberts' response was first published in *The Christian Guardian* of Toronto on July 12, 1837. See Ripley, *The Black Abolitionist Papers*, 2:65–66.

4. "Fugitive Slave – Arrest – Rescue – Loss of Life: The Petition of the Inhabitants of the Town of Niagara," *Genius of Universal Emancipation* (Baltimore, MD), October 1837, American Periodicals Series II; David Murray, "Hands Across the Border: The Abortive Extradition of Solomon Moseby," *Canadian Review of American Studies* 30, no. 2 (January 2000): 187–188, 190–192.

5. "Fugitive Slave – Arrest – Rescue – Loss of Life: The Petition of the Inhabitants of the Town of Niagara," *Genius of Universal Emancipation* (Baltimore, MD), October 1837, American Periodicals Series II.

6. "British and Foreign Anti-Slavery Convention," *The Philanthropist* (Cincinnati, OH), August 25, 1840, Slavery and Anti-Slavery: A Transnational Archive.

7. Murray, "Hands Across the Border," 189–191, 200; Historian Roman Zorn argues that the publicity surrounding the 1842 extralegal extradition of Nelson Hacket from Canada had a more immediate effect on the Webster–Ashburton Treaty. See Roman J. Zorn, "Criminal Extradition Menaces the Canadian Haven for Fugitive Slaves, 1841–1861," *Canadian Historical Review* 38, no. 4 (December 1957): 284–294. However, an

abolitionist orator speaking of the fugitives in Upper Canada at the 1840 British and Foreign Anti-Slavery Convention asserted that it was the Moseby case, specifically, that had kept him in "a long correspondence both with the colonial and foreign secretaries of state" on the topic of securing the border against similar threats. See, "British and Foreign Anti-Slavery Convention," *The Philanthropist* (Cincinnati, OH), August 25, 1840, Slavery and Anti-Slavery: A Transnational Archive.

8. See, for example, "They Don't Know What is Good for Them," *The Liberator* (Boston, MA), August 25, 1837, American Periodicals Series II; and "Interesting Correspondence," *The Philanthropist* (Cincinnati, OH), August 4, 1837, Slavery and Anti-Slavery: A Transnational Archive.

9. Anderson Ruffin Abbott, Notebook II (*c.* 1899), Toronto Public Library, Anderson Ruffin Abbott Collection, 32–36.

10. Murray, "Hands Across the Border," 190; see also Jason H. Silverman, "Kentucky, Canada, and Extradition: The Jesse Happy Case," *The Filson Club History Quarterly* 54 (January 1980): 50–60.

11. For examples of the coverage of runaway slave escapes during the mid- to late-1830s by the abolitionist press, see "Thrilling Anecdote," *The New York Evangelist* (New York), May 14, 1836, American Periodicals Series II; "The Anti-Slavery Record for August Contains a Highly Interesting Narration of David Barrett a Slave Who Escaped from Kentucky into Canada," *New England Spectator* (Boston, MA), August 23, 1837, Slavery and Anti-Slavery: A Transnational Archive; "Extraordinary Case," *The Liberator* (Boston, MA), September 22, 1837, American Periodicals Series II; "An Authentic Narrative of the Adventures and Sufferings of a Fugitive Slave," *The Liberator* (Boston, MA), December 28, 1838, American Periodicals Series II; "From the Herald of Freedom: The Slave, Robert," *The Liberator* (Boston, MA), May 10, 1839, American Periodicals Series II; "We give an account of the recent fugitive slave who passed through here to Canada," *The Colored American* (New York), June 1, 1839, Slavery and Anti-Slavery: A Transnational Archive.

12. Although the term "Underground Railroad" does not appear in print until 1842, when *The Liberator* announced the escape of twenty-six slaves, it was already a familiar concept. In 1839, for example, the well-known abolitionist Hiram Wilson suggested that American slaves would willingly flee to Canada upon a "great republican railroad" at the rate of 500 per day if given the chance. See "Twenty-Six Slaves in One Week," *The Liberator* (Boston, MA), October 14, 1842, American Periodicals Series II; and "Anti-Slavery. From the *Friend of Man*," *The Liberator* (Boston, MA), October 11, 1839, American Periodicals Series II. On the apocryphal origin stories for the term, see Blight, *Passages to Freedom*, 3.

13. "Fugitive Slaves," *New England Spectator* (Boston, MA), May 10, 1837, Slavery and Anti-Slavery: A Transnational Archive.

14. Targeted keyword searches for complete runs of *The Liberator* (Boston, MA) and *The National Anti-Slavery Standard* (New York) suggest that neither influential anti-slavery newspaper contains mention of free emigration to Canada between January 1, 1841 and December 31, 1849. Although this methodology is not foolproof, it does

convincingly indicate that coverage of Upper Canada as a destination for free African Americans had severely, if not entirely, diminished by the early 1840s.

15. "Judge Jay on the Bloodhound Bill," *National Anti-Slavery Standard* (New York), October 17, 1850, Slavery and Anti-Slavery: A Transnational Archive.

16. Hannah Townsend, *The Anti-Slavery Alphabet* (Philadelphia, PA: Printed for the Anti-Slavery Fair by Merrihew & Thompson, 1846), 14.

17. "Thrilling Anecdote," *The New York Evangelist* (New York), May 14, 1836, American Periodicals Series II.

18. "The Runaway," *The Anti-Slavery Record* (London), June 1836, American Periodicals Series II.

19. "Poetry: The Fugitive," *The Friend of Man* (Utica, NY), July 28, 1836, Slavery and Anti-Slavery: A Transnational Archive.

20. *The American Anti-Slavery Almanac for 1839* (New York and Boston, MA: S. W. Benedict and Isaac Knapp for the American Anti-Slavery Society, 1839), 9.

21. Samuel Ringgold Ward, *Autobiography of a Fugitive Negro: His Anti-Slavery Labours in the United States, Canada and England* (London: John Snow, 1855), 163–164.

22. Historian Stanley Harrold emphasizes that these three men were radicals because of their willingness to work outside established institutions to end slavery, and that their advocacy of self-emancipation in their addresses to enslaved people during the 1840s "capture[s] an American anti-slavery movement in tension between its peaceful past and violent future." See Stanley Harrold, *The Rise of Aggressive Abolitionism: Addresses to the Slaves* (Lexington: University Press of Kentucky, 2004), 4.

23. Blackett, *The Captive's Quest for Freedom*, 5.

24. For recent work on the human cost of kidnapping free African Americans into slavery (what historian Richard Bell calls the "Reverse Underground Railroad"), see Richard Bell, *Stolen: Five Free Boys Kidnapped into Slavery and Their Astonishing Odyssey Home* (New York: Simon & Schuster, 2019); Caleb McDaniel, *Sweet Taste of Liberty: A True Story of Slavery and Restitution in America* (New York: Oxford University Press, 2019).

25. "Speech of Lewis Richardson," full text from John W. Blassingame, ed., *Slave Testimony: Two Centuries of Letters, Speeches, Interviews, and Autobiographies* (Baton Rouge: Louisiana State University Press, 1977), 164–166.

26. "The Star-Led Fugitives," *The Liberator* (Boston, MA), March 17, 1843, Slavery and Anti-Slavery: A Transnational Archive.

27. "A Suggestion for the South," *The Liberator* (Boston, MA), May 10, 1839, Slavery and Anti-Slavery: A Transnational Archive.

28. See Smith's "Address of the Anti-Slavery Convention of the State of New York, Held in Peterboro, January 19th, 1842, TO THE SLAVES IN THE U. STATES OF AMERICA," in Harrold, *The Rise of Aggressive Abolitionism*, 155.

29. "Jonathan Walker and Charles T. Torrey," *The American and Foreign Anti-Slavery Reporter* (New York), November 1, 1844, Slavery and Anti-Slavery: A Transnational Archive.

30. "Refuge of Oppression," *The Liberator* (Boston, MA), December 20, 1844, Slavery and Anti-Slavery: A Transnational Archive.

31. For a full account of Torrey's trial, incarceration, and death, see E. Fuller Torrey, *The Martyrdom of Abolitionist Charles Torrey* (Baton Rouge: Louisiana State University Press, 2013), 127–166.

32. *Barre Patriot* (Barre, MA), June 12, 1846; reprinted from the *Essex Transcript* (Amesbury, MA).

33. Stanley Harrold, *Border War: Fighting over Slavery before the Civil War* (Chapel Hill: University of North Carolina Press, 2010), 125. For more on the relationship between abolitionists' rhetorical strategies in print media and slaveholders' property-protection strategies at the U.S. sectional border, see ibid., 122–127.

34. Henry Bibb, *Narrative of the Life and Adventures of Henry Bibb, an American Slave, Written by Himself* (New York: The Author, 1849), 78.

35. Josiah Henson, *The Life of Josiah Henson, Formerly a Slave, Now an Inhabitant of Canada, As Narrated by Himself*, ed. Samuel A. Eliot (Boston: A. D. Phelps, 1849), 70.

36. Troutman, "Grapevine in the Slave Market," 203–204.

37. "An Asylum for the Oppressed," *The Colored American* (New York), March 29, 1838.

38. Drew, *A North-Side View of Slavery*, 50.

39. Lewis Clarke, *Narrative of the Sufferings of Lewis Clarke, During a Captivity of More than Twenty-Five Years, among the Algerines of Kentucky, One of the So Called Christian States of North America. Dictated by Himself* (Boston, MA: David H. Ela, 1845), 31, 39.

40. Ward, *Autobiography of a Fugitive Negro*, 161.

41. Clarke, *Narrative of the Sufferings of Lewis Clarke*, 39–41.

42. Kelley, "Mexico in His Head," 719.

43. Of the original 164 enslaved Americans aboard the *Comet*, eleven immediately swam ashore after the disabled ship arrived at Nassau (and thus were technically escaped slaves rather than liberated slaves), five decided to return to the United States as slaves, and two died. The remaining 146 were freed by a government agent in Nassau. See Royal Commission on Fugitive Slaves (Great Britain), *Report of the Commissioners, Minutes of the Evidence, and Appendix, with General Index of Minutes of Evidence and Appendix* (George Edward Eyre and William Spottiswoode, 1876), 231.

44. For a detailed examination of cases in which the enslaved passengers of American ships were freed in the Caribbean, as well as their overall impact on the domestic slave trade, see Kerr-Ritchie, *Rebellious Passage*, especially 66–76.

45. Ibid. In the case of the *Encomium*, twelve of the enslaved decided to return to the United States.

46. "Another Seizure of American Slaves in Bermuda" (from the *New York Journal of Commerce*), *Salem Gazette* (Salem, MA), March 20, 1835, America's Historical Newspapers.

47. Ibid.

48. "Remarks of Mr. Calhoun, of South Carolina," *Appendix to the Congressional Globe*, 24th Congress, 2nd Session, [March 2] 1837, 318. In addition to their inclusion in the *Congressional Globe*, Calhoun's remarks (and variants of them) were widely reprinted. See *Daily National Intelligencer* (Washington, DC), March 10, 1837; the *Mercury* (Charleston, SC), March 17, 1837; the *Globe* (Washington, DC), July 17, 1837; the *Reformer* (Washington, DC), March 2, 1837; the *Daily National Intelligencer*

(Washington, DC), March 3, 1837; and the *Morning Courier and New-York Enquirer* (New York), March 4, 1837. See Clyde Norman Wilson, ed., *The Papers of John C. Calhoun* (Columbia: University of South Carolina Press, 1959), 13:486.

49. The British reached this sum based on the average insurance payment made in both cases for the slaves who had been insured prior to the voyages. See Royal Commission on Fugitive Slaves (Great Britain), *Report of the Commissioners*, 230–231; Rugemer, *The Problem of Emancipation*, 199–200.

50. Royal Commission on Fugitive Slaves (Great Britain), *Report of the Commissioners*, 230–231.

51. "Another Seizure of American Slaves in Bermuda" (from the *New York Journal of Commerce*), *Salem Gazette* (Salem, MA), March 20, 1835, America's Historical Newspapers.

52. Hendrick and Hendrick, *The Creole Mutiny*, 77–120.

53. "The Domestic Slave Trade," *The Liberator* (Boston, MA), December 24, 1841, Slavery and Anti-Slavery: A Transnational Archive.

54. *The Friend of Man*, for example, ran an informational series on Madison Washington's life in which it celebrated the "Immortal Nineteen" and framed the *Creole* rebellion as slaves' heroic effort to fight for their liberty. See "From the Friend of Man. Madison Washington. Another Chapter in His History," *The Liberator* (Boston, MA), June 10, 1842, Slavery and Anti-Slavery: A Transnational Archive. On the rise of "aggressive abolitionism" and abolitionists' increasing comfort with violence as an anti-slavery strategy, see Kellie Carter Jackson, *Force and Freedom: Black Abolitionists and the Politics of Violence* (Philadelphia: University of Pennsylvania Press, 2019); Harrold, "Romanticizing Slave Revolt."

55. "From the Friend of Man. Madison Washington. Another Chapter in His History," *The Liberator* (Boston, MA), June 10, 1842, Slavery and Anti-Slavery: A Transnational Archive.

56. Winsboro and Knetsch, "Florida Slaves, the 'Saltwater Railroad' to the Bahamas, and Anglo-American Diplomacy," 52–53.

57. "Jonathan Walker and Charles T. Torrey," *The American and Foreign Anti-Slavery Reporter* (New York), November 1, 1844, Slavery and Anti-Slavery: A Transnational Archive.

58. Winsboro and Knetsch, "Florida Slaves, the 'Saltwater Railroad' to the Bahamas, and Anglo-American Diplomacy."

59. Drew, *A North-Side View of Slavery*, 84.

60. On the reputation of Mexico among enslaved people, see Kelley, "Mexico in His Head."

61. Cornell, "Citizens of Nowhere," 356–357.

62. Kelley, "Mexico in His Head," 716; Nichols, *The Limits of Liberty*, 68–69.

63. On the perils faced by fugitive slaves in the Nueces Strip, see Audain, "Design His Course to Mexico," 137.

64. Nichols, *The Limits of Liberty*, 127, 139–143, 159; Audain, "Mexican Canaan," 149–150. See also Baumgartner, *South of Freedom*.

65. Nichols, *The Limits of Liberty*, 70–71, 127, 137–139, 151; Audain, "Design His Course to Mexico," 241.

66. Rugemer, *The Problem of Emancipation*, 211–214; Horne, *Negro Comrades of the Crown*, 148–163.

67. "Mr. Calhoun to Mr. Packenham," April 18, 1844, *Reports and Public Letters of John C. Calhoun*, ed. Richard K. Crallé (New York: D. Appleton and Co., 1883), 333–339.

68. Ashbel Smith to John C. Calhoun, June 19, 1843, as quoted in Horne, *Negro Comrades of the Crown*, 148.

69. Rugemer, *The Problem of Emancipation*, 211–214; Horne, *Negro Comrades of the Crown*, 148–163.

70. "Texas and Mexico," in *The Legion of Liberty: Remonstrance of Some Free Men, States, and Presses, to the Texas Rebellion, Against the Laws of Nature and of Nations* (Albany, 1843).

71. American Anti-Slavery Society, *The Legion of Liberty! And Force of Truth, Containing the thoughts, word, and deed, of some prominent Apostles, Champions and Martyrs*, 2nd ed. (New York, 1843).

72. "Hillsborough Counsellor Convention," *New Hampshire Patriot and State Gazette* (Concord, NH), January 8, 1846. Senator Robert Walker of Mississippi was a southern politician who shared the view that Texas annexation would eventually contribute to ending slavery in the Upper South. As historian Edward Rugemer points out, however, while this sort of argument was intended to ease northern anxiety regarding Texas annexation, pro-slavery politicians in favor of annexation (like Calhoun) would not have found the argument acceptable. See Rugemer, *The Problem of Emancipation*, 214–215.

73. Nichols, *The Limits of Liberty*, 129.

74. William Ellery Channing, *The Duty of the Free States, or, Remarks Suggested by the Case of the Creole, First Part* (Boston, MA: William Crosby & Co., 1842), 7.

75. "Americans, Blush!" *The Liberator* (Boston, MA), April 12, 1839, American Periodicals Series II.

76. For current scholarship on southern slaveholders' political power within the U.S. government and their shared vision for American foreign policy, see Matthew Karp, *This Vast Southern Empire: Slaveholders at the Helm of American Foreign Policy* (Cambridge, MA: Harvard University Press, 2016).

77. William Jay, *A View of the Action of the Federal Government in Behalf of Slavery* (New York: J. C. Jackson for the American Anti-Slavery Society, 1844); Joshua R. Giddings, *The Rights of the Free States Subverted, or, An Enumeration of Some of the Most Prominent Instances in Which the Federal Constitution Has Been Violated by Our National Government, for the Benefit of Slavery* ([Washington, DC?], 1844); Loring Moody, *Facts for the People: Showing the Relations of the United States Government to Slavery, Embracing a History of the Mexican War, Its Origin and Objects* (Boston, MA: Dow and Jackson's Anti-Slavery Press, 1847).

7 FREE SOIL, FICTION, AND THE FUGITIVE SLAVE ACT

1. William Wells Brown, *The Escape, Or, A Leap for Freedom A Drama in Five Acts (1858)* (Knoxville: University of Tennessee Press, 2001), 34.

2. Ward, *Autobiography of a Fugitive Negro*, 158.

3. Eric J. Sundquist, Introduction to *New Essays on Uncle Tom's Cabin*, ed. Eric J. Sundquist, The American Novel (Cambridge: ProQuest LLC, 2000), 18. Of course, taking into account the way books were circulated and shared in the nineteenth century, readership far surpassed the number of copies sold. Declaring *Uncle Tom's Cabin* "the book of the age," for example, Boston abolitionist Amos Lawrence sent his friend Mark Hopkins, the president of Williams College, twelve copies. These copies circulated among the whole of the college's population. Amos Lawrence (Boston) to Mark Hopkins (Williams College), April 7, 1852 and April 22, 1852, Amos Lawrence papers II, 1811–1851, "Hopkins Letters," vol. 4, Massachusetts Historical Society.

4. "Speech of Hon. Joshua R. Giddings of Ohio, in the House of Representatives," *Frederick Douglass' Paper* (Rochester, NY), January 7, 1853, Accessible Archives; David S. Reynolds, *Mightier than the Sword: Uncle Tom's Cabin and the Battle for America* (New York: W. W. Norton, 2011), x.

5. Harriet Beecher Stowe, *Uncle Tom's Cabin, or, Life Among the Lowly*, vol. 2 (Boston: J. P. Jewett, 1852), 234, 238–239.

6. On the Congressional debates surrounding the Compromise of 1850 and the passage of the Fugitive Slave Act, see Stanley W. Campbell, *The Slave Catchers: Enforcement of the Fugitive Slave Law, 1850–1860* (Chapel Hill: University of North Carolina Press, 1970), 3–25, 110–147; and Fergus M. Bordewich, *America's Great Debate: Henry Clay, Stephen A. Douglas, and the Compromise that Preserved the Union* (New York: Simon & Schuster, 2013). For scholarship that centers fugitive slaves, resistance to the Fugitive Slave Act, and northern opposition, see Blackett, *The Captive's Quest for Freedom*; Foner, *Gateway to Freedom*, 119–150; R. J. M. Blackett, *Making Freedom: The Underground Railroad and the Politics of Slavery* (Chapel Hill: University of North Carolina Press, 2013); Angela F. Murphy, *The Jerry Rescue: The Fugitive Slave Law, Northern Rights, and the American Sectional Crisis* (Oxford: Oxford University Press, 2014).

7. Harriet Beecher Stowe was not the first author to use fiction in the service of antislavery. Literary scholar Celeste-Marie Bernier has shown that Frederick Douglass, for example, began to develop techniques in the late 1840s and early 1850s to fictionalize and dramatize the history of the *Creole* rebellion to elicit political and moral responses from his audience. Bernier emphasizes that while Douglass first began this narrative transition, it went against the grain of mainstream white abolitionists' prioritization of "truth" in ex-slave narratives, *Uncle Tom's Cabin* made it impossible to ignore the rhetorical value of dramatizing and fictionalizing slavery's horrors. Celeste-Marie Bernier, "From Fugitive Slave to Fugitive Abolitionist," *Atlantic Studies* 3, no. 2 (October 2006): 203, 205.

8. Sarah Meer, *Uncle Tom Mania: Slavery, Minstrelsy, and Transatlantic Culture in the 1850s* (Athens, GA: University of Georgia Press, 2005), 1–3.

9. Howard Holman Bell, ed., "Proceedings of the Colored National Convention, 1853" (Rochester: Printed at the Office of Frederick Douglass' Paper, 1853), in *Minutes of the Proceedings of the National Negro Conventions, 1830–1864* (New York: Arno Press, 1969), 4; Meer, *Uncle Tom Mania*, 4.

10. Meer, *Uncle Tom Mania*, 75–76, 81.

11. Stowe, *Uncle Tom's Cabin, or, Life Among the Lowly*, vol. 2, 234, 238–239.

12. Quotes, in order, Stowe, *Uncle Tom's Cabin, or, Life Among the Lowly*, vol. 2, 292, 299, 300.

13. Based on census data from 1852, historian Gary Collison concluded that few fugitive slaves arrived in Montreal in the early 1850s. For those who did not go to Upper Canada when they crossed the U.S.–Canada border, evidence from the Boston Vigilance Committee account book suggests that destinations in the Maritimes (St. Johns and Halifax) were more typical than destinations in Quebec (of which none were noted). See Gary L. Collison, *Shadrach Minkins: From Fugitive Slave to Citizen* (Cambridge, MA: Harvard University Press, 1998), 172–173, 196.

14. Stowe, *Uncle Tom's Cabin, or, Life Among the Lowly*, vol. 2, 302.

15. Martin B. Pasternak, *Rise Now and Fly to Arms: The Life of Henry Highland Garnet* (New York: Routledge, 1994), 60.

16. Power-Greene, *Against Wind and Tide*, 97–102; Brandon Mills, "'The United States of Africa': Liberian Independence and the Contested Meaning of a Black Republic," *Journal of the Early Republic* 34, no. 1 (Spring 2014): 84–85.

17. Power-Greene, *Against Wind and Tide*, 97–102.

18. Abraham Lincoln, "Reply to Stephen A. Douglas in Their First Debate, 21 August 1858," in *The Lincoln–Douglas Debates*, ed. Rodney O. Davis and Douglas L. Wilson (Urbana: Knox College Lincoln Studies Center and the University of Illinois Press, 2008), 19.

19. Stowe, *Uncle Tom's Cabin, or, Life Among the Lowly*, vol. 2, 302.

20. Ibid., 300.

21. See Nicholas Guyatt, "'The Outskirts of Our Happiness': Race and the Lure of Colonization in the Early Republic," *Journal of American History* 95, no. 4 (March 2009): 987–988.

22. Guyatt, "The Outskirts of Our Happiness," 987; See also Everill, *Abolition and Empire*, Mills, "The United States of Africa," 79–107, quote 92.

23. See "Professor Stowe on Colonization," *African Repository and Colonial Journal* (Washington, DC), December 1, 1834, Slavery and Anti-Slavery: A Transnational Archive.

24. Mills, "The United States of Africa," 100–101, 92; Carl Patrick Burrowes, "Black Christian Republicanism: A Southern Ideology in Early Liberia, 1822 to 1847," *Journal of Negro History* 86, no. 1 (2001): 30–44.

25. Stowe, *Uncle Tom's Cabin, or, Life Among the Lowly*, vol. 2, 301.

26. Quoted in Reynolds, *Mightier than the Sword*, 130 (original emphasis).

27. See, for example, "The Refugees' Home Society," *Frederick Douglass' Paper* (Rochester, NY), April 22, 1853, America's Historical Newspapers.

28. "Mrs. Stowe's Position," *Frederick Douglass' Paper* (Rochester, NY), May 6, 1853, America's Historical Newspapers.

29. "Uncle Tom's Cabin – Objectionable Characteristics," *The Liberator* (Boston, MA), July 9, 1852, Slavery and Anti-Slavery: A Transnational Archive.

30. "Reply to H. C. Wright on 'Uncle Tom's Cabin,'" *The Liberator* (Boston, MA), September 17, 1852, Slavery and Anti-Slavery: A Transnational Archive.

31. "The Letter of M. R. Delany," *Frederick Douglass' Paper* (Rochester, NY), May 6, 1853, America's Historical Newspapers.

32. *Provincial Freeman* (Toronto, Upper Canada), July 22, 1854, Accessible Archives.

33. Stowe, *Uncle Tom's Cabin, or, Life Among the Lowly*, vol. 2, 234, 238–239.

34. Ibid., 238–239.

35. William L. Andrews, *To Tell a Free Story: The First Century of Afro-American Autobiography, 1760–1865* (Urbana: University of Illinois Press, 1986), 97.

36. The number of slave narratives per decade was sourced from the North American Slave Narratives Collection from the University of North Carolina's "Documenting the American South" project (docsouth.unc.edu). This collection is self-described as including "all the existing autobiographical narrative of fugitive and former slaves published as broadsides, pamphlets, or books in English up to 1920." For the chronological breakdown of included narratives, see: http://docsouth.unc.edu/neh/chron autobio.html.

37. Regarding the ability of slave autobiographers' firsthand accounts to sway "the uncommitted mass of readers" to the anti-slavery cause, African American autobiography scholar William Andrews points out, specifically, that the slave narrative "answered a felt need for a rhetorical mode that would conduct the battle against racism and slavery on grounds other than those already occupied by pro- and antislavery polemics." Andrews, *To Tell a Free Story*, 5.

38. Reynolds, *Mightier than the Sword*, 103.

39. According to literary historian Charles Heglar, nineteenth-century narratives were intended to depict the overcoming of a particular ordeal or turning point. For self-emancipated slaves, this ordeal was passing from slavery to freedom, which became the recognizable form of the slave narrative genre. Charles J. Heglar, Introduction to *The Life and Adventures of Henry Bibb: An American Slave* (Madison: University of Wisconsin Press, 2001), vii.

40. William Wells Brown, *Narrative of William W. Brown, A Fugitive Slave. Written by Himself* (Boston, MA: The Anti-Slavery Office, 1847), 31.

41. Ibid., 84.

42. Ibid., 71–72 (original emphasis).

43. Ibid., 105.

44. Ibid., 108–109.

45. Andrews, *To Tell a Free Story*, 107.

46. William Wells Brown, *Narrative of William W. Brown, A Fugitive Slave. Written by Himself*, 4th ed. (London: Charles Gilpin, 1849), 133–162.

47. Brown, "A Song for Freedom."

48. Bibb, *Narrative of the Life and Adventures of Henry Bibb, an American Slave*, 78.

49. Ibid., ii; Andrews, *To Tell a Free Story*, 98, 106.

50. Henson, *The Life of Josiah Henson*, 47, 58–59.

51. Andrews, *To Tell a Free Story*, 97; Winks, *The Blacks in Canada*, 187–193; Josiah Henson, *Truth Is Stranger than Fiction. Father Henson's Story of His Own Life*, ed. Samuel A. Eliot (Boston, MA: J. P. Jewett, 1858).

52. For example, Stowe lifts text from the 1848 narrative of Lewis Clarke to anchor George's reaction upon reaching Canadian shores. See Harriet Beecher Stowe, *A Key to Uncle Tom's Cabin; Presenting the Original Facts and Documents Upon Which the Story is Founded. Together with Corroborative Statements Verifying the Truth of the Work* (Boston, MA: J. P. Jewett, 1853), 17.

53. "Fugitive Slaves in Canada," *The Anti-Slavery Reporter* (London), January 1, 1851, Slavery and Anti-Slavery: A Transnational Archive; Mary Ann Shadd, *A Plea for Emigration; or Notes of Canada West* [1852], ed. Phanuel Antwi (Peterborough, Ontario: Broadview Press, 2016), 48; Drew, *A North-Side View of Slavery*, v; Ward, *Autobiography of a Fugitive Negro*, 154; *The Fugitive Slaves in Canada*, Wilson Anti-Slavery Collection (1858) (London: Seeley, Jackson & Halliday, 1858), 6.

54. Ward, *Autobiography of a Fugitive Negro*, 163–164.

55. Audain, "Mexican Canaan," 127.

56. Nichols, *The Limits of Liberty*, 142.

57. Audain, "Mexican Canaan," 141–146.

58. Blackett, *Building an Antislavery Wall*, 5.

59. For the full text of William Craft's 1860 narrative situated with a foreword and culminating essay by R. J. M. Blackett, see William Craft, *Running a Thousand Miles for Freedom: The Escape of William and Ellen Craft*, ed. R. J. M. Blackett (Baton Rouge: Louisiana State University Press, 1999).

60. James Theodore Holly, C. Freeman, and Lewis Clark, "Report on Emigration," in *Minutes and Proceedings of the General Convention for the Improvement of the Colored Inhabitants of Canada, Held by Adjournments in Amhrstburgh [sic], C.W., June 16th and 17th, 1853* (Windsor, Canada West: Bibb & Holly, 1853), 14.

61. "The Slave-Catching Law," *The Liberator* (Boston, MA), October 4, 1850, Slavery and Anti-Slavery: A Transnational Archive.

62. "The Slave-Catching Law," and "Fugitive Slave Excitement," *The Liberator* (Boston, MA), October 4, 1850, Slavery and Anti-Slavery: A Transnational Archive.

63. *The Liberty Almanac for 1852* (New York: American and Foreign Anti-Slavery Society, 1852), 32. On the disputed claim, see Blackett, *The Captive's Quest for Freedom*, 47.

64. "From the Anti-Slavery Standard. Letter from Canada," *Provincial Freeman* (Toronto, Canada West), January 13, 1855, Accessible Archives.

65. John Henry Hill to William Still, Letters 1–13, quotation from "Third Letter," published sometime between October 20, 1853 and November 12, 1853, all in William Still, *The Underground Railroad: A Record of Facts, Authentic Narrative, Letters, &c., Narrating the Hardships, Hair-Breadth Escapes and Death Struggles of the Slaves in Their Efforts of Freedom, as Related by Themselves and Others, or Witnessed by the Author; Together with Sketches of Some of the Largest Stockholders, and Most Liberal Aiders and Advisers, of the Road* (Philadelphia: Porter & Coates, 1872).

66. While Canada featured prominently in only three of the twenty-four narratives published over the course of the 1840s, nine of the twenty-nine ex-slave narratives published in the 1850s celebrated Canada as an escape from American slavery and racial persecution. Most of these stories specifically revolved around the narrator's efforts to reach Canada

and claim freedom under the British flag. See William Anderson, *Life and Narrative of William J. Anderson, Twenty-Four Years a Slave; Sold Eight Times! In Jail Sixty Times!! Whipped Three Hundred Times!!! Or The Dark Deeds of American Slavery Revealed. Containing Scriptural Views of the Origin of the Black and of the White Man. Also, a Simple and Easy Plan to Abolish Slavery in the United States. Together with an Account of the Services of Colored Men in the Revolutionary War – Day and Date, and Interesting Facts* (Chicago: Daily Tribune, 1857); William Green, *Narrative of Events in the Life of William Green, (Formerly a Slave.) Written by Himself* (Springfield, MA: L. M. Guernsey, 1853); Henson, *Truth Is Stranger Than Fiction*; Steward, *Twenty-Two Years a Slave and Forty Years a Freeman*; Thomas Smallwood, *A Narrative of Thomas Smallwood, Coloured Man: Giving an Account of His Birth – The Period He Was Held in Slavery – His Release – And Removal to Canada, Etc. Together with an Account of the Underground Railroad. Written by Himself* (Toronto: The Author, 1851); Ward, *Autobiography of a Fugitive Negro*; James Watkins, *Narrative of the Life of James Watkins, Formerly a "Chattel" in Maryland, U.S. Containing an Account of His Escape from Slavery, Together with an Appeal on Behalf of Three Millions of Such "Pieces of Property," Still Held Under the Standard of the Eagle* (Bolton: Kenyon & Abbatt, 1852).

67. Smallwood, *A Narrative of Thomas Smallwood*, 18–33, quote on 33. On Underground Railroad activities in Washington, DC, see Stanley Harrold, *Subversives: Antislavery Community in Washington, D.C., 1828–1865* (Baton Rouge: Louisiana State University Press, 2002).

68. Smallwood, *A Narrative of Thomas Smallwood*, 33.

69. "New Publications," *National Anti-Slavery Standard* (New York), June 26, 1858, Slavery and Anti-Slavery: A Transnational Archive.

70. Wells Brown, *The Escape, Or, A Leap for Freedom*, 34.

71. "Poetry: Away to Canada," *The Liberator* (Boston, MA), December 10, 1852, Slavery and Anti-Slavery: A Transnational Archive.

72. On the complex relationship between Stephen Foster's minstrelsy music and his views on African Americans and slaves, see Matthew Shaftel, "Singing a New Song: Stephen Foster and the New American Minstrelsy," *Music and Politics* 1, no. 2 (2007): 1–27.

73. "Poetry: Away to Canada," *The Liberator* (Boston, MA), December 10, 1852, Slavery and Anti-Slavery: A Transnational Archive.

8 EMIGRATION AND ENMITY: THE MEANING OF FREE SOIL IN A NATION DIVIDED

1. "Emigration," *Provincial Freeman* (Toronto, Canada West), January 20, 1854, Accessible Archives.

2. "Proceedings of the North American Convention Convened at St. Lawrence Hall, Toronto, Canada West, 11–13 September 1851. Voice of the Fugitive. 24 September 1851," in Ripley, *The Black Abolitionist Papers*, vol. 2.

3. Ibid.

4. Rhodes, "The Contestation over National Identity," 180–182.

5. On the Colored Conventions of the nineteenth century, see: http://coloredconven tions.org.

6. Toyin Falola, "Introduction," in *The Condition, Elevation, Emigration, and Destiny of the Colored People of the United States and Official Report of the Niger Valley Exploring Party (Martin Delany)*, ed. Toyin Falola (Amherst, NY: Humanity Books, 2004), 7–10, 24 (fn. 3); Robert S. Levine, ed., *Martin R. Delany: A Documentary Reader* (Chapel Hill: University of North Carolina Press, 2003), 1–2.

7. Falola, "Introduction," 7–10, 24; Levine, *Martin R. Delany*, 1–2.

8. Martin R. Delany, *The Condition, Elevation, Emigration, and Destiny of the Colored People of the United States. Politically Considered* (Philadelphia, PA: Martin Robison Delany, 1852), 190.

9. As historian Tunde Adeleke points out, this interpretation of Delany's ideology stemmed, in large part, from the resuscitation of Delany's work during the civil rights movement, when black American scholars and thinkers looked to historical characters like Delany whose lives were "consistent with radical antiestablishment values." For both a complete treatment of Delany historiography and a more comprehensive examination of the man's ideological complexity, see Tunde Adeleke, *Without Regard to Race: The Other Martin Robison Delany* (Jackson: University Press of Mississippi, 2003), quote p. xx.

10. Delany, *The Condition, Elevation, Emigration, and Destiny of the Colored People of the United States*, 190.

11. Rhodes, *Mary Ann Shadd Cary*, 1–5.

12. Bell, "Minutes and Proceedings of the First Annual Convention of the People of Colour (1831)."

13. "Wilmington," *The North Star* (Rochester, NY), March 23, 1859, Accessible Archives.

14. Rhodes, *Mary Ann Shadd Cary*, 33–34.

15. Mary Ann Shadd, *A Plea for Emigration; or, Notes of Canada West, in Its Moral, Social, and Political Aspect: With Suggestions Respecting Mexico, West Indies, and Vancouver Island* (Detroit, MI: George W. Pattison, 1852).

16. Shadd, *A Plea for Emigration*, 41.

17. Rhodes, "The Contestation over National Identity," 180, 181.

18. "Letter from John N. Still," *Frederick Douglass' Paper* (Rochester, NY), April 28, 1854, Slavery and Anti-Slavery: A Transnational Archive; Simpson, *Under the North Star*, 93.

19. Delany, *The Condition, Elevation, Emigration, and Destiny of the Colored People of the United States*, 169; Shadd, *A Plea for Emigration*, 19.

20. Shadd, *A Plea for Emigration*, 19.

21. Delany, *The Condition, Elevation, Emigration, and Destiny of the Colored People of the United States*, 170–171.

22. Ibid., 174–175.

23. Leading colonizationist James G. Birney, for example, expressed this concern in a letter published for the public, causing Canadian emigrationist Samuel Ringgold Ward to publish a refutation in *Frederick Douglass' Paper*. See "Communications," *Frederick*

Douglass Paper (Rochester, NY), March 11, 1852, Slavery and Anti-Slavery: A Transnational Archive.

24. Delany, *The Condition, Elevation, Emigration, and Destiny of the Colored People of the United States. Politically Considered*, 179–181.

25. "Call for a National Emigration Convention of Colored Men," *Frederick Douglass' Paper* (Rochester, NY), September 9, 1853, Slavery and Anti-Slavery: A Transnational Archive.

26. Martin R. Delany, "The Political Destiny of the Colored Race on the American Continent," in *Martin R. Delany: A Documentary Reader*, ed. Robert S. Levine (Chapel Hill: University of North Carolina Press, 2003), 245–279; "Colored Convention at Cleveland," *The African Repository* (Washington, DC), January 1, 1855, Slavery and Anti-Slavery: A Transnational Archive.

27. "National Emigration Convention of Colored Men," *The Liberator* (Boston, MA), September 29, 1854, Slavery and Anti-Slavery: A Transnational Archive.

28. *Report of the Select Committee on Emancipation and Colonization, with an Appendix (House of Representatives, 37th Congress, 2nd Session)* (Washington, DC: Government Printing Office, 1862), 37–59. On Lincoln's wartime colonizationism, see Sebastian N. Page, "'A Knife Sharp Enough to Divide Us': William H. Seward, Abraham Lincoln, and Black Colonization," *Diplomatic History* 41, no. 2 (April 2017): 362–391; James D. Lockett, "Abraham Lincoln and Colonization: An Episode that Ends in Tragedy at L'Ile a Vache, Haiti, 1863–1864," *Journal of Black Studies* 21, no. 4 (June 1991): 428–444; Michael Vorenberg, "Abraham Lincoln and the Politics of Black Colonization," *Journal of the Abraham Lincoln Association* 14, no. 2 (1993): 22–45.

29. Delany, "The Political Destiny of the Colored Race on the American Continent," 279.

30. Shadd, *A Plea for Emigration*, 43.

31. Roger W. Hite, "Voice of a Fugitive: Henry Bibb and Ante-Bellum Black Separatism," *Journal of Black Studies* 4, no. 3 (March 1974): 275.

32. Shadd, *A Plea for Emigration; or Notes of Canada West* [1852], 59.

33. Mitchell, *Raising Freedom's Child*, 28–34.

34. Nichols, *The Limits of Liberty*, 127, 143, 159.

35. Mitchell, *Raising Freedom's Child*, 34–35.

36. Shadd, *A Plea for Emigration*, 59.

37. Ibid., 43.

38. Ibid., 53, 36.

39. Archives Ontario (AO), Ontario Department of Education Incoming General Correspondence, RG 2-12, Container 11, Petition of colored inhabitants of Simcoe to Egerton Ryerson, December 12, 1851; RG 2-12, Container 12, Committee of Colored Citizens of Chatham to Egerton Ryerson and George Duck, March 31, 1852; RG 2-12, Container 14, Dennis Hill to Egerton Ryerson, November 22, 1852; RG 2-12, Container 20, William P. Newman to Egerton Ryerson, January 13, 1856; RG 2-12, Container 26, Committee for the Colored People of Windsor to Egerton Ryerson, March 2, 1859.

40. AO, Ontario Department of Education Incoming General Correspondence, RG 2-12, Container 11, Petition of colored inhabitants of Simcoe to Egerton Ryerson, December 12, 1851.

41. Shadd, *A Plea for Emigration*, 62.
42. "Our Free Colored Emigrants," *Provincial Freeman* (Toronto, Canada West), May 20, 1854, Accessible Archives.
43. "To the Editor of the Provincial Freeman," *Provincial Freeman* (Toronto, Canada West), August 12, 1854, Accessible Archives.
44. Drew, *A North-Side View of Slavery*, vi.
45. Ibid., 15.
46. Ibid., 239–247, 30.
47. "Letter from Rev. Hiram Wilson," *The Liberator* (Boston, MA), January 11, 1856, Slavery and Anti-Slavery: A Transnational Archive; "Anti-Slavery Men and Women!" *The Liberator* (Boston, MA), November 16, 1855, Slavery and Anti-Slavery: A Transnational Archive; "Anti-Slavery Men and Women!" *National Anti-Slavery Standard* (New York, NY), December 1, 1855, Slavery and Anti-Slavery: A Transnational Archive; "Anti-Slavery Men and Women!" *National Era* (Washington, DC), December 6, 1855, Slavery and Anti-Slavery: A Transnational Archive.
48. "Attention!!!" *Provincial Freeman* (Toronto, Canada West), March 25, 1854, Accessible Archives.
49. Drew, *A North-Side View of Slavery*, 15.
50. This term was coined by historian Ibram X. Kendi in *Stamped from the Beginning*.
51. Hite, "Voice of a Fugitive," 272–273.
52. It is worth noting that Cooper also credits the *Voice of the Fugitive* for creating a "black transnational antislavery awareness and culture, in respect not only to Canada and the United States but beyond." As the present work demonstrates, Cooper's assessment is perhaps overly focused on Canada in the 1850s, as a robust "black transnational antislavery awareness and culture" had existed since at least the mid-1820s. Nonetheless, Cooper's general assessment of the significance of the Bibbs' newspaper for black anti-slavery activists is irrefutable. Afua Cooper, "The Voice of the Fugitive: A Transnational Abolitionist Organ," in *A Fluid Frontier: Slavery, Resistance, and the Underground Railroad in the Detroit River Borderland*, eds. Karolyn Smardz Frost and Veta Smith Tucker (Detroit, MI: Wayne State University Press, 2016), 136.
53. Note: Henry Bibb wrote this address in conjunction with two other delegates. Despite its co-authorship, it reflects Bibb's perspective and pen. "An Address to the Colored Inhabitants of North America (Henry Bibb)," *The Anti-Slavery Reporter* (London), December 1, 1851, Slavery and Anti-Slavery: A Transnational Archive.
54. "A Recent Tour," *Provincial Freeman* (Toronto, Canada West), March 24, 1854, Accessible Archives. Notably, my reading of Shadd's views on prejudice and discrimination differ substantively from Shadd's biographer, Jane Rhodes. Rhodes suggests that Shadd saw racial prejudice as a rarity in Canadian life. I argue that her authorial and editorial choices suggest she was very aware of it. She truly believed, however, that its pernicious effects could be overcome by integration and by using the legal means that British subjects' legal equality entitled them to. In the article cited, Shadd blames the effects of prejudice on those who would "rather cringe than contend for what law and right entitle them to." See, Rhodes, *Mary Ann Shadd Cary*, 44.

55. See, for example, Shadd, *A Plea for Emigration*, 39.

56. Roger W. Hite, a communications scholar, has described Bibb's ideology as separatism, in contrast to Shadd's integrationism. Though Bibb certainly advocated for black settlements and uplift projects, I argue that this terminology seems a bit misleading. Unlike Delany, for example, who advocated that African Americans should remove themselves from white influence, Bibb worked with white allies and seemed to view his interventions as means to an end, rather than an end in and of themselves. See Hite, "Voice of a Fugitive," 275–281.

57. "Report of the Refugee's Home Society," *Frederick Douglass' Paper* (Rochester, NY), October 15, 1852, Slavery and Anti-Slavery: A Transnational Archive; "Homes for the Refugees," *The Liberator* (Boston, MA), June 11, 1852, Slavery and Anti-Slavery: A Transnational Archive.

58. "Homes for the Refugees," *The Liberator* (Boston, MA), June 11, 1852, Slavery and Anti-Slavery: A Transnational Archive.

59. "No More Begging for Farms or Clothes for Fugitives in Canada," *The Liberator* (Boston, MA), October 15, 1852, Slavery and Anti-Slavery: A Transnational Archive.

60. "The Colored People in Canada – Do They Need Help?" *The Liberator* (Boston, MA), December 24, 1852, Slavery and Anti-Slavery: A Transnational Archive (original emphasis).

61. "Refugee's Home Society," *The Liberator* (Boston, MA), March 4, 1853, Slavery and Anti-Slavery: A Transnational Archive.

62. "No More Begging for Farms or Clothes for Fugitives in Canada," *The Liberator* (Boston, MA), October 15, 1852, Slavery and Anti-Slavery: A Transnational Archive.

63. "The Fugitives and their Needs," *National Anti-Slavery Standard* (New York), January 20, 1853, Slavery and Anti-Slavery: A Transnational Archive.

64. Ibid.

65. Ward, *Autobiography of a Fugitive Negro*, 3–4.

66. "Samuel Ringgold Ward to Henry Bibb and James Theodore Holly, October 1852" (published in Bibb's *Voice of the Fugitive*)," in Ripley, *The Black Abolitionist Papers*, 2:226.

67. Jeffrey R. Kerr-Ritchie, "Samuel Ward and the Making of an Imperial Subject," *Slavery & Abolition* 33, no. 2 (May 2012): 213.

68. Gale L. Kenny, "Manliness and Manifest Racial Destiny: Jamaica and African American Emigration in the 1850s," *Journal of the Civil War Era* 2, no. 2 (2012): 169; Kerr-Ritchie, "Samuel Ward and the Making of an Imperial Subject," 209.

69. Faulkner, "The Root of the Evil," 378–379, 401–403; Elizabeth A. O'Donnell, "'There's Death in the Pot!' The British Free Produce Movement and the Religious Society of Friends, with Particular Reference to the North-East of England," *Quaker Studies; Liverpool* 13, no. 2 (March 2009): 189.

70. "An Address to the Colored Inhabitants of North America (Henry Bibb)," *The Anti-Slavery Reporter* (London), December 1, 1851, Slavery and Anti-Slavery: A Transnational Archive; "23. Proceedings of the North American Convention Convened at St. Lawrence Hall, Toronto, Canada West, 11–13 September 1851. Voice of the Fugitive. 24 September 1851," in Ripley, *The Black Abolitionist Papers*, vol. 2; "Agricultural Union,"

Voice of the Fugitive (Windsor, Canada West), December 3, 1831, Black Abolitionist Archive, accessed March 16, 2014.

71. "Letter from H. H. Garnet" (from the *New York Tribune*), *Frederick Douglass' Paper* (Rochester, NY), September 2, 1853, Accessible Archives; Kenny, "Manliness and Manifest Racial Destiny," 169.

72. Kenny, "Manliness and Manifest Racial Destiny," 168.

73. Martin R. Delany, "Official Report of the Niger Valley Exploring Party (1861)," in *Martin R. Delany: A Documentary Reader*, ed. Robert S. Levine (Chapel Hill: University of North Carolina Press, 2003), 351–357; Levine, *Martin R. Delany*, 316–318; Miller, *The Search for a Black Nationality*, 170–231.

74. Chief Justice Roger Taney, "Opinion of the Chief Justice," in *The Case of Dred Scott in the United States Supreme Court with the Full Opinions of Chief Justice Taney and Justice Curtis, and the Abstracts of the Opinions of the Other Judges* (New York: Horace Greeley, 1860), 7–22. On *Dred Scott* v. *Sandford*, see David Thomas Konig, Paul Finkelman, and Christopher Alan Bracey, eds., *The Dred Scott Case: Historical and Contemporary Perspectives on Race and Law* (Athens, OH: Ohio University Press, 2010); Paul Finkelman, *Dred Scott v. Sandford: A Brief History with Documents*, 2nd ed. (New York: Bedford Books, 2016); Don Edward Fehrenbacher, *Slavery, Law, and Politics: The Dred Scott Case in Historical Perspective* (New York: Oxford University Press, 1981).

75. Holly, Freeman, and Clark, "Report on Emigration," 15.

76. Miller, *The Search for a Black Nationality*, 232.

77. Dixon, *African America and Haiti*, 90–91, 103–110; Miller, *The Search for a Black Nationality*, 161–169, 232–235.

78. James Theodore Holly, *A Vindication of the Capacity of the Negro for Self-Government and Civilized Progress, as Demonstrated by Historical Events of the Haytian Revolution; and the Subsequent Acts of That People since Their National Independence* (New Haven, CT: Afric-American Printing Co., 1857), 46, 45.

79. "Hayti Inviting the Free Negroes of the United States," *The Liberator* (Boston, MA), September 17, 1858, Accessible Archives.

80. On James Redpath and the Haitian Bureau of Emigration, see Dixon, *African America and Haiti*, 129–169.

81. Martin R. Delany, "Letter to James T. Holly, 15 January 1861," in *Martin R. Delany: A Documentary Reader*, ed. Robert S. Levine (Chapel Hill: University of North Carolina Press, 2003), 365–367; "Haytian Emigration," *Weekly Anglo-African*, October 26, 1861.

82. Dixon, *African America and Haiti*, 129; "1860 Census," Minnesota Population Center, National Historical Geographic Information System, Version 11.0.

83. "George Cary to James Redpath, 26 August 1861," in Ripley, *The Black Abolitionist Papers*, 2:449–450.

84. "William Wells Brown to James Redpath" (October 1861), in Ripley, *The Black Abolitionist Papers*, 2:458–459.

85. "'The Colored People of Canada,' by William Wells Brown," in Ripley, *The Black Abolitionist Papers*, 2:461–498.

86. Ripley, *The Black Abolitionist Papers*, 2:449.

87. Dixon, *African America and Haiti*, 129–130.

88. "Emigration to Mexico," *The National Era* (Washington, DC), October 8, 1857, Accessible Archives; "Emigration Movement to New Mexico," *The Vincennes Weekly Western Sun* (Vincennes, IN), October 10, 1857, Accessible Archives. Emigration to Mexico in the late 1850s seems to have comprised quite small numbers and was relatively restricted to the free black population of New Orleans. See Mitchell, *Raising Freedom's Child*, 12–13, 29–30.

89. "Emigration to Hayti," *Douglass' Monthly* (Rochester, NY), January 1861, Accessible Archives.

90. Ibid.

91. Holly, Freeman, and Clark, "Report on Emigration," 14.

92. "William Whipper to Gerrit Smith, 22 April 1856," in *The Black Abolitionist Papers*, ed. C. Peter Ripley, *Vol. 4: The United States, 1847–1858* (Chapel Hill: University of North Carolina Press, 1985), 336.

93. Harrold, *Border War*, 168–173; John Stauffer and Zoe Trodd, eds., *The Tribunal: Responses to John Brown and the Harpers Ferry Raid* (Cambridge, MA: Belknap Press, 2012), xxvi–xxviii.

94. Dixon, *African America and Haiti*, 131–133.

95. Interestingly, in 1867, Martin Delany reported to his biographer, Frances Rollin, that the plan regarding Harper's Ferry was not discussed at the Chatham convention. Osborne P. Anderson, *A Voice from Harper's Ferry: A Narrative of Events at Harper's Ferry; with Incidents Prior and Subsequent to Its Capture by Captain Brown and His Men* (Boston, MA, 1861), 13, Slavery and Anti-Slavery: A Transnational Archive; Robert S. Levine, ed., "Canada. – Captain John Brown," in *Martin R. Delany: A Documentary Reader* (Chapel Hill: University of North Carolina Press, 2003), 330.

96. Stephen B. Oates, *To Purge This Land with Blood: A Biography of John Brown*, 2nd ed. (Amherst, MA: University of Massachusetts Press, 1984), 244.

97. Anderson, *A Voice from Harper's Ferry*, 21–22.

98. Stauffer and Trodd, *The Tribunal*, xix, xxxiii.

99. Steven Hahn, "Did We Miss the Greatest Slave Rebellion in Modern History?" in *The Political Worlds of Slavery and Freedom* (Cambridge, MA: Harvard University Press, 2009), 55–114.

CONCLUSION

1. Samuel Gridley Howe, *The Refugees from Slavery in Canada West: Report to the Freedmen's Inquiry Commission* (Boston, MA: Wright & Potter, Printers, 1864), 1.

2. Although Edwin Stanton was officially in charge of the AFIC, Massachusetts Senator Charles Sumner was its true "patron." It was Sumner who likely hand-picked the three commissioners. On the AFIC, see Manning, *Troubled Refuge*, 22–23. See also John G. Sproat, "Blueprint for Radical Reconstruction," *Journal of Southern History* 23(1) (February 1957): 34; Matthew Furrow, "Samuel Gridley Howe, the Black Population of

Canada West, and the Racial Ideology of the 'Blueprint for Radical Reconstruction,'" *Journal of American History* 97, no. 2 (2010): 348.

3. On the AFIC in the South, especially in relation to the interviews they conducted with – and related to – the black men and women who formed "contraband camps" behind Union Army lines during the Civil War, see Chandra Manning's *Troubled Refuge*. Reference to Jamaica and Honduras on p. 205.

4. Howe, *The Refugees from Slavery in Canada West*, 2.

5. Ibid., 1.

6. U.S. Department of War, *Letters Received by the Office of the Adjutant General, Main Series, 1861–1870* (M619: reels 199–102, file No. 10), RG 94 (National Archives, Washington, DC), hereafter AFIC Upper Canada Reports (NARA).

7. United States American Freedmen's Inquiry Commission Box 1, Folder 25, Houghton Library, Harvard University; United States American Freedmen's Inquiry Commission Box 1, Folder 5, Houghton Library, Harvard University; Jeff Strickland, "The American Freedmen's Inquiry Commission, 19th-Century Racial Pseudoscience, and the False Assessment of Black America, 1863–1864," *Federal History* 11 (2019): 118–120.

8. Hiram Wilson, "Letter to the Commission, St. Catharines, Canada, 1863 Dec. 10," United States American Freedmen's Inquiry Commission Records (MS Am 702–122), Houghton Library, Harvard University.

9. U.S. Department of War, *Letters Received by the Office of the Adjutant General, Main Series, 1861–1870* (M619: reels 199–102, file No. 10), RG 94 (National Archives, Washington, DC), hereafter AFIC Upper Canada Reports (NARA). Referenced is the testimony of Mrs. Hannah Fairfax.

10. Frankel, *States of Inquiry*, 205. It has been suggested, based on surveys of Howe's personal records, that Howe and Yerrinton conducted many more interviews than they submitted to the AFIC. See Furrow, "Samuel Gridley Howe, the Black Population of Canada West, and the Racial Ideology of the 'Blueprint for Radical Reconstruction,'" 353–354.

11. AFIC Upper Canada Reports (NARA).

12. Howe, *The Refugees from Slavery in Canada West*.

13. Historian John G. Sproat first identified the AFIC's influence on Reconstruction policy, calling it a "blueprint" for the government's policy toward freed people after the Civil War. See Sproat, "Blueprint for Radical Reconstruction."

14. Furrow, "Samuel Gridley Howe, the Black Population of Canada West, and the Racial Ideology of the 'Blueprint for Radical Reconstruction,'" 352, 358–360.

15. Howe, *The Refugees from Slavery in Canada West*, 55.

16. On labor competition with Irish immigrants, see Silverman, *Unwelcome Guests*, 62; Winks, *The Blacks in Canada*, 484. On the topic of black emigrants' evaluation of their labor in relationship to their ideas about liberty and equality, see, for example, Hepburn, *Crossing the Border*, 22. Hepburn cites an 1854 episode in which black hotel waiters went on strike to protest the hotels' discriminatory practice of disallowing black riders from riding on their coaches. In this case, the work stoppage was successful, and

offers insight into how black emigrants might use their labor (or lack of it) to demand more equitable treatment.

17. See, for example, the testimony of James W. Hall (wagon and carriage builder), John Shipton, and Andrew Smith (blacksmith), AFIC Upper Canada Reports (NARA).

18. Howe, *The Refugees from Slavery in Canada West*, 45.

19. Ibid., 46.

20. Ibid., 45.

21. See, for example, the testimony of J. H. Bland and Washington Thomas, AFIC Upper Canada Reports (NARA).

22. Based on estimates of Canada's black population in the 1850s in comparison with census data from 1871, historians have long believed that a significant majority of Canada's black population returned to the United States after the Civil War. Offering a possible corrective, historian Michael Wayne suggests that a strict comparison between the censuses of 1861 and 1871 suggest that no such exodus took place. In either case, however, it is clear that a noticeable number did make a return migration to the United States, and it was clearly due to the changes effected by the Civil War. See Winks, *The Blacks in Canada*, 234; Silverman, *Unwelcome Guests*, 161; Michael Wayne, "The Black Population of Canada West on the Eve of the American Civil War: A Reassessment Based on the Manuscript Census of 1861," *Social History/Histoire Sociale* 28, no 56 (1995): 470–471.

23. Howe, *The Refugees from Slavery in Canada West*, 103, 104.

24. Sproat, "Blueprint for Radical Reconstruction," 39–40.

25. "Jamaica Royal Commission Report," *Parliamentary Papers*, 1866, xxx [C.3683], 14, quoted in Philip D. Curtin, *Two Jamaicas: The Role of Ideas in a Tropical Colony, 1830–1865* (Cambridge, MA: Harvard University Press, 1955), 197.

26. Rugemer, *The Problem of Emancipation*, 291–293; Nichola Clayton, "Managing the Transition to a Free Labor Society: American Interpretations of the British West Indies during the Civil War and Reconstruction," *American Nineteenth Century History* 7, no. 1 (March 2006): 89–90.

27. Clayton, "Managing the Transition to a Free Labor Society."

28. Although the sugar economies of several West Indian islands had recovered from their precipitous decline in the immediate aftermath of emancipation, Jamaica was still only exporting 38 percent of its pre-abolition levels by 1865. Clayton, "Managing the Transition to a Free Labor Society," 91.

29. "Refuge of Oppression: The British West India Negro System," *The Liberator* (Boston, MA), April 25, 1856, Slavery and Anti-Slavery: A Transnational Archive.

30. Clayton, "Managing the Transition to a Free Labor Society," 92; Chandra Manning, *What This Cruel War was Over: Soldiers, Slavery, and the Civil War* (New York: Random House, 2007).

31. Rugemer, *The Problem of Emancipation*, 294–300; Clayton, "Managing the Transition to a Free Labor Society," 89–90, 94–95.

32. Eric Foner, *Nothing But Freedom: Emancipation and Its Legacy* (Baton Rouge: Louisiana State University Press, 2007), 39–73; Eric Foner, *Reconstruction: America's Unfinished Revolution, 1863–1877* (New York: Harper & Row, 1988).

33. Steven Hahn, *A Nation Under Our Feet: Black Political Struggles in the Rural South from Slavery to the Great Migration* (Cambridge, MA: Belknap Press, 2005), 320–321, 328–331, 337.

34. A. B. Coleman to William Coppinger, 13 April 1880, 1 Apr.–30 June 1880, MS American Colonization Society: A Register of its Records in the Library of Congress, I. Incoming Correspondence, 1819–1917; A. Domestic Letters, 1823–1912 (Library of Congress), Slavery and Anti-Slavery: A Transnational Archive.

35. Hahn, *A Nation Under Our Feet*, 355.

APPENDIX

1. Wigmore, "Before the Railroad," 438–439.

2. Staudenraus, *The African Colonization Movement*, 11.

3. Cornell, "Citizens of Nowhere," 356–357; Kelley, "Mexico in His Head," 714–716.

4. Power-Greene, *Against Wind and Tide*, 97–102.

5. Fanning, *Caribbean Crossing*, 17.

6. Drew, *A North-Side View of Slavery*, 246; "African Colony in Canada," *Genius of Universal Emancipation* (Baltimore, MD), February 5, 1830, American Periodicals Series II.

7. Bell, "Minutes and Proceedings of the First Annual Convention of the People of Colour (1831)," 12–13; Winks, *The Blacks in Canada*, 156.

8. "An Asylum for the Oppressed," *The Colored American* (New York), March 29, 1838, Slavery and Anti-Slavery: A Transnational Archive; "British and Foreign Anti-Slavery Convention," *The Philanthropist* (Cincinnati, OH), August 25, 1840, Slavery and Anti-Slavery: A Transnational Archive.

9. Royal Commission on Fugitive Slaves (Great Britain), *Report of the Commissioners*, 230–231; Hendrick and Hendrick, *The Creole Mutiny*, 77–120.

10. "Return of Immigrants," "Journals of the Council, Dec. 1840–Feb. 1844," National Archives of Jamaica, Spanish Town, JA, 1B/5/4; Higman, "Jamaican Census of 1844," 5.

11. Winks, *The Blacks in Canada*, 486; "Colored Population of Canada, according to the Census of 1847," *African Repository and Colonial Journal* (Washington, DC), January 1849, American Periodicals Series II; "Colored Voters," *The Liberator* (Boston, MA), September 20, 1844, Slavery and Anti-Slavery: A Transnational Archive; "Communications. For the Liberty Standard. Canada Mission," *Liberty Standard* (Hallowell, ME), Slavery and Anti-Slavery: A Transnational Archive.

12. Winsboro and Knetsch, "Florida Slaves, the 'Saltwater Railroad' to the Bahamas, and Anglo-American Diplomacy," 52–53.

13. Power-Greene, *Against Wind and Tide*, 97–102.

14. Audain, "Mexican Canaan," 127; Nichols, *The Limits of Liberty*, 127.

15. "Fugitive Slaves in Canada," *The Anti-Slavery Reporter* (London), January 1, 1851, Slavery and Anti-Slavery: A Transnational Archive; Shadd, *A Plea for Emigration* (2016), 48; Drew, *A North-Side View of Slavery*, v; Ward, *Autobiography of a Fugitive Negro*, 154; *The*

Fugitive Slaves in Canada, Wilson Anti-Slavery Collection (London: Seeley, Jackson & Halliday, 1858), 6.

16. Kenny, "Manliness and Manifest Racial Destiny," 168.

17. Mitchell, *Raising Freedom's Child*, 12–13, 29–30.

18. Dixon, *African America and Haiti*, 129.

19. Winks, *The Blacks in Canada*, 486; Wayne, "The Black Population of Canada West on the Eve of the American Civil War," 470–471.

20. Hahn, *A Nation Under Our Feet*, 355.

Bibliography

ARCHIVE COLLECTIONS

BOSTON

Houghton Library, Harvard University
  American Freedmen's Inquiry Commission Records
Boston Public Library Special Collections
  Anti-Slavery Collection

JAMAICA

National Archives of Jamaica
  Journals of the Council

ONTARIO

Toronto Public Library Special Collections
  Anderson Ruffin Abbott Collection
  Robert Baldwin Correspondence Papers
Archives Ontario
  Ontario Department of Education Incoming General Correspondence
City of Toronto Archives
  Toronto City Council Communications from the 19th Century

WASHINGTON, DC

National Archives of the United States
  U.S. Department of War. Letters Received by the Office of the Adjutant
  General

DIGITIZED COLLECTIONS

American Colonization Society. Incoming Correspondence, 1819–1917, Library of Congress, Washington, DC, *Slavery and Anti-Slavery: A Transnational Archive.* Gale, Georgetown University.

American Missionary Association. Archives, 1839–1882, Amistad Research Center, Tulane University, New Orleans, LA. *Slavery and Anti-Slavery: A Transnational Archive.* Gale, Georgetown University.

Black Abolitionist Archive. University of Detroit Mercy, Detroit, MI, available at: https://libraries.udmercy.edu/find/special_collections/digital/baa.

Boston Public Library Anti-Slavery Collection, Boston, MA, available at: https://archive.org/details/bplscas.

Colored Conventions Project. University of Delaware, Wilmington, DE, available at: http://coloredconventions.org.

Frederick Douglass Project. University of Rochester, Department of Rare Books and Special Collections, Rochester, NY, available at: https://rbscp.lib.rochester.edu/2494.

James Birney Collection of Anti-Slavery Pamphlets, Johns Hopkins University, Baltimore, MD, available at: https://archive.org/details/birney.

Letters of Hiram Wilson. Huron University College, Hiram Wilson Project, London, Ontario, Canada, available at: https://hiramwilson.wordpress.com.

North American Slave Narratives. *Documenting the American South,* University of North Carolina, Chapel Hill, NC, available at: http://docsouth.unc.edu/neh.

Oberlin College Anti-Slavery Library. Oberlin College, Oberlin, OH, available at: https://archive.org/details/antislavery.

Samuel J. May Anti-Slavery Collection. Cornell University Library, Division of Rare and Manuscript Collections, Ithaca, NY, available at: http://ebooks.library.cornell.edu/m/mayantislavery.

DIGITAL DATABASES

19th-Century U.S. Newspapers. Gale Digital Collections, available at: https://www.gale.com/c/19th-century-us-newspapers.

Accessible Archives, Inc. Malvern, PA, available at: http://www.accessible-archives.com.

America's Historical Newspapers. Readex: A Division of Newsbank, available at: http://www.readex.com/content/americas-historical-newspapers.

American Periodicals Series Online. Proquest, available at http://www.proquest.com/products-services/aps.html.

Hathi Trust Digital Library, available at: https://www.hathitrust.org.

Minnesota Population Center. National Historical Geographic Information System, Version 11.0 (database), University of Minnesota, Minneapolis, 2016, available at: http://doi.org/10.18128/D050.V11.0.

ProQuest Civil War Era. ProQuest, available at: https://www.proquest.com/products-services/cwe.html.

Slavery and Anti-Slavery: A Transnational Archive. Gale, Georgetown University, available at: http://www.gale.com/primary-sources/slavery-and-anti-slavery.

PRINTED PRIMARY SOURCES

NEWSPAPERS AND PERIODICALS

Advocate of Freedom (Brunswick, ME)
African Repository and Colonial Journal (Washington, DC)
American Anti-slavery Reporter (New York)
American and Foreign Anti-Slavery Reporter, The (New York)
Annals of Congress (Washington, DC)
Anti-Slavery Examiner, The (New York)
Anti-Slavery Record, The (London, UK)
Anti-Slavery Reporter, The (London, UK)
Banner of the Constitution, The (Washington, DC)
Barre Patriot (Barre, MA)
Boston Recorder (Boston, MA)
British and Foreign Anti-Slavery Reporter, The (London, UK)
Christian Register, The (Boston, MA)
Colored American, The (New York)
Congressional Globe (Washington, DC)
Connecticut Courant (Hartford, CT)
Daily Cincinnati Gazette, The (Cincinnati, OH)
Daily National Intelligencer (Washington, DC)
Daily Picayune, The (New Orleans, LA)
Dial, The: A Monthly Magazine for Literature, Philosophy and Religion (Cincinnati, OH)
Douglass' Monthly (Rochester, NY)
Eastern Argus (Portland, ME)
Emancipator, The (New York)
Farmer's Cabinet, The (Amherst, NH)
Frederick Douglass' Paper (Rochester, NY)
Freedom's Journal (New York)
Friend, The (Philadelphia, PA)
Friend of Man, The (Utica, NY)
Genius of Universal Emancipation (Greensboro, TN and Baltimore, MD)
Globe, The (Washington, DC)
Haverhill Gazette and Patriot (Haverhill, MA)
Liberator, The (Boston, MA)
Liberty Standard (Hallowell, ME)
Mercury, The (Charleston, SC)
Morning Courier and New-York Enquirer (New York)
National Anti-Slavery Standard (New York)
National Era, The (Washington, DC)
New-Bedford Mercury (New Bedford, MA)
New England Spectator (Boston, MA)
New Hampshire Patriot and State Gazette (Concord, NH)
New Hampshire Sentinel (Keene, NH)

New York Evangelist (New York)
New York Observer and Chronicle (New York)
Newport Mercury (Newport, RI)
Niles' Weekly Register (Baltimore, MD)
North Star, The (Rochester, NY)
Norwich Courier (Norwich, CT)
Philanthropist, The (Cincinnati, OH)
Pittsfield Sun (Pittsfield, MA)
Portsmouth Journal of Literature and Politics (Portsmouth, NH)
Provincial Freeman (Toronto, Canada West)
Reformer, The (Washington, DC)
Religious Intelligencer, The (New Haven, CT)
Richmond Enquirer (Richmond, VA)
Rights of All (New York)
Salem Gazette (Salem, MA)
Vincennes Weekly Western Sun, The (Vincennes, IN)
Weekly Intelligencer (Philadelphia, PA)
Zion's Herald (Boston, MA)
Zion's Watchman (New York)

BOOKS AND PAMPHLETS

American Anti-Slavery Almanac for 1839, The. New York and Boston, MA: S. W. Benedict and Isaac Knapp for the American Anti-Slavery Society, 1839.
American Anti-Slavery Society. *Fourth Annual Report of the American Anti-Slavery Society, with the Speeches Delivered at the Anniversary Meeting Held in the City of New York on the 9th May, 1837.* New York: William S. Dorr, 1837.
American Anti-Slavery Society. *The Legion of Liberty! And Force of Truth, Containing the thoughts, word, and deed, of some prominent Apostles, Champions and Martyrs.* 2nd ed. New York, 1843.
American Convention for Promoting the Abolition of Slavery and Improving the Condition of the African Race. *Minutes of the proceedings of the Fifteenth American Convention for Promoting the Abolition of Slavery and Improving the Condition of the African Race, Assembled at Philadelphia, on the fifth day of August, 1817, and continued by adjournments until the eighth of the same month, inclusive.* Philadelphia: Merritt, 1817.
American Convention for Promoting the Abolition of Slavery and Improving the Condition of the African Race. *Minutes of the proceedings of a special meeting of the fifteenth American Convention for Promoting the Abolition of Slavery and Improving the Condition of the African Race, Assembled at Philadelphia, on the tenth day of December, 1818, and continued by adjournments until the fifteenth of the same month, inclusive.* Philadelphia: Hall & Atkinson, 1818.
Anderson, Osborne P. *A Voice from Harper's Ferry: A Narrative of Events at Harper's Ferry; with Incidents Prior and Subsequent to Its Capture by Captain Brown and His Men.* Boston, MA, 1861.

Anderson, William. *Life and Narrative of William J. Anderson, Twenty-Four Years a Slave; Sold Eight Times! In Jail Sixty Times!! Whipped Three Hundred Times!!! Or The Dark Deeds of American Slavery Revealed. Containing Scriptural Views of the Origin of the Black and of the White Man. Also, a Simple and Easy Plan to Abolish Slavery in the United States. Together with an Account of the Services of Colored Men in the Revolutionary War – Day and Date, and Interesting Facts.* Chicago, IL: Daily Tribune, 1857.

Bibb, Henry. *Narrative of the Life and Adventures of Henry Bibb, an American Slave, Written by Himself.* New York: The Author, 1849.

Birney, William. *James G. Birney and His Times: The Genesis of the Republican Party with Some Account of Abolition Movements in the South before 1828.* New York: D. Appleton and Co., 1890.

Bleby, Henry. "Speech of Rev. Henry Bleby, Missionary from Barbadoes, on the Results of Emancipation in the British W. I. Colonies, Delivered at the Celebration of the Massachusetts Anti-Slavery Society, Held at Island Grove, Abington, July 31st, 1858." R. F. Wallcut, 1858.

Brown, Isaac V. *Memoirs of the Rev. Robert Finley, D.D.* New Brunswick, NJ: Terhune & Letson, 1819.

Brown, William Wells. *Narrative of William W. Brown, A Fugitive Slave. Written by Himself.* Boston, MA: The Anti-Slavery Office, 1847.

Brown, William Wells. *The Anti-Slavery Harp: A Collection of Songs for Anti-Slavery Meetings.* Boston, MA: Bela Marsh, 1848.

Brown, William Wells. *Narrative of William W. Brown, A Fugitive Slave. Written by Himself.* 4th ed. London: Charles Gilpin, 1849.

Brown, William Wells. *The Escape, Or, A Leap for Freedom: A Drama in Five Acts (1858).* Knoxville: University of Tennessee Press, 2001.

Channing, William Ellery. *The Duty of the Free States, or, Remarks Suggested by the Case of the Creole, First Part.* Boston, MA: William Crosby, 1842.

Child, Lydia Maria. *The Right Way the Safe Way, as Proved by Emancipation in the British West Indies.* New York, 1862.

Clarke, Lewis. *Narrative of the Sufferings of Lewis Clarke, During a Captivity of More than Twenty-Five Years, among the Algerines of Kentucky, One of the So Called Christian States of North America. Dictated by Himself.* Boston, MA: David H. Ela, Printer, 1845.

Craft, William. *Running a Thousand Miles for Freedom: The Escape of William and Ellen Craft.* Edited by R. J. M. Blackett. Baton Rouge: Louisiana State University Press, 1999.

Crallé, Richard K., ed. *Reports and Public Letters of John C. Calhoun.* New York: D. Appleton and Company, 1883.

Delany, Martin R. *The Condition, Elevation, Emigration, and Destiny of the Colored People of the United States. Politically Considered.* Philadelphia, PA: Martin Robison Delany, 1852.

Dewey, Loring D. *Correspondence Relative to the Emigration to Hayti, of the Free People of Colour, in the United States. Together with the Instructions to the Agent Sent Out by President Boyer.* New York: Mahlon Day, 1824.

Drew, Benjamin. *A North-Side View of Slavery. The Refugee: Or The Narratives of Fugitive Slaves in Canada. Related by Themselves, with an Account of the History and Condition of the Colored Population of Upper Canada.* Boston, MA: J. P. Jewett, 1856.

Earle, Thomas. *The Life, Travels and Opinions of Benjamin Lundy: Including His Journeys to Texas and Mexico; with a Sketch of Contemporary Events, and a Notice of the Revolution in Hayti.* Philadelphia, PA: William D. Parrisi, 1847.

Exposition of the Object and Plans of the American Union for the Relief and Improvement of the Colored Race. Boston, MA, 1835.

Forten, James and Russell Perrott. "Address to the humane and benevolent Inhabitants of the city and county of Philadelphia" (1817). In *Minutes of the proceedings of a special meeting of the fifteenth American Convention for Promoting the Abolition of Slavery and Improving the Condition of the African Race, Assembled at Philadelphia, on the tenth day of December, 1818, and continued by adjournments until the fifteenth of the same month, inclusive,* i–iv. Philadelphia, PA: Hall & Atkinson, 1818.

Giddings, Joshua R. *The Rights of the Free States Subverted, or, An Enumeration of Some of the Most Prominent Instances in Which the Federal Constitution Has Been Violated by Our National Government, for the Benefit of Slavery.* [Washington, DC?], 1844.

Green, William. *Narrative of Events in the Life of William Green, (Formerly a Slave.) Written by Himself.* Springfield, MA: L. M. Guernsey, 1853.

Gurney, Joseph John. *Familiar Letters to Henry Clay of Kentucky, Describing a Winter in the West Indies.* New York: Mahlon Day & Co., 1840.

Henson, Josiah. *The Life of Josiah Henson, Formerly a Slave, Now an Inhabitant of Canada, As Narrated by Himself.* Edited by Samuel A. Eliot. Boston, MA: A. D. Phelps, 1849.

Henson, Josiah. *Truth Is Stranger than Fiction. Father Henson's Story of His Own Life.* Edited by Samuel A. Eliot. Boston, MA: J. P. Jewett, 1858.

Holly, James Theodore. *A Vindication of the Capacity of the Negro for Self-Government and Civilized Progress, as Demonstrated by Historical Events of the Haytian Revolution; and the Subsequent Acts of That People since Their National Independence.* New Haven, CT: Afric-American Printing Co., 1857.

Holly, James Theodore, C. Freeman, and Lewis Clark. "Report on Emigration." n *Minutes and Proceedings of the General Convention for the Improvement of the Colored Inhabitants of Canada, Held by Adjournments in Amhrstburgh [Sic], C.W., June 16th and 17th, 1853,* 11–16. Windsor, Canada West: Bibb & Holly, 1853.

Hovey, Sylvester. *Letters from the West Indies. Relating Especially to the Danish Island St. Croix, and to the British Islands Antigua, Barbados, and Jamaica.* New York: Gould & Newman, 1838.

Howe, Samuel Gridley. *The Refugees from Slavery in Canada West: Report to the Freedmen's Inquiry Commission.* Boston, MA: Wright & Potter, 1864.

Jay, William. *An Inquiry into the Character and Tendency of the American Colonization, and American Anti-Slavery Societies.* New York: Leavitt, Lord, 1835.

Jay, William. *A View of the Action of the Federal Government in Behalf of Slavery.* New York: J. C. Jackson for the American Anti-Slavery Society, 1844.

Lundy, Benjamin. *The life, travels, and opinions of Benjamin Lundy: including his journeys to Texas and Mexico, with a sketch of contemporary events, and a notice of the revolution in Hayti.* Philadelphia, PA: William D. Parrish, 1847.

Malvin, John. *Autobiography of John Malvin: A Narrative, Containing an Authentic Account of His Fifty Years' Struggle in the State of Ohio in Behalf of the American Slave and the Equal Rights of All Men Before the Law Without Reference to Race or Color; Forty-*

Seven Years of Said Time Being Expended in the City of Cleveland. Cleveland, OH: Leader Printing Co., 1879.

Martineau, Harriet. *The Martyr Age of the United States.* Boston, MA: Weeks, Jordan & co., 1839.

Moody, Loring. *Facts for the People: Showing the Relations of the United States Government to Slavery, Embracing a History of the Mexican War, Its Origin and Objects.* Boston, MA: Dow and Jackson's Anti-Slavery Press, 1847.

New York City Anti-Slavery Society. *Address of the New-York City Anti-Slavery Society, to the People of the City of New-York.* New York: West & Trow, 1833.

Phillippo, James M. *Jamaica: Its Past and Present State.* London: John Snow, 1843.

Prince, Nancy. *The West Indies: Being a Description of the Islands, Progress of Christianity, Education, and Liberty among the Colored Population Generally.* Boston, MA: Dow & Jackson, 1841.

Report of the Select Committee on Emancipation and Colonization, with an Appendix (House of Representatives, 37th Congress, 2nd Session). Washington, DC: Government Printing Office, 1862.

Royal Commission on Fugitive Slaves (Great Britain). *Report of the Commissioners, Minutes of the Evidence, and Appendix, with General Index of Minutes of Evidence and Appendix.* George Edward Eyre and William Spottiswoode, 1876.

Saunders, Prince. *Haytian Papers: A Collection of the Very Interesting Proclamations and Other Official Documents: Together with Some Account of the Rise, Progress, and Present State of the Kingdom of Hayti.* London: W. Reed, law bookseller, 1816.

Saunders, Prince. *A Memoir Presented to the American Convention for Promoting the Abolition of Slavery, and Improving the Condition of the African Race, December 11th, 1818.* Philadelphia: Dennis Heartt, 1818.

Shadd, Mary Ann. *A Plea for Emigration; or, Notes of Canada West, in Its Moral, Social, and Political Aspect: With Suggestions Respecting Mexico, West Indies, and Vancouver Island.* Detroit, MI: George W. Pattison, 1852.

Shadd, Mary Ann. *A Plea for Emigration; or Notes of Canada West.* Edited by Phanuel Antwi. Peterborough, Ontario: Broadview Press, 2016.

Smallwood, Thomas. *A Narrative of Thomas Smallwood, Coloured Man: Giving an Account of His Birth – The Period He Was Held in Slavery – His Release – And Removal to Canada, Etc. Together with an Account of the Underground Railroad. Written by Himself.* Toronto: The Author, 1851.

Steward, Austin. *Twenty-Two Years a Slave and Forty Years a Freeman; Embracing a Correspondence of Several Years, While President of Wilberforce Colony, London, Canada West.* Rochester, NY: W. Alling, 1857.

Still, William. *The Underground Railroad: A Record of Facts, Authentic Narrative, Letters, &c., Narrating the Hardships, Hair-Breadth Escapes and Death Struggles of the Slaves in Their Efforts of Freedom, as Related by Themselves and Others, or Witnessed by the Author; Together with Sketches of Some of the Largest Stockholders, and Most Liberal Aiders and Advisers, of the Road.* Philadelphia, PA: Porter & Coates, 1872.

Stowe, Harriet Beecher. *Uncle Tom's Cabin, or, Life Among the Lowly.* Boston, MA: J. P. Jewett, 1852.

Stowe, Harriet Beecher. *A Key to Uncle Tom's Cabin; Presenting the Original Facts and Documents Upon Which the Story is Founded. Together with Corroborative Statements Verifying the Truth of the Work.* Boston, MA: J. P. Jewett, 1853.

Stuart, Charles. *Remarks on the Colony of Liberia and the American Colonization Society, with some account of the settlement of Colored People at Wilberforce, Upper Canada, by C. Stuart.* London: J. Messeder, 1832.

Sturge, Joseph and Thomas Harvey. *The West Indies in 1837; Being a Journal of a Visit to Antigua, Montserrat, Dominica, St. Lucia, Barbadoes, and Jamaica; Undertaken for the Purpose of Ascertaining the Actual Condition of the Negro Population of Those Islands.* 2nd ed. London: Hamilton, Adams, 1838.

Taney, Chief Justice, Roger. *The Case of Dred Scott in the United States Supreme Court with the Full Opinions of Chief Justice Taney and Justice Curtis, and the Abstracts of the Opinions of the Other Judges.* New York: Horace Greeley, 1860.

The Legion of Liberty: Remonstrance of Some Free Men, States, and Presses, to the Texas Rebellion, Against the Laws of Nature and of Nations. Albany, NY, 1843.

The Fugitive Slaves in Canada. London: Seeley, Jackson & Halliday, 1858.

Thome, James A. and Joseph Horace Kimball. *Emancipation in the West Indies: A Six Months' Tour in Antigua, Barbadoes, and Jamaica in the Year 1837.* New York: American Anti-Slavery Society, 1838.

Thome, James A. and Joseph Horace Kimball. "Emancipation in the West Indies: A Six Months' Tour in Antigua, Barbadoes, and Jamaica in the Year 1837" (Pamphlet). *The Anti-Slavery Examiner,* 1838.

Townsend, Hannah. *The Anti-Slavery Alphabet.* Philadelphia, PA: Merrihew & Thompson, 1846.

Two Hundred Coloured Persons. "A Petition, Discovered by the Honourable William Renwick Riddell, Justice of Appeal, Ontario, Canada (June 18, 1828)." *Journal of Negro History* 15, no. 1 (January 1930): 115–116.

Walker, David. *Walker's Appeal, in Four Articles; Together with a Preamble, to the Colored Citizens of the World, but in Particular, and Very Expressly, to Those of the United States of America.* Boston, MA, 1829.

Ward, Samuel Ringgold. *Autobiography of a Fugitive Negro: His Anti-Slavery Labours in the United States, Canada and England.* London: John Snow, 1855.

Watkins, James. *Narrative of the Life of James Watkins, Formerly a "Chattel" in Maryland, U.S. Containing an Account of His Escape from Slavery, Together with an Appeal on Behalf of Three Millions of Such "Pieces of Property," Still Held Under the Standard of the Eagle.* Bolton: Kenyon & Abbatt, 1852.

EDITED DOCUMENT COLLECTIONS

Bell, Howard Holman, ed. *Minutes of the Proceedings of the National Negro Conventions, 1830–1864.* The American Negro: His History and Literature. New York: Arno Press, 1969.

Blassingame, John W., ed. *Slave Testimony: Two Centuries of Letters, Speeches, Interviews, and Autobiographies.* Baton Rouge: Louisiana State University Press, 1977.

Davis, Rodney O. and Douglas L. Wilson, eds. *The Lincoln–Douglas Debates.* Urbana: Knox College Lincoln Studies Center and the University of Illinois Press, 2008.

Levine, Robert S., ed. *Martin R. Delany: A Documentary Reader.* Chapel Hill: University of North Carolina Press, 2003.

Mallory, Daniel, ed. *The Life and Speeches of the Hon. Henry Clay, in Two Volumes.* Vol. 2. 2nd ed. New York: R. P. Bixby, 1843.

McCarthy, Timothy Patrick and John Stauffer, eds. *Pamphlets of Protest: Reconsidering the History of American Abolitionism.* New York: New Press, 2006.

Ripley, C. Peter, ed. *The Black Abolitionist Papers.* Vol. 2, *Canada, 1830–1865.* Chapel Hill: University of North Carolina Press, 1985.

Ripley, C. Peter, ed. *The Black Abolitionist Papers.* Vol. 4, *The United States, 1847–1858.* Chapel Hill: University of North Carolina Press, 1985.

Wiggins, Rosalind Cobb. *Captain Paul Cuffe's Logs and Letters, 1808–1817: A Black Quaker's "Voice from Within the Veil."* Washington, DC: Howard University Press, 1996.

Wilson, Clyde Norman, ed. *The Papers of John C. Calhoun.* Vol. 13. Columbia: University of South Carolina Press, 1959.

SECONDARY SOURCES

Adderley, Rosanne Marion. *"New Negroes from Africa": Slave Trade Abolition and Free African Settlement in the Nineteenth-Century Caribbean.* Bloomington, IN: Indiana University Press, 2006.

Adeleke, Tunde. *Without Regard to Race: The Other Martin Robison Delany.* Jackson: University Press of Mississippi, 2003.

Adler, Judith. "Travel as Performed Art." *American Journal of Sociology* 94, no. 6 (1989): 1366–1391.

Andrews, William L. *To Tell a Free Story: The First Century of Afro-American Autobiography, 1760–1865.* Urbana: University of Illinois Press, 1986.

Appadurai, Arjun. *Fear of Small Numbers: An Essay on the Geography of Anger.* Durham, NC: Duke University Press, 2006.

Audain, Mekala. "Mexican Canaan: Fugitive Slaves and Free Blacks on the American Frontier, 1804–1867." PhD diss., Rutgers, 2014.

Audain, Mekala. "'Design His Course to Mexico': The Fugitive Slave Experience in the Texas–Mexico Borderlands, 1850–1853." In *Fugitive Slaves and Spaces of Freedom in North America*, edited by Damian Alan Pargas, 232–250. Gainesville: University of Florida Press, 2018.

Bacon, Jacqueline. *Freedom's Journal: The First African-American Newspaper.* Lanham, MD: Lexington Books, 2007.

Ball, Erica. *To Live an Antislavery Life: Personal Politics and the Antebellum Black Middle Class.* Athens, GA: University of Georgia Press, 2012.

Baptist, Edward E. *The Half Has Never Been Told: Slavery and the Making of American Capitalism.* New York: Basic Books, 2016.

Baumgartner, Alice. *South to Freedom: Runaway Slaves to Mexico and the Road to the Civil War.* New York: Basic Books, 2020.

Bell, Richard. *Stolen: Five Free Boys Kidnapped into Slavery and Their Astonishing Odyssey Home.* New York: Simon & Schuster, 2019.

Bernier, Celeste-Marie. "From Fugitive Slave to Fugitive Abolitionist." *Atlantic Studies* 3, no. 2 (October 2006): 201–224.

Bethel, Elizabeth Rauh. "Images of Hayti: The Construction of an Afro-American Lieu De Mémoire." *Callaloo* 15, no. 3 (July 1992): 827–841.

Blackett, R. J. M. *Building an Antislavery Wall: Black Americans in the Atlantic Abolitionist Movement, 1830–1860.* Baton Rouge: Louisiana State University Press, 1983.

Blackett, R. J. M. *Making Freedom: The Underground Railroad and the Politics of Slavery.* Chapel Hill: University of North Carolina Press, 2013.

Blackett, R. J. M. *The Captive's Quest for Freedom: Fugitive Slaves, the 1850 Fugitive Slave Law, and the Politics of Slavery.* New York: Cambridge University Press, 2018.

Blight, David, ed. *Passages to Freedom: The Underground Railroad in History and Memory.* Washington, DC: Harper, 2006.

Bolland, O. Nigel. "The Politics of Freedom in the British Caribbean." In *The Meaning of Freedom: Economics, Politics, and Culture after Slavery,* edited by Frank McGlynn and Seymour Drescher, 113–146. Pittsburgh, PA: University of Pittsburgh Press, 1992.

Bordewich, Fergus M. *Bound for Canaan: The Underground Railroad and the War for the Soul of America.* New York: Amistad, 2005.

Bordewich, Fergus M. *America's Great Debate: Henry Clay, Stephen A. Douglas, and the Compromise that Preserved the Union.* New York: Simon & Schuster, 2013.

Brown, Christopher Leslie. *Moral Capital: Foundations of British Abolitionism.* Chapel Hill: University of North Carolina Press, 2006.

Browning, Andrew H. *The Panic of 1819: The First Great Depression.* Columbia, MO: University of Missouri Press, 2019.

Buchanan, Thomas C. *Black Life on the Mississippi: Slaves, Free Blacks, and the Western Steamboat World.* Chapel Hill: University of North Carolina Press, 2004.

Burin, Eric. *Slavery and the Peculiar Solution: A History of the American Colonization Society.* Gainesville: University Press of Florida, 2008.

Burrowes, Carl Patrick. "Black Christian Republicanism: A Southern Ideology in Early Liberia, 1822 to 1847." *Journal of Negro History* 86, no. 1 (2001): 30–44.

Byrd, Alexander X. *Captives and Voyagers: Black Migrants Across the Eighteenth-Century British Atlantic World.* Baton Rouge: Louisiana State University Press, 2008.

Calloway-Thomas, Carolyn. "Mary Ann Shadd Cary: Crafting Black Culture Through Empirical and Moral Arguments." *Howard Journal of Communications* 24, no. 3 (July 2013): 239–256.

Campbell, Lyndsay. "The Northern Borderlands: Canada West." In *Freedom's Conditions in the U.S.–Canadian Borderlands in the Age of Emancipation,* edited by Tony Freyer and Lyndsay Campbell, 196–226. Durham, NC: Carolina Academic Press, 2011.

Campbell, Randolph B. *An Empire for Slavery: The Peculiar Institution in Texas, 1821–1865.* Baton Rouge: Louisiana State University Press, 1991.

Campbell, Stanley W. *The Slave Catchers: Enforcement of the Fugitive Slave Law, 1850–1860.* Chapel Hill: University of North Carolina Press, 1970.

Claybaugh, Amanda. *The Novel of Purpose: Literature and Social Reform in the Anglo-American World.* Ithaca, NY: Cornell University Press, 2007.

Clayton, Nichola. "Managing the Transition to a Free Labor Society: American Interpretations of the British West Indies during the Civil War and Reconstruction." *American Nineteenth Century History* 7, no. 1 (March 2006): 89–108.

Clegg, Claude Andrew. *The Price of Liberty: African Americans and the Making of Liberia.* Chapel Hill: University of North Carolina Press, 2004.

Cohen, Lara Langer and Jordan Alexander Stein, eds. *Early African American Print Culture*. Philadelphia: University of Pennsylvania Press, 2012.

Collison, Gary L. *Shadrach Minkins: From Fugitive Slave to Citizen*. Cambridge, MA: Harvard University Press, 1998.

Cooper, Afua. "The Voice of the Fugitive: A Transnational Abolitionist Organ." In *A Fluid Frontier: Slavery, Resistance, and the Underground Railroad in the Detroit River Borderland*, edited by Karolyn Smardz Frost and Veta Smith Tucker, 135–153. Detroit, MI: Wayne State University Press, 2016.

Cordell, Ryan. "Reprinting, Circulation, and the Network Author in Antebellum Newspapers." *American Literary History* 27, no. 3 (September 2015): 417–445.

Cornell, Sarah E. "Citizens of Nowhere: Fugitive Slaves and Free African Americans in Mexico, 1833–1857." *Journal of American History* 100, no. 2 (September 2013): 351–374.

Curtin, Philip D. *Two Jamaicas: The Role of Ideas in a Tropical Colony, 1830–1865*. Cambridge, MA: Harvard University Press, 1955.

Curtis, Bruce. "Preconditions of the Canadian State: Educational Reform and the Construction of a Public in Upper Canada, 1837–1846." In *Historical Essays on Upper Canada: New Perspectives*, edited by J. K. Johnson and Bruce G. Wilson, 341–368. Ottawa: Carleton University Press, 1989.

Davis, David Brion. *The Problem of Slavery in the Age of Emancipation*. New York: Knopf, 2014.

DeBoer, Clara Merritt. *Be Jubilant My Feet: African American Abolitionists in the American Missionary Association, 1839–1861*. New York: Garland, 1994.

Delbanco, Andrew. *The Abolitionist Imagination*. Cambridge, MA: Harvard University Press, 2012.

DeLombard, Jeannine Marie. *Slavery on Trial: Law, Abolitionism, and Print Culture*. Chapel Hill: University of North Carolina Press, 2007.

Deyle, Steven. *Carry Me Back: The Domestic Slave Trade in American Life*. Oxford: Oxford University Press, 2005.

Diemer, Andrew. *The Politics of Black Citizenship: Free African Americans in the Mid-Atlantic Borderland, 1817–1863*. Athens, GA: University of Georgia Press, 2016.

Dillon, Merton L. *Benjamin Lundy and the Struggle for Negro Freedom*. Urbana: University of Illinois Press, 1966.

Dixon, Chris. *African America and Haiti: Emigration and Black Nationalism in the Nineteenth Century*. Westport, CT: Greenwood Press, 2000.

Downey, Arthur T. *The Creole Affair: The Slave Rebellion that Led the U.S. and Great Britain to the Brink of War*. Lanham, MD: Rowman & Littlefield, 2014.

Drescher, Seymour. *The Mighty Experiment: Free Labor versus Slavery in British Emancipation*. Oxford: Oxford University Press, 2002.

Drescher, Seymour. *Abolition: A History of Slavery and Antislavery*. Cambridge: Cambridge University Press, 2009.

Earle, Jonathan Halperin. *Jacksonian Antislavery and the Politics of Free Soil, 1824–1854*. Chapel Hill: University of North Carolina Press, 2004.

Everill, Bronwen. *Abolition and Empire in Sierra Leone and Liberia*. Basingstoke: Palgrave Macmillan, 2012.

Fagan, Benjamin. *The Black Newspaper and the Chosen Nation*. Athens, GA: University of Georgia Press, 2018.

Falola, Toyin. Introduction to *The Condition, Elevation, Emigration, and Destiny of the Colored People of the United States and Official Report of the Niger Valley Exploring Party*, by Martin Delany, 7–25. Amherst, NY: Humanity Books, 2004.

Fanning, Sara C. "The Roots of Early Black Nationalism: Northern African Americans' Invocations of Haiti in the Early Nineteenth Century." *Slavery & Abolition* 28, no. 1 (April 2007): 61–85.

Fanning, Sara C. *Caribbean Crossing: African Americans and the Haitian Emigration Movement*. New York: New York University Press, 2015.

Faulkner, Carol. "The Root of the Evil: Free Produce and Radical Antislavery, 1820–1860." *Journal of the Early Republic* 27, no. 3 (2007): 377–405.

Faust, Drew Gilpin. "A Southern Stewardship: The Intellectual and the Proslavery Argument." In *Proslavery Thought, Ideology, and Politics*, edited by Paul Finkelman, 129–146. New York: Garland, 1989.

Fehrenbacher, Don Edward. *Slavery, Law, and Politics: The Dred Scott Case in Historical Perspective*. New York: Oxford University Press, 1981.

Ferrer, Ada. "Haiti, Free Soil, and Antislavery in the Revolutionary Atlantic." *American Historical Review* 117, no. 1 (February 2012): 40–66.

Ferrer, Ada. *Freedom's Mirror: Cuba and Haiti in the Age of Revolution*. New York: Cambridge University Press, 2014.

Finkelman, Paul. *Dred Scott v. Sandford: A Brief History with Documents*. 2nd ed. New York: Bedford Books, 2016.

Fitz, Caitlin. *Our Sister Republics: The United States in an Age of American Revolutions*. New York: Liveright, 2016.

Foner, Eric. *Reconstruction: America's Unfinished Revolution, 1863–1877*. New York: Harper & Row, 1988.

Foner, Eric. *Free Soil, Free Labor, Free Men: The Ideology of the Republican Party before the Civil War*. New York: Oxford University Press, 1995.

Foner, Eric. *Nothing But Freedom: Emancipation and Its Legacy*. Baton Rouge: Louisiana State University Press, 2007.

Foner, Eric. *Gateway to Freedom: The Hidden History of the Underground Railroad*. New York: W. W. Norton, 2016.

Foner, Philip S. "Alexander Von Humboldt on Slavery in America." *Science & Society* 47, no. 3 (October 1983): 330–342.

Forbes, Robert Pierce. *The Missouri Compromise and Its Aftermath: Slavery and the Meaning of America*. Chapel Hill: University of North Carolina Press, 2007.

Ford, Lacy. "Reconfiguring the Old South: 'Solving' the Problem of Slavery, 1787–1838." *Journal of American History* 95, no. 1 (June 2008): 95–122, 14–15.

Foreman, P. Gabrielle, Jim C. Casey, and Sarah L. Peterson, eds. *The Colored Conventions Movement: Black Organizing in the Nineteenth Century*. Chapel Hill: University of North Carolina Press, 2021, forthcoming.

Frankel, Oz. *States of Inquiry: Social Investigations and Print Culture in Nineteenth-Century Britain and the United States*. Baltimore, MD: Johns Hopkins University Press, 2006.

Frost, Karolyn Smardz. *I've Got a Home in Glory Land: A Lost Tale of the Underground Railroad*. New York: Farrar Strauss & Giroux, 2008.

Frost, Karolyn Smardz and Veta Smith Tucker, eds. *A Fluid Frontier: Slavery, Resistance, and the Underground Railroad in the Detroit River Borderland.* Detroit, MI: Wayne State University Press, 2016.

Furrow, Matthew. "Samuel Gridley Howe, the Black Population of Canada West, and the Racial Ideology of the 'Blueprint for Radical Reconstruction.'" *Journal of American History* 97, no. 2 (2010): 344–370.

Gaines, Kevin K. *Uplifting the Race: Black Leadership, Politics, and Culture in the Twentieth Century.* Chapel Hill: University of North Carolina Press, 1996.

Gara, Larry. *The Liberty Line: The Legend of the Underground Railroad.* Lexington: University Press of Kentucky, 1996.

Garvey, Ellen Gruber. *Writing with Scissors: American Scrapbooks from the Civil War to the Harlem Renaissance.* New York: Oxford University Press, 2012.

Geggus, David P., ed. *The Impact of the Haitian Revolution in the Atlantic World.* Columbia: University of South Carolina Press, 2001.

Gellman, David N. *Emancipating New York: The Politics of Slavery and Freedom, 1777–1827.* Baton Rouge: Louisiana State University Press, 2006.

Genovese, Eugene D. *Fatal Self-Deception: Slaveholding Paternalism in the Old South.* New York: Cambridge University Press, 2011.

Gilbert, Alan. *Black Patriots and Loyalists: Fighting for Emancipation in the War for Independence.* Chicago: University of Chicago Press, 2013.

Gonzalez, Johnhenry. "Defiant Haiti: Free-Soil Runaways, Ship Seizures and the Politics of Diplomatic Non-Recognition in the Early Nineteenth Century." *Slavery & Abolition* 36, no. 1 (2015): 124–135.

Gosse, Van. "'As a Nation, the English Are Our Friends': The Emergence of African American Politics in the British Atlantic World, 1772–1861." *American Historical Review* 113, no. 4 (October 2008): 1003–1028.

Green, William A. *British Slave Emancipation: The Sugar Colonies and the Great Experiment, 1830–1865.* Oxford: Oxford University Press, 1976.

Griggs, Earl Leslie and Clifford H. Prator, eds. Introduction to *Henry Christophe and Thomas Clarkson: A Correspondence.* New York: Greenwood, 1968.

Gross, Robert A. and Mary Kelley, eds. *An Extensive Republic: Print, Culture, and Society in the New Nation, 1790–1840.* Chapel Hill: University of North Carolina Press, 2007.

Guyatt, Nicholas. "'The Outskirts of Our Happiness': Race and the Lure of Colonization in the Early Republic." *Journal of American History* 95, no. 4 (March 2009): 986–1011.

Hahn, Steven. *A Nation Under Our Feet: Black Political Struggles in the Rural South from Slavery to the Great Migration.* Cambridge, MA: Belknap Press, 2005.

Hahn, Steven. "Did We Miss the Greatest Slave Rebellion in Modern History?" In *The Political Worlds of Slavery and Freedom*, 55–114. Cambridge, MA: Harvard University Press, 2009.

Hall, Catherine. *Civilising Subjects: Metropole and Colony in the English Imagination 1830–1867.* Chicago: University of Chicago Press, 2002.

Harris, Leslie M. *In the Shadow of Slavery: African Americans in New York City, 1626–1863.* Chicago: University of Chicago Press, 2003.

Harrold, Stanley. "Romanticizing Slave Revolt: Madison Washington, the Creole Mutiny, and Abolitionist Celebration of Violent Means." In *Antislavery Violence:*

Sectional, Racial, and Cultural Conflict in Antebellum America, edited by John R. McKivigan and Stanley Harrold, 89–107. Knoxville: University of Tennessee Press, 1999.

Harrold, Stanley. *Subversives: Antislavery Community in Washington, D.C., 1828–1865*. Baton Rouge: Louisiana State University Press, 2002.

Harrold, Stanley. *The Rise of Aggressive Abolitionism: Addresses to the Slaves*. Lexington: University Press of Kentucky, 2004.

Harrold, Stanley. *Border War: Fighting Over Slavery Before the Civil War*. Chapel Hill: University of North Carolina Press, 2010.

Harrold, Stanley. *American Abolitionism: Its Direct Political Impact from Colonial Times into Reconstruction*. Charlottesville: University of Virginia Press, 2019.

Heglar, Charles J. Introduction to *The Life and Adventures of Henry Bibb: An American Slave*, v–xxxv. Madison: University of Wisconsin Press, 2001.

Hendrick, George and Willene Hendrick. *The Creole Mutiny: A Tale of Revolt Aboard a Slave Ship*. Chicago, IL: Ivan R. Dee, 2003.

Henry, Natasha L. *Emancipation Day: Celebrating Freedom in Canada*. Toronto: Dundurn Press, 2010.

Hepburn, Sharon A. Roger. *Crossing the Border: A Free Black Community in Canada*. Urbana: University of Illinois Press, 2007.

Herschthal, Eric. "Slaves, Spaniards, and Subversion in Early Louisiana: The Persistent Fears of Black Revolt and Spanish Collusion in Territorial Louisiana, 1803–1812." *Journal of the Early Republic* 36, no. 2 (June 2016): 283–311.

Higman, B. W., ed. "Jamaican Census of 1844." In *The Jamaican Censuses of 1844 and 1861*. Mona, JA: Department of History, University of the West Indies, 1980.

Hinks, Peter B. "'Frequently Plunged into Slavery': Free Blacks and Kidnapping in Antebellum Boston." *Historical Journal of Massachusetts* (Winter 1992): 16–31.

Hirschman, Albert O. *Exit, Voice, and Loyalty: Responses to Decline in Firms, Organizations, and States*. Cambridge, MA: Harvard University Press, 1970.

Hite, Roger W. "Voice of a Fugitive: Henry Bibb and Ante-Bellum Black Separatism." *Journal of Black Studies* 4, no. 3 (March 1974): 269–284.

Hodges, Graham Russell Gao. *David Ruggles: A Radical Black Abolitionist and the Underground Railroad in New York City*. Chapel Hill: University of North Carolina Press, 2010.

Hoffer, Peter Charles, *Cry Liberty: The Great Stono River Slave Rebellion of 1739*. New York: Oxford University Press, 2011.

Holt, Thomas C. *The Problem of Freedom: Race, Labor, and Politics in Jamaica and Britain, 1832–1938*. Baltimore, MD: Johns Hopkins University Press, 1992.

Horne, Gerald. *Negro Comrades of the Crown: African Americans and the British Empire Fight the U.S. Before Emancipation*. New York: New York University Press, 2012.

Horton, James Oliver and Lois E. Horton. *In Hope of Liberty: Culture, Community, and Protest among Northern Free Blacks, 1700–1860*. New York: Oxford University Press, 1997.

Horton, Lois E. "From Class to Race in Early America: Northern Post-Emancipation Racial Reconstruction." *Journal of the Early Republic* 19, no. 4 (December 1999): 629–649.

Hunt, Alfred N. *Haiti's Influence on Antebellum America: Slumbering Volcano in the Caribbean*. Baton Rouge: Louisiana State University Press, 1988.

Hurwitz, Samuel J. and Edith F. Hurwitz. "A Token of Freedom: Private Bill Legislation for Free Negroes in Eighteenth-Century Jamaica." *William and Mary Quarterly* 24, no. 3 (1967): 423–431.

Jackson, Kellie Carter. *Force and Freedom: Black Abolitionists and the Politics of Violence.* Philadelphia: University of Pennsylvania Press, 2019.

James, Winston. *The Struggles of John Brown Russwurm: The Life and Writings of a Pan-Africanist Pioneer, 1799–1851.* New York: New York University Press, 2010.

Jasanoff, Maya. *Liberty's Exiles: American Loyalists in the Revolutionary World.* New York: Alfred A. Knopf, 2011.

Johnson, Walter. *River of Dark Dreams: Slavery and Empire in the Cotton Kingdom.* Cambridge, MA: Belknap Press, 2013.

Jones, Martha S. "Time, Space, and Jurisdiction in Atlantic World Slavery: The Volunbrun Household in Gradual Emancipation New York." *Law and History Review* 29, no. 4 (2011): 1031–1060.

Jones, Martha S. *Birthright Citizens: A History of Race and Rights in Antebellum America,* New York: Cambridge University Press, 2018.

Kachun, Mitchell A. *Festivals of Freedom: Memory and Meaning in African American Emancipation Celebrations, 1808–1915.* Amherst: University of Massachusetts Press, 2003.

Kantrowitz, Stephen. *More Than Freedom: Fighting for Black Citizenship in a White Republic, 1829–1889.* New York: Penguin, 2012.

Karp, Matthew. *This Vast Southern Empire: Slaveholders at the Helm of American Foreign Policy.* Cambridge, MA: Harvard University Press, 2016.

Kelley, Sean. "'Mexico in His Head': Slavery and the Texas–Mexico Border, 1810–1860." *Journal of Social History* 37, no. 3 (2004): 709–723.

Kendi, Ibram X. *Stamped from the Beginning: The Definitive History of Racist Ideas in America.* New York: Nation Books, 2016.

Kennington, Kelly M. *In the Shadow of Dred Scott: St. Louis Freedom Suits and the Legal Culture of Slavery in Antebellum America.* Athens, GA: University of Georgia Press, 2017.

Kenny, Gale L. *Contentious Liberties: American Abolitionists in Post-Emancipation Jamaica, 1834–1866.* Athens, GA: University of Georgia Press, 2010.

Kenny, Gale L. "Manliness and Manifest Racial Destiny: Jamaica and African American Emigration in the 1850s." *Journal of the Civil War Era* 2, no. 2 (2012): 151–178.

Kerr-Ritchie, Jeffrey R. *Rites of August First Emancipation Day in the Black Atlantic World.* Baton Rouge: Louisiana State University Press, 2007.

Kerr-Ritchie, Jeffrey R. "Samuel Ward and the Making of an Imperial Subject." *Slavery & Abolition* 33, no. 2 (May 21, 2012): 205–219.

Kerr-Ritchie, Jeffrey R. *Rebellious Passage: The Creole Revolt and America's Coastal Slave Trade.* New York: Cambridge University Press, 2018.

Kinshasa, Kwando Mbiassi. *Emigration vs. Assimilation: The Debate in the African American Press, 1827–1861.* Jefferson, NC: McFarland, 1988.

Konig, David Thomas, Paul Finkelman, and Christopher Alan Bracey, eds. *The Dred Scott Case: Historical and Contemporary Perspectives on Race and Law.* Athens, OH: Ohio University Press, 2010.

Landers, Jane. *Black Society in Spanish Florida*. Urbana: University of Illinois Press, 1999.

Lightfoot, Natasha. *Troubling Freedom: Antigua and the Aftermath of British Emancipation*. Durham, NC: Duke University Press, 2015.

Lockett, James D. "Abraham Lincoln and Colonization: An Episode That Ends in Tragedy at L'Ile a Vache, Haiti, 1863–1864." *Journal of Black Studies* 21, no. 4 (June 1991): 428–444.

Lohse, Russell. "Reconciling Freedom with the Rights of Property: Slave Emancipation in Colombia, 1821–1852, with Special Reference to La Plata." *Journal of Negro History* 86, no. 3 (2001): 203–227.

Loughran, Trish. *The Republic in Print: Print Culture in the Age of U.S. Nation Building, 1770–1870*. New York: Columbia University Press, 2007.

Lynch, John. *Simón Bolívar: A Life*. New Haven, CT: Yale University Press, 2006.

Mahar, William J. *Behind the Burnt Cork Mask: Early Blackface Minstrelsy and Antebellum American Popular Culture*. Urbana: University of Illinois Press, 1998.

Manning, Chandra. *What This Cruel War Was Over: Soldiers, Slavery, and the Civil War*. New York: Random House, 2007.

Manning, Chandra. *Troubled Refuge: Struggling for Freedom in the Civil War*. New York: Alfred A. Knopf, 2016.

McDaniel, W. Caleb. *The Problem of Democracy in the Age of Slavery: Garrisonian Abolitionists and Transatlantic Reform*. Baton Rouge: Louisiana State University Press, 2013.

McDaniel, Caleb. *Sweet Taste of Liberty: A True Story of Slavery and Restitution in America*. New York: Oxford University Press, 2019.

McGill, Meredith L. *American Literature and the Culture of Reprinting, 1834–1853*. Philadelphia: University of Pennsylvania Press, 2003.

McPherson, James. *The Struggle for Equality*. Princeton: Princeton University Press, 1964.

Meer, Sarah. *Uncle Tom Mania: Slavery, Minstrelsy, and Transatlantic Culture in the 1850s*. Athens, GA: University of Georgia Press, 2005.

Melish, Joanne Pope. *Disowning Slavery: Gradual Emancipation and "Race" in New England, 1780–1860*. Ithaca, NY: Cornell University Press, 1998.

Miller, Floyd J. *The Search for a Black Nationality: Black Emigration and Colonization, 1787–1863*. Urbana: University of Illinois Press, 1975.

Mills, Brandon. "'The United States of Africa': Liberian Independence and the Contested Meaning of a Black Republic." *Journal of the Early Republic* 34, no. 1 (Spring 2014): 79–107.

Mitchell, Mary Niall. *Raising Freedom's Child: Black Children and Visions of the Future after Slavery*. New York: New York University Press, 2010.

Murphy, Angela F. *The Jerry Rescue: The Fugitive Slave Law, Northern Rights, and the American Sectional Crisis*. Oxford: Oxford University Press, 2014.

Murray, Alexander Lovell. "Canada and the Anglo-American Anti-Slavery Movement: A Study in International Philanthropy." PhD diss., University of Pennsylvania, 1960.

Murray, David. "Hands Across the Border: The Abortive Extradition of Solomon Moseby." *Canadian Review of American Studies* 30, no. 2 (January 2000): 185–208.

Nash, Gary B. *Forging Freedom: The Formation of Philadelphia's Black Community, 1720–1840.* Cambridge, MA: Harvard University Press, 1988.

Newman, Richard S. *The Transformation of American Abolitionism: Fighting Slavery in the Early Republic.* Chapel Hill: University of North Carolina Press, 2001.

Newman, Richard S. *Freedom's Prophet: Bishop Richard Allen, the AME Church, and the Black Founding Fathers.* New York: New York University Press, 2008.

Newman, Richard S. "'Lucky to Be Born in Pennsylvania': Free Soil, Fugitive Slaves and the Making of Pennsylvania's Anti-Slavery Borderland." *Slavery & Abolition* 32, no. 3 (2011): 413–430.

Newman, Richard and James Mueller, eds. *Antislavery and Abolition in Philadelphia: Emancipation and the Long Struggle for Racial Justice in the City of Brotherly Love.* Baton Rouge: Louisiana State University Press, 2011.

Nichols, James David. "Freedom Interrupted: Runaway Slaves and Insecure Borders in the Mexican Northeast." In *Fugitive Slaves and Spaces of Freedom in North America,* edited by Damian Alan Pargas, 251–274. Gainesville: University of Florida Press, 2018.

Nichols, James David. *The Limits of Liberty: Mobility and the Making of the Eastern U. S.–Mexico Border.* Lincoln: University of Nebraska Press, 2018.

Novak, William J. "The Legal Transformation of Citizenship in Nineteenth-Century America." In *The Democratic Experiment,* edited by Meg Jacobs, William J. Novak, and Julian E. Zelizer, 85–119. Princeton: Princeton University Press, 2003.

Oates, Stephen B. *To Purge This Land with Blood: A Biography of John Brown,* 2nd ed. Amherst, MA: University of Massachusetts Press, 1984.

O'Donnell, Elizabeth A. "'There's Death in the Pot!' The British Free Produce Movement and the Religious Society of Friends, with Particular Reference to the North-East of England." *Quaker Studies; Liverpool* 13, no. 2 (March 2009): 184–204.

Oldfield, J. R. *Transatlantic Abolitionism in the Age of Revolution: An International History of Anti-Slavery, c. 1787–1820.* New York: Cambridge University Press, 2013.

Page, Sebastian N. "'A Knife Sharp Enough to Divide Us': William H. Seward, Abraham Lincoln, and Black Colonization." *Diplomatic History* 41, no. 2 (April 2017): 362–391.

Pargas, Damian Alan, ed. *Fugitive Slaves and Spaces of Freedom in North America.* Gainesville: University Press of Florida, 2018.

Pasternak, Martin B. *Rise Now and Fly to Arms: The Life of Henry Highland Garnet.* New York: Routledge, 1994.

Peabody, Sue and Keila Grinberg. "Free Soil: The Generation and Circulation of an Atlantic Legal Principle." *Slavery & Abolition* 32, no. 3 (2011): 331–339.

Pease, Jane H. and William Henry Pease. *They Who Would Be Free: Blacks' Search for Freedom, 1830–1861.* New York: Atheneum, 1974.

Power-Greene, Ousmane K. *Against Wind and Tide: The African American Struggle against the Colonization Movement.* New York: New York University Press, 2014.

Pryor, Elizabeth Stordeur. *Colored Travelers: Mobility and the Fight for Citizenship before the Civil War.* Chapel Hill: University of North Carolina Press, 2016.

Pybus, Cassandra. *Epic Journeys of Freedom: Runaway Slaves of the American Revolution and the Their Global Quest for Liberty.* Boston, MA: Beacon Press, 2007.

Quarles, Benjamin. *Black Abolitionists.* New York: Da Capo Press, 1991.

Rael, Patrick. *Black Identity and Black Protest in the Antebellum North.* Chapel Hill: University of North Carolina Press, 2002.

Reynolds, David S. *Mightier than the Sword: Uncle Tom's Cabin and the Battle for America.* New York: W. W. Norton, 2011.

Rhodes, Jane. *Mary Ann Shadd Cary: The Black Press and Protest in the Nineteenth Century.* Bloomington: Indiana University Press, 1999.

Rhodes, Jane. "The Contestation over National Identity: Nineteenth-Century Black Americans in Canada." *Canadian Review of American Studies* 30, no. 2 (January 2000): 173–184.

Risley, Ford. *Abolition and the Press: The Moral Struggle Against Slavery.* Evanston, IL: Northwestern University Press, 2008.

Rose, Willie Lee. "The Domestication of Domestic Slavery." In *Slavery and Freedom,* edited by William W. Freehling, 18–36. New York: Oxford University Press, 1982.

Rugemer, Edward Bartlett. *The Problem of Emancipation: The Caribbean Roots of the American Civil War.* Baton Rouge: Louisiana State University Press, 2008.

Sanneh, Lamin O. *Abolitionists Abroad: American Blacks and the Making of Modern West Africa.* Cambridge, MA: Harvard University Press, 1999.

Sayre, Robert Duane. "The Evolution of Early American Abolitionism: The American Convention for Promoting the Abolition of Slavery and Improving the Condition of the African Race, 1794–1837." PhD diss., Ohio State University, 1987.

Schmidt-Nowara, Christopher. *Slavery, Freedom, and Abolition in Latin America and the Atlantic World.* Albuquerque: University of New Mexico Press, 2011.

Schuler, Monica. *"Alas, Alas, Kongo": A Social History of Indentured African Immigration into Jamaica, 1841–1865.* Baltimore, MD: Johns Hopkins University Press, 1980.

Schwartz, Rosalie. *Across the Rio to Freedom: U.S. Negroes in Mexico.* El Paso: Texas Western Press, 1975.

Scott, Julius Sherrard. "The Common Wind: Currents of Afro-American Communication in the Era of the Haitian Revolution," PhD dissertation, Duke University, 1986.

Shaftel, Matthew. "Singing a New Song: Stephen Foster and the New American Minstrelsy." *Music and Politics* 1, no. 2 (2007): 1–27.

Sidbury, James. *Becoming African in America: Race and Nation in the Early Black Atlantic.* New York: Oxford University Press, 2009.

Silverman, Jason H. "Kentucky, Canada, and Extradition: The Jesse Happy Case." *The Filson Club History Quarterly* 54 (January 1980): 50–60.

Silverman, Jason H. *Unwelcome Guests: Canada West's Response to American Fugitive Slaves, 1800–1865.* Millwood, NY: Associated Faculty Press, 1985.

Simpson, Donald George. *Under the North Star: Black Communities in Upper Canada Before Confederation (1867),* edited by Paul E Lovejoy. Harriet Tubman Resource Center on the African Diaspora, York University. Trenton, NJ: Africa World Press, 2005.

Sinha, Manisha. *The Slave's Cause: A History of Abolition.* New Haven, CT: Yale University Press, 2016.

Sio, Arnold A. "Race, Colour, and Miscegenation: The Free Coloured of Jamaica and Barbados." *Caribbean Studies* 16, no. 1 (April 1976): 5–21.

Spires, Derrick R. *The Practice of Citizenship: Black Politics and Print Culture.* Philadelphia: University of Pennsylvania Press, 2019.

Sproat, John G. "Blueprint for Radical Reconstruction." *Journal of Southern History* 23, no. 1 (February 1957): 25–44.

Staudenraus, P. J. *The African Colonization Movement 1816–1865.* New York: Columbia University Press, 1961.

Stauffer, John. *The Black Hearts of Men: Radical Abolitionists and the Transformation of Race.* Cambridge, MA: Harvard University Press, 2004.

Stauffer, John and Zoe Trodd, eds. *The Tribunal: Responses to John Brown and the Harper's Ferry Raid.* Cambridge, MA: Belknap Press, 2012.

Stewart, James Brewer. *Abolitionist Politics and the Coming of the Civil War.* Amherst: University of Massachusetts Press, 2008.

Stouffer, Allen P. *The Light of Nature and the Law of God: Antislavery in Ontario, 1833–1877.* Baton Rouge: Louisiana State University Press, 1992.

Strickland, Jeff. "The American Freedmen's Inquiry Commission, 19th-Century Racial Pseudoscience, and the False Assessment of Black America, 1863–1864." *Federal History* 11 (2019): 109–128.

Sundquist, Eric J. Introduction to *New Essays on Uncle Tom's Cabin,* edited by Eric J. Sundquist, 1–44. Cambridge: ProQuest LLC, 2000.

Tamarkin, Elisa. "Black Anglophilia; or, The Sociability of Antislavery." *American Literary History* 14, no. 3 (2002): 444–478.

Taylor, Nikki Marie. *Frontiers of Freedom: Cincinnati's Black Community, 1802–1868.* Athens, OH: Ohio University Press, 2005.

Thomas, Lamont D. *Paul Cuffe: Black Entrepreneur and Pan-Africanist.* Urbana: University of Illinois Press, 1988.

Thornton, John K. "'I Am the Subject of the King of Congo': African Political Ideology and the Haitian Revolution." *Journal of World History* 4, no. 2 (1993): 181–214.

Tise, Larry E. *Proslavery: A History of the Defense of Slavery in America, 1701–1840.* Athens, GA: University of Georgia Press, 1987.

Tomek, Beverly C. *Colonization and Its Discontents: Emancipation, Emigration, and Antislavery in Antebellum Pennsylvania.* New York: New York University Press, 2012.

Torrey, E. Fuller. *The Martyrdom of Abolitionist Charles Torrey.* Baton Rouge: Louisiana State University Press, 2013.

Trent, James W. *The Manliest Man: Samuel G. Howe and the Contours of Nineteenth-Century American Reform.* Amherst: University of Massachusetts Press, 2012.

Troutman, Phillip. "Grapevine in the Slave Market: African American Geopolitical Literacy and the 1841 Creole Revolt." In *The Chattel Principle: Internal Slave Trades in the Americas,* edited by Walter Johnson, 203–233. New Haven, CT: Yale University Press, 2004.

Turner, Mary. *Slaves and Missionaries: The Disintegration of Jamaican Slave Society, 1787–1834.* Urbana: University of Illinois Press, 1982.

Vorenberg, Michael. "Abraham Lincoln and the Politics of Black Colonization." *Journal of the Abraham Lincoln Association* 14, no. 2 (1993): 22–45.

Waldinger, Roger. *The Cross-Border Connection: Immigrants, Emigrants, and Their Homelands*. Cambridge, MA: Harvard University Press, 2015.

Wayne, Michael. "The Black Population of Canada West on the Eve of the American Civil War: A Reassessment Based on the Manuscript Census of 1861." *Social History/Histoire Sociale* 28, no. 56 (1995): 465–485.

Weiner, Dana Elizabeth. *Race and Rights: Fighting Slavery and Prejudice in the Old Northwest, 1830–1870*. DeKalb, IL: Northern Illinois University Press, 2013.

White, Arthur O. "Prince Saunders: An Instance of Social Mobility Among Antebellum New England Blacks." *Journal of Negro History* 60, no. 4 (October 1975): 526–535.

White, Ashli. *Encountering Revolution: Haiti and the Making of the Early Republic*. Baltimore, MD: Johns Hopkins University Press, 2010.

White, Shane. *Somewhat More Independent: The End of Slavery in New York City, 1770–1810*. Athens, GA: University of Georgia Press, 1991.

Whitfield, Harvey Amani. *Blacks on the Border: The Black Refugees in British North America, 1815–1860*. Burlington: University of Vermont Press, 2006.

Wigmore, Gregory. "Before the Railroad: From Slavery to Freedom in the Canadian–American Borderland." *Journal of American History* 98, no. 2 (September 2011): 437–454.

Wilson, Henry. *Rise and Fall of the Slave Power in America*. Vol. 2. Boston, MA: James R. Osgood, 1874.

Winks, Robin W. *The Blacks in Canada: A History*. 2nd ed. Montreal: McGill-Queen's University Press, 1997.

Winsboro, Irvin D. S. and Joe Knetsch. "Florida Slaves, the 'Saltwater Railroad' to the Bahamas, and Anglo-American Diplomacy." *Journal of Southern History* 79, no. 1 (February 2013): 51–78.

Wong, Edlie L. *Neither Fugitive nor Free: Atlantic Slavery, Freedom Suits, and the Legal Culture of Travel*. New York: New York University Press, 2009.

Wood, Peter H. *Black Majority: Negroes in Colonial South Carolina from 1670 through the Stono Rebellion*. New York: Knopf, 1974.

Yingling, Charlton W. "No One Who Reads the History of Hayti Can Doubt the Capacity of Colored Men: Racial Formation and Atlantic Rehabilitation in New York City's Early Black Press, 1827–1841." *Early American Studies: An Interdisciplinary Journal* 11, no. 2 (2013): 314–348.

Young, Jeffrey Robert. *Domesticating Slavery: The Master Class in Georgia and South Carolina, 1670–1837*. Chapel Hill: University of North Carolina Press, 1999.

Zboray, Ronald J. *A Fictive People: Antebellum Economic Development and the American Reading Public*. New York: Oxford University Press, 1993.

Zorn, Roman J. "Criminal Extradition Menaces the Canadian Haven for Fugitive Slaves, 1841–1861." *Canadian Historical Review* 38, no. 4 (December 1957): 284–294.

Index